A COGNITIVE APPROACH TO SITUATION AWARENESS:
THEORY AND APPLICATION

A Cognitive Approach
to Situation Awareness:
Theory and Application

Edited by
SIMON BANBURY
School of Psychology, Cardiff University, United Kingdom

SÉBASTIEN TREMBLAY
École de Psychologie, Université Laval, Canada

ASHGATE

Published by
Ashgate Publishing Limited
Gower House
Croft Road
Aldershot
Hampshire GU11 3HR
England

Ashgate Publishing Company
Suite 420
101 Cherry Street
Burlington, VT 05401-4405
USA

Ashgate website: http://www.ashgate.com

British Library Cataloguing in Publication Data
A cognitive approach to situation awareness : theory and
    application
    1.Human engineering 2. Awareness
    I.Banbury, Simon II.Tremblay, Sébastien
    620.8'2

Library of Congress Cataloging-in-Publication Data
A cognitive approach to situation awareness : theory and application / by Simon Banbury, Sébastien Tremblay.
        p. cm.
    Includes index.
    ISBN 0-7546-4198-8
    1. Human engineering. 2. Awareness. 3. Cognition. I. Banbury, Simon. II Tremblay, Sébastien.

    TA166.C58 2004
    620.8--dc22

                                            2004011838

ISBN 0 7546 4198 8

Reprinted 2006

Printed and bound in Great Britain by MPG Books Ltd, Bodmin, Cornwall

Contents

PART II: APPLICATION

List of Contributors

Henrik Artman is currently Senior Lecturer in Human-Computer Interaction at the Department of Numerical Analysis and Computer Science the Royal Institute of Technology (KTH), Sweden. His current research is focusing on procurement of usability in complex systems design. He earned his Ph.D. at the Department of Communication Studies, Linköping University in 1999, researching coordination and Situation Awareness (SA) in control rooms and micro-world systems. In between positions he worked as researcher at the National Defence College as well as Usability Consultant.

Simon P. Banbury is currently a Lecturer at the School of Psychology, Cardiff University and a Senior Human Factors Consultant at the Centre for Human Sciences, QinetiQ, UK. From 1996 to 2000, he was a Senior Psychologist at the Defence and Evaluation and Research Agency (DERA), UK. He received his Ph.D. in Psychology from the University of Reading in 1996.

Joseph V. Baranski is a Defence Scientist and Head of the Judgment and Decision Making Group at Defence R & D Canada – Toronto. His research interests include individual and team decision making and confidence in human judgment. He received his Ph.D. in Psychology from Carleton University in 1992.

Dianne C. Berry is Pro-Vice-Chancellor (Research) and Professor of Psychology at the University of Reading, having previously been Dean of the Faculty of Economic and Social Sciences. Prior to coming to Reading in 1990, she was a research fellow at the University of Oxford and Lecturer in Psychology at Baliol College Oxford. Professor Berry is an Academician of the Academy of Social Sciences, and a Chartered Psychologist and Associate Fellow of the British Psychological Society.

Robert S. Bolia is currently a Computer Scientist in the Air Force Research Laboratory's Human Effectiveness Directorate, where he studies military decision making, and command and control from historical, cultural, and psychological perspectives. He received an M.A. in Military Studies (joint warfare) from American Military University in 2004.

Richard Breton is currently a Defence Scientist at Defence R & D Canada – Valcartier, and an Associate Professor at the School of Psychology, Université Laval, Québec, Canada. He received his Ph.D. in Psychology from Université Laval in 1997. His research interests are related to SA and situation assessment, decision making and cognitive system engineering.

Johnell O. Brooks is currently a Ph.D. student in the Psychology Department at Clemson University. She is supported by a Dwight D. Eisenhower Graduate Transportation Fellowship from the US Department of Transportation.

David J. Bryant received his Ph.D. in Psychology from Stanford University in 1991. He has conducted research on human spatial cognition, human factors of aviation security, and decision-making as it is related to military command and control. Dr. Bryant is currently a Defence Scientist with Defence R & D Canada – Toronto, where he is pursuing research on inferential processes involved in situation assessment and tactical picture compilation.

Laurie T. Butler is a Lecturer at the School of Psychology, University of Reading. He received his Ph.D. in Psychology from the University of Reading in 1999.

Darryl G. Croft is a Senior Human Factors Consultant, and team leader for the Cognitive Technologies Capability Group, at the Centre for Human Sciences, QinetiQ, UK. Previously, he was a Senior Psychologist at DERA, UK. He is nearing completion of his Ph.D. in Psychology at the University of Reading.

Andrew R. Dattel is a Ph.D. candidate in Texas Tech's Human Factors program, after obtaining a Master's degree from the University of Connecticut. He maintains a commercial pilot's license and is a certified flight instructor.

Sidney Dekker is Professor of Human Factors at the Linköping Institute of Technology, Sweden. He gained his Ph.D. in Cognitive Systems Engineering from The Ohio State University, USA. He has previously worked in Australia, New Zealand, Singapore and the UK.

Helen J. Dudfield is a Technical Manager in Human System Technologies, Simulation and Training at QinetiQ, UK, where she has worked for 19 years. She received her Ph.D. in Aviation Psychology from Cranfield University in 1992.

Frank T. Durso is Professor of Psychology at Texas Tech University where he directs the Cognitive Ergonomics Laboratory. He is senior editor of the *Handbook of Applied Cognition* and serves on a number of editorial boards. He received his B.S. from Carnegie-Mellon University and his Ph.D. from SUNY at Stony Brook in 1980.

Mica R. Endsley is President of SA Technologies in Marietta, Georgia, USA, conducting SA research and development in the aviation, military and medical fields. She received her Ph.D. in Industrial and Systems Engineering from the University of Southern California. Her most recent book is entitled *Designing for Situation Awareness*.

John Flach received his Ph.D. (Human Experimental Psychology) from The Ohio State University in 1984. John was an Assistant Professor at the University of Illinois from 1984 to 1990 where he held joint appointments in the Department of Mechanical & Industrial Engineering, the Psychology Department, and the Institute of Aviation. In 1990 he joined the Psychology Department at Wright State

University where he currently holds the rank of Professor. He is interested in coordination and control in cognitive systems and their application to aviation and medicine.

Han Tin French heads the Human Sciences Discipline in the Land Operations Division of Australia's Defence Science and Technology Organisation. Her research areas, spanning 16 years, include the effects of blast overpressures on humans, collective training and SA in the land environment. She gained her Ph.D. in Physical Chemistry from the University of New England, NSW, Australia.

Christer Garbis holds a position as Project Manager for usability coordination at Siemens AB, Sweden. He earned his Ph.D. in 2002 at the Department of Communication Studies, Linköping University, Sweden, researching distributed cognition and communication in control rooms. His main research interests focus on communication and design of computer systems in underground control systems.

Leo Gugerty is currently an Associate Professor in the Department of Psychology, Clemson University. Previously, he was a Research Psychologist for Galaxy Scientific Corporation, USA, where he worked in the US Air Force Research Laboratory. He received his Ph.D. in Psychology from the University of Michigan in 1989.

Justin G. Hollands is a Defence Scientist at Defence R&D Canada – Toronto, and leads the Centre's Human-Computer Interaction Group. From 1994 to 1999, he was an Assistant Professor in the Psychology Department at the University of Idaho. He received a Ph.D. in Psychology from the University of Toronto in 1993.

Hans-Jürgen Hörmann is currently the Team Leader for the Safety and Human Factors Group at Boeing Research and Technology Europe, where he coordinates research activities on training design and crew performance. In 1987, he received his Ph.D. in Applied Psychology from the Free University in Berlin. He then worked for 17 years as Aviation Psychologist for the German Aerospace Center (DLR) where he was involved in pilot selection, cross-cultural research, and CRM training methods. He is representing the European Association of Aviation Psychology on the Editorial Board of the *International Journal of Aviation Psychology*.

Mark S. Horswill has been a Lecturer at the School of Psychology, University of Queensland since 2002. Previous to that he was a Lecturer at the School of Psychology, University of Reading, and obtained his Ph.D. at Reading in 1994.

Nic James is currently a Lecturer in the Department of Sports Science, University of Wales, Swansea. His research interests involve cognitive performance of teams and individuals, having recently been working with professional rugby and soccer teams as well as elite squash players. He received his Ph.D. in Psychology from Cardiff University in 1995.

Dylan M. Jones (Professor) is Head of School at Cardiff University School of Psychology; he obtained a Ph.D. in Human Cognition at Cardiff and was fortunate enough to become Donald Broadbent's research assistant at the University of Oxford. His main interests are in human performance particularly the role of linguistic and perceptual factors in short-term memory.

Frederick M.J. Lichacz is an Experimental Cognitive Psychologist with the Canadian Forces Experimentation Centre in Ottawa, Canada. He received his Ph.D. in Psychology from Carleton University in 1996.

Mike Lodge studied Modern Languages at University College North Wales and Tuebingen, Germany. He began his flying career with British Airways (then BEA) in 1966 and flew both short and long-haul, completing his 30+ piloting years as a Base Training Captain and Instrument Rating Examiner on Boeing 747s. He was the project pilot for British Airways on a number of European Commission sponsored initiatives. He is now an independent consultant, designing and delivering non-technical skills training to airlines and other safety critical organizations.

Margareta Lützhöft is a Ph.D. student at the Linköping Institute of Technology. Previously a Captain with 13 years of experience at sea, she received a degree in Cognitive Science from Skövde University in Sweden.

Alastair M. McGowan is currently undertaking his Ph.D. at the School of Psychology, Cardiff University. He received his M.Sc. in Occupational Psychology from Cardiff University in 2002.

William J. Macken is currently a Senior Lecturer in the School of Psychology, Cardiff University, from where he received his Ph.D. in 1996.

Frank P. McKenna is currently a Professor at the School of Psychology, University of Reading. He did his Ph.D. on Psychophysics at University College London after which he worked at the Medical Research Council Applied Psychology Unit in Cambridge. His work is mainly on risk perception and risk taking.

Michael D. Matthews is a Professor of Engineering Psychology at the US Military Academy. His primary research interests include infantry small unit decision-making and leadership, and command and control issues in homeland security. Prior to joining the West Point faculty, he was a Research Psychologist at the US Army Research Institute, and an Associate Professor of Human Factors Engineering at the US Air Force Academy.

Max Mulder received his Ph.D. (Aerospace Engineering) from the Delft University of Technology in 1999, for his work on the cybernetics of perspective flight-path displays. He is currently an Assistant Professor at the Control & Simulation division of the Faculty of Aerospace Engineering at Delft University of Technology. His research interests include cybernetics and its use in modeling human performance and the application of cognitive systems engineering principles in the design of interfaces for professionals working in the transport domain.

W. Todd Nelson is a Senior Engineering Research Psychologist in the Collaborative Interfaces Branch, Warfighter Interface Division, Human Effectiveness Directorate of the Air Force Research Laboratory, Wright-Patterson Air Force Base, Ohio. He received his Ph.D. in Experimental Psychology/Human Factors from the University of Cincinnati in 1996.

Marinus M. (René) van Paassen received his Ph.D. (Aerospace Engineering) from the Delft University of Technology in 1994, for his work on biomechanics of manual control of aircraft. He worked as a post-doctoral researcher at the University of Kassel and the Danish Technical University on means-ends visualization for process control in cement mills, and as a researcher at Delft University of Technology, Mechanical Engineering on alarm management. He is currently an Assistant Professor at the Control & Simulation division of the Faculty of Aerospace Engineering at Delft University of Technology. His research interests include cognitive systems engineering for the transport domain, cybernetics, flight simulation and real-time software engineering.

John Patrick is a Senior Lecturer in the School of Psychology at Cardiff University and is an experienced researcher in the area of Applied Cognitive Psychology.

Elizabeth S. Redden is currently serving as the Chief of the US Army Research Laboratory Infantry School Field Element and the manager for the Army's Situation Understanding Science and Technology Objective. She has served as the Field Element Chief for 22 years. She received her Ph.D. in Management from Auburn University.

Robert Rousseau has joined the Decision Support System section at R&D Canada – Valcartier as a Senior Defense Scientist in 2003. His work deals with cognitive issues in evaluation of DSS, decision-making in C^2, SA and teamwork. He has been a faculty at the School of Psychology at Universitié Laval from 1968 to 2003, where he has done experimental research on timing and attention in humans and performed applied cognition projects on work automation, information systems implementation and knowledge management.

Henning Soll studied Psychology at the Christian-Albrecht-Universität in Kiel, Germany, and received his Master's degree in 1999. He started working for the German Aerospace Center (DLR) in 1998 and since then his main working fields include pilot selection, simulator testing and psychophysiology. His research interests include the implementation of psychophysiological testing into the selection process for pilots. He has held a private pilot license since 1989.

Craig A. Treadaway is currently a M.S. student in the Psychology Department at Clemson University.

Sébastien Tremblay is currently an Assistant Professor at the School of Psychology, Université Laval. His main research interests relate to human cognition and performance. Prior to his appointment at Laval, Dr Tremblay held a postdoctoral fellowship at Cardiff University, funded by DERA, UK. He holds a Ph.D. in Psychology (1999, Cardiff University, UK).

Michael A. Vidulich is a Senior Research Psychologist in the Collaborative Interfaces Branch, Warfighter Interface Division, Human Effectiveness Directorate of the Air Force Research Laboratory, Wright-Patterson Air Force Base, Ohio. He received his Ph.D. in Experimental Psychology from the University of Illinois at Urbana-Champaign in 1983.

Preface

The test of Situation Awareness as a construct will be in its ability to be operationalized in terms of objective, clearly specified independent and dependent variables ... Otherwise, SA will be yet another buzzword to cloak scientists' ignorance. (Flach, J., *Human Factors*, 1995, 37(1), p. 155)

The importance of Situation Awareness (SA) in assessing and predicting operator competence in complex environments has become increasingly apparent in recent years. For example, it has been widely established that SA is a contributing factor to many commercial and military accidents and incidents. However, determining exactly what constitutes SA is a very difficult undertaking given the complexity of the construct itself and the many different psychological processes involved with its acquisition and maintenance. The quote above is taken from an article within a special issue of the journal *Human Factors* published almost ten years ago and devoted to the newly-emerging topic of SA. The special issue should be considered a landmark in SA research given the large amount of citations that these articles have received; approximately 350 peer-reviewed journal publications citations to date. Resonating with the quote from John Flach, a number of other articles in the special issue also stressed that SA research should proceed with strong theoretical underpinnings. For example, Richard Gilson wrote in the foreword that SA 'clearly suffers from a lack of empirical data' and hoped that the articles within the special issue 'will stimulate more research aimed at clarifying the theoretical picture and that they will provide recommendations for transfer to current and future applications' (*Human Factors*, 1995, 37(1), p. 3). But how much progress has been made towards these goals? Are we still building our house on poor foundations almost ten years later?

A cursory Internet search on the term 'Situation(al) Awareness' conducted at the time of writing compiled over 100,000 hits, whilst a search for 'Situation(al) Awareness Model' compiled 130, and 'Situation(al) Awareness Theory' compiled just 68. On this rather clumsy metric it does appear that we have made surprisingly little progress in ten years towards a clearer theoretical account of SA.

Like many researchers in the field of SA, our approach is guided by principles and theories from cognitive psychology. We feel that it is a strong and rigorous approach within which our understanding of the capabilities and limitations of human cognition can be applied to gaining a better understanding of SA. Indeed, it could be argued that SA is an epiphenomenon of cognition. Despite this, in our view cognitive psychology has had rather less impact that we might have expected. Although cognitive processes are an integral part of many frameworks of SA, their description is at a rather superficial level. Indeed, models of SA refer to cognitive processes in general terms, but do not specify exactly what processes are involved and to what to extent. Instead, the major impetus of research has been on the development of techniques to measure SA, at the expense of a more rigorous understanding of *why* SA varies under certain psychological and environmental conditions. But why might this be so?

> The basic science of psychology and human performance, generally considered to be the foundation upon which human factors stands, is largely a science of nonsense syllables ... It is a science where meaning has been considered a confounding factor, not an integral part of the problem. (Flach, *CSERIAC Gateway*, 1996, 6(6), p. 85)

So perhaps one reason why the wealth of knowledge between the covers of cognitive psychology journals is rarely seen in the context of SA research is due to its *apparent* lack of application; studies devoid of meaning and involving 'nonsense symbols' seem to have little to say about operators engaging in complex activities, such as driving a car or piloting an aircraft.

This book attempts to address this perceived imbalance and highlight how cognitive psychology has improved our understanding of SA and how it has been successfully applied to many real-world applications, such as driving, aviation, military operations, the nuclear power industry and sport. The volume is concerned primarily with human cognition and its application to understanding the processes and structures that underlie SA. The general aim of the book was to bring together recent developments from researchers and practitioners from around the world who are studying SA from a cognitive perspective. Our 41 contributors to this book thus represent a broad diversity of theoretical perspectives, research approaches and domains of application. The contributors are from academic departments and industrial organizations; giving a blend between academic and practitioner approaches. Two of the contributors appeared in the *Human Factors* special issue, whilst a significant number of contributors became involved with SA research a little more recently. Clearly, SA research is very much alive and well. Finally, all contributors are familiar with the core of each others' contributions and share the common interest of approaching SA from a cognitive perspective. To bring further coherence to the book, all of our contributors received draft manuscripts of those chapters most relevant to their own for consideration during the revision stage.

Echoing Gilson, the book is organized around two themes; theory and application. Part I addresses theory and takes a critical view on issues relating to defining and modeling SA. Chapter 1, by *Robert Rousseau, Sébastien Tremblay* and *Richard Breton*, considers descriptive and prescriptive modeling with the aim of clarifying the status of SA models with reference to the current understanding of information-processing, mental models, situation models and team cognition. In Chapter 2, *Sidney Dekker* and *Margareta Lützhöft* describe an ecological, relational account of SA where awareness, or consciousness, is not the contents of mind but an intrinsic feature of the functional relationship between the environment and the person. Their account is consistent with more recent ideas about 'sensemaking' as an active strategy for dealing with a dynamic, complex world. In Chapter 3, *John Flach, Max Mulder* and *Marinus van Paassen* focus on what is meant by 'situation'. Inspired by the ecological approach of Gibson, they argue that a clear understanding of what we mean by the term 'situation' is an essential first step toward a theory of SA. Similarly, *John Patrick* and *Nic James* in Chapter 4 review critically the nature of SA and discuss evidence from the process control domain that SA involves situation-specific phenomena. They argue in context of both individual and team SA, that it is useful to conceptualize SA as the product of successfully accomplishing an important yet specific task. In Chapter 5, *Darryl Croft, Simon Banbury, Laurie Butler* and *Dianne Berry* focus on what is meant by 'awareness' and argue that the knowledge that guides our behavior may sometimes be unavailable to conscious inspection and therefore cannot be articulated as 'awareness'. After outlining key evidence for the implicit/explicit distinction they describe a number of approaches that have been used to measure implicit knowledge in complex situations. In Chapter 6, *David Bryant, Frederick Lichacz, Justin Hollands* and *Joseph Baranski* examine how SA theory has been profitably used as a descriptive model that summarizes important concepts for application to military and industrial domains but offer criticisms of how the theory has been misused as a prescriptive model. They go on to discuss the Critique, Explore, Compare, and Adapt (CECA) descriptive model of C^2 decision making as a competing framework in which to address issues of SA. Finally, *Simon Banbury, Darryl Croft, William Macken* and *Dylan Jones* conclude this section in Chapter 7. They outline a contemporary account of selective attention and short-term memory, Cognitive Streaming, and argue how it might be extended to explain key phenomena of SA; particularly how operators are able to anticipate the future states of objects.

Part II is concerned with the application of SA and covers a wide range of SA research currently being conducted in the applied context; including research in well-established domains such as aviation, command and control and driving, and research in emerging domains such as infantry operations and sport. In Chapter 8, *Frank Durso* and *Andrew Dattel* discuss the Situation Present Assessment Method (SPAM) procedure for measuring SA. Their chapter reviews the SPAM procedure's strengths and limitations, and compares SPAM to other query procedures. In Chapter 9, *Mark Horswill* and *Frank McKenna* review research into hazard perception, including an examination of expert/novice driver differences, and risk-taking behavior. Their chapter reviews attempts to provide training for hazard perception and discusses the different real-world applications of hazard perception tests training. *Alastair McGowan* and *Simon Banbury*, Chapter 10, adapted McKenna and Horswill's driving hazard perception test to measure SA using both embedded measures of anticipation and interruption-based SA probes. The work described in their chapter tested predictions derived from current accounts of task interruption and SA. Continuing the theme of driving, *Leo Gugerty, Johnell Brooks* and *Craig Treadaway* in Chapter 11, focus on individual differences in operators' ability to perform transportation tasks, such as driving and flying. They investigate cognitive abilities and strategies in two transportation sub-tasks; navigation and maneuvering to avoid local hazards. In Chapter 12, *Hans-Jürgen Hörmann, Simon Banbury, Helen Dudfield, Mike Lodge* and *Henning Soll* describe the experimental evaluation of a training solution for SA. They report the results of a study with 32 airline pilots to evaluate the effects of training SA on different measures of pilots' behavior, skills and attitudes related to SA. *Michael Vidulich, Robert Bolia* and *Todd Nelson* in Chapter 13 propose that a critical feature in the implementation of new technology will be ensuring that SA is maintained at all levels of the decision-making chain. They provide theoretical perspectives and historical examples to argue that over-reliance on or misuse of technology may in fact lead to reduced SA, compromising decision quality and mission effectiveness. In Chapter 14, *Han Tin French, Michael Matthews* and *Elizabeth Redden* review research and development in infantry SA; the challenges of the infantry environment and mission and how SA is vital to mission success, specific SA information requirements for infantry operations, and SA metrics appropriate to the infantry domain. Continuing the team theme, *Christer Garbis* and *Henrik Artman* in Chapter 15 argue that it is necessary to study the communicative and coordinative practices in order to understand how the successful team operation of dynamic systems is constituted. Through field studies they demonstrate how team SA is actively constructed via the communicative practices. In Chapter 16, *Nic James* and *John Patrick* review the nature of various sports situations together with their varying SA requirements and accompanying SA processes. Studies in sports psychology are reviewed with respect to SA in terms of different training methods and the nature of the available contextual cues. Specific examples of the role of SA are also discussed. Finally, the book is concluded by *Mica Endsley* in Chapter 17. She provides a critical review of recent research in SA, including the research outlined in the previous chapters, and discusses progress that has been made towards providing useful inputs into SA theory, measurement, training and system design.

   This book allows practitioners, academics or students to gain an appreciation of state-of-the-art, international research on SA theory and application from a cognitive perspective. Those seeking to measure and apply SA in real-world settings, for example equipment design, personnel training and so on, will benefit from work directed at understanding the cognitive mechanisms underlying SA. Ten years on from the special issue of *Human Factors*, we hope to demonstrate that cognitive psychology has assisted us in making significant progress towards a better understanding of SA.

   Finally, we would like to express our gratitude to John Hindley of Ashgate for his encouragement throughout this project, to John Marsh, Shaun Helman, Nick Mosdell and Alastair McGowan for their assistance in the preparation of this volume, and to our contributors for their support and patience.

Simon Banbury
Sébastien Tremblay

PART I
THEORY

Chapter 1

Defining and Modeling Situation Awareness: A Critical Review

Robert Rousseau, Sébastien Tremblay and Richard Breton

Introduction

The concept of Situation Awareness (SA) is now well established in the domain of human factors studies in complex environments. In practice, a long list of examples exists to persuade someone that SA has its own reality and its own importance. Indeed, knowledge of the information relevant to efficient task performance is critical to safety and productivity in a wide variety of situations such as air-traffic controllers, jet pilots, nuclear power plant operators and military commanders (see Durso and Gronlund, 1999). However, when an attempt is made to define SA, the result is highly variable. Reviews of definitions from varied sources (e.g., Dominguez, 1994; Breton and Rousseau, 2001) provide a clear indication of the variety of viewpoints about SA. One might not be too concerned with that situation. As Pew pointed out:

> The term *situation awareness* shares a common history with several psychological concepts such as intelligence, vigilance, attention, fatigue, stress, compatibility, or workload. During decades, all these terms were poorly defined. However, each became important because they attracted attention on critical processes or mental states that were previously unknown. Ultimately, they changed the ways to study human factors problems, and they brought new benefits. (Pew, 2000, p. 33)

Defining SA

Surveying definitions of SA reveals the variety of conceptions currently conveyed in the literature. Breton and Rousseau (2001) performed a systematic classification of 26 SA definitions. These definitions turned out to be evenly divided in two classes corresponding to the now accepted duality of SA as a *State* or as a *Process*.

State and Process-oriented Definitions

SA is often considered a 'buzzword' that serves as a label for a range of cognitive processes (see Prince, Salas and Brannick, 1999). Sarter and Woods (1995, p. 16) proposed that: 'the term *situation awareness* should be viewed just as a label for a variety of *cognitive processing activities* that are critical to dynamic, event-driven, and multitasks fields of practice'. Endsley (1988, 1995) takes an opposite position reflected in the well-known definition of SA as: 'the perception of the elements in the environment within a volume of time and space, the comprehension of their meaning, and the projection of their status in the near future.'

Endsley further claims that SA is a *state of knowledge* that needs to be distinguished from the processes used to achieve that state. These processes should be referred to as *situation assessment*. That distinction between *'Process'* and *'State'* definitions is of considerable importance. One of the major difficulties in working with SA is to avoid confusion between SA knowledge and the underlying cognitive processes such as perception, memory, attention or categorization that underlie the production of SA. The proposition of Endsley (1995) to distinguish between *situation awareness* (a state) and *situation assessment* (a process) has been very influential on development of measures and modeling efforts (Pew and Mavor, 1998). Unfortunately, as pointed out by Pew and Mavor, the similarity in acronym for situation awareness and situation assessment has led to some confusion. Moreover, situation assessment is included in a number of decision-making models without any reference to Situation Awareness. For instance, Klein (1997) refers to situation assessment as central to decision-making and as including appropriate goals, cue salience, expectations and identification of typical actions. Given such a definition, it is apparent that in Klein's view, situation assessment is a very broad concept that covers situation awareness content as defined by Endsley as well as actions. Thus, simply identifying the processes supporting Situation Awareness as a Situation Assessment process is likely to bring some confusion given the way situation assessment is already defined in the broader literature on decision-making.

Similarly, defining SA as the relevant knowledge of which an operator is aware is not without problems. According to Smith and Hancock (1995), SA cannot be equated with the momentary knowledge of which an operator is aware. Clearly, SA cannot simply be equated to any verbal report of the content of consciousness about a situation. Even more fundamentally, the question remains as to whether SA should be considered as meaning conscious mental content, precluding all forms of tacit knowledge (see Banbury, Andre and Croft, 2001; Croft, Banbury, Butler and Berry, Chapter 5, this volume).

As pointed out by Durso and Gronlund (1999) that difficulty could very likely stem from the existence of two basic approaches to the question. One approach, the Operator-focused approach, is concerned with the properties, basically mechanisms, of the operator as they determine SA. The second approach, the Situation-focused approach, views SA as determined by the environment or situation in which the operator is at work. The interest of that point of view is that it resets the issue of SA definition around the two basic factors on which SA depends. A State-oriented definition could then be associated with a Situation-focused approach and characterized as driven by the properties of the Situation aspect of the SA concept. On the other hand, a Process-oriented definition, associated with an Operator-focused approach, would be centered on the properties of the operator or agent. The distinction between Operator and Situation focused approaches helps to reframe the classical state-process distinction.

Operator-focused Approach

An Operator-focused point of view is more concerned with the set of cognitive processes supporting the production of the mental representation corresponding to the SA state. These processes are by definition a general property of the human agent. That approach follows an information-processing framework that considers a mental representation of the world to be based on a processing with specific functions (e.g., Marr, 1982; Dawson, 1998). That framework requires an explicit description of the processes involved in providing humans with cognition. As an example, Dominguez (1994) includes a set of processes on which SA depends: *information extraction, information integration, mental picture formation,* and *projection and anticipation.* In a way, it could be argued that Endsley (1988) also describes three cognitive processes or functions: *perception, comprehension* and *projection,* even though she defines SA as a State. Most of these Process-based definitions do not rely on available generally accepted human information processing (HIP) models like the one described in Wickens and Hollands (2000). The HIP models identify a network of processes like perception, attention and memory.

Situation-focused Approach

A *Situation-focused* point of view is clearly concerned with the mapping of the relevant information in the situation onto a mental representation of that information within the agent. *State*-oriented definitions limit the description of processes involved in SA. In fact, they are on line with the fundamental concept of *direct perception* derived from the work of Gibson (1979). *Direct perception* is based on a number of principles two of them being of interest for SA: (i) all the information necessary for perception is contained in the environment; (ii) perception is immediate and spontaneous. Based on these principles one can assume that in order to understand perception, the priority must be on understanding the environment without concern for possible underlying processes.

The Situation-focused approach provides a more factual basis on which to define SA as a State. The *Situation* can be defined in terms of events, objects, systems, other persons and their mutual interactions. However, this is complicated by the fact that a Situation is domain-dependent and that elements of the situation that should be within SA in aircraft control will be different from the ones that are required for an anesthesiologist.

Pew (2000, p. 34) provides an example of what could be included in a generic definition of Situation, even though it is somewhat specific to aircraft piloting. He defines a situation as 'a set of environmental conditions and system states with which the participant is interacting that can be characterized uniquely by a set of information, knowledge, and response options.' Pew then proposes that SA should integrate, when applicable, five aspects of the situation:

- the surrounding environment;
- the mission's goals;
- the system;
- the available physical and human resources;
- the crew.

In that view, 'situation' takes a very large meaning. It includes task and mission features, as well as the other human agents in the significant environment. It is much more than the awareness of the distribution in space of objects within a contextual environment. Actually, Smith and Hancock (1995) view SA as a concept that is centered on task goals. They explicitly include task goals, criteria of performance and cues in the environment or situation.

From Defining to Modeling

In the context of developing the concept of SA, one is then left with a double-edged sword problem. If SA is a state, it is essential to give a precise definition of the knowledge that defines the state. There should be a certain mapping between a situation schema and a knowledge schema. If one is to improve SA, the elements of the situation critical for SA should be specified, and the SA content definition should follow from these elements. On the other hand, if SA depends on a set of processes that are not an intrinsic part of SA as a state but on which SA depends, it becomes important to specify which processes are essential to SA. SA improvement, for instance, will depend upon changes in the operation of these processes.

The debate remains as to whether a definition of SA should be limited to content or should include the processes or functions linked to the awareness of the situation. Should SA include (or not) what some authors refer to as situation assessment? It is not possible to provide an answer to that question from the strict analysis of SA definitions. However, many authors have expanded their definition of SA by developing models of SA. These models are reviewed in the next section.

Modeling SA

In its most generic form, a model is a representation or description, more or less complete, of an object or a process. The representation of an object refers to a statement, formula or image that depicts or describes that object. A model describing a process will include one, or a series of operations, that accomplish an end. Models are useful to support reflection about the effectiveness of action or of a particular device with which a human interacts. They provide a logic that lends itself to measurement or experimentation about a problem related to the model. Many different types of models have been developed that address specific aspects of performance, particular processes or goal-directed actions. For the sake of reviewing, models of SA will be divided in two groups: descriptive models and prescriptive (computational, numerical or simulation-based) models (Zacharias, Miao, Illgen, Yara and Siouris, 1996).

Descriptive Models

Most SA models are descriptive. Descriptive models of SA are driven by an effort to describe the actual SA process. A good descriptive model will reflect the operator's, or most often the pilot's, decision-making processes. It is very flexible and can take into account most constraints that are typical in an operational setting. However, the descriptive models are difficult to represent in formal prescriptive terms. They will provide rather general predictions. Their main strength resides in the analytic power they carry. They provide a systematic description of what SA is and how it is produced.

A systematic analysis of SA descriptive models is provided in Endsley, Holder, Leibrecht, Garland, Wampler and Matthews (2000). They provide a list of eight models presented as '… models of how people achieve SA in complex domains …' (Endsley et al., p. 34). Amongst these models, Endsley's model (1988, 1995, 2000a) clearly stands as the reference for most work done on SA. It is the prototypical descriptive model for SA. A number of other models focus on specific aspects of SA but remain within the constraints of Endsley's model (e.g., Endsley and Jones, 1997; McGuinness and Foy, 2000). Given the tremendous influence of Endsley's SA model on the evolution of the concept and its acceptance by field experts, we will briefly describe the model and then address the basic aspects of Endsley's model.

Endsley (1988, 1995) presents an SA model with two main parts: a core SA model and a set of various factors affecting SA. The first part, the *Core SA model* represents the processes directly responsible for SA. The second and much more elaborate part describes in detail the various factors affecting SA grouped into four broad classes: external world, task and environmental factors, individual factors, and a set of domain factors. These factors also include contributions of all components of current HIP models like goals, active schemas, past experience, attentional processes and memory. The core SA model is what is usually referred to as the SA model. The core model of SA presented in Endsley (1995) is the basis for much of the current modeling of core SA. It is a three-level system that can be described as follows.

Level one, *Perception of the Elements in the Environment*, is the first step in *achieving* SA. It provides information about the status of the relevant elements in the environment. The interaction with long-term memory knowledge makes possible the inclusion of classification of information into understood representations. The subset is under attentional selection based on task requirements. The elements are structured into meaningful events situated in time and space. This content is active in working memory thereby providing a basis for its awareness.

Level two, *Comprehension of the Current Situation*, is a synthesis of disjointed elements of Level one. It provides an organized picture of the elements with a comprehension of the significance of objects and events. Schemata or mental models stored in long-term memory are the basis for level two SA. Level two SA is then defined as a situational model depicting the current state of the mental model.

Level three, *Projection of Future Status*, is achieved through knowledge of the status and the dynamics of the elements and comprehension of the situation. It enables predictions about the states of the environment in the near future.

Endsley's model is a complex model in which State and Process aspects are meshed. Endsley et al. (2000) describe an extended version of Endsley's (1995) model, adapted to infantry operations. It is, by far, the most extensive SA model currently available including an impressive set of cognitive and non-cognitive contributing factors. While this makes the model all-encompassing in terms of factors affecting SA, it does not push the modeling of core SA any further.

Process Aspects of Descriptive SA

The essential aspect of the Endsley family of SA models about process issues is that SA is achieved through a hierarchical linear processing system. This sets SA within a well-known approach on descriptive modeling of decision-making in the context of control by experts in dynamic situations. The approach is characterized by the representation of decision-making as operating through a series of processes somewhat similar to Endsley's model (e.g., Klein, 1997; Rasmussen, Pejtersen and Goodstein, 1994). For example, the Rassmussen et al's model describes a decision ladder on which information processing goes from a simple perception of the environment to progressive contact with stored knowledge, for comprehension and then to the development of an appropriate action. Although analogous in part with Endsley's model they differ on two basic points. First, there are 'short-cuts' in the system allowing an action to be implemented without full processing. It follows that the processing path is not strictly sequential. The actual processing path depends on the joint properties of the situation and expertise of the operator. So, the processing systems analogous to the SA descriptive models are much more flexible. Descriptive models of SA should be modified to take into account the basic properties of related cognitive processing models, mainly by providing flexible links between SA process and action selection/implementation.

A second aspect of SA models in relation to processes concerns the position and role of SA in the cognitive processing system supporting SA. Two main points are currently debated about this issue, namely that SA provides direct control of the information gathering processes and attention, and that SA is determined by the actions of an operator in a given situation. Klein (2000) proposed that SA development is an active process of guided information seeking, rather than a passive receipt and storage of details. He points out that SA is not only determined by the situation but also by what the person is doing. Information is considered to be part of SA if it is required to achieve a goal. This is very much in line with Adams, Tenney, and Pew (1995). Their model is based on Neisser's (1976) perception-action cycle which includes three basic processes: perceived environment (P), memory schema (M), and active exploration (A). An essential element of that approach is that these three processes form a cycling network in which perception is controlled, in part, by the action process. Adams et al., consider that SA is limited to the state of the *active memory schema*, the other two processes being the active processes that determine SA at a given point in time. This approach makes it possible to define a linear but less hierarchical SA model since the Perception cycle is a closed network in which each process can be seen as the beginning of the cycle. These types of consideration lead to the inclusion of the decision-making and action implementation processes within a complete SA model. It remains that by setting SA within a cognitive processing system, models of SA carry with them the basic question about the architecture of the processes. This double question of identifying both the processes and their architecture is a fundamental problem in cognitive modeling. The tri-level hypothesis for cognitive modeling proposed by Marr (1982) and developed by Dawson (1998) defines three levels of analysis of a cognitive system: Computational, Algorithmic and Implementational.

The level of concern for descriptive SA models is the algorithmic level addressing the issue of identifying the information-processing steps being used to solve a problem. At that level, the information-processing system is described from a functional perspective. The functional perspective has two basic aspects: the identification of the functions and the identification of the functional architecture. Given the difficulties with the identification of an architecture for the processes supporting SA, limiting modeling to the identification of the functions could help to simplify the problem of SA modeling.

A model of SA developed by McGuinness and Foy (2000) provides an example of that approach. Their model proposes to distinguish between functions, content, and processes. The three levels of Endsley's model are labeled here as *functions*. The functions provide the content and processes are typical of processes described in HIP models of the type described in Wickens and Hollands (2000). McGuinness and Foy also include a fourth function, 'Resolution'. Far from being trivial, going from levels to functions is a basic change in the model. Indeed, if each function were to be linked to a structural level, the model would fast become intractable with the addition of new functions since the number of levels would increase with each new function, thus complicating the processing architecture. By shifting from levels to functions, McGuinness and Foy question a basic feature of Endsley's model: SA is generated through a linear hierarchical network of three basic processes. Indeed, McGuinness and Foy (2000) explicitly argue that in Endsley's model: '...*we should not interpret these (the levels) as a linear or hierarchical sequence but more as a network of parallel functions serving a common purpose.*' Nonetheless, it does appear as though SA is supported by a number of functions with an unknown system of composition rules. It is on the output of these functions that SA is based.

Functions have a logic structured in terms of agents and intentions or goals. For Boy (1998), a *cognitive function* transforms a task into an activity. Functions are not organized as an input/output system, as is the case for processes, they are defined by the task. Their structure parallels the structure of the task as identified through a task analysis procedure. They are context sensitive and they operate on content (representation) in order to achieve a task goal. It would be worth considering the concept of functions in descriptive SA models since their properties are very much in line with the contribution of SA to task execution.

State Aspects of Descriptive SA

In a number of papers since 1995 (e.g., Endsley, 1995, 2000b; Shebilske, Goettl and Garland, 2000) SA is referred to as a situational model. The situational model is then defined as *a schema depicting the current state of the mental model of the system*. Both the mental model and the situational models are concepts that have been developed outside the domain of SA. For these models to provide a strong contribution to the modeling of SA as a mental representation, they have to be used in a manner consistent with their status outside SA modeling. It is always the case in scientific modeling that models borrowed from a relevant domain show their usefulness in the host model where they are implemented by providing a logic of objects, relations and operations that is an enrichment to the host model. Thus, it is important in analyzing SA models to describe situational and mental models and see how they are put to use in SA modeling.

The situational model concept has been developed within the domain of discourse comprehension, mainly in the works of van Dijk and Kintsch (1983), van Dijk (1999) and Kintsch (1998). When applied to SA modeling, text is considered analogous to situation. van Dijk and Kintsch as well as Kintsch distinguish between *text representation* and *situational representation.* Text representations are in terms of text structure and components of text information. Situation models result from the connection of text representation with prior knowledge stored in long-term memory. Furthermore, Kintsch proposes that the comprehension of a text is based on an episodic text memory that includes both text representation and situation model. He claims that the episodic text memory and consequently the comprehension of a text results from a mixture of text-derived and knowledge-derived information, not necessarily in equal parts. Given that approach in text comprehension, we would argue that SA would more likely be an analogue of episodic memory representation rather that of the situation model. That episodic memory representation would be the active component of the Level two comprehension process in Endsley's model. Similarly, van Dijk proposes the concept of *experienced mental models* including domain information and situation information. The situation information contains setting parameters (time, location …), participants' parameters (roles) and action and cognition parameters. Within the context of discourse comprehension, situation models are not defined as mere extensions of mental models.

Even without referring to situational models, SA can still be viewed as a form of *mental model* (see Hendy, 1995). The concept of mental models has a very long tradition in cognition and reviewing that concept is beyond the scope of the present chapter. However, we would like to stress the point that the concept of mental models has generated a number of interpretations that have resulted in confusion. Rouse and Morris (1986) provide a now classical definition of *mental models*. Mental models are the mechanisms whereby humans are able to generate: descriptions of system purpose and form; explanations of system functioning and observed system states; and predictions of future system states. These functions are very much compatible with Endsley (1988; 1995). For Rouse and Morris, the mental model is not a state but a set of functions.

Rasmussen (1983) describes the SRK model of cognitive control of human activities in terms of a hierarchically organized three-level cognitive control system: Skill-based, Rule-based, and Knowledge-based. Rasmussen et al., (1994) propose to limit the definition of *mental models* at the Knowledge-based level. The Knowledge-based level relies on a conscious symbolic mental model, forming the reference on which information is interpreted. The mental model is then defined as declarative (semantic and explicit) representations of the environment and the constraints governing the regularity of its behavior.

For Moray (1996), mental models operate at all levels of information processing and not only at the knowledge level. He claims that there are many mental models of a system going from a model of the physical form or physical function of the system to models of general functions and goals/means/ends of a system. These models may even form a hierarchical network of mental models going from concrete to abstract functional content.

The efforts for modeling SA as a state are interesting in as much as they underline the fundamental contribution of prior knowledge to SA. However, they also bring some difficulty mainly related to the status of perception as SA. The discussion from discourse comprehension models or even from the mental models tends to limit SA to Level two and consequently questions the actual status of the other two processes in the descriptive SA model of the Endsley's family of models.

Prescriptive Models

The prescriptive models are theory driven. SA is set in formal models of the operator cognitive model. They are characterized by the formal representation of processes leading to some computational modeling of SA. SA level is construed as a numerical metric derived from some combination of information from the environment and information already present in the operator's long-term memory. Their development is costly since it requires building a database providing a model of the mental model, for each specific situation and integrating the corresponding mental models into the model SA. However, it remains that these formal modeling efforts have been more or less ignored in the literature and that they are worth being reviewed.

Zacharias and his colleagues (Zacharias et al., 1996; Mulgund, Harper, Zacharias and Menke, 2000) have developed the SAMPLE model. SA is modeled as the central part of the Pilot model in SAMPLE. It is defined as essentially a diagnostic reasoning process. SA starts with the detection of event occurrence. The events are cues about the current status of the situation. Then, the beliefs about the possible impacts of the events on the situation are evaluated by using mental models which maintain in long-term memory the structure and parameters defining the events/situation relationship. The Pilot mental model is modeled as a belief network that represents knowledge as a set of event/situation relationships. SA reflects the belief that a given event will play a more or less important role in a situation. One can see that such a model does not include a perception process as the basis on which SA relies.

Shively, Brickner and Silbiger (1997) have developed an SA module within the MIDAS architecture (Man-machine Integration Design and Analysis System). MIDAS enables the modeling and simulation of the human-machine interaction when executing a task. SA is modeled within the Operator model of MIDAS. Situation is defined as in Pew (1995) and more specifically, it is represented by a set of defining situation elements connected to contextual information setting the relevance of a given element. For instance, a context node can be identified as threat/target on the battlefield. The importance of an element in defining a situation is weighted as a function of the level of processing performed on an element. Perceived SA is the weighted average over all situation elements. High value reflects the level of SA a pilot thinks he/she has on the situation. The model computes an actual SA that corrects perceived SA for these two erroneous or incomplete sources of information. This model deliberately does not consider the projection aspect of SA.

McCarley, Wickens, Goh and Horrey (2002) have presented a prescriptive model of SA with the objective of mitigating pilot error in aviation operations. The model bears some similarity with the previous ones namely that SA reflects the degree of correct awareness about a current situation. Actually, correct awareness is seen as a belief about the state of a situation determined by the weights given to a particular event as a function of event conspicuity, information value and attention allotted to the event. The model is strongly based on scientific theories of visual attention and of memory decay. Actually, the model is more aligned with plausible cognitive processes than other computational models. It addresses two basic aspects of SA namely SA changes in a dynamic environment and SA guidance of attentional processes. In a way, that model remains more in line with the descriptive models of SA in as much as it links SA with attention and working memory. While it does not refer to long-term memory mental models as a means to achieve SA, the role of the mental model is included in the model. Application of the model yields a numerical estimate of correct SA. The SA value will be affected by the pilot attending to events of low information value or operating in environmental conditions reducing the salience of the events.

Other attempts at developing a prescriptive model have been made. For instance, Finnie and Taylor (1998) proposed the IMPACT SA model, based on Powers's (1973) Perceptual Control Theory. In that model, SA is controlled by the operator's behavior and the maintenance of SA is related to behaviors involved in reducing the difference between perceived and desired levels of SA.

Although different from each other, the prescriptive models share a number of characteristics. All models use some form of ideal SA resulting from an analysis of the situation by subject matter experts and providing a baseline against which the actual SA is computed. Second, they all compute an index of correct SA giving an indication of the quality of the internal representation of the information determining SA and consequently the behavior. SA is modeled, in most of these models, as a belief network representing what the operator relies on for determining action at a given point in time. Most models are concerned with the handling of dynamic changes in SA as a function of changes in the environment. They also take into account the reduction in SA errors.

As pointed out by McCarley et al., (2002), prescriptive models do not bring radical changes in the understanding of the SA concept. However, such models provide a particular view of SA. For instance, the concept of multilevel SA, prominent in descriptive SA models, is not explicit in prescriptive models. They tend to downplay issues such as the conscious content of the operator's mind and the internal image of the world, usually associated with SA. It is interesting to note that SAMPLE as well as the McCarley et al., (2002) model take into account information that is not present in the environment but that is expected to be there. The operator's expectations are part of SA. This stresses the importance prescriptive models place on the role of SA in directing action since it follows that the unavailable information will be sought for by the operator. As is always the case with prescriptive modeling, the existing mathematical or formal methods of a particular modeling approach put an important constraint as to how aspects of SA should be modeled. That is the case, for instance, with the use of belief networks in many models.

Team Situation Awareness

Defining and modeling SA has recently evolved to take into account the emerging concept of team cognition (see Salas and Fiore, 2004, for a review). In fact, although some authors argue that Team Situation Awareness (TSA) originates from individual SA, it is from the analysis of pilot crew performance that stems the interest in SA (see Bolman, 1979). Over the last decade team related issues have drawn increasing interest from a wide range of organizations that rely on teamwork. There are many definitions of team but they all seem to agree that teamwork is about several individuals working toward a shared goal (Dickinson and McIntyre, 1997). As situations get more complex, more people are required for information gathering and actions. Teamwork requires information sharing among team members and coordination activities (e.g., Brannick and Prince, 1997). The importance of teams in the workforce has been well documented (see, e.g., Thomas and Helmreich, 2002). In such settings, SA is often reported to affect a team's functioning and performance.

While the importance of teamwork is recognized, experimental psychology has not traditionally addressed team related variables such as communication, shared information and coordination (see Waern, 1998; Hauland, 2002, for a discussion). At the conceptual level there is some relevant work on the applicability of distributed cognition to learning and system design (see Hutchins, 1991) and the notion of 'sharedness' with regards to mental representations (e.g., Klimoski and Mohammed, 1994). More recently, some researchers have adopted an experimental approach to investigate such questions (e.g., Stout, Cannon-Bowers, Salas and Milanovich, 1999) and characterize team processes such as communication and coordination, mainly with the intention of developing methodologies for measurement (e.g., Cooke and Stout, 2001).

According to many researchers and practitioners, defining and modeling SA in the context of teamwork is constrained by the fact that it involves two key but poorly understood concepts: individual SA and team cognition (see, e.g., Gilson, 1995; Sarter and Woods, 1991; see also Nofi, 2000). The operational definition of SA is still a matter of debate and the precise nature of team cognition is yet to be clarified. Nevertheless, there is a consensus about the assumption that TSA is *more* than the sum of the team member's individual SA (e.g., Salas, Stout and Cannon-Bowers, 1994; Schwartz, 1990). This premise has led to the suggestion that individual SA and TSA models should remain two distinct models (Endsley et al., 2000). Hence, modeling efforts should begin with highlighting the characteristics of TSA that make it distinct from individual SA.

One such distinction is that most models and definitions of individual SA are based on information processing constructs (e.g., Endsley, 1995), whereas descriptions of TSA are derived from the distributed cognition framework (e.g., Fink, 2000; Hauland, 2002). According to Endsley (1995), individual SA relies on cognitive processes such as perception, comprehension and projection but TSA involves additional and unique activities such as communication and coordination. Indeed, TSA is often seen as individual SA plus a number of processes that serve to share part of that SA with team members. Some authors claim that the first step in developing TSA is for team members to build their own individual SA (e.g., Nofi, 2000). The following step is for them to share their SA with team members. One question is whether team elements could simply be considered as part of the specific situation of a team setting, and thus be part of each team member's individual SA, as any other relevant information. The latter suggestion brings us to argue that, even if considered distinct, both TSA and individual SA models may share the same foundation. It is clear that both TSA and individual SA models must include a knowledge structure and a set of processes or functions that serve to develop that knowledge. According to Stout, Cannon-Bowers and Salas (1997), shared knowledge, necessary for team members to perform their team tasks, and its development constitute the basis of TSA.

Structure of Knowledge and Team Processes

A number of researchers have focused on the knowledge possessed by teams (e.g., Cooke, Salas, Cannon-Bowers and Stout, 2000). Part of the research effort is concerned with the content of such a collective knowledge base. One suggestion is to extend the mental models framework to teams (e.g., Klimoski and Mohammed, 1994; Langan-Fox, 2000). According to Cannon-Bowers, Salas and Converse (1993), team mental models can be conceived as organized bodies of knowledge that are shared across members of the team. A degree of redundancy in task-related knowledge among team members is necessary for communication, coordination, and in some cases, cross-checking purposes (Wellens, 1993).

So-called team mental models encompass team and task information, and there is evidence that such knowledge must be acquired before task performance (e.g., Bolstad and Endsley, 1999). However, in the context of any complex and dynamic situations, as soon as team members are engaged in their tasks, the specific situation will evolve and change. Thus, team members constantly update their collective understanding of the specific situation (e.g., Blickensderfer, Cannon-Bowers and Salas, 1999), as is the case in single-operator situations. The nature of the latter set of knowledge is dynamic and episodic rather than semantic. Those properties are typically associated with the concept of situational models (e.g., Orasanu, 1990). According to some researchers situational models could represent the knowledge structure of TSA, as it represents, in part, the shared understanding of a situation among team members at one point in time (see Cooke et al., 2000). In view of the questions regarding the appropriate status and applicability of situational models in individual SA, caution should be exercised when applying this concept to TSA.

There are several team behaviors or processes that serve to develop and update the body of knowledge that team members must possess in order to perform their task. As mentioned above, in addition to the processes usually associated with individual SA, TSA involves unique behaviors, such as coordination (Endsley and Jones, 2001; Muniz, Salas, Stout and Bowers, 1999), information sharing (Wagner and Simon, 1990; McIntyre and Salas, 1995) and cross-checking information (Bolman, 1979). There is empirical evidence that communication and coordination activities are essential to updating shared knowledge and links to team performance have been established (e.g., Prince and Salas, 1993; Schwartz, 1990; Stout et al., 1999).

Hauland (2002) pointed out that most descriptions of TSA are concerned with team processes but fail to take into account interpersonal relations. Indeed, a number of TSA descriptions appear to carry the assumption that overall TSA is good if every team member has good individual SA. However, social and organizational factors can impede accurate TSA, and should also be considered in modeling efforts (e.g., Endsley and Jones, 2001). The contribution of such factors to TSA highlights the considerable difference between individual and team processes.

The Notion of Sharedness

Significant progress in modeling TSA has been hampered by the lack of understanding of so-called shared cognition. The reference to terms such as shared or team cognition is increasing with frequency but it is also rising with confusion. It is not quite clear whether the notion of cognition shared among team members implies that cognitive processes, as characterized within the information processing architecture, take place outside the human mind. For example, some authors claim that encoding and retrieval of information is applicable to teams as well as individuals (e.g., Tindale and Kameda, 2000). The metaphor of 'sharedness' has embraced well-established information processing constructs such as attention (e.g., joint attention; Butterworth and Jarret, 1991) and memory (e.g., transactive memory; Wegner, 1986). Although it is unequivocal that team members share their knowledge with other team members through communication and multiparty displays, the existence of shared cognition as such is questionable. Furthermore, the difference between 'shared' and 'distributed' is often ambiguous.

With regards to role of shared cognition in TSA (or the integration of TSA within the more general concept of team cognition), there is a number of unresolved issues. A key issue is the distinction between 'shared awareness of a situation' and 'awareness of a shared situation':

> Used in the sense of 'awareness of a shared situation,' shared situational awareness implies that we understand that we are in a shared situation. In contrast, when used in the sense of 'shared awareness of a situation,' shared situational awareness implies that we all understand a given situation in the same way. (Nofi, 2000, p. 12)

The latter represents the sense in which most definitions and models portray SA. One question is whether a similar distinction is applicable to cognitive processes (e.g., 'encoding of shared information' and 'shared encoding of information').

Conclusion

Despite the difficulty in reaching a consensus about definitions of SA, the concept has evolved and a number of models have recently emerged from existing cognitive frameworks. Some of the key issues highlighted in the review had already been identified and discussed in previous documents. However, we made the attempt to provide an exhaustive and up to date analysis of the literature from a cognitive psychology perspective.

The classical view of SA is based on Endsley's seminal work, and over the last two decades that view has led research efforts. From the beginning of the interest in SA, the concept has been cleaved along the distinction between state and process. In relation to modeling, that distinction is often reset onto an operator-situation distinction. The latter approach is closely linked to the application of mental models and situational models to SA.

The multi-level model of SA (Endsley, 1988; 1995) proposes a system in which processing is hierarchical and linear. One alternative is to reframe the analysis of SA based on a network of parallel functions (McGuinness and Foy, 2000) as opposed to a hierarchical line of processes. Whether information gathering is accomplished through serial processing or a set of functions acting in parallel, SA is often described as a state, rather passive, influenced by the actions of the operator. An alternative approach is to allocate an active role to SA. Indeed, SA could act as some executive unit that controls the gathering of information (e.g., McCarley et al., 2002).

Most researchers and practitioners agree that SA represents a body of knowledge with a set of processes (or functions) that serve to develop and update that knowledge. Hence, the integration of mental models to SA and more recently the addition of the situational models. Within the context of SA research, the situational model is often regarded as the current state of the mental model (e.g., Endsley, 2000b). The problem with considering SA as a situational model is that it is not compatible with the status of perception as described in the original multilevel model of SA. A novel and promising approach that has received little attention in the literature is the use of prescriptive models. Applying assumptions associated with prescriptive modeling to the study of SA has raised some challenging questions. For instance, in such models awareness is not explicitly considered and a role is given to expected information.

The extension of SA related concepts such as mental models and situational models to a team SA is of great interest. These constructs are candidates to represent the so-called team knowledge structure. In order to develop that knowledge structure, TSA must rely on functions that are specific to team settings, in addition to the functions or processes usually associated with individual SA. One point of view that has emerged from our survey of the literature is that clarifying the operational definition of TSA may actually shed some light on individual SA. Even though it is clear that the two concepts are distinct, the same approach seems applicable to modeling TSA and individual SA. However, progress in modeling TSA is limited by the lack of understanding of team cognition. A key issue is to clarify the notion of sharedness.

Acknowledgement

Thanks are due to Katherine Guérard for critical reading of an earlier draft.

References

Adams, M.J., Tenney, Y.J. and Pew, R.W. (1995), 'Situation Awareness and the Cognitive Management of Complex Systems', *Human Factors*, vol. 37(1), pp. 85-104.

Banbury, S.P. Andre, A.D. and Croft, D.G. (2001), *Do We 'Know' All That We 'Know'? The Role of Implicit Knowledge in Situation Awareness*, paper presented at the 44th Annual Human Factors and Ergonomics Society Conference, HFES, San Diego.

Blickensderfer, E., Cannon-Bowers, J.A. and Salas, E. (1999, May), 'The Relationship Between Shared Knowledge and Team Performance: A Field Study', in K.A. Smith-Jenthsch and L.L. Levesque (Co-chairs), *Shared Cognition in Teams: Predictors, Processes, and Consequences, Symposium conducted at the 14th annual meeting of the Society Industrial and Organizational Psychology*, Atlanta.

Bolman, L. (1979), 'Aviation Accidents and the Theory of the Situation', in G.E. Cooper, M.D. White and J.K. Lauder (eds), *Resource Management on the Flight Deck: Proceedings of a NASA Industry workshop*, NASA Ames Research Center, Moffett Field, pp. 31-58.

Bolstad, C.A. and M.R. Endsley (1999), *Shared Mental Models and Shared Displays: An Empirical Evaluation of Team Performance*, paper presented at the 43th Meeting of the Human Factors and Ergonomics Society, Marietta.

Boy, G.A. (1998), *Cognitive Function Analysis*, Ablex Publishing, Westport.

Brannick, M.T. and Prince, C. (1997), 'An Overview of Team Performance Measurement', in M. Brannick, E. Salas and C. Prince (eds), *Team Performance Assessment and Measurement: Theory, Methods and Applications*, Erlbaum, Hillsdale, pp. 331-356.

Breton, R. and Rousseau, R. (2001), *Situation Awareness: A Review of the Concept and its Measurement*, Technical Report No. 2001-220, Defence Research and Development Canada, Valcartier.

Butterworth, G. and Jarret, N. (1991), 'What Minds Have in Common is Space: Spatial Mechanisms Serving Joint Visual Attention in Infancy', *British Journal of Developmental Psychology*, vol. 9, pp. 55-72.

Cannon-Bowers, J.A., Salas, E. and Converse, S.A. (1993), 'Shared Mental Models in Expert Team Decision Making', in N.J. Castellan (ed.), *Current Issues in Individual and Group Decision Making*, Erlbaum, Hillsdale, pp. 221-246.

Cooke, N.J., Salas, E., Cannon-Bowers, J.A. and Stout, R.J. (2000), 'Measuring Team Knowledge', *Human Factors*, vol. 42(1), pp. 151-173.

Cooke, N.J. and Stout, R.J. (2001), 'A Knowledge Elicitation Approach to the Measurement of Team Situation Awareness', in M. McNeese, E. Salas and M.R. Endsley (eds), *New Trends in Cooperative Activities: Understanding System Dynamics in Complex Environments*, HFES, Santa Monica, pp. 114-139.

Dawson, M.R.W. (1998), *Understanding Cognitive Science*, Blackwell, Malden.

Dickinson, T.L. and McIntyre, R.M. (1997), 'A Conceptual Framework for Teamwork Measurement', in M.T. Brannick, E. Salas and C. Prince (eds), *Team Performance Assessment and Measurement: Theory, Methods and Applications*, Erlbaum, Hillsdale, pp. 19-44.

Dominguez, C. (1994), 'Can SA Be Defined?', in M. Vidulich, C. Dominguez, E. Vogel and G. McMillan (eds), *Situation Awareness: Papers and Annotated Bibliography*, United States Air Force Armstrong Laboratory, Brooks Air Force Base, pp. 5-15.

Durso, F.T. and Gronlund, P. (1999), 'Situation Awareness', in F.T. Durso, R. Nickerson, R. Schvaneveldt, S. Dumais, S. Linday and M. Chi (eds), *Handbook of Applied Cognition*, John Wiley and Sons, New York, pp. 283-314.

Endsley, M.R. (1988), *Design and Evaluation for Situation Awareness Enhancement*, paper presented at the Human Factors Society 32nd Annual Meeting, Santa Monica.

Endsley, M.R. (1995), 'Toward a Theory of Situation Awareness in Dynamic Systems', *Human Factors*, vol. 37(1), pp. 32-64.

Endsley, M.R. (2000a), 'Theoretical Underpinnings of Situation Awareness: A Critical Review', in M.R. Endsley and D.J. Garland (eds), *Situation Awareness Analysis and Measurement*, Lawrence Erlbaum Associates, Mahwah, pp. 3-32.

Endsley, M.R. (2000b), *Situation Models: An Avenue to the Modelling of Mental Models*, paper presented at the 14th triennial congress of the International Ergonomics Association and 44th annual meeting of the Human Factors and Ergonomics Society, Santa Monica.

Endsley, M.R., Holder, L.D., Leibrecht, B.C., Garland, D.J., Wampler, R.L. and Matthews, M.D. (2000), *Modeling and Measuring Situation Awareness in the Infantry Operational Environment*, US Army Research Institute for the Behavioral and Social Sciences, Alexandria.

Endsley, M.R. and Jones, W.M. (1997), *Situation Awareness, Information Dominance and Information Warfare*, Technical Report No. 0156, United States Air Force Armstrong Laboratory, Brooks Air Force Base.

Endsley, M.R. and Jones, W.M. (2001), 'A Model of Inter and Intrateam Situation Awareness: Implications for Design, Training and Measurement', in M. McNeese, E. Salas and M.R. Endsley (eds), *New Trends in Cooperative Activities: Understanding System Dynamics in Complex Environments*, HFES, Santa Monica, pp. 46-67.

Fink, A.A. (2000), *Toward a Model of Team Situation Awareness*. Old Dominion University. Unpublished thesis.

Finnie, S. and Taylor, R. (1998), 'The Cognitive Cockpit', *Flight Deck International*, International Press, UK.

Gibson, J.J. (1979), *The Ecological Approach to Visual Perception*, Houghton-Mifflin, Boston.

Gilson, R.D. (1995), 'Introduction to the Special Issue on Situation Awareness', *Human Factors*, vol. 37(1), pp. 3-4.

Hauland, G. (2002), *Measuring Team Situation Awareness in Training of En Route Air Traffic Control*, Technical Report No. 1343, Riso National Laboratory, Denmark.

Hendy, K.C. (1995), 'Situation Awareness and Workload: Birds of a Feather?', in *Proceedings (CP–575) of the AGARD AMP Symposium on Situation Awareness: Limitations and Enhancement in the Aviation Environment*, Advisory Group for Aerospace Research and Development, Neuilly-sur-Seine, pp. 211-217.

Hutchins, E. (1991), 'The Social Organization of Distributed Cognition', in L.B. Resnick, J.M. Levine and S. Teasley (eds), *Perspectives on Socially Shared Cognition*, American Psychological Association, Washington, pp. 283-307.

Kintsch, W. (1998), *Comprehension: A Paradigm for Cognition*, Cambridge University Press, Cambridge.

Klein, G. (1997), 'The Recognition-Primed Decision (RPD) Model: Looking Back, Looking Forward', in C.E. Zsambock and G. Klein (eds), *Naturalistic Decision Making*, Lawrence Erlbaum Associates, Mahwah, pp. 285-292.

Klein, G. (2000), 'Cognitive Task Analysis of Teams', in J.M. Schraagen, S.F. Chipman and T.D. Shalin (eds), *Cognitive Task Analysis,* Lawrence Erlbaum Associates Inc, Mahwah, pp. 417-30.

Klimoski, R. and Mohammed, S. (1994), 'Team Mental Model: Construct or Metaphor?', *Journal of Management*, vol. 20, pp. 403-437.

Langan-Fox, J. (2000), 'Team Mental Models: Techniques, Methods, and Analytic Approaches', *Human Factors*, vol. 42(2), pp. 242-271.

Marr, D. (1982), *'Vision'*, W.F. Freeman, San Francisco.

McCarley, J.S., Wickens, C.D., Goh, J. and Horrey, W.J. (2002), 'A Computational Model of Attention / Situation Awareness', in *Proceedings of the 46th Annual Meeting of the Human Factors and Ergonomics Society*, Human Factors and Ergonomics Society, Santa Monica, pp. 1669-1673.

McGuinness, B. and Foy, J.L. (2000, October), *A Subjective Measure of SA: The Crew Awareness Rating Scale (CARS)*, paper presented at the First Human Performance, Situation Awareness, and Automation Conference, Savannah.

McIntyre, R.M. and Salas, E. (1995), 'Measuring and Managing for Team Performance: Emerging Principles From Complex Environments', in R.A. Guzzo and E. Salas (eds), *Team Effectiveness and Decision Making in Organizations*, Jossey-Bass, San Francisco, pp. 9-45.

Moray, N. (1996), 'Mental Models in Theory and Practice', in D. Gopher and A. Koriat (eds), *Attention and Performance XVII*, MIT Press, Cambridge, pp. 223-258.

Mulgund, S., Harper, K., Zacharias, G. and Menke, T. (2000, May), *SAMPLE: Situation Awareness Model for Pilot-In-The-Loop Evaluation*, paper presented at the 9th Conference on Computer Generated Forces and Behavior Representation, Orlando.

Muniz, E.J., Salas, E., Stout, R.J. and Bowers, C.A. (1999), 'The Validation of a Team Situational Awareness Measure', in *Proceedings for the Third Annual Symposium and Exhibition on Situation Awareness in the Tactical Air Environment*, Naval Air Warfare Center Aircraft Division, Patuxent River, pp. 183-190.

Neisser, U. (1976), *Cognition and Reality*, W.H. Freeman and Co, San Francisco.

Nofi, A.A. (2000), *Defining and Measuring Shared Situational Awareness*, Center for Naval Analyses, Alexandria.

Orasanu, J. (1990), *Shared Mental Models and Crew Decision Making*, Technical Report No. 46, Princeton University, Cognitive Sciences Laboratory, Princeton.

Pew, R.W. (1995), 'The State of Situation Awareness Measurement: Circa 1995', in D. Garland and M. Endsley (eds), *Experimental Analysis and Measurement of Situation Awareness*, Embry-Riddle, Daytona Beach, pp. 7-16.

Pew, R.W. (2000), 'The State of Situation Awareness Measurement: Heading Toward the Next Century', in M.R. Endsley and D.J. Garland (eds), *Situation Awareness Analysis and Measurement*, Lawrence Erlbaum Associates Inc, Mahwah, pp. 33-47.

Pew, R.W. and Mavor, A. (1998), *Modeling Human and Organizational Behaviour*, National Academy of Sciences Press, Washington.

Powers, W.T. (1973), *Behavior: The Control of Perception*, Aldine DeGruyter, Hawthorne.

Prince, C. and Salas, E. (1993), 'Training and Research for Teamwork in the Military Aircrew', in E.L. Weiner, B.G. Kanki and R.L. Helmreich (eds), *Cockpit Resource Management*, Academic Press, San Diego, pp. 337-366.

Prince, D., Salas, E. and Brannick, M. (1999), 'Situation Awareness: What Do We Know Now That the 'Buzz' Has Gone?', in D. Harris (ed.), *Engineering Psychology and Cognitive Ergonomics*, Ashgate Publishing Ltd, Aldershot, vol. 3, pp. 216-221.

Rasmussen, J. (1983), 'Skills, Rules, and Knowledge; Signals, Signs, and Symbols, and Other Distinctions in Human Performance Models', *IEEE Transactions on Systems, Man and Cybernetics*, vol. 13(3), pp. 257-266.

Rasmussen, J., Pejtersen, A. and Goodstein, L.P. (1994), *Cognitive Systems Engineering*, John Wiley and Sons, New York.

Rouse, W.B. and Morris, N.M. (1986), 'On Looking into the Black Box: Prospects and Limits in the Search for Mental Models', *Psychological Bulletin*, vol. 100(3), pp. 349-363.

Salas, E. and Fiore S.M. (2004), *Team Cognition: Understanding the Factors That Drive Process and Performance*, American Psychological Association, Washington.

Salas, E., Stout, R.J. and Cannon-Bowers, J.A. (1994), 'The Role of Shared Mental Models in Developing Shared Situational Awareness', in R.D. Gilson, D.J. Garland, and J.M. Koonce (eds), *Situational Awareness in Complex System*, Aeronautical University Press, Embry-Riddle, pp. 297-304.

Sarter, N.B. and Woods, D.D. (1991), 'Situation Awareness: A Critical But Ill-Defined Phenomenon', *International Journal of Aviation Psychology*, vol. 1(1), pp. 45-57.

Sarter, N.B. and Woods, D.D. (1995), 'How in the World Did I Ever Get Into That Mode: Mode Error and Awareness in Supervisory Control', *Human Factors*, vol. 37(1), pp. 5-19.

Schwartz, D. (1990), *Training for Situational Awareness*, Flight Safety International, Houston.

Shebilske, W.L., Goettl, B.P. and Garland, D.J. (2000), 'Situation Awareness, Automaticity, and Training', in M.R. Endsley and D.J. Garland (eds) *Situation Awareness Analysis and Measurement*, Lawrence Erlbaum Associates Inc, Mahwah, pp. 303-323.

Shively, R.J., Brickner, M. and Silbiger, J. (1997), 'A Computational Model of Situational Awareness Instantiated in MIDAS', in *Proceedings of the Ninth International Symposium on Aviation Psychology*, University of Ohio, Columbus, pp. 1454-1459.

Smith, K. and Hancock, P.A. (1995), 'Situation Awareness is Adaptive, Externally Directed Consciousness', *Human Factors*, vol. 37(1), pp. 137-148.

Stout, R.J., Cannon-Bowers, J.A. and Salas, E. (1997), 'A Team Perspective on Situational Awareness (SA): Cueing Training', in *Proceedings of the 19th annual Interservice/ Industry Training, Simulation and Education Conference*, Orlando, pp. 174-182.

Stout, R.J., Cannon-Bowers, J.A, Salas, E. and Milanovich, D.M. (1999), 'Planning, Shared Mental Models, and Coordinated Performance: An Empirical Link is Established', *Human Factors*, vol. 41, pp. 61-71.

Thomas, E.J. and Helmreich, R.L. (2002), 'Will Airline Safety Models Work in Medicine?', in K.M. Sutcliffe and M.M. Rosenthal (eds), *Medical Error*, Jossey-Bass, San Francisco, pp. 217-234.

Tindale, R.S. and Kameda, T. (2000), ''Social Sharedness' as a Unifying Theme for Information Processing in Groups', *Group Processes and Intergroup Relations*, vol. 3, pp. 123-140.

van Dijk, T. (1999), 'Context Models in Discourse Processing', in H. van Oostendorp and S.R. Goldman (eds), *The Construction of Mental Representations During Reading*, Laurence Erlbaum Associates Inc, Mayhaw, pp. 123-148.

van Dijk, T. and Kintsch, W. (1983), *Strategies of Discourse Comprehension*, Academic Press, New York.

Waern, Y. (1998), 'Analysis of a Generic Dynamic Situation', in Y. Waern (ed.), *Co-operative Process Management: Cognition and Information Technology*, Taylor and Francis, Bristol, pp. 7-20.

Wagner, M. and Simon, R. (1990), *Development of Measures of Crew Coordination*, Technical Report No. 0030, Dynamics Research Corporation, Wilmington.

Wegner, D.M. (1986), 'Transactive Memory: A Contemporary Analysis of the Group Mind', in B. Mullen and G.R. Goethals (eds), *Theories of Group Behaviour*, Springer-Verlag, New York, pp. 185-208.

Wellens, A.R. (1993), 'Group Situation Awareness and Distributed Decision Making from Military to Civilian Applications', in N.J. Castellan (ed.), *Individual and Group Decision Making: Current Issues*, Erlbaum, Hillsdale, pp. 267-291.

Wickens, C.D. and Hollands, J.G. (2000), *Engineering Psychology and Human Performance*, (3rd ed.), Prentice Hall, Upper Saddle.

Zacharias, G., Miao, A., Illgen, C., Yara, J. and Siouris, G. (1996), *SAMPLE: Situation Awareness Model for Pilot-In-The-Loop Evaluation*, paper presented at the First Annual Conference on Situation Awareness in the Tactical Air Environment, Naval Air Warfare Center, Patuxent River.

Chapter 2

Correspondence, Cognition and Sensemaking: A Radical Empiricist View of Situation Awareness

Sidney Dekker and Margareta Lützhöft

SA as the Difference Between Matter and Mind

The relationship between mind and matter has dominated many struggles in the history of psychology. All psychological theories, including those on Situation Awareness (SA), implicitly or explicitly choose a position with respect to this relationship. Virtually all theories of SA rely on the idea of correspondence – a match, or correlation, between an external world of stimuli and an internal world of mental representations. Such theories are dualist because they separate the notion of an outside, 'objective' material world, and a subjective, mental mirror or simile of that world.

Situation awareness is not just about awareness of a situation (i.e., the mental existence of that simile), but about the accuracy of that awareness. A good match, or a close correspondence between the mental and the material, is thought to produce 'good SA'; a bad match is synonymous to bad SA, or to having 'lost SA'. In many contributions to SA research, this idea is illustrated with Venn diagrams, which indicate the difference between what people were aware of in a particular situation, and what they could, or should have been aware of. While not all authors apply the same terms, Venn diagrams point out the mismatch between 'actual' or 'ideal' SA (see Figure 2.1 for an example). The labels 'actual' and 'ideal' could also be replaced by 'mind' and 'matter'. 'Mind' is the small circle (this is the scope and contents of the mental mirror of the outside world). 'Matter' is the larger circle, which refers to all available material out there that would be interesting and relevant for the observer to look at and know about in that particular situation.

The Venn diagram notation (Figure 2.1) illustrates the normativism inherent in today's theories of SA. These theories aim to understand mental processes by reference to ideals or normative standards that describe optimal strategies. Common expressions such as 'deficient SA' or 'loss of SA' are evidence of this subtractive model, where researchers seek to understand or model SA in terms of how far short if falls from some 'ideal'. SA is nothing in and of itself: it can only be expressed in relation to some norm. SA, in other words, is the difference between what people apparently knew about a situation and what they could or

22

should have known about that situation. The mind-matter problem is closed by mapping the delta, the gap between matter and mind: there was all this matter (how could they have missed it!) and there was only this much of it in the mind.

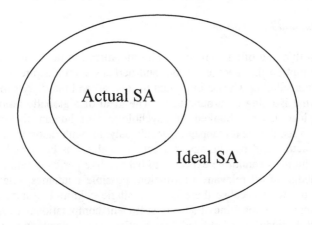

Figure 2.1 The typical depiction of SA (Situation Awareness): as a difference between that which is 'in awareness' currently versus that which could or should be

The Venn notation confirms the idea that situation awareness is about accuracy – about achieving an accurate mapping between some objective, outside world (the large circle) and the inner representation of that world (the small circle). The idea of an 'objective' environment somewhere out there, independent of the observer, is a necessary ingredient for this characterization of SA. Accuracy, per definition, is about a relationship. Yet the notion of accuracy is not necessarily sustainable if we have as a goal to model cognitive processes that lead to an understanding of dynamic situations. Weick (1995) reminds us that such sensemaking is not about accuracy, but rather about plausibility. What matters to people is not to produce a precise internalized simile of an outside situation, but to account for their sensory experiences in a way that supports action and goal achievement.

Seeing SA as a measure of the accuracy of correspondence between an outer world and an inner representation carries with it a number of irresolvable problems – latter-day instantiations of the mind-matter problem. We will deal with these in turn here. First, accuracy ideals imply rationalism, which has long since lost credibility as a basis for modeling psychological processes. Second, the dualist pursuit of accuracy is born out of what Varela, Thompson and Rosch (1991) have called 'Cartesian anxiety' – rife in human factors, but unable to deal with the more complex problems of sensemaking. Third, there are problems related to the presumed perception of 'elements' in the world and the construction of meaning in the head. Is that really what happens? This spins off into various subsidiary problems, for example the role of history in SA that most current theories do not satisfactorily take into account. As this chapter hopes to illustrate, the radical empiricist position is one reply to these problems: it does away with dualism and notions of accuracy, but we will test it against a case study to see what 'sense' this position makes for creating progress in our understanding of SA.

Normativism and Rationalism

Normativist thinking often coincides with rationalism: in the case of SA there is a hidden assumption that people can be (and perhaps should aspire to be) perfectly rational in considering what is important to look at, and that they can be perfectly aware of what is going on around them. The ideal of a globally rational observer has long since been debunked in psychology and human factors, and it is interesting to see the ideal reappear, if insidiously, through theories of SA. In much of human factors and psychology, perfect rationality has been replaced by local rationality: humans cannot be expected to behave like perfectly rational observers. Full knowledge of all relevant information, possible outcomes, relevant goals is impossible to attain because there is not a single cognitive system in the world (neither human nor machine) that has sufficient computational capacity to deal with that all. Rationality is bounded. Observations and understanding what is going on are governed by people's local focus of attention, which in turn is governed by goals, expectations and knowledge, rather than some global ideal, or full rationality.

'Rationality thus has interpretive flexibility: what is locally rational does not need to be globally rational. If a focus of attention is locally rational, it makes sense from the point of view of the observer – which is what matters if we want to learn about the underlying reasons for what from the outside looks like 'deficient SA'. The notion of local rationality removes the need to rely on irrational or motivational explanations of 'deficient SA' or the 'loss of SA'. Such performance makes sense; it is rational, if only locally so, when seen from the inside of the situation in which it occurred.

Knowing about and guarding against this fallacy, this mixing of realities (a normative one versus the inside-out one, if you will), is critical to understanding 'SA'. When looked at from the position of retrospective outsider, the 'loss of SA' can look so very real, so compelling. They failed to notice, they did not know, they should have done this or that. But from the point of view of people inside the situation, as well as potential other observers, this same 'loss of SA' is often nothing more than normal work. If we want to begin to understand why it made sense for people to do what they did, we have to reconstruct their local rationality. Behavior is rational within situational contexts: people do not come to work to do a bad job, to 'lose SA'.

To begin to understand the awareness of other people at another time and place, a precondition is to make this switch, this inversion of perspectives. We have to submit to putting ourselves in the shoes of other people. This context becomes the constraint on what meaning we, who were not there when it happened, can now give to past controversial assessments and actions. Forget the Venn diagram and the difference between what was known and what could or should have been known. In hermeneutics this is known as the difference between exegesis (reading out of the text) and eisegesis (reading into the text). The point is to read out of the text what it has to offer about its time and place, not to read into the text what we want it to say or reveal now. Jens Rasmussen is among the foremost advocates of this in human factors: if we cannot find a satisfactory answer to questions such as 'how could they not have known?', then this is not because these people were behaving bizarrely. It is because we chose the wrong frame of reference for understanding their behavior. The outside circle of a Venn diagram is the wrong frame, as it artificially imposes a normative rendering of reality on what other people were seeing at the time. Instead, the frame of reference for understanding people's behavior is their own normal, individual work context, the context they are deeply embedded in and from which point of view the decisions and assessments made are mostly normal, daily, unremarkable, unnoticeable even. A challenge is to understand how assessments and actions that from the outside look like 'deficient SA' become neutralized or normalized, so that from the inside they appear non-remarkable, routine, normal. Some in sociology too, promote the search beyond individual failure, for example by framing puzzling behavior in complex organizations as individuals struggling to make sense (Snook, 2000).

Anthropologists assert that the adequacy of an insider's representation of the situation cannot be called into question. The reason is that there are no objective features in the domain on which we can base such a judgment. In fact, as soon as we make such a judgment, we have imported criteria from the outside – from another time and place, from another rationality. Ethnographers have always championed the point of view of the person on the inside. Emerson, as did Rasmussen, advised that instead of using criteria from outside the setting to examine mistake and error, we should investigate and apply local notions of competent performance that are honored and used in particular social settings (Vaughan, 1996). The ethnographic distinction between *etic* and *emic* perspectives was coined in the 1950s, to capture the difference between how insiders view a setting and how outsiders view it. Emic originally referred to the language and categories used by people in the culture studied, while etic language and categories were those of the outsider (e.g., the ethnographer) based on their analysis of important distinctions. Today, emic is often understood to be the view of the world from the inside-out, i.e., how the world looks from the eyes of the person studied. The point of ethnography is to develop an insider's view of what is happening. Etic is contrasted as the perspective from the outside-in, where researchers or observers attempt to gain access to some portions of an insider's knowledge through psychological methods such as surveys or laboratory studies.

Empiricism and Radical Empiricism

Most theories of SA actually leave the processes by which the gap between mind and matter is closed, by which such correspondence comes about, to the imagination, other than appealing to information processing psychology. Information processing theories begin with the primitive, meaningless nature of stimuli in the world (they are 'elements' in the words of one SA theory). The human mind has to engage in various kinds of work (including retrieving data from mental stores and matching it with the incoming stimuli) to make sense of the sensory impressions through successive stages of processing (or 'levels' of SA). Figure 2.2 illustrates the typical idea of SA as a process of mental addition to impoverished stimuli from the outside world.

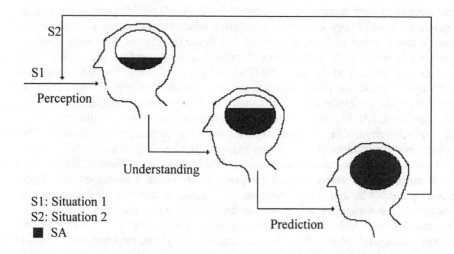

S1: Situation 1
S2: Situation 2
■ SA

Figure 2.2 SA seen as additive process, where meaning is constructed from impoverished stimuli through successive stages of mental processing. (Loyola, 2004; reproduced with permission)

A side effect of using the information processing metaphor (as is the focus on accuracy versus plausibility) is that SA is seen as a problem of getting more information into people, and more information processed through their limited intrapsychic channels. Yet sensemaking, as Weick (1995) and others (e.g., Woods, Patterson and Roth, 2002) point out, is not about more information, about more data, more elements. 'That is not what people need when they are overwhelmed by equivocality. Instead, they need values, priorities, and clarity about preferences to help them be clear about' what matters (Weick, 1995, p. 27).

Most SA theories are product-oriented. Even their methods of inquiry reflect an interest in the end result, as indicated by the Venn diagrams. Methodological concerns center on questions such as 'do you remember what you saw?' over an investigation of the processes that produce(d) such awareness. SA thus refers to the present or immediately past contents of mind relative to then available matter. Understanding cognition (or understanding SA) is synonymous to the mapping of those contents in relation to the objective matter available to the person at the time. Such thinking resembles the controlled Wundtian introspection used in German laboratories at the start of experimental psychology in the 19th century. Wundt's concern for the 'elements' of sensations brought him to the same types of introspective questions that SA researchers are pursuing nowadays.

On the Perception of 'Elements'

Theories of SA borrow from empiricism (particularly British empiricism), which assumed that the organized character and the meaningfulness of our perceptual world are achieved by matching incoming stimuli with prior experience, through a process called association The idea was that stimuli are meaningless; that the world as experienced is disjointed (consisting of 'elements') except when mediated by previously stored knowledge. Correspondence between mind and matter is made by linking incoming impressions through earlier associations.

Consistent with the tenets of empiricism, most theories of SA begin with a perception of 'elements' in the environment, in the situation. It is on the basis of these 'elements' that we gradually build up an understanding of the situation, by processing such elementary stimulus information through multiple stages of consciousness or awareness ('levels of SA'). But do we perceive 'elements'? Wundt may have liked to think so, and British empiricists certainly claimed that we do. The idea that we perceive elements was given further credence through the late 19th century discovery of photoreceptors in the human eye. Their mosaic already chunks up the percepts coming into the eyeball, sending the subsequent neural signals for further processing up the perceptual path, all the way to the visual cortex where finally a (conscious) percept appears. But if we perceive elements, then how does order in our perceptual experience come about? Order, according to most SA theories (and information processing) is an end-product, it is the output of mental, or cognitive work; the result of an internal trade in representations. During the flow from periphery (eyeball) to center (visual cortex) a number of operations are applied on the elementary stimulus material, gradually converting elements into meaning. According the empiricists, a large part of this meaning results from our ability to make associations – to link previous perceptions of elements with current stimuli and understand their connection.

But, again, do we perceive elements? The Gestalt tradition, launched in part as a response or protest to Wundtian elementarism, claimed that we actually perceive meaningful wholes; that we immediately experience those wholes. We cannot help but to see these patterns, these wholes. Max Wertheimer (1880-1934), one of the founding fathers of Gestaltism, illustrates this:

> I am standing at the window and see a house, trees, sky. And now, for theoretical purposes, I could try to count and say: there are … 327 nuances of brightness [and hue]. Do I see '327'? No; I see sky, house, trees. (Wertheimer 1923/1950; translated from the original by N. Sarter in Woods et al., 2002, p. 28)

The gestalts that Wertheimer sees (house, trees, sky) are primary to their parts (their elements), and they are more than the sum of their parts. There is an immediate orderliness in experiencing the world. Wertheimer inverts the empiricist claim: rather than meaning being the result of mental operations on elementary stimuli, it actually takes painstaking mental effort (counting 327 nuances of brightness and hue) to reduce primary sensations to their primitive elements. We do not perceive elements: we perceive meaning. Meaning comes effortlessly, prerationally. In contrast, it takes cognitive work to see elements. In the words of William James' senior Harvard colleague Chauncey Wright, there is no antecedent chaos that requires some intrapsychic glue to prevent percepts from falling apart.

Empiricism does not recognize the immediate orderliness of experience because it does not see relations as real aspects of immediate experience (Heft, 2001). Relations are a product of mental (information) processing. This is true too for theories of SA. For them, relations between elements are mental artifacts. They get imposed through stages of processing. Subsequent 'levels of SA' add relationships to elements by linking those elements to current 'meanings' and future projections. The problem of the relationship between matter and mind is not at all solved through empiricist responses. But perhaps engineers and designers, as well as many experimental psychologists, are happy to hear about 'elements' (or 327 nuances of brightness and hue). For those can be manipulated in a design prototype and experimentally tested on subjects. Wundt would have done the same thing.

Information processing theories have lost much of their appeal and credibility (having corrupted the spirit of the post-behaviorist cognitive revolution by losing sight of mind and meaning-making) (Bruner, 1990; Clark, 1997). Empiricism (or British empiricism) has slipped into history as another school of thought at the beginning of psychological theorizing. But both form apparently legitimate offshoots in current understandings of SA. Notions similar to those of empiricism and information processing are reinvented under new guises, which reintroduce the same type of foundational problems, while leaving some of the really hard problems unaddressed. The problem of the nature of stimuli is one of those, and associated with it is the problem of meaning-making. How does the mind 'make sense' of those stimuli? Is meaning the end-product of a processing pathway that flows from periphery to center? These are enormous problems in the history of psychology, all of them problems of the relationship between mind and matter, and all essentially still unresolved. Perhaps they are fundamentally unsolvable within the dualist tradition that psychology has inherited from Descartes and Newton.

If dualist approaches are not helpful, then what alternatives are there? Radical empiricism is one way of circumventing the insurmountable problems associated with psychologies based on dualistic traditions, and William James introduced it as such at the beginning of the 20th century (Heft, 2001). Radical empiricism rejects the notion of separate mental and material worlds; it rejects dualism. British empiricism (as does information processing) relies to a great extent on internal mental operations (that provide that intrapsychic glue) to make sense of percepts. In fact, elements in the world are only the starting point, the input data. For empiricists, the interesting (associationist) processes ironically happen in a mental realm, not a material one. This actually makes empiricism less empirical, not more. And, for James, not quite empirical enough.

Radical Empiricism

James adheres to an empiricist philosophy, which holds that our knowledge comes (largely) from our discoveries, our experience (in other words, we are not born omniscient, as the nativists would have it). But, as Heft (2001) points out, James' philosophy is radically empiricist. What is experienced, according to James, is not elements, but relations – meaningful relations. Experiencible relations are what perception is made up of. Such a position can account for the orderliness of experience, as it does not rely on subsequent, or a-posteriori mental processing. Orderliness is an aspect of the ecology, of our world as we experience it and act in it. The world as an ordered, structured universe is experienced as such, not constructed as such through mental work. James thus deals with the matter-mind problem by letting the knower and the known coincide during the moment of perception (which itself is a constant, uninterrupted flow, rather than a moment). Ontologies (our being in the world) are characterized by continual transactions between knower and known where order is not imposed on experience, but is itself experienced.

Weick (1995) uses the term 'enactment' to indicate how people often produce the environment they face: people create environments which in turn constrain their actions and possible interpretations. This cyclical, ongoing nature of cognition and sensemaking has been recognized by many (see Neisser, 1976) and challenges common interpretations rooted in information processing psychology where stimuli precede meaning-making and (only then) action, and where frozen snapshots of environmental status can be taken as legitimate 'input' to the human processing system. Instead, activities of individuals are only partially triggered by stimuli, because the stimulus itself is produced by activity of the individual. This moves Weick to comment that sensemaking never starts; that people always are in the middle of things. While we may look back on our own experience as consisting of discrete 'events', the only way to get this impression is to step out of that stream of experience and look down on it from a position of outsider, or retrospective outsider.

It is only possible, really, to pay direct attention to what already exists (that which has already passed). 'Whatever is now, at the present moment, under way will determine the meaning of whatever has just occurred' (Weick, 1995, p. 27). SA is in part about constructing a plausible story of the process by which an outcome came about, and the reconstruction of immediate empirical history plays a dominant role in this. Few theories of SA acknowledge this, however, instead directing their attention to the creation of meaning from elements and the future projection of that meaning.

Radical empiricism does not take the stimulus as its starting point, as does information processing, and neither has it need for a posteriori processes (mental, representational) to impose orderliness on sensory impressions. We already experience orderliness and relationships through ongoing, goal-oriented transaction of acting and perceiving. Indeed what we experience during perception is not some cognitive end-product 'in the head'. Rather we are aware of the world, and its structure, in the world, (just) outside of our heads. What is perceived, according to

James, is not a replica, not a simile of something out there. What is perceived is already out there. There are no intermediaries between perceiver and percept; perceiving is direct. This position forms the groundwork of ecological approaches in psychology and even human factors. There are currently no well-developed ecological theories of SA.

Ontological Relativism and 'Cartesian Anxiety'

If there is no separation between matter and mind, then there is no gap that needs bridging; there is no need for reconstructive processes in the mind that make sense of elementary stimuli. In addition, the Venn diagram with a little and a larger circle that depict 'actual' and 'ideal SA' is unnecessary. Radical empiricism allows human factors to stick closer to the anthropologist's ideal of describing and capturing insider accounts. If there is no separation between mind and matter, between 'actual' and 'ideal SA', then there is no risk of getting trapped in judging performance by use of extrogenous criteria; criteria imported from outside the setting (informed by hindsight or some other source of omniscience about the situation which opens up that delta, or gap, between what the observer inside the situation knew and what the researcher knows). What the observer inside the situation knows must be seen as canonical – it must be understood not in relation to some normative ideal. For the radical empiricist, there would not be two circles in the Venn diagram, but rather different rationalities, different understandings of the situation—none of them right or wrong or necessarily better or worse, but all of them coupled directly to the interests, expectations, knowledge and goals of the respective observer.

This is known as ontological relativism: there is plasticity or flexibility associated with what it means to be in the world or in a particular situation. While people live in the same empirical world (actually, the radical empiricist would argue that there is no such thing), they may arrive at rather different, yet equally valid, conclusions about what is going on inside of it, and propose different vocabularies and models to capture those phenomena and activities. There is not a fixed environment out there (the outer circle of the Venn diagram) that exists detached from and external to people. Yet the loss of such 'common denominators' is deeply unsettling to many, even in various sciences. This is Varela's Cartesian anxiety: people seem to need the notion of an outside world, an objective environment, out there independent of them or their constructions of it. Without such stability, such groundedness of our being, our knowing, there is only subjectivism, relativism and ultimately nihilism. Radical empiricism is not deterred by such anxiety. It is entirely anti-dualist and provides a simple solution: even if there is an objective reality out there, some kind of common denominator, we could not know it.

To quell some of the anxiety, philosophers sometimes use the example of a tree. While at first sight an objective, stable entity in some external reality, separate from us as observers, the tree can mean entirely different things to someone in the logging industry as compared to, say, a wanderer in the Sahara. Both interpretations can be valid because validity is measured in terms of local relevance, situational applicability and social acceptability – not in terms of correspondence with a 'real, external world'. Among different characterizations of the world there is no 'more real' or 'more true'. Validity is a function of how the interpretation conforms to the worldview of those to whom the observer makes his appeal (including him- or herself). The question is: why did it make sense to them, at their time and place? The ontological relativist submits that the meaning of observing a particular situation depends entirely on what the observer brings to it. The tree is not just a tree. It is a source of shade, sustenance, survival. Reality, says Weick (1995), is an ongoing project.

Drifting Off Track: A Case for Radical Empiricism

Traditionalist ideas about a lack of correspondence between a material and mental world get a boost from cases where people clearly did not understand what the real nature of the situation was. Navigational accidents are one such category of cases. In hindsight it is easy to see where people were versus where they thought they were. In hindsight, it is easy to point to the cues and indications that people should have picked up in order to update or correct or even form their understanding of the unfolding situation around them. Hindsight has a way of amplifying the importance of those 'elements' that people missed, but should not have missed. Hindsight also helps tremendously in creating cognitive distance between people's understanding at another time and place (which obviously proved wrong because of the outcome of the accident) and our understanding now (which is always right since we have unencumbered access to the real nature of the situation, and, given the outcome, know exactly which elements were critical and should have been picked up).

One such accident is the one that happened to the Royal Majesty, a cruise ship that left Bermuda to set 'sail' for Boston in the summer of 1995. Instead of in Boston, the Royal Majesty ended up on a sandbank close to the Massachusetts shore. It had drifted 17 miles off course during a day and a half of sailing, as the ship's autopilot had defaulted to DR (Dead Reckoning) mode instead of NAV (Navigation) mode. The DR mode does not compensate for the effects of wind and other drift (e.g., swell) like the NAV mode. In DR mode, a north easterly wind meant that the ship was slowly but steadily pushed off course, off to the side of its intended track. Predictably, the NTSB (National Transportation Safety Board) investigation into the accident confirmed that 'despite repeated indications…the crew failed to recognize … numerous opportunities to detect … that the vessel had drifted off track' (NTSB, 1997). The eventual 17 miles between the intended and actual track serves as an emulation of the gap between material and mental worlds: this is where you were, versus this is where you thought you were. With 17 nautical miles in between. The lack of correspondence between these two can only be explained through a 'lack of SA', or a 'loss of SA'. In the dualist tradition, that is.

Why Did It Make Sense to Them?

In the remainder of this chapter, we trace some of the key the events of the Royal Majesty once again. Rather than trying to force find the lack of correspondence between actual and experienced worlds (which is an artificial, retrospective, meaningless exercise), we want to take a radically empiricist's look at the crew's unfolding experience of the situation in which they found themselves. At relevant twists in the plot, we start with the crew's assessments and actions that befuddle and surprise outside observers; where there is a clear mismatch, a lack of correspondence between 'matter' as we know it now, and 'mind' as displayed by peoples understanding and actions back them. How could they not have noticed? Yet rather than wondering why the crew failed to close the gap between matter and mind in a way that we now could do (with full knowledge of the outcome and true nature of the circumstances surrounding them at the time), we try to understand why they experienced the situation they way they did. After all, saying what people should have seen or done does not explain why they did what they did, or why what they saw 'made sense' to them at the time.

Departure from Bermuda

The Royal Majesty departed Bermuda bound for Boston at 12:00 noon on the 9th of June 1995 (NTSB, 1997). The visibility was good, the winds slight and the sea calm. Before the departure the navigator checked the navigation and communication equipment and found it in 'perfect operating condition'. About half an hour after departure the harbor pilot disembarked and the course was set towards Boston. Just before 13:00 there was a cut-off in the signal from the GPS (Global Positioning System) antenna, routed on the fly bridge (the roof of the bridge), to the receiver – leaving the receiver without satellite signals. Post accident examination showed that the antenna cable had separated from the antenna connection.

When it lost the satellite signals, the GPS promptly defaulted to dead reckoning (DR) mode, sounded a brief aural alarm and displayed two codes on the display: DR and SOL. These alarms and codes were not noticed (DR means that the position is estimated, or deduced, hence 'ded', or now 'dead', reckoning. SOL means that satellite positions cannot be calculated). Why was no one 'aware' that a loss of satellite data would automatically lead to DR mode, and that this in turn would affect the whole navigation system? How is it possible that not one of the crew members on the bridge heard the alarm, or 'attended to' the indications on the display? After all, if the visual indications were in plain view on the screen for 34 hours, monitoring must have been deficient? Such questions test SA in the extreme: they would seem to confirm that all data were available (the large circle of the Venn diagram), but that people simply did not direct attention to it. Their SA was 'deficient'; there was a lack of correspondence between a world of matter (indications on a display) and mind. Or?

About 15 years ago, when this particular GPS receiver was manufactured, the GPS satellite system was not as reliable as it is today. Therefore the receiver could, when satellite data was unreliable, use a DR mode in which it estimated positions using an initial position, the gyrocompass for course input and a log for speed input. The GPS thus had two modes, 'normal' and DR, between which it switched autonomously depending on the accessibility of satellite signals.

GPS satellite coverage had, at the time of the incident, been all-inclusive and working well for many years, and the crew did not expect anything out of the ordinary. The GPS antenna was moved in February, since parts of the superstructure occasionally would block the incoming signals, which caused temporary and short (a few minutes, according to the captain) periods of DR navigation. This was to a great extent remedied by the antenna move, as the Majesty Cruise Line's electronics technician testified, and nothing in the officers' testimonies suggests that this had been a problem during the present trip. Several of the officers also testified that they relied on the GPS position data and considered other systems to be back-up systems, and that the only times the GPS positions could not be depended on for accuracy were during these brief episodes. Thus, the whole bridge crew was 'aware' of the DR mode option and how it worked, but none of them ever imagined or were prepared for loss of satellite data caused by a cable break – no previous loss of satellite data was ever so swift and so absolute.

When the GPS switched from normal to DR, an aural alarm sounded and a tiny visual mode annunciation appeared on the display. The aural alarm sounded like that of a digital wristwatch and was less than a second long. This was the first opportunity to notice that the mode had changed. The time of the mode change was a busy time (shortly after departure), with multiple tasks and distracters competing for the crew's attention. A departure involves complex maneuvering, there are several crewmembers on the bridge and there is a great deal of communication. When a pilot disembarks, the operation is highly time-constrained and risky. In such situations, the aural signal could easily have been drowned out, and assuming that it was, no one would be expecting the DR mode, and thus the visual indications were not seen either. From the insider perspective, there was no alarm, as there was not going to be a mode default. There was neither a history, nor an expectation of its occurrence.

Yet even if the initial alarm was missed, the mode indication was continuously available on the GPS display. None of the bridge crew saw it, according to their testimonies. If they had seen it, they knew what it meant, literally translated – dead reckoning means no satellite fixes. But there is a crucial difference between data that with hindsight can be shown to have been available and data that was observable at the time. The indications on the display (DR and SOL) were placed between the two rows of numbers, latitude and longitude, that indicate the ship's position on the screen, and were about one-sixth the size of those numbers. There was no difference in the size and character of the position indications after the switch to DR. The size of the display screen was about 7.5 by 9 centimeters, and the receiver was placed at the aft part of the bridge on a chart table, behind a curtain. The location is reasonable, since it places the GPS, which supplies raw position data, next to the chart, which is normally placed on the chart table. Only in combination with a chart would the GPS data make sense, and furthermore the data was forwarded to the integrated bridge system and displayed there (quite a bit more outstanding) as well.

For the crew of the Royal Majesty, this meant that they would have to leave the forward console, actively look at the display, and expect to see more than a prominent series of digits representing the latitude/longitude position. Even then, if they had seen the two-letter code and translated it into the expected behavior of the ship, it is not a certainty that the immediate conclusion would have been 'this ship is not heading towards Boston anymore'. When the officers did leave the forward console to plot a position on the chart, they looked at the display and saw a position, and nothing but a position, because that is what they were expecting to see. It is not a question of 'not attending to the indications' – they were attending to the indications, the position indications, since plotting the position it is the professional thing to do – and so the mode change continued to pass unnoticed.

If the mode change was so non-observable on the GPS display, why was it not shown more clearly somewhere else? How could the loss of signals reverberate throughout the system, and have such consequences? How could one small failure have such an effect – were there no back-ups, and if not – why not? The Royal Majesty had a modern integrated bridge system, of which the main component was the navigation and command system (NACOS). The NACOS consisted of two parts, an autopilot part to keep the ship on course and a map construction part, where simple maps could be created and displayed on a radar screen. When the Royal Majesty was being built, the NACOS and the GPS receiver were delivered by different manufacturers, and they, in turn, used different versions of the electronic communication standards.

Due to these differing standards and versions, valid position data and invalid DR data sent from the GPS to the NACOS were both 'labeled' with the same code (GP). The installers of the bridge equipment were not told, nor did they expect, that position data (GP-labeled) sent to the NACOS would be anything but valid position data. The designers of the NACOS expected that if invalid data were received it would have another format. Due to this misunderstanding the GPS used the same 'data label' for valid and invalid data, and thus the autopilot could not distinguish between them. Since the NACOS could not detect that the GPS data was invalid the ship sailed on an autopilot that was using estimated positions until a few minutes before the grounding.

A principal function of an integrated bridge system is to collect data such as depth, speed and position from different sensors, which are then shown on a centrally placed display to provide the officer of the watch with an overview of most of the relevant information. The NACOS on the Royal Majesty was placed at the forward part of the bridge, next to the radar screen. Current technological systems commonly have multiple levels of automation with multiple mode indications on many displays. An adaptation of work strategy is to collect these in the same place and another solution is to integrate data from many components into the same display surface (Cook and Woods, 1996). This presents an integration problem for shipping in particular, where quite often components are delivered by different manufacturers.

The centrality of the forward console in an integrated bridge system also sends the implicit message to the officer of the watch that: navigation may have taken place at the chart table in times past, but as of now the work is performed at the console. The chart should still be used, to be sure, but only as a back-up option and at regular intervals (customarily every half-hour or every hour). The forward console is perceived to be a place for all the information needed to safely navigate the ship.

As mentioned, the NACOS consisted of two main parts. The GPS sent position data (via the radar) to the NACOS in order to keep the ship on track (autopilot part) and to position the maps on the radar screen (map part). The autopilot part had a number of modes that could be manually selected; NAV and COURSE. NAV mode kept the ship within a certain distance of a track, and corrected for drift caused by wind, sea, and current. COURSE mode was similar but the drift was calculated in an alternative way. The NACOS also had a DR mode, in which the position was continuously estimated. This backup calculation was performed in order to compare the NACOS DR with the position received from the GPS. To calculate the NACOS DR position, data from the gyro compass and Doppler log was used, but the initial position was regularly updated with GPS data. When the Royal Majesty left Bermuda, the navigation officer chose the NAV mode and the input came from the GPS, normally selected by the crew during the three years the vessel had been in service.

If the ship had deviated from her course more than a pre-set limit, or if the GPS position differed from the DR position calculated by the autopilot, the NACOS would have sounded an aural and clearly shown a visual alarm at the forward console (position-fix alarm). There were no alarms since the two DR positions calculated by the NACOS and the GPS were identical. The NACOS DR, which was the perceived backup, was using GPS data, believed to be valid, to refresh its DR position at regular intervals. This is because the GPS was sending DR data, estimated from log and gyro data, but labeled as valid data. Thus, the radar chart and the autopilot were using the same inaccurate position information and there was no display or warning of the fact that DR positions (from the GPS) were used. Nowhere on the integrated display could the officer on watch confirm what mode the GPS was in, and what effect the mode of the GPS was having on the rest of the automated system, not to mention the ship.

In addition to this, there were no immediate and perceivable effects on the ship since the GPS calculated positions using the log and the gyrocompass. It cannot be expected that a crew should become suspicious of the fact that the ship actually is keeping her speed and course, since that is why the automation was installed in the first place. The combination of a busy departure, an unprecedented event (cable break) together with a non-event (course keeping) and the change of the locus of navigation (including the intra-system communication difficulties) shows that it made perfect sense, in the situation and at the time, not to 'attend to' the mode change.

The Ocean Voyage

Given that the mode change was hard to notice, there was still a long voyage at sea where the problem could have been detected. Why did not one of the officers cross check the GPS position against another source, such as the Loran-C receiver that was placed close to the GPS? (Loran-C is a radio-based navigation system which relies on land-based transmitters.) Why did nobody notice that the Royal Majesty was drifting further from her route with every passing hour? Why were the procedures (e.g., cross checking, alerting the captain of any uncertainty related to the ship's position) not followed? Why did the officers, inappropriately, rely solely on the position-fix alarm to warn them of problems with GPS data? Why did the master not notice that something was wrong?

Until the very last minutes before the grounding, the ship did not act strangely – it was a routine trip, the weather was good and the watches and watch changes uneventful. There were, but only with hindsight, further cues indicating that the situation was not completely under control, and further mechanisms will be invoked to explain why they were not perceived as warnings at the time.

Several of the officers claim to have checked the displays of both receivers, but only used the GPS data to plot positions on the paper chart. Without plotting, assessing a possible error in position by looking at two sets of numbers is a significant cognitive operation. It was virtually impossible to actually observe the implications of the difference between numbers alone. Apart from this, there actually was some cross checking, whether 'conscious' or not. The position on the radar map was checked against the position on the paper chart hourly and the first officer most likely perceived sighting the first buoy as cross checking with GPS data. Another powerful, but unintentional, reassurance was that the master on a number of occasions spent several minutes checking the position and progress of the ship, and did not make any corrections.

Before the GPS antenna was moved, the short spells of signal degradation that lead to DR mode also caused the radar map to 'jump around' on the radar screen (the crew called it chopping) since the position would change erratically. The reason chopping was not observed on this particular occasion was that the position did not change erratically, but in a manner consistent with dead reckoning. It is entirely possible that the satellite signal was lost before the autopilot was switched on, thus causing no shift in position. The crew had developed a strategy to deal with this occurrence in the past. When the position-fix alarm sounded they first changed modes (from NAV to COURSE) on the autopilot and then they acknowledged the alarm. This had the effect of stabilizing the map on the radar screen so that it could be used until the GPS signal returned. It was an unreliable strategy, since the map was being used without knowing the extent of error in its positioning on the screen. And, it also led to the belief that, as mentioned earlier, the only time the GPS data was unreliable was during chopping. Chopping was more or less alleviated by moving the antenna, which means that by eliminating one problem a new pathway for accidents was created. The strategy of using the position-fix alarm as a safeguard no longer covered all or most of the instances of GPS unreliability.

This locally efficient procedure would almost certainly not be found in any manuals, but gained legitimacy through successful repetition becoming common practice over time. It may have sponsored the belief that a stable map is a good map, with the crew concentrating on the visible signs instead of being wary of the errors hidden below the surface. The chopping problem had been resolved for about four months, and trust in the automation slowly grew. The officers made sensible decisions given the constraints on their tasks, at the time, in the specific situation and context.

First Buoy to Grounding

Why did the chief officer and the second officer not follow 'longstanding watch keeping practices when approaching land'? Why did the first officer not positively identify the first buoy? How come the error in position was not detected, given that the vessel was so close to the shore? Furthermore, why did the second officer not take any action after hearing the lookouts report red lights and later blue and white water? Why did he not understand that the warning broadcasted on the VHF concerned his vessel? For what reason did he ignore the fact that he did not see the second buoy on the radar, and even told the master that it had been sighted? In short – why did the crew consistently fail to recognize all warnings, repeated indications that the vessel was not on its intended track and numerous opportunities to avoid the grounding?

The first buoy ('BA') in the Boston traffic lanes was passed at 19:20 on the 10th of June, or so the chief officer thought. The buoy identified by the first officer as the 'BA' turned out to be the 'AR' buoy placed about 15 miles to the west-south-west of the 'BA'. A traffic lane is a separation scheme delineated on the chart to keep meeting and crossing traffic at safe distance and to keep ships away from dangerous areas. It made perfect sense to the first officer to identify the 'AR' as the correct buoy since the echo on the radar screen coincided perfectly with the mark on the radar map that signified the 'BA'. This was in fact a stochastic fit; he expected to see it, and there it was, and the influence of local rationality further strengthened his belief that they were on the right track. At this point in time the first officer probably even believed he had cross checked his position by two independent means; the radar map and the buoy. An uncontrollable factor and an unfortunate coincidence was the sun glare on the ocean surface that made it impossible to visually identify the 'BA'.

An especially problematic aspect of keeping track of an evolving situation manifests itself when several people use an automated system, simultaneously as in an aircraft, or consecutively as the watch keeping officers on a ship. At 20:00 the second officer took over the watch from the chief officer. The chief officer must have provided the vessel's assumed position, as is good watch keeping practice. The second officer had no reason to doubt that this was a correct position, especially given that the chief officer had been at sea for 21 years, spending 30 of the last 36 months on board the Royal Majesty. Shortly after the take-over, the second officer reduced the radar scale from 12 to six nautical miles. This is normal and even canonical practice as vessels come closer to shore or other restricted waters. By reducing the scale, there is less to monitor, thereby increasing the likelihood to see anomalies and dangers. Instead of reducing his scope, it was an act to create safety.

When the lookouts later reported lights, these reports may with hindsight be construed as additional 'elements' that could have helped the crew perceive (understand) the meaning of their situation and its projection in the future (i.e., drifting off track, a potential grounding). But when seen from the inside of the situation, the second officer had no expectation that there was anything wrong, as for him the vessel was safely in the traffic lane. Also, lookouts are liable to report everything indiscriminately; it is always up to the officer of the watch to decide whether to take action or not. There is also a cultural and hierarchical gradient between the officer and the lookouts – they come from different nationalities and backgrounds. At this time, the master also visited the bridge, and just after he left, there was a radio call. This escalation of work may well have distracted the second officer from considering the lookouts' report, even if he had wanted to.

After the accident investigation was concluded, it was discovered that two Portuguese fishing vessels had been trying to call the Royal Majesty on the radio to warn her of the imminent danger. The calls were made not long before the grounding, at which time the Royal Majesty was already 16.5 nautical miles from where the crew knew her to be. At 20:42, one of the fishing vessels called 'fishing vessel, fishing vessel call cruise boat' on channel 16 (an international distress channel for emergencies only). Immediately following this first call in English the two fishing vessels started talking to each other in Portuguese. One of the fishing vessels tried to call again a little later; giving the position of the ship he was calling.

Calling on the radio without positively identifying the intended receiver can lead to mix-ups with disastrous results. Or in this case, if the second officer heard the first English call and the ensuing conversation he most likely disregarded it since it seemed to be two other vessels talking to each other. Furthermore, as he was using the six-mile scale, he could not see the fishing vessels on his radar. If he heard the second call and checked the position he might well have decided that the call was not for him, as it appeared that he was far from that position.

At about this time, the second buoy should have been seen and around 21:20 it should have been passed, but was not. The second officer assumed that the radar map was correct when it showed that they were on course. To him the buoy signified a position – a distance traveled in the traffic lane – and reporting that it had been passed may have amounted to the same thing as reporting that they had passed the position it was (supposed to have been) in. The second officer did not, at this time, experience an accumulation of anomalies, warning him that something was going wrong. In his view this buoy, which was perhaps missing or not picked up by the radar, was the first anomaly, and not perceived as a large one. Paraphrasing the 'Bridge Procedures Guide', it is said that the master should be called when a) something unexpected happens, b) when something expected does not happen (e.g., a buoy), and c) at any other time of uncertainty. It is all very well to define an unexpected event, but when it happens, people tend to quickly rationalize it. This is even more so in the case of not seeing what was expected:

'well, I guess the X isn't doing Y ...', and clearly an act of local rationality. The NTSB report, on the other hand, lists at least five actions that the officer should have taken. He did not take any of these actions, because he was not missing opportunities to avoid the grounding. He was navigating the vessel safely to Boston.

The second officer suspected the radar of being unreliable ('perhaps the radar did not reflect the buoy'), but the radar map was perceived as very reliable. So reliable in fact, that the crew, including the master, had 'sailed it' the entire trip, despite the view that fundamental seamanship practices caution against relying on one source of position information. Then again, the second officer saw and experienced the whole crew doing just this, during his time on board. Everyone trusted the radar map, the GPS, and the position-fix alarm.

The master visited the bridge just before the radio call, called the bridge about one hour after it, and made a second visit around 22:00. The times at which he chose to visit the bridge were calm and uneventful, and did not prompt the second officer to voice any concerns, nor did they trigger the master's interest in more closely examining the apparently safe handling of the ship. Five minutes before the grounding, a lookout reported blue and white water. For the second officer, these indications alone were no reason for taking action. They were no warnings of anything about to go amiss, because nothing was going to go amiss. The crew knew where they were. Nothing in their situation suggested to them that they were not doing enough or that they should question the 'accuracy' of their awareness of the situation.

At 22:20 the ship started to veer, which brought the captain to the bridge. The second officer, still certain that they were in the traffic lane, believed that there was something wrong with the steering. This interpretation would be consistent with his experiences of cues and indications during the trip so far. The master, however, came to the bridge and saw the situation differently, but was too late to correct the situation. The Royal Majesty ran aground east of Nantucket at 22:25, at which time she was 17 nautical miles from her planned and presumed course. None of the over 1000 passengers was injured, but repairs and lost revenues cost the company $7 million.

Drifting off Track: A Case for Sensemaking

With a discrepancy of 17 miles at the premature end to the journey of the Royal Majesty, and a day and a half to discover the growing gap between actual and intended track, the case of 'loss of SA', or 'deficient SA' looks like it is made. But the 'elements' that make up all the cues and indications that the crew should have seen, and should have understood, are mostly products of hindsight; products of our ability to look at the unfolding sequence of events from the position of retrospective outsiders. In hindsight, we wonder how these repeated 'opportunities to avoid the grounding', these repeated invitations to undergo some kind of epiphany about the real nature of the situation was never experienced by the people who most needed it. But the revelatory nature of the cues, as well as the structure or coherence that they apparently have in retrospect, are not products of the situation itself or the actors in it. They are retrospective imports. One effect of hindsight is that 'people who know the outcome of a complex prior history of tangled, indeterminate events, remember that history as being much more determinant, leading 'inevitably' to the outcome they already knew' (Weick, 1995, p. 28). Hindsight allows us to change past indeterminacy and complexity into order, structure, and oversimplified causality.

When looked at from the position of retrospective outsider, the 'deficient SA' can look so very real, so compelling. They failed to notice, they did not know, they should have done this or that. But from the point of view of people inside the situation, as well as potential other observers, these deficiencies do not exist in and of themselves; they are artifacts of hindsight, 'elements' removed retrospectively from a stream of action and experience. To people on the inside, it is often nothing more than normal work. If we want to begin to understand why it made sense for people to do what they did, we have to put ourselves in their shoes. What did they know? What was their understanding of the situation?

Rather than construing the case as a 'loss of SA' (which simply judges other people for not seeing what we, in our retrospective omniscience, would have seen), there is more explanatory leverage in seeing the crew's actions as normal processes of sensemaking – of transactions between goals, observations and actions. As Weick (1995) points out, sensemaking is:

> Something that preserves plausibility and coherence, something that is reasonable and memorable, something that embodies past experience and expectations, something that resonates with other people, something that can be constructed retrospectively but also can be used prospectively, something that captures both feeling and thought... In short, what is necessary in sensemaking is a good story. A good story holds disparate elements together long enough to energize and guide action, plausibly enough to allow people to make retrospective sense of whatever happens, and engagingly enough that others will contribute their own inputs in the interest of sensemaking. (p. 61)

Even if one does make the concessions to the existence of 'elements', as Weick does in the above quote, it is only for the role they play in constructing a plausible story of what is going on, not for building an accurate mental simile of an external world somewhere out there.

References

Bruner, J. (1990), *Acts of Meaning*, Harvard University Press, Cambridge, MA.

Clark, A. (1997), *Being There*, MIT Press, Cambridge, MA.

Cook, R.I. and Woods, D.D. (1996), 'Adapting to New Technology in the Operating Room', *Human Factors*, vol. 38(4), pp. 593-613.

Heft, H. (2001), *Ecological Psychology in Context: James Gibson, Roger Barker, and the Legacy of William James' Radical Empiricism*, Lawrence Erlbaum Associates, Mahwah, NJ.

Loyola, M. (2004), *Integrating Qualitative and Quantitative Research Methods: Situation Awareness, Cognitive Systems and Experimental Design*, Unpublished MSc thesis (in Swedish), Department of Computer Sciences, Linköping University, Sweden.

National Transportation Safety Board (1997), *Marine Accident Report: Grounding of the Panamanian Passenger Ship Royal Majesty on Rose and Crown Shoal near Nantucket, Massachusetts, June 10, 1995* (NTSB/MAR-97/01), NTSB, Washington, DC.

Neisser, U. (1976), *Cognition and Reality: Principles and Implications of Cognitive Psychology*, Freeman, San Francisco, CA.

Snook, S.A. (2000), *Friendly Fire: The Accidental Shootdown of US Black Hawks over Northern Iraq*, Princeton University Press, Princeton, NJ.

Varela, F.J., Thompson, E. and Rosch, E. (1991), *The Embodied Mind: Cognitive Science and Human Experience*, MIT Press, Cambridge, MA.

Vaughan, D. (1996), *The Challenger Launch Decision: Risky Technology, Culture and Deviance at NASA*, University of Chicago Press, Chicago, IL.

Weick, K.E. (1995), *Sensemaking in Organizations*, Sage Publications, Thousand Oaks, CA.

Woods, D.D., Patterson, E.S. and Roth, E.M. (2002), 'Can we ever Escape from Data Overload? A Cognitive System Diagnosis', *Cognition, Technology and Work*, vol. 4, pp. 22-36.

Chapter 3

The Concept of the Situation in Psychology

John Flach, Max Mulder and Marinus M. van Paassen

Introduction

> The emphasis on finding and describing 'knowledge structures' that are somewhere 'inside' the individual encourages us to overlook the fact that human cognition is always situated in a complex sociocultural world and cannot be unaffected by it. (Hutchins, 1995, p. xiii)

In the previous chapter, Dekker and Lützhöft introduced the dichotomy of mind and matter that is typically suggested by discussions of Situation Awareness (SA). In some respects this chapter provides another tactic for escaping this dichotomy to address the issue of 'what matters.' That is, we propose an approach to *situations* that reflects the relations associated with satisfying functional goals in work ecologies. This approach is based on Rasmussen's (1986) Abstraction Hierarchy and is consistent with Simon's concept of problem space and Gibson's concept of ecology. Note that the concepts of problem space and ecology do not reflect environments independent of observers. Rather, they describe situation constraints that are intimately related to observers in terms of intentions and intrinsic constraints on perception and action. Similarly, these constraints reflect the environments in terms of consequences and external constraints on perception and action. The abstraction hierarchy describes the confluence of internal and external constraints as a nested hierarchy of means-ends relations.

In his famous parable of the ant traveling across a cluttered beach, Herbert Simon (1981; see also Vicente, 1999) offered a hypothesis that should be a challenge to all who are interested in SA. He wrote,

> Viewed as a geometric figure, the ant's path is irregular, complex and hard to describe. But its complexity is really a complexity in the surface of the beach, not a complexity in the ant. (Simon, 1969, p. 64)

Consistent with this observation, building a description of the problem space (in terms of states, operators, and constraints) was at the center of Simon's approach to engineering intelligent systems.

In a similar vein, Gibson's (e.g., 1966, 1979) ecological approach has been characterized by Mace (1977) as asking the question, 'what is the head inside of?' in contrast to the more conventional approach to psychology of asking 'what is inside the head?' For Gibson, a key to understanding behavior was an analysis of the stimulus or ecology. The title of this chapter was inspired by Gibson's (1960) paper on the concept of the stimulus in psychology. Paraphrasing from that work,

> There is a weak link in the chain of reasoning by which we explain experience and behavior [situation awareness], namely, our concept of stimulus [situation]. The aim of this paper is to find out what psychologists mean by the term stimulus [situation], with the hope of deciding what they ought to mean by it. (Gibson, 1960)

In contrast to the advice of Simon and Gibson about the need for clear descriptions of the problem space or the ecology, it appears that the concept of 'situation' is almost completely missing in discussions of Situation Awareness (SA). It seems that the dialogue has crystallized around questions of 'awareness.' And that awareness has been operationalized in terms of information processing stages in the head of the human operator – somewhere between the perception and decision-making stages (e.g., Endsley, 1995). The emphasis has been on the content of the boxes in these stage models, rather than on the nature of the situation that the processing system is embedded within. The thesis of this chapter is that a clear understanding of what we mean by the term 'situation' is essential for any progress toward a coherent theory of SA.

It is important to be clear that we believe the phenomena associated with an operator's feelings of being in control of events (high SA) or of being lost in events (low SA) are important phenomena to study. And that we think that the term 'situation awareness' is a good term to represent this phenomenon. However, we worry that the term is inappropriately treated as an explanation, rather than as a simple label of the phenomenon (Flach, 1994; 1995). Psychologists from James (1890) to Underwood (1957) have warned that this temptation to reify descriptions of phenomena as mechanisms in the head is a major threat to the development of a scientific approach to mind. It is important that we don't slip into using the description of a phenomenon (i.e., high or low situation awareness) as an explanation for the phenomenon.

Also, it is not our intention to dismiss the role of internal constraints that are typically associated with or implied by the term 'awareness.' As Rasmussen (1978) has noted, the human may be more complex than suggested by Simon's ant analogy. This complexity can be reflected in the different strategies that the human can use for navigating through the problem space. Our thesis has to do with the logic of research and inference about the nature of 'awareness' (Flach, 1995). Our claim is that we must start by defining the events of interest. We claim that a clear approach to measuring situations is an essential ingredient in any empirical attack on the problem of 'awareness.'

We also claim that the properties of situations may be more important for generalizing from one work domain to another, than properties of awareness. In part, this claim reflects our appreciation for the flexible, adaptive nature of humans. Because of this adaptive nature, we believe that internal human processing constraints will rarely be a limiting factor on work. We realize that this notion is contrary to the conventional wisdom that tends to treat the human as the weak link in any complex system and that treats human information processing limitations as the basis for generalizing from one domain to another (e.g., Wickens, 1984).

Norman (1993) has attributed the focus on human limitations to a 'machine bias' in our normative image of cognition. This bias tends to hold the capabilities of computers as a gold standard against which, humans are found wanting. This bias can be illustrated in the context of Miller's (1956) Magic Number (seven plus or minus two). The observation that humans have a 'limited' capacity in terms of the number of 'chunks' that they can keep in 'working memory.' Conventional wisdom tends to emphasize the number seven plus or minus two as a hard limitation (i.e., information processing bottleneck) that humans bring to complex systems. However, the research clearly shows that human experts have a unique ability to reduce very complex stimuli into a set of coherent chunks [in Dreyfus's (1992) terms an ability to zero-in on relevant properties]. Thus, expert chess players are able to remember complete layouts of a chessboard and are able to 'see' good moves as the first options that they consider (de Groot, 1965; Chase and Simon, 1973). Because of the capacity of humans to parse complex situations into a few coherent chunks, the seven plus or minus two constraint will rarely be a limit on the performance of experts in their natural domains.

It is important to note that the ability to see the chessboard as a coherent set of chunks is destroyed when the pieces are placed randomly. Thus, the high levels of situation awareness depend on the structure of the game of chess (i.e., the situation). The structure of the game is the analog to the beach landscape in Simon's parable. It is our claim that building a description of that landscape is an essential first step toward understanding both the impressive ability of chess experts to make sense of complex situations and the learning challenge that novices face.

The purpose of this chapter is not to defend these claims. In fact, the claims may be indefensible, in that they reflect 'first principles' guiding our research. Rather, our goal is to begin exploring ways for describing situations. In doing this, it is important that we acknowledge our debt to Rasmussen (1986; Rasmussen, Pejtersen, and Goodstein, 1994) and the important things that he has taught us about levels of abstraction and decomposition for describing work situations. We will define a situation as a nested set of constraints that have the potential to shape performance. In this context, high skill or high situation awareness will reflect a tight coupling to these constraints. That is, the skilled operator will take advantage of the constraints to 'chunk' complex stimuli in order to make sense of situations. Low skill or low situation awareness will reflect a de-coupling from the constraints, so that the complex stimuli do not cohere into a structured whole. We will use Rasmussen's Abstraction Hierarchy as a framework for describing the constraints.

The Abstraction Hierarchy is typically presented as a tool for work analysis. That is, it is a tool used by Cognitive Systems Engineers to describe work demands. However, it can also be considered as a description of how experts organize or chunk complex information (e.g., Vicente and Wang, 1998). In this sense, higher levels of abstraction provide categories for 'chunking' information at lower levels of abstraction. For discussions of situation awareness, it is this aspect of the Abstraction Hierarchy that is most interesting. In some sense, the Abstraction Hierarchy provides a means for describing the survey knowledge that an operator has of the work landscape. Can a description of the situation constraints in terms of nested levels of abstraction help us to appreciate human expertise? Can it help us to explain the ability of experts to handle complex situations and can it help us to explain how both experts and novices can be over taken by the complexity of events?

The remainder of this chapter will be organized around different levels of abstraction and the implications of each level for our understanding of situations. In applying the Abstraction Hierarchy to the concept of situation, it is important to note that we will be focusing on the space of possibilities, not on specific trajectories of activity. Again, we hope to understand the survey knowledge of the landscape that potentially shapes and bounds behavior. We believe that a rich description of this landscape provides the best context for understanding specific behavioral events. It helps us to understand both how and why people do what they do. In addition, it suggests norms for what people can do and for what people ought to do. We appreciate the cautions offered by Dekker and Lützhöft (Chapter 2, this volume) that these norms should not be used to assign blame. However, we believe that such norms may help us to better understand the complexity that operators are faced with and they may serve as important guides for the design of interfaces and training programs to help operators to manage that complexity.

Functional Purpose

Perhaps the composition and layout of surfaces constitute what they afford. If so, to perceive them is to perceive what they afford. This is a radical hypothesis, for it implies that the 'values' and 'meanings' of things in the environment can be directly perceived. Moreover, it would explain the sense in which values and meanings are external to the perceiver. (Gibson, 1986/1979, p. 127)

Wiener's (1961) Cybernetic Hypothesis formalized the role of goals, intentions, or purpose as a critical dimension of behavioral dynamics. Miller, Galanter, and Pribram (1960) introduced this concept to cognitive psychology as the TOTE Unit. And William Powers's (1973, 1998) work on Perceptual Control Theory (PCT) has continued to remind us of the significance of goals for understanding behavior. For these authors, the goal is operationalized as the reference signal (or signals) in a feedback control system. However, in defining situations, it may be important to take a broader perspective on functional purpose that includes not only the explicit references, but that also includes any dimension that reflects value. That is, any dimension that might be used to 'score' performance or that might index the motives and preferences that a complex system is directed toward.

For example, in the formulation of 'optimal control' problems, in addition to the 'references' in the feedback control system, there is also a 'cost functional.' This cost functional is an explicit statement about the values used to compare one solution with another. Optimization typically refers to the maximization or minimization of the cost functional. The 'quadratic cost functional' used in optimal control models of human tracking performance (e.g., Pew and Baron, 1978) was expressed in terms of minimizing a weighted combination of squared tracking error and squared control velocity. In essence, the goal was defined as a tradeoff between minimizing tracking error and minimizing control effort. In Power's PCT model, the dimensions of the cost functional would be incorporated as outer loops in a hierarchical control system.

Thus, the cost functional is an example of a kind of 'speed-accuracy' tradeoff that is typical of many situations. An important aspect of skill in these situations is to find the right balance between the value of 'effort' and the value of 'precision' (error).

At the Functional Purpose level, we are essentially interested in describing situations in terms of the value constraints. This can include identification of specific end states or goals. But it also includes any other dimensions that impact tradeoffs associated with the accomplishment of those goals. The term 'tradeoffs' is particularly important in the context of the phenomenon of situation awareness. We doubt whether the construct of situation awareness would be necessary in a world of simple servomechanisms designed around single, specific goals. Situation awareness is more likely to be an issue when there are multiple dimensions of value. And where the pursuit of one value comes at the expense of another value. For example, in a game of chess where offensive and defensive goals need to be balanced and resources have to be distributed across the board.

A person with a clear understanding of the trade-offs among the multiple value dimensions might be able to balance or manage these trade-offs more effectively. In some sense, this person might be said to 'have their priorities in order.' Whereas, someone who is unclear about these tradeoffs may have great uncertainty about which of many alternatives might lead to satisfactory results. Such a person may be vulnerable to the classic 'paralysis of analysis' as they laboriously weigh one option against another. The person with the clear understanding would exhibit a higher degree of SA (all other things being equal).

In comparing among situations for the purposes of scientific generalization and design guidance there are several obvious dimensions related to functional purpose. The number of value dimensions and the degree of dependence among the various dimensions are obvious attributes for comparing situations. It is not unreasonable to expect that as the number of dimensions and the degree of dependence increases the more likely there are to be problems of situation awareness.

Another property that may be of significance for generalizing across situations is the degree to which the values are defined around explicit, objective dimensions versus implicit subjective dimensions. For example, one might contrast the problem of controlling a commercial aircraft with the problem of finding an interesting book in a library. For the commercial aircraft pilot, the functional values can be explicitly identified in terms of objective physical (e.g., energy, positions, velocities, fuel, time) and economic (e.g., costs) dimensions. And, for the most part, the highest-level goals are shared by everyone who participates in the work domain – there is a shared value system. For a library, however, the functional values may be far from explicit – and although a patron might be able to recognize a good book when she finds it, she may have great difficultly articulating the values that determine whether a book is satisfactory or not. And each patron that enters the library may have different goals or values in terms of what they consider to be interesting or enjoyable.

Thus, it might be expected that intuitions developed within the domain of aviation are more likely to generalize to other domains where the functional purpose is well defined in terms of shared, objective physical and economic goals (e.g., nuclear power, chemical process control). On the other hand, it may be more likely that intuitions developed within the library domain will generalize to other domains where goals reflect more individual discretion (e.g., web browsers and collaborative design tools).

Functional Measurement

> ... the nature of the computations that underlie perception depends more upon the computational problems that have to be solved than upon the particular hardware in which their solutions are implemented. To phrase the matter another way, an algorithm is likely to be understood more readily by understanding the nature of the problem being solved than by examining the mechanism (and the hardware) in which it is embodied.
>
> In a similar vein, trying to understand perception by studying only neurons is like trying to understand bird flight by studying only feathers: It just can't be done. In order to understand bird flight, we have to understand aerodynamics: only then do the structures of feathers and the different shapes of birds' wings make sense. (Marr, 1982, p. 27)

A second level of description that may be important for a deep understanding of situations concerns the issue of how the goals can be accomplished. In addressing this question at the functional measurement level – the questions are framed in terms of what Marr (1982) called the *computational level* of description. The focus at this level is to describe the situation constraints independently from the algorithms or mechanisms that might be involved. What are the fundamental limits associated with the situation? In the aviation context this would be reflected in general theories of aerodynamics, rather than in particular theories of any specific flying machine. In some respects, this boils down to fundamental issues of measurement: 'how to measure progress toward achieving the functional purposes?' In the language of systems theory, the problem of measurement is reflected in the term 'state' variables. The state dimensions index the 'position' in the problem-space relative to the goals.

Note that there may be many choices for how to describe the 'state' of a system. For example, the state of an aircraft with respect to vertical descent could be described using the variables of altitude, speed, and their derivatives or it could be described using the variables of potential and kinetic energy and their derivatives. Either set of variables will completely span the problem space and it would be possible to map from points in one state space to points in the other. However, in relating these states to other levels of abstraction, one choice of variables may allow a more obvious parsing than the other. For a complete analysis at the level of functional measurement, we believe it is important to explore multiple sets of state variables. Each set of variables (in effect, each coordinate system) may offer unique insights into the situation.

It is tempting to hypothesize that an ability to shift from one coordinate system to another may be a critical factor determining creativity and flexibility. Research on problem solving clearly illustrates how a shift in representation (coordinate systems) can be the key to 'seeing' solutions (e.g., Wertheimer, 1945). A person who can easily shift from one representation to another may be less likely to become 'fixated' on a representation that is not productive. In the present context, a shift in coordinate systems may be the difference between low or high situation awareness.

In the context of Simon's language for describing problem spaces, the abstract measurement level of description will generally reflect the 'constraints' associated with different operators. That is, abstract measurement levels of description provide the general conditions that must be satisfied before an operator can be applied.

In the context of control theory, the measurement problem reflects the need for feedback to guide action with respect to the goals. This feedback must index 'error' with respect to goals as well as the 'potential' for different actions to reduce that error. Where the term 'potential' refers to measures that allow potential actions (operations) to be prioritized in terms of their prospects for effecting movement toward goal states. Flach, Smith, Stanard and Dittman (2003) refer to this as the comparator problem. That is, to have measures so that the states of the system that are fed back can be compared to reference values to yield appropriate commands for actions that will reduce discrepancies (Figure 3.1).

Gibson's (1979) term, 'affordance,' reflects this need for the measures to reflect both ends (i.e., goals or values) and means (i.e., operators or action constraints) of the situation. Gibson's (1979) concept of 'ecological physics' was an expression of the need for a description of stimuli and events (i.e., situations) relative to both means and ends.

In the context of Simon's parable of the ant, a functional purpose might be to efficiently gather food. The measurement issues at the second level of description would be associated with what qualifies as food and what are the indexes of efficiency. For example, how can the functional distance to the goal be measured? Is it linear distance? Is it time? Is it energy required? To be more specific, is the path over the steep rise more or less efficient than an alternative path that goes around the rise. Which path would or should the ant with high SA choose? Similar questions could be framed with respect to the game of chess. What are appropriate measures of the 'strength' of a position, a game situation, or an alternative move?

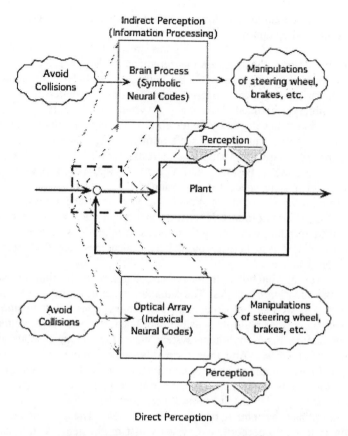

Figure 3.1 For closed-loop control to be possible information feedback must be compared to intentions to yield specification for actions to reduce discrepancies. The comparator problem is to find a common currency for relating intentions, feedback, and action commands

In systems where the goals reflect objective physical states, the physical laws that govern the process will be very important in the choice of state variables. For example, in controlling motion, the laws of motion (e.g., Newton's second law) will be important concerns (e.g., for controlling an inertia system, position and velocity will be critical to any description of a situation). However, as noted above, other levels of description (choices of state variables) may also provide important insights into the dynamics of situations. Vicente's (1992) work on feedwater control and Amelink, Mulder, van Paassen, and Flach's (submitted) (see also Flach, Jacques, Patrick, Amelink, van Paassen, and Mulder, 2003) analysis of aircraft landing illustrate the value of including energy variables in the state description. Vicente found that mass and energy balance relations provided important insights for the feedwater control problem. Amelink et al. found that the balance between potential and kinetic energy provided important insights for controlling the landing approach.

In the case of situations where the goals are related to more discretional or subjective dimensions, the issue of measurement is also critical for a complete description. This is nicely illustrated by Pejtersen's (1984) explorations in the domain of libraries. A critical aspect of characterizing the search for 'interesting' books in a library, involved developing a system for classifying fiction. The classification system developed by Pejtersen (1984) can be thought of as a system for 'measuring' books. This nominal scale of measurement provided categories for describing books relative to people's interests. Similarly, the MDS interface developed by Stappers, Pasman, and Groenen (2000) used multidimensional scaling to build a state space for exploring different features of large product databases (e.g., roller skates or whiskeys). The MDS interface allows customers to learn about the different product dimensions that might make a difference in terms of how well the product will satisfy their needs. It might be said that explorations using the MDS interface help to build better 'awareness' of the nature of the functional 'product space.'

At the level of functional measurement, the key is to find measures for describing the situation dynamics. The situation dynamics reflect both the action (or operations) as well as the perceptual (or feedback) constraints on situations. It is important to consider multiple possible coordinate systems for describing these situation dynamics. Each coordinate system may offer unique insights about the possibilities of situations. And trajectories that look complex in one coordinate system may appear simple in another coordinate system. The essence of Simon's parable of the ant is that when the ant's trajectory is taken out of its natural coordinate system (the beach), it becomes very complex. However, when placed in the right coordinate system, it becomes very simple. The goal at this level of abstraction is to explore coordinate systems that might help us to visualize the landscape of the beach through the eyes and body of the ant. This aspect of description is nicely crystallized in Gibson's construct of 'affordance' and also in von Uexküll's (1957) construct of 'umwelt.'

Functional Organization

> Behavior mission analysis is the process by which system requirements are analyzed to determine their behavioral implications. The logical-deductive process partitions gross requirements into finer detail by asking at each step of the process the following questions: To accomplish this requirement or this function, to satisfy this constraint, what is needed in the way of inputs and outputs and implementing mechanisms? (Meister, 1985)

The next level for describing situations focuses on their functional organization. This level of description comes closest to the classical idea of 'function/task analysis' as described by Meister (1985). This level addresses how resources are organized to link information, action, and purposes. This type of description is often expressed in terms of block diagrams that illustrate the flow of activity within a situation. Rasmussen's (1986) Decision Ladder provides a good framework for thinking about the different possible flows of information as a function of the situation semiotics (Figure 3.2). In this context, semiotics refers to the mapping from the functional purposes and states of the situation (i.e., the meanings) onto the flow of information and activity (i.e., the representations). Rasmussen (1986) suggested three types of mappings that can be important for the flow of activity – signal, sign, and symbol.

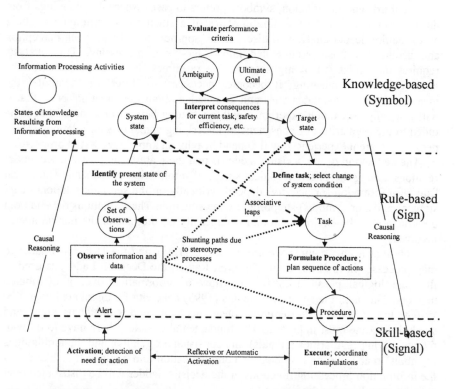

Figure 3.2 The decision ladder after Rasmussen (1986) suggests a framework for thinking about the functional organization of a cognitive system. There are many logical paths through this network of processing stages

Signal refers to cases where there is a direct mapping from aspects of the representation to the meaningful states of the situation. For example, in driving there is a direct mapping from the motion of a steering wheel to the change in direction of an automobile and conversely there is a direct mapping from the flow of optical texture that specifies motion relative to the landscape. This allows the possibility for skill-based or automatic processing. That is, there is little need for inference or dependence on high-level cognitive resources. In this context, it is possible for an operator to 'see' the way through the complexity, without the need for complex 'analysis' of the situation.

Sign refers to cases where there is a consistent history (a correlation over time) between aspects of representations and meaningful states of a situation. These consistencies allow short cuts across the Decision Ladder that Rasmussen called rule-based processing. As with signal mappings, the consistent mapping reflected in sign relations allows a connection between perception and action without the need for a deep analysis of the situation.

The third semiotic relation, symbolic, refers to cases where the mappings from the representation to the meaningful states of a situation are ambiguous. These cases require deeper analysis to discover the appropriate links between perception and action that Rasmussen called knowledge-based processing. This analysis requires the utilization of higher cognitive resources. It is not possible for the observer to 'see' meaning. It becomes necessary to 'infer' or 'compute' the meaning from the available cues and knowledge about the situation. Note that it will generally take much experience with a situation before someone will become tuned to the regularities or consistencies underlying signal or sign relations. Thus, people who are inexperienced will depend heavily on knowledge-based processes.

The key lesson of the decision ladder is that there are many possible sequential relations among the different logical stages of information processing. The actual flow of information (or activity) depends critically on the semiotic relations (e.g., signals, signs, or symbols) supported by the situation. These relations depend both on structure in the environment and perspicacity on the part of the human agents involved.

Note that in this context we are not necessarily using the Decision Ladder to map processes in the head of an observer. Rather, the Decision Ladder is used to illustrate logical possibilities for the flow of information over a distributed network. This is in the spirit of Hutchins (1995) concept of a distributed cognitive system. In this context, the semiotic constraints associated with signals, signs, and symbols become most important. The fundamental questions here have to do with the underlying regularities (signals), the consistencies (signs), and the ambiguities (symbols) that have implications for communication and control. It is likely that the information processing functions in the decision ladder will be distributed over multiple people and technologies.

These kinds of concerns are nicely illustrated in Hutchins's (1995) description of different types of map projections. For example, some maps are designed to allow direct inferences about course and heading through plotting lines on the surface (at the expense of area). Other maps are designed to preserve areas. The point is that the various projections determine whether the maps function as signals, signs, or symbols with respect to various meanings. This in turn has obvious implications for the meanings that can easily be 'seen' using the map versus other meanings that have to be 'figured out.'

Another useful tool for visualizing the functional flow in complex systems is Lind's (1994) language for multilevel flow analysis. This formalism for mapping the signal flows and the control loops is particularly useful for visualizing the organizational constraints in relation to lower and higher levels within the abstraction hierarchy.

In general, the level of situation awareness will be inversely related to the level of processing demanded. That is, feelings of low situation awareness will be highly correlated with the need for higher, knowledge-based processing. Feelings of high situation awareness will be correlated with contexts where the perception-action loop is closed at lower levels in the decision ladder (rule- and skill-based processing). However, the patterns that support rule- and skill-based performance under normal operating circumstances can sometimes lead operators down a garden path to disaster in unusual situations.

Again, as Rasmussen (1978) notes the human is simple in a complex way. An important lesson of the Decision Ladder is that there are many possible paths through the human information processing system (i.e., many degrees of freedom). This allows great flexibility in adapting to a wide range of problems. However, managing many degrees of freedom creates a problem for stable control. Runeson (1977) suggests that a 'smart' system can utilize the flexibility of high degrees of freedom and minimize the management demands on control by organizing itself into various simple machines that are tuned to specific problems. That is, the smart system takes advantage of natural constraints in a problem space and chooses the fewest degrees of freedom required to satisfy the functional goals. This tuning to natural constraints may be a characteristic of high situation awareness. But it can also be a threat to situation awareness when the system moves outside the bounds of the local rationality that guided the design of a normally 'smart' mechanism.

Physical Function

The listing of system functions does not determine how these functions are to be carried out. A function is initially neutral in the sense that it may be implemented by a human, by a machine, or by some combination of both. The process of determining which shall implement the function, and more particularly *how*, is known as *function allocation* (FA). (Meister, 1985)

At the level of general function, the primary concern was a logical decomposition to reflect the flow of information through a network of functions. At the level of physical function, the physical decomposition of the situation into distinct technological systems is considered. What kind of technologies will be implemented to carry out the various functions? Which of the functions are allocated to humans? Which to automation? What types of modalities link the various physical entities? In other words, what kinds of 'agents' are involved in the situation and what are the attributes of the different agents? These questions are classically addressed in the process of function allocation.

At the physical function level, specific 'devices' can be identified that support the achievement of the general functionality that was identified in the previous level. For example for the aircraft, fixed wings are a specific kind of lift-generating device. Without exception, the choice of a specific component involves compromises. Wings for example have maximum load carrying capabilities, and there are minimum and maximum speeds at which they can provide the required function. Analysis of a system at this level typically gives insight to limitations of the system, either because the boundaries of functionality are reached (at low speeds, there simply is not more lift possible with this wing), or because the system integrity is threatened (at high speeds, maximum lift will break the wing). In the aviation domain some specific 'devices' might include:

- wings, for lift;
- control surfaces, to enable maneuverability;
- engines, for sustained flight and acceleration;
- wings and body, for producing drag and deceleration, possibly with additional drag-generating control surfaces;
- the pilots or the autopilot, for control of the aircraft;
- a navigation system, for determination of the own aircraft's position;
- ADSB (Automatic Dependent Surveillance Broadcast) receivers and transmitters, for communication of travel;
- the FMS, for calculation of projected path, storage of ADSB tracks from other aircraft, and possibly for autopilot guidance;
- instrumentation, for communication of information to the pilots.

Note that this is just a small sample of the functions we could identify here, e.g., fuel tanks have not been mentioned. Each of these components has its limitations of functionality, and constraints to ensure continued integrity. Note that most also carry their own non-functional requirements. For example, pilots need a habitable environment, and therefore a functioning pressurization and heating/cooling system. These non-functional purposes are normally not defined at the start of a top-down approach to developing an AH, and it is not customary to express these 'condition for functioning' relationships in the AH. Other methods for expressing functional models, such as Multilevel Flow Modeling, do have explicit language for expressing a function's demands on prior goal achievement.

In terms of SA, the compromises and non-functional requirements associated with a particular choice of device can be critical aspects of the work context. Understanding these limits and demands can be critical for diagnosing problems or for generating creative solutions when systems fail. This reflects one of the biggest challenges in modern socio-technical systems – many of the specific devices, (e.g., Flight Management Systems) are themselves complex systems and few people have the knowledge or training to fully understand the limits of the devices that they depend on. Incomplete or incorrect knowledge about these devices can sometimes lead to loss of situation awareness. This kind of concern is reflected in Sarter and Woods' (1995) discussion of mode awareness.

Physical Form

> For want of a nail the shoe was lost.
> For want of a shoe the horse was lost.
> For want of a horse the rider was lost.
> For want of a rider the battle was lost.
> For want of a battle the kingdom was lost.
> And all for want of a horseshoe nail.
>
> (Classical Nursery Rhyme)

As the classical nursery rhyme suggests, the key to success can often be in the details. The level of physical form considers the details of a situation. At this level the micro-structures of space-time interactions within the situation landscape are considered. At this level, a system is often best described by technical drawings, materials specifications, pictures and similar topological descriptions. Since laboratory systems are normally simulated, and there are a lot of (dreary?) details to be specified at this level, many reports of AHs do not cover this level. However, descriptions at this level are obviously of importance in actual operation of a system, especially when considering maintenance and communication with 'field operators'.

An important aspect of this level of description is the identification of interactions that are not function related. At the physical function level the interaction between the functions is normally identified at a 'systems' level. For example the ADSB transceiver has a maximum capacity and range (functional limits), and a certain energy consumption and cooling requirements (behavioral needs). At the physical form level, however, one can check for interactions across systems (e.g., relative to location). For example, the wing configuration of a specific aircraft might block the signals from the ADSB antenna in certain directions. Or the collocation of electronic and hydraulic systems may lead to an interaction where leaking hydraulic fluids short out electronic circuits.

Again, the potential for surprise or unexpected events may lie in the nonfunctional interactions between components that may appear 'irrational' when considered in light of the functional logic of the work situation. Many critical accidents can be linked to interactions at this level (Rasmussen and Svedung, 2000; Snook, 2000; Woo and Vicente, 2003). For example, in the case of the friendly fire accident described by Snook, the simple fact that the F15s and the Black Hawks were on different radio frequencies was one of the 'lost nails' that set the stage for disaster.

Cognition in the wild is 'situated' in the context of the nonfunctional interactions that can happen at the physical function and physical form levels. These interactions are often 'invisible' to operators since interfaces and training programs are typically designed around functional models of work domains. Thus, as mentioned in the previous section, these 'invisible' aspects of the work can often lead to loss of situation awareness. Although with hindsight, these details may loom large as obvious factors in a causal chain leading to disaster.

The Big Picture

> ... the universal can only be perceived in the particular, while the particular can be
> thought of only in reference to the universal. (Cassirer, 1953, p. 86)

Each level in the Abstraction Hierarchy outlined in this chapter provides a different
perspective on a situation. However, a coherent picture of the situation requires
integration across these levels. That is, the mappings across the various levels
become important for understanding coordinated adaptation to the situation
constraints. One way to think about this mapping across levels is as a nested
hierarchy in which the higher levels provide a categorical structure for chunking
detailed information at lower levels of abstraction.

For example, to understand the meaning of a particular action (pilot adjusting
the throttle during a landing approach) it is useful to place the action in the context
of the physical functions (manual or fly-by-wire control system); in the context of
the general function (following a glide path); in the context of abstract
measurement (the impact on the energy distribution); and the implications for the
goal (safe landing).

Conversely, to know what to do in order to reach a specific goal (safe landing),
it is important to understand the implications for functional measurement (the
appropriate energy balance); to map this balance onto general functions (tracking
speed and altitude with respect to prescribed values); allocated to different physical
components (pilot, co-pilot, or autopilot); requiring specific physical actions
(manipulating throttle), and depending on the proper functioning of specific
devices (fly-by-wire computers).

The mappings across the levels of abstraction can be a key to understanding
what a pilot means when he says he has good or bad SA. We believe that good SA
is associated with the ability to see the connections across levels of abstraction.
This allows the pilot to see what matters; to organize the complexity into coherent
chunks; to see where to go; and to see satisfactory ways to get there. In designing
systems with the goal of good SA, it is the designers' responsibility to make the
mapping across level of abstraction visible to the operators. This is the main theme
of 'ecological interface design' – to make the functional constraints (at all levels of
abstraction) visible to the operators (Amelink et al., submitted; Rasmussen and
Vicente, 1989; Vicente and Rasmussen, 1992).

Poor SA refers to an inability of the pilot to see what matters. Pilots describe
this phenomenon in terms of events being 'unconnected' or 'incoherent.' That is,
the links across levels of abstraction are not clear. Thus, there is no basis for
decomposing the complexity into coherent chunks. It is difficult to see what
matters; to see where to go, or how to get there.

Thus, a model of the situation in terms of the different levels of abstraction and
the mappings from one level to another provides a normative model for assessing
awareness. This model should suggest how skilled operators might 'chunk'
information so that they can smoothly navigate through the problem space. And it
might suggest where operators might be led astray by local regularities that mask
the hidden dangers of exceptional cases. This model also should provide an anchor

against which to measure a novice's understanding of a situation. What links are missing in the novice's understanding of the situation? Are there superstitious links or unnecessary constraints in the novice's image of the situation?

A normative model of situations should also suggest interface and training interventions. In either case, the goal would be to make it easier for the operator to have a coherent image of the situation (to have a basis for chunking complex information into a coherent picture of the situation). In the case of interface design, the goal is to make the connections across levels of abstraction explicit in the configuration of displays and controls. In the case of training, the goal is to provide awareness of the natural patterns (signals) and consistencies (signs) that link levels of abstraction and to provide the knowledge needed to bridge those links that are not apparent as signs or signals.

Summary

I hope to evoke with this metaphor a sense of an ecology of thinking in which human cognition interacts with an environment rich in organizing resources. (Hutchins, 1995, p. xiv)

Consistent with Hutchins' hope, the main theme of this chapter was to show how Rasmussen's Levels of Abstraction could be used to build a description of the rich organizing resources within situations. We believe that a thorough description of these organizing resources is an essential first step to any comprehensive theory of SA. We expect that the humans in complex cognitive systems have many more degrees of freedom than Simon's ant. Thus, this description of situations may not be the whole story, but nevertheless, we claim that it is a critical part of the story.

It is important to note that a 'complete' description of a situation will only be possible for simple, closed-systems (e.g., missionary and cannibals) or isolated micro-worlds (Vicente's DURESS). In more natural work situations, the best we can hope for is an asymptotic approach to a full description. This is in part due to the dynamics of natural work environments that are constantly evolving and in part due to the complexity associated with the rich interactions in natural systems. The idea of an asymptotic approach suggests that you can't learn everything about a situation, but a lot can be learned. Further, we believe a lot can be gained from even a small investment in situation analysis. An iterative process of design and evaluation can be an important path to deeper levels of situation analysis.

In support of the iterative design and evaluation process, we believe it is important to develop 'living abstraction hierarchies' for any complex system (but especially for safety critical systems. By 'living abstraction hierarchies' we mean that the AH should not be an exercise that is conducted in the early design phases and then put aside when a system is fielded. Rather, we believe that it is important to explore ways to build databases that are maintained and updated over the operational life of the system. These databases should be organized to reflect the AH. These databases could be an important resource for upgrading interfaces, for accident investigations, for performance research, and for guiding the development of training curricula as the functionality of the system evolves to take advantage of new technologies and to meet the demands of a changing world.

In sum, we think it is a mistake to treat SA as the answer to the problems of complexity associated with modern socio-technical systems. Rather, SA is a question or a challenge that demands a deeper understanding of situations. We believe that Rasmussen's AH offers a promising direction for addressing this challenge!

References

Amelink, M.H.J., Mulder, M.M., van Paassen, M.M. and Flach, J.M. (Submitted), 'Theoretical Foundations for a Total Energy-based Perspective Flight-path Display', *Journal of Aviation Psychology.*

Cassirer, E. (1953), *The Philosophy of Symbolic Forms,* Yale University Press, New Haven, CT, (Original 1923).

Chase, W.G. and Simon, H.A. (1973), 'The Minds Eye in Chess', In W.G. Chase (ed.), *Visual Information Processing,* Academic Press, New York.

de Groot, A.D. (1965), *Thought and Choice in Chess,* Mouton, The Hague.

Dreyfus, H.L. (1992), *What Computers still can't do: A Critique of Artificial Reason,* MIT Press, Cambridge, MA.

Endsley, M. (1995), 'Toward a Theory of Situation Awareness in Dynamic Systems', *Human Factors,* vol. 37, pp. 32–64.

Flach, J.M. (1994), 'Situation Awareness: The Emperor's New Clothes', In M. Mouloua and R. Parasuaman (eds), *Human Performance in Automated Systems: Current Research and Trends,* Erlbaum, Hillsdale, NJ, pp. 241–248.

Flach, J.M. (1995), 'Situation Awareness: Proceed with Caution', *Human Factors,* vol. 37, pp. 149–157.

Flach, J.M., Jacques, P.F., Patrick, D.L. Amelink, M.H.J., van Paassen, M.M. and Mulder, M.M. (2003), 'A Search for Meaning: A Case Study of the Approach-to-landing'. In E. Hollnagel (ed.), *The Handbook of Cognitive Task Design,* Erlbaum, Mahwah, NJ, pp. 171–192.

Flach, J.M., Smith, M.R.H., Stanard, T. and Dittman, S.M. (2003), 'Collision: Getting them Under Control'. In H. Hecht and G.J.P. Savelsbergh (eds), *Theories of Time to Contact,* Advances in Psychology Series, Elsevier, North-Holland, pp. 67–91.

James, W. (1890), *Principles of Psychology,* Holt, New York.

Gibson, J.J. (1960), 'The Concept of the Stimulus in Psychology'. *American Psychologist,* vol. 15, pp. 694–703.

Gibson, J.J. (1966), *The Senses Considered as Perceptual Systems.* Houghton-Mifflin, Boston.

Gibson, J.J. (1986), *The Ecological Approach to Visual Perception,* Erlbaum, Hillsdale, NJ, (Original work published in 1979).

Hutchins, E. (1995), *Cognition in the Wild,* MIT Press, Cambridge, MA.

Lind, M. (1994), 'Modeling Goals and Functions of Industrial Plant', *Applied Artificial Intelligence,* vol. 7.

Mace, W. (1977), 'James J. Gibson's Strategy for Perceiving: Ask not what's inside your head but what your head's inside of'. In R.E. Shaw and J. Bransford (eds), *Perceiving, Acting, and Knowing,* Hillsdale, NJ, Erlbaum, pp. 43–65.

Marr, D. (1982), *Vision,* Freedman, New York.

Meister, D. (1985), *Behavior Analysis and Measurement Methods,* Wiley, New York.

Miller, G.A. (1956), 'The Magic Number Seven Plus or Minus Two: Some Limits on our Capacity to Process Information, *Psychological Review,* vol. 63, pp. 81–96.

Miller, G.A., Galanter, E. and Pribram, K. (1960), *Plans and the Structure of Behavior,* Holt, Rinehart, and Winston, New York.

Norman, D.A. (1993), *Things that make us Smart,* Addison-Wesley, Boston.

Pejtersen, A.M. (1984), 'Design of a Computer-aided User-system Dialogue based on an Analysis of Users' Search Behavior', *Social Science Information Studies,* vol. 4, pp.167–183.

Pew, R.W. and Baron, S. (1978), 'The Components of an Information Processing Theory of Skilled Performance based on an Optimal Control Perspective'. In G.E. Stelmach (ed.), *Information Processing in Motor Control and Learning,* Academic Press, New York, pp. 71–78.

Powers, W.T. (1973), *Behavior: The Control of Perception,* Aldine, New York.

Powers, W.T. (1998), *Making Sense of Behavior: The Meaning of Control,* Benchmark, New Canaan, CT.

Rasmussen, J. (1978), *Operator/Technician Errors in Calibration, Setting, and Testing Nuclear Power Plant Equipment.* (Report No. N-17-78). Risø National Laboratory, Electronics Department, Roskilde, Denmark.

Rasmussen (1986), *Information Processing and Human-machine Interaction: An Approach to Cognitive Engineering,* North Holland, New York.

Rasmussen, J., Pejtersen, A.M. and Goodstein, L.P. (1994), *Cognitive Systems Engineering,* Wiley, New York.

Rasmussen, J. and Svedung, I. (2000), *Proactive Risk Management in a Dynamic Society,* Swedish Rescue Services Agency, Karlstad, Sweden.

Rasmussen, J. and Vicente, K.J. (1989), 'Coping with Human Errors through System Design: Implications for Ecological Interface Design', *International Journal of Man-Machine Studies,* vol. 31, 517–534.

Runeson, S. (1977), 'On the Possibility of "Smart" Perceptual Mechanisms', *Scandinavian Journal of Psychology,* vol. 18, pp. 172–179.

Sarter, N.B. and Woods, D.D. (1995), 'How in the world did we ever get into that mode? Mode Error and Awareness in Supervisory Control', *Human Factors,* vol. 37, pp. 5–19.

Simon, H. (1981), *Sciences of the Artificial,* (2nd ed.), MIT Press, Cambridge, MA.

Snook, S.A. (2000), *Friendly Fire. The Accidental Shootdown of US Black Hawks over Northern Iraq,* Princeton University Press, Princeton, NJ.

Stappers, P.J., Pasman, G. and Groenen, P.J.F. (2000), Exploring Databases for Taste or Inspiration with Interactive Multi-dimensional Scaling, In *Proceedings of the XIV triennial congress of the International Ergonomics Association and 44th annual meeting of the Human Factors and Ergonomics Society.* San Diego, CA, July 29 – August 4, pp. 3-575–3-578.

Underwood, B.J. (1957), *Psychological Research,* Prentice-Hall, Englewood Cliffs, NJ.

Vicente, K.J. (1992), 'Memory Recall in a Process Control System: A Measure of Expertise and Display Effectiveness', *Memory and Cognition,* vol. 20, pp. 356–373.

Vicente, K.J. (1999), *Cognitive Work Analysis,* Erlbaum, Mahwah, NJ.

Vicente, K.J. and Rasmussen, J. (1992), 'Ecological Interface Design: Theoretical Foundations', *IEEE Transactions on System, Man, and Cybernetics,* vol. 22(4), pp. 589–606.

Vicente, K.J. and Wang, J.H. (1998), 'An Ecological Theory of Expertise Effects in Memory Recall', *Psychological Review,* vol. 105, pp. 33–57.

von Uexküll. J. (1957), 'A Stroll through the Worlds of Animals and Man'. In C.H. Schiller (ed.), *Instinctive Behavior,* International Universities Press, New York, pp. 5–80.

Wertheimer, M. (1945), *Productive Thinking,* Harper, New York.

Wickens, C.D. (1984), *Engineering Psychology and Human Performance,* Merrill, Columbus, OH.

Wiener, N. (1961), *Cybernetics or Control and Communication in the Animal and the Machine,* (2nd ed.), MIT Press, Cambridge, MA.

Woo, D.M. and Vicente, K.J. (2003), 'Sociotechnical Systems, Risk Management, and Public Health: Comparing the North Battleford and Walkerton Outbreaks', *Reliability Engineering and Systems Safety,* vol. 80, pp. 253–269.

Chapter 4

A Task-Oriented Perspective of Situation Awareness

John Patrick and Nic James

Introduction

This chapter reviews critically the nature of SA and discusses evidence from the process control domain that it involves situation specific phenomena. Despite the vast literature concerning SA uncertainty still exists concerning the status of SA as a construct and whether it should be conceptualized as psychological in nature. It is argued, in context of both individual and team SA, that it is useful to conceptualize SA as the product of successfully accomplishing an important yet specific task. This argument is developed in the context of the processes versus the products of achieving awareness and whether SA can be conceptualized as a cause of error. Evidence is discussed from both theoretical and practical perspectives that suggest the situation specific nature of SA. Relevant literature from cognitive psychology is cited and Newell and Simon's model of problem solving is adapted to explain potential SA problems that may develop in nuclear control room teams. In particular, operators' interactions, sometimes involving procedures, not only with a complex interface but also with colleagues provide many opportunities for error, including lack of awareness. Some nuclear incidents are discussed in terms of their SA problems and the extent that they depend on specific contextual details. Some studies that experimentally investigate the SA of control room teams are discussed. Empirical evidence is cited concerning the lack of intra- and inter-team consistency of SA. In addition, qualitative data are discussed from process tracing of operators' problem solving during unusual simulated events, together with how training can be designed to switch representations, thus facilitating awareness and successful diagnosis.

Definition and Nature of SA Construct

A reasonable scientific aim is to define a construct before proceeding to measure it and then to investigate empirically its nature. Undoubtedly the most frequently cited definition of SA is that by Endsley (e.g., 1995):

The perception of the elements in the environment within a volume of time and space, the comprehension of their meaning and the projection of their status in the near future. (Endsley, 1995, p. 36)

However the frequency of this citation belies the considerable confusion and disagreement in the literature concerning what is meant by the term SA. Some, as Endsley, define SA as referring to certain aspects of knowledge (e.g., Fracker, 1988; Whitaker and Klein, 1988) whereas Smith and Hancock (1995) refer to it as 'adequate, externally directed consciousness', the product of which is a person's knowledge about a situation. Forrester (1978) seems to envisage SA as an unmeasurable psychic ability by defining it as a 'sixth sense' while Sarter and Woods (1995) have argued that 'there is no point in trying to define SA'. These apparently different perspectives are somewhat surprising as SA has been the subject of much investigation in many contexts over the last decade. Indeed it will be suggested that Flach's (1995) careful discussion of the concept of SA and his warning 'Situation Awareness: Proceed with Caution' have not been heeded sufficiently.

Product versus Process

The first issue to be addressed is the dichotomy frequently drawn in the literature between a person's knowledge or awareness of a situation (product) and the information processes including perception, comprehension etc., which are responsible for generating that knowledge. Pew (1994) and Endsley (1995) preserve this distinction by labelling the former, situation awareness, and the latter, situation(al) assessment. Theoretically, this distinction is clear, although operationally it is difficult, if not impossible, for psychology to separate the many cognitive processes from their associated products, particularly in complex, dynamic performance situations. Adams, Tenney, and Pew (1995) also adopt this perspective, suggesting that the key is to appreciate the interdependence between the processes and products of awareness. There are at that least three reasons. First, cognitive processes can only be measured indirectly by evaluating their products. Second, in supervisory control of, say, a plane or process plant, there are many attention, perceptual and reasoning processes that contribute to a person's SA at any point in time. Each cognitive process has its own product that will in turn influence the next process undertaken and vice versa. These processes and products cannot be disentangled operationally although their aggregation will determine a person's SA. Dominguez (1994) came to a similar conclusion having compared fifteen definitions of SA, arguing that any useful definition of SA has to embrace not only a person's knowledge of a situation but also the processes responsible for such knowledge, given that in supervisory control, persons are involved in continuously extracting information from a changing environment.

Finally, another reason that it is problematic separating processes and products stems from a hierarchical perspective of skilled performance in which skilled behavior at one level can be divided into various sub-skills at a lower level, and these can be further subdivided, and so on. Thus achieving awareness (i.e., product) described at one level of description can be decomposed into various skilled subunits, each comprising its own product and process. Such a decomposition process can continue until the postulated products and processes are too fleeting and short in duration to divide further (i.e., milliseconds). For example, achieving awareness of the time of day may involve various products and processes. At one level within the skill hierarchy the person will need to be aware of what sources exist for telling the time (i.e., products) and this in itself may involve both cognitive processes (memory of what sources exist and their location, deciding what sources to access) and actions (moving hands, body and eyes as appropriate). At a lower level of description, detecting visually the position of the hands of a clock could be decomposed into a series of fast eye movements, each of which delivers its own product concerning visual-spatial knowledge. Therefore, whilst we agree that situation awareness involves knowledge that is task-relevant, attempting to separate processes from products in a rigorous manner is not feasible even with experimental and psychophysiological techniques. We therefore conclude that any useful understanding of SA has to embrace not only a person's knowledge of a situation but also the processes responsible for producing such knowledge, which will depend on the situation and its context.

A Task-Oriented Perspective

The question arises as to how best conceptualize the status of the concept of SA and the processes associated with the acquisition of SA. Our solution is to adopt a task-oriented perspective, which we believe is consistent with Endsley's approach, and to consider that SA is the product of performing satisfactorily the task of 'achieving and maintaining SA'. The task is therefore defined in terms of its goal, as advocated by task analysis techniques such as Hierarchical Task Analysis (HTA) (e.g., Shepherd, 2001). Endsley (1995) has stressed the importance of separating this task concerned with the achievement of SA from the subsequent tasks of decision making and performance. In task analytic-terms, the former task is a logical prerequisite for the latter tasks. If we adopt the rules and vocabulary advocated by HTA, then we can represent these three tasks (1.1 – 1.3) together with their associated plan 1 in the hierarchical diagram of Figure 4.1. This spells out that performance of supervisory control task 1 (or indeed any task) can be broken down into three sub-tasks 1.1 – 1.3 that should be carried out in the sequence specified by plan 1. This cycle of task behaviors will be repeated for each of the many actions that are required to control any complex and dynamic system. The important point is that the achievement of SA is a prerequisite for successful action.

Let us take this task-analytic approach a stage further. Endsley's (1995) model, as suggested by her definition of SA quoted above, comprises what she terms 'three hierarchical phases', namely: perception of elements in the current situation; comprehension of the current situation; and projection of its future status. These three hierarchical phases of Endsley's SA model correspond to what would normally be referred to in HTA terms as the three sub-tasks that comprise the task of 'achieving and maintaining SA' (i.e., sub-tasks 1.1.1 – 1.1.3 of Figure 4.1).

Again there is a logical sequence in which these three sub-tasks should be performed and this is specified by plan 1.1 in Figure 4.1. Hence sub-task 1.1.1 is defined by its goal ('to perceive elements of the current situation') and it has to be accomplished before sub-task 1.1.2 ('to comprehend the current situation'), which in turn precedes sub-task 1.1.3 ('to project future status of system').

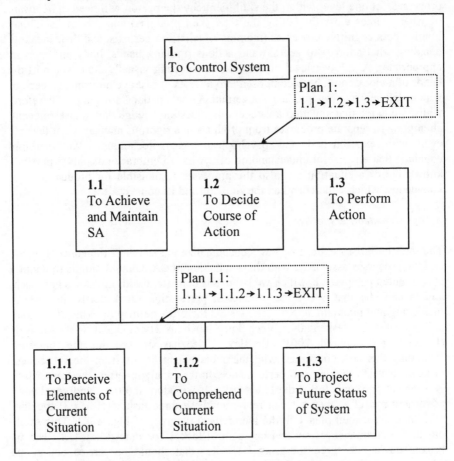

Figure 4.1 The task hierarchy of supervisory control, including the achievement of SA

Two important questions arise. How far should this decomposition process go? How are the task-related actions and strategies, involving particular knowledge and skills, specified? The answers to these questions are related to each other. In HTA the extent of decomposition is governed by the p (probability) x c (cost) rule that concerns the probability that satisfactory performance can be achieved at a specified level of description and, if it is not feasible, that the cost to system performance is acceptable. If either probability or cost is judged unacceptable, then the task hierarchy is broken down into another level of description and the rule is reapplied. In order for the analyst to make such judgments, it is necessary to be able to detail how the task should be performed including all the specific strategies and actions necessary to accomplish that particular task goal. This would be a requirement, for example, for subtask 1.1.1, and if all the necessary detail could not be prescribed for the achievement of this goal then it would be decomposed further. The point to stress is that in order to analyze any task and improve performance of it, all of the detail of the task situation and context need to be specified.

Whilst this task-oriented perspective may seem straightforward and uncontentious, various important ramifications emanate from it, which may help towards reducing some of the confusion in the literature.

SA is not a Psychological Construct

The task-oriented perspective emphasizes that SA is the outcome of performing a task and this task (i.e., achieving and maintaining SA) can be broken down into three constituent sub-tasks together with their plan. All of these tasks and subtasks are defined by their goals (i.e., what has to be achieved), corresponding to Endsley's hierarchical phases of SA, rather than by the processes involved in achieving these goals (i.e., how). These processes, both cognitive and actions, may be heterogeneous with respect to the same task goal, depending upon the task situation and context. For example, in a nuclear power plant, in order to perceive the elements of the situation (task 1.1.1), an operator will need to *decide* what aspects of plant operation to examine (e.g., logs, colleagues and instruments) before examining them. Despite the goal being to *perceive* elements of the situation, any or all psychological processes may be involved in achieving this goal besides perceptual ones, including, attention, memory, decision making and action. It is easy to confuse the task-oriented model of Figure 4.1 with information processing models described in the 1960s and 70s, in which each stage represented only one specific psychological process. In contrast, none of the tasks represented in Figure 4.1 are bounded by specific psychological processes, which cannot be specified without a close examination of the interaction between the task performer and their situation/context. This explains why Sarter and Woods (1995), as quoted above, argued that there is no point in trying to pinpoint the goal/task of achieving SA as constituting particular cognitive processes. They stated:

> Rather it [SA] should be viewed as a label for a variety of cognitive processing activities that are critical to dynamic, event-driven and multitask fields of practice. (Sarter and Woods, 1995, p. 16)

This does not mean that it is not worthwhile in adopting an information processing perspective to explain the nature of the difficulties that might occur in performing the task of achieving and maintaining SA. However this is impossible to theorize about in the absence of details of the specific situation and context (see

Flach, Mulder and van Paassen, Chapter 3, this volume, for a discussion of possible dimensions of the situation).

Another ramification of the task-oriented perspective of SA elaborated above is that statements that a person has poor or good SA can be misleading if this suggests a particular psychological skill or any generality in level of performance from one situation to another. When we state that a person has poor SA, this should be interpreted as shorthand for saying that the person has failed to perform the task of achieving SA satisfactorily in a particular situation and, conversely, a person with good SA has accomplished the task of achieving and maintaining SA. It is tempting to then conclude that a person has skill, or not, in achieving SA. However the difficulty of using the term skill in this way is that the task of achieving SA is psychologically so variable in nature, between situations and contexts, that the term would have no unitary meaning. Consequently it is important that the situation and a person's awareness of it are always linked, and the details of the task of achieving SA are not discarded. From this it follows that it is unlikely to be useful to conceptualize SA as a personal attribute or ability. Similarly the use of psychometric measures in the attempt to identify individual differences and abilities involved in SA will be problematic given the potential variation in the underpinning psychological processes involved in different situations.

SA is the Cause of Poor Performance

Endsley (2000, p. 24) considers SA to be 'an intervening variable between stimulus and response'. However if SA can be the result of a plethora of psychological processes, it is difficult to envisage how it can be cited as a causal mechanism of poor performance. Flach (1995), in a useful discussion of this issue, also rejects this notion. Using Underwood's (1957) five levels of concepts, Flach argues that thinking of SA as a potential cause of poor performance results in a circular argument with no added explanatory value. Flach makes this evident in the following quotation:

> How does one know that SA was lost? Because the human responded inappropriately? Why did the human respond inappropriately? Because SA was lost. (Flach, 1995, p. 150)

There already exists a wide-ranging set of psychological constructs, such as attention, perception, decision making and memory that can be used to explain deficiencies in performance. If we attribute the same status to the concept of SA, then it becomes problematic to differentiate SA from traditional psychological concepts.

Given the task-oriented perspective, the only sense that SA can be conceptualized as a cause of poor performance is if the prerequisite task of achieving SA is not accomplished (i.e., a person or team does not have the necessary and relevant awareness) then this task failure, in turn, may lead to human error in performance of the subsequent tasks of decision making and performance (see Figure 4.1).

Conclusions and the Way Forward

If we agree to reject SA as a facet of information processing, a personal attribute or skill, then what is the status of the concept of SA? The solution offered here is that the concept is best interpreted within the task-oriented perspective elaborated above. Flach's (1995) paper is again helpful. He argues persuasively that if we reject SA as a causal mediating variable, then it is still possible to use it at a phenomenological level (i.e., level 2 in Underwood's taxonomy). In this way one does not make strong claims about causality etc., but the concept bounds the phenomenon or task of achieving SA and invites researchers to examine it for possible similarities and differences in findings. It also emphasizes an important point that seems to have become lost by some research into SA. As a phenomenon, it is necessary to examine the relationship between the dynamically changing situation *and* a person's understanding or awareness of it. The two sides of this equation are *inseparable*. As the task specification varies in terms of the external environment, so also does the skill requirement. Useful generalizations concerning SA will only emerge when analyses preserve the link between characteristics of a particular situation and a person's awareness of it. The same exhortation has been made by others (e.g., Flach, 1995; Pew, 2000; Wickens, 2000). For example, Flach (1995) argues that the main benefit of the SA construct is:

> To draw attention to the inseparability of situations and awareness when addressing issues of meaning or functionality. (Flach, 1995, p. 152)

If situations and a person's accompanying awareness are indivisible, one has to face what Pew (1994) terms a critical question. Is there any generality in solutions relating to SA or does every task/situation require a unique solution? If the latter case is true, it is not necessary to even invoke the concept of SA at a phenomenological level. This issue of generality versus specificity is a thorny problem in all areas of both pure and applied science. Pew's (1994) answer sits in the middle of the specific versus general dimension. Our perspective is that to a large extent the jury is still out and the answer will depend on empirical work, some of which is discussed below.

Awareness of Process Control Teams

Control room teams are required to manage complex process plant, including Nuclear Power Plants (NPP's), and maintain them within steady state. Critical features of this environment are that it is dynamic, uncertain, risky and has a large number of interconnected parts (Woods, 1988). It is therefore inevitable that the task of achieving and maintaining SA (task 1.1, Figure 1), together with its constituent sub-tasks (1.1.1 – 1.1.3, Figure 4.1), is important yet difficult within this environment. In order to explore some of these difficulties, Newell and Simon's (1972) problem solving model is adapted for our discussion of the awareness of control room teams. Subsequently some nuclear incidents are highlighted in terms of how such teams failed to maintain SA of various aspects of plant operation. Finally some data are presented concerning intra- and inter-team differences in SA with respect to scenarios tackled on full-scope high fidelity simulators.

Difficulties of Control Room Teams Achieving SA

The nature of what is often referred to as team SA has been discussed by many researchers (e.g., Bolman, 1979; Salas, Prince, Baker, and Shrestha, 1995; Artman, 2000; Endsley and Jones, 2001) although only a few have considered this in the context of the process control industry (Hogg, Folleso, Strand-Volden, and Torralba, 1995; Kaber and Endsley, 1998; Sebok, 2000). A control room team comprises normally a minimum of two desk operators and a control room supervisor, each of whom has different responsibilities within the control room. Therefore, depending upon the tasks in hand, awareness will be distributed throughout the team with some being shared between all or some individuals and some remaining in scope to only one member. This view is consistent with Artman (2000) who proposed team SA to be:

> Two or more agents active construction of a situation model, which is partly shared and partly distributed and, from which they can anticipate important future states in the near future. (Artman, 2000, p. 1113)

This perspective not only emphasizes the interpretative and distributed nature of the types of knowledge that constitute the awareness of the team but also hints at the importance of communication and other team processes that underpin the development of that awareness. These are particularly important as the nature of the required awareness, both shared and individual, will fluctuate with the nature of the operations undertaken by the control room team together with the changing state of the plant.

Further insights into the difficulty of achieving SA in these dynamic and potentially costly situations can be gleaned from adopting Newell and Simon's (1972) perspective of problem solving. Their perspective emphasizes that the difficulty of achieving awareness is always relative to the skills and experience that the individual and team bring to bear upon performing this task. These can best be illustrated with respect to the problem solving model in Figure 4.2 that suggests various potential sources of difficulty for an individual operator (represented by the shaded square box of Figure 4.2). The operator works in a multi-task environment that is shaped by organizational factors, which include different procedures concerning plant operation, and by team factors (both formal and informal) relating to the role of the operator within the team and how the team functions. We will focus only on the sources of difficulty associated with perceiving and understanding elements of this environment, for example, when some type of plant event occurs.

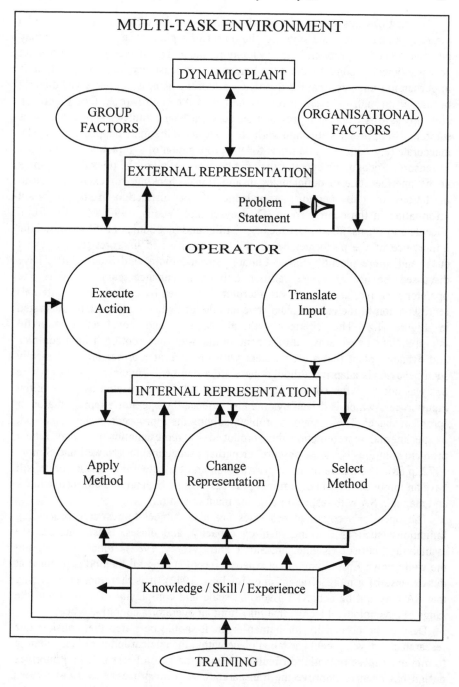

Figure 4.2 Newell and Simon's (1972) approach to problem solving (adapted)

The first obvious source of difficulty stems from the fact that a team has to be aware of a changing plant state. At the outset of a plant event, the operator may perceive a need or problem in the task environment. This perceived need does not necessarily correspond to the actual need for at least two reasons. First, it is important to remember that the dynamic state of the plant is not perceived directly but rather through its external representation in the control room (see Figure 2). Not only is this external representation necessarily incomplete, although it does sample all important states and variables, but, as sometimes happens, it may be inaccurate (e.g., due to cycle times for the propagation of symptoms or the failure of sensors). Second, the operator may not be aware of all of the relevant symptoms at the interface due to deficiencies in attentional checking, for example, due to limitations in the operator's knowledge of, or distraction from, important information in the control room (De Keyser and Woods, 1990; Mumaw, Roth, Vicente and Burns, 2000). Decades ago Miller and Slebodnick (1958) stressed the importance of the performer being able to identify and interpret 'task relevant cues' and, more recently, Salas, Cannon-Bowers, Fiore, and Stout (2001) have discussed the use of cue-recognition training to enhance team SA. What the operator perceives and how this is interpreted is driven by the operator's (internal) representation of the current plant state and the goals being pursued, as illustrated in Figure 4.2. The operator will always try and construct meaningful interpretations or patterns out of the multitude of signals coming from a complex and dynamic plant that are consistent with his current representation. Typically such behavior is adaptive although there are a number of nuclear incidents where this was not so. After some problem is perceived, it is translated by some initial input process which is driven by, and also affects, the operator's representation or 'problem space'. The operator's problem solving then 'proceeds in the framework of the internal representation thus produced - a representation that may render problem solutions obvious, obscure, or perhaps unattainable' (Newell and Simon, 1972, p.88). The nature of this representation and the extent that it is accurate will have an important role in determining the ease with which an operator can achieve and maintain SA with respect to ongoing plant operation.

The operator's cognitive processes are also subject to resource processing limitations, such as working memory capacity, and biases. Biases include the availability heuristic (Kahneman, Slovic and Tversky, 1982), 'tunnel vision', and the well-known Einstellung effect where a recent successful method is pursued at the expense of a more efficient one (Luchins, 1942). It is therefore unsurprising that SA may not be achieved given the scale and complexity of a plant and the range of psychological factors that may limit an operator's cognitive processes.

Despite the propensity for human error, it should be stated that considerable research and development has taken place within the nuclear industry in an attempt to minimize these potential difficulties. Whilst the goal of research into interface design has been to improve the transparency of plant processes, various writers have noted that increased automation has often made it more difficult for the person to achieve SA (e.g., Bainbridge, 1987). Research has investigated two main types of display; status displays that provide the operator with information regarding the state of various aspects of the process, and predictor displays that predict the future status of aspects of the process (e.g., Bennett, Woods, Roth and Haley, 1986). Status displays can be seen to serve the perception and comprehension sub-tasks of achieving SA (i.e., 1.1.1 – 1.1.2, Figure 4.1), whilst predictor displays relate to the third, (i.e., 1.1.3, predicting future states). However, understanding of plant status is more than awareness of plant elements which, many years ago, led Goodstein (1981) to advocate the use of holistic displays that provide the operator with higher-level representations and abstractions of plant state. Monitoring of plant status and failure detection are also supported by the use of displays concerning critical parameters (e.g., Kishi, Nagaoka, Yoneda, Fukuzaki, Kiyokowa, Serizawa and Nigawara, 1976) or functions (e.g., Marshall, Makkonen, Kautto and Rohde, 1983). In the nuclear industry this idea has been implemented as control room responsibilities are allocated so that the supervisor is able to maintain an overview of plant operation by monitoring a high-level display of critical plant parameters. Also much research has investigated how failure detection can be enhanced in process control through the use of alarm handling and filtering systems such as HALO (Baker, Gertman, Hollnagel, Holmstrom, Marshall, and Owre, 1985) and CASH developed at the Halden OECD Reactor Project. Also there has been much excitement concerning so-called 'ecological interface design' (Rasmussen and Vicente, 1988; Pawlack and Vicente, 1996) and direct perception interfaces. The goal of these designs has been to minimize the need for data to be transformed and to provide the operator with more direct information concerning process variables and their interactions. However it is difficult to ensure that such displays are sufficiently versatile to support the full range of activities likely to be encountered by the operator.

Evidence from some Nuclear Incidents and Events

All nuclear incidents, by definition, have involved the control room team being unaware of some important aspect of plant operation that has contributed to the incident. However this lack of awareness needs to be understood in the context of the operator's overall representation of plant operation that may lead to an incorrect rationalization concerning, for example, an anomalous instrument reading or the status of one part of the plant. Evidence is cited from some incidents concerning this type of problem.

Operators may believe incorrectly that an instrument reading is valid or invalid. Either the operator believes it to be valid when it is invalid, or vice versa. Generally there are more instances of the former type, which is not surprising as instruments rarely fail and therefore an operator's default representation would suggest that an instrument reading should be believed. Two incidents involving the former situation are Davis-Besse 1985 (Grime, Wood and Mominee, 1986; NUREG 1154, 1985) and Biblis 1987 (Becker, 1990). During the later stage of the Davis-Besse incident, operators mistakenly believed that a signal was valid, indicating a pressure relief valve was shut. This was partly because they mistakenly reasoned that the steady pressure level in the pressurizer confirmed that the valve was indeed shut. In the Biblis incident an operator inferred incorrectly that no message from the safety valve sensor indicated that the plant was OK. In fact the alarm had failed. The cause of this performance deficiency was the operator's representation, which was wrong, that the plant state was OK and therefore would not trigger this safety valve. Similarly during the well documented TMI incident, reactor temperature rose tripping the reactor and the electromatic relief valve. When levels returned to normal, a signal in the control room indicated that the relief valve had closed when, in fact, it had not. Operators were unaware that it was open for more than two hours despite contraindications. This lack of awareness was partly due to their knowledge of a persistent leak of reactor coolant, which they had been dealing with previously, to which they rationalized the contraindications.

Two incidents in which operators believed mistakenly that an instrument reading was invalid were Biblis and Oyster Creek, 1979 (Pew, Miller and Feeher, 1981). In the Biblis incident there was an example when an instrument reading indicated that the valve was open, which indeed it was, although the operator believed that this was incorrect. There were various possible reasons for this wrong inference. First, the operators had knowledge that this unusual type of valve was more likely to fail and they had experienced such failures previously. Second, they were unable to corroborate their inference because there was no additional indicator against which the valve signal could be checked. The Oyster Creek incident provides another example where an operator failed to believe a signal that was indeed correct. During this incident, two pump discharge valves were inadvertently shut so that there was no natural circulation to the core area. Because of lack of awareness of this, operators assumed that a subsequent low level water alarm was spurious when it was not. It appears that operators' internal representation of the problem was seriously flawed and confirmation bias resulted in contradictory evidence being explained away.

These incidents illustrate how reasoning errors can occur as a consequence of an inaccurate representation. However a wide variety of reasons, besides misreasoning, can lead to a failure to achieve SA. We carried out a search of an industrial database of nuclear events and identified an opportunistic sample of forty events that involved instances in which control teams failed to achieve or maintain SA. Four proximate causes were responsible for these failures to achieve SA, two of which were further subdivided (Figure 4.3). Deficits in communication were often problematic, although more from written information (procedures, work cards, reports and logs) than from verbal communication. This is somewhat surprising as written information is normally subject to greater scrutiny and regulation than verbal communication. Over half the events involved lack of attention due to distraction or involvement in multiple tasks causing lack of SA. Perceptual, mostly visual deficits were the least frequent category and concerned poor layout, redundant indicators, bad visibility and poor labeling, ergonomic factors largely outside the influence of the control room team. Given the complexity of nuclear plant and the evidence from incidents discussed above, it is not surprising that just under half of the proximate causes related to knowledge deficits from either inaccurate knowledge or the failure to reason effectively. These knowledge deficits, through lack of training or experience, referred to minor and specialized items of information that resulted in an operator being not fully aware of some evolving aspect of plant operation. Finally, one interesting result was that, on average, there were nearly five proximate causes per event and this is consistent with the suggestions by Perrow (1984) and Reason (1990) that many events are the result of an aggregation of many small, sometimes latent errors.

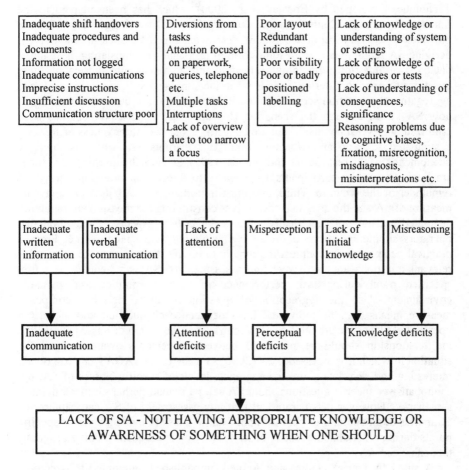

Figure 4.3 Proximate causes of lack of SA

Empirical Evidence from Simulation Studies

The evidence from nuclear incidents and events is necessarily speculative as it depends upon retrospective accounts of what happened. Stronger empirical evidence is available from simulation studies in which operators' awareness has been investigated (Decortis 1992; Hogg et al., 1995; Patrick, Grainger, Gregov, Halliday, Handley, James and O'Reilly, 1999; Sebok, 2000). Evidence will be discussed from two of our simulation studies in the nuclear industry in terms of how SA can be measured, whether generalizations emerge concerning different control room teams' achievement of SA, and how training can help.

Measuring SA is controversial. The most frequently used measure of SA involves probing, via questions, a person's recalled knowledge of a situation. The most well known example is SAGAT (Situation Awareness Global Assessment Technique) developed by Endsley (e.g., 2000), which has been adapted to the Situation Awareness Control Room Inventory (SACRI) by Hogg et al., (1995) in the nuclear industry. Both techniques derive an aggregate measure of SA by: deriving SA requirements from some form of task analysis; translating these into a database of questions; randomly selecting and administering subsets of these questions to operators during periods when the simulated scenario is 'frozen'; and aggregating the question scores from each administration to develop a measure of how SA varies through the scenario. This approach to measurement has been criticized on several counts. There are concerns about the intrusiveness of freezing a simulated scenario and whether or not this disrupts SA, which is the very phenomenon of interest (Sarter and Woods, 1995). Second, the questions or probes are liable to cue the participants as to where to direct their attention during the remainder of the scenario. Third, and most important, SAGAT uses an aggregate measure of SA and the questions themselves constituting the measure are randomly generated and do not specifically address the critical aspects of operation that operators should be aware of in a given situation at a specific time. From a practical perspective it is almost impossible to ensure that a comprehensive set of relevant questions are used when the assessment of SA is scheduled at a pre-specified point during task performance in such a complex and dynamic environment. Also the aggregation of question scores to derive a composite measure means that the individual links between each question and the actual operational plant state are broken. This contravenes the notion discussed above that the relationship should be preserved between a person's awareness and the situation in which it is assessed. Pew (2000) said 'by using SAGAT one can obtain interesting and rich data about the aggregate levels of specific classes of SA, but cannot answer specific questions about SA at a particular, perhaps critical, point in a scenario'. However it is paramount that any assessment of SA can capture the awareness of an operator or control room team in a task relevant manner at specific points during a simulated event in order to develop subsequent training programs that enhance SA.

A study by Patrick, James and Ahmed (unpublished) attempted to overcome these methodological difficulties by following suggestions by Sarter and Woods (1994) and, more recently, Pritchett and Hansman (2000) both of whom have advocated the use of task-relevant, performance-based measures of SA that obviate the need for 'freezes' of a scenario. Probe events that require not only the achievement of SA but also specific behavioral consequences were scripted into a scenario, in a similar fashion to the TARGETS methodology (Fowlkes, Lane, Salas, Franz and Oser, 1994). Six control room teams were observed and rated in terms of whether critical target behaviors occurred whilst tackling three simulated scenarios, each containing specified probe events where it was predicted that operators would be vulnerable to loss of SA. Reliability of the scores from three raters was assessed by calculating, where statistically feasible, intraclass correlation coefficients (ICCs) and interrater correlations. The five ICCs were high, ranging from 0.89 - 0.99, and the average interrater correlation for the three pairs of raters was 0.79, 0.86 and 0.91. These two sources of evidence indicated satisfactory interrater reliability concerning the rating of team's SA during the scenarios.

The most striking finding was the variability of awareness, both within and between control room teams. Statistically significant differences were found between teams in their rated SA although there was no discernible consistency to these differences. There was at least one instance where one team was better than another for one target event and yet worse than another team at a second event. One might expect less variability in team performance when the probe events shared the same potential proximate cause. For example, there were three probe events in the scenarios that involved each team being subjected to some form of potential distraction, which might have resulted in SA not being achieved satisfactorily. Again, there was no consistent pattern of differences between teams even within these situations. The same lack of trend occurred elsewhere and the average correlation between awareness of all pairs of target events, using the mean rating for each team, was only 0.16. This evidence taken together suggests that SA should be viewed as a task-specific phenomenon, even within the same scenario, and generalizations about SA should be avoided.

Another study by Patrick, Grainger et al., (1999), whilst not investigating SA explicitly, examined operators' awareness of unusual events and devised training to improve this. Unusual plant events may be difficult to comprehend because they require an operator to shift from his normal reasoning and thinking habits that may act as a barrier to effective diagnostic reasoning. Difficulties in performance due to habit or frequent 'routine' behavior were originally recognized by William James (1890). Reason (1990) discussed the use of 'strong but wrong' rules, which whilst good in most situations, can be inappropriately applied in unusual ones, resulting in error. He suggested that the incidents at both Oyster Creek and Three Mile Island in 1979 fell into this category. From Newell and Simon's (1972) problem solving perspective, discussed above, an operator's habitual representation will limit the range of hypotheses that are considered, thus making some events difficult or impossible to diagnose. Such difficulty is consistent with that produced by the availability heuristic (Kahneman et al., 1982) and also the tendency to default to high frequency responses in cognitively underspecified situations (Reason, 1990). The plant events that were the focus of the Patrick, Grainger et al., study were multiple faults, which were unusual but not unknown to the operators used in the study.

A process tracing approach was developed in order to investigate operators' difficulties in diagnostic reasoning (for a review of process tracing methodology, see Patrick and James, in press). During each fault scenario, operators were required to 'think aloud' and these verbal reports were collected together with a video recording of their actions, including the plant areas viewed on the simulator. The process tracing involved:

- transcription of these verbalizations and actions onto a timeline;
- coding of their responses into behavioral and subsequently, psychological categories;
- use of a technique named MAPS (Mental States and Activities in the Problem Space) developed by Patrick, Gregov, Halliday, Handley and O'Reilly (1999) that provides a visuo-spatial representation of an operator's reasoning during a scenario.

Operators were unable to diagnose multiple faults and it was striking that all of the operators' hypotheses generated during the scenarios were confined to single fault explanations. This is illustrated by the performance of one typical operator tackling the scenario in which a control rod had dropped into the reactor and some instruments had failed, thus masking this problem. This person's reasoning, including the hypotheses generated, is represented in the MAPS diagram (Figure 4.4). The MAPS technique represents the operator's behavior as a search for the nature of the fault, accumulating knowledge through various activities. A distinction is made between mental states and activities. Activities are so called because they involve the active collection or processing of information. They refer to both mental and physical processes (e.g., reflecting on the evidence, and testing a hypothesis by inspecting instrumentation). Mental states, represented as nodes, concern having or expressing knowledge about plant information, fault symptoms and operators' explanations for them. Particularly important are operators' hypotheses concerning the cause of the event. Hypotheses are numbered sequentially in the order that they are proposed by the operator during the scenario but if an earlier hypothesis is regenerated the original number is retained. The node which represents a regenerated hypothesis is aligned vertically beneath the original one. Alarms are distinguished from other symptoms as they are 'announced' rather than discovered through information gathering activities. Identification of an alarm can lead to a change in the direction of an operator's reasoning. A MAPS diagram starts at the top left hand corner and the passage of time is indicated by movement either to the right or down where it indicates the generation of a hypothesis. Spaces between activities and nodes represent two sequences that are not directly connected, for instance, where an alarm causes an operator to begin a new search.

The operator's first hypothesis that a control rod had failed was generated after only two minutes, immediately after identification of the excess margins alarm (Figure 4.4). However, this was quickly rejected after inspection of the control rod indicator panel that had been failed, masking the symptoms of the rod drop. His second hypothesis was generated without any new evidence but provided an alternative explanation for the same symptoms, that is, that he had activated the control rods and had left them moving. In fact the operator had made no control actions up to this point. This hypothesis was rejected on inspection of the relevant control panel. The operator searched for more alarms but as before only identified the power and temperature symptoms. He then regenerated his first hypothesis and rejected it yet again on accessing the control rod indicator panel. He recognized the drop in pressure as being consistent with the other symptoms but was unable to propose a satisfactory explanation. Therefore, for the fourth time, the operator inspected the control rod panel to see 'if I've missed something the first time I looked.' When he confirmed that he had not, he then took one more look at the alarm panel and then appeared to abandon his attempts at diagnosis in favor of system control. At no point did the operator consider that the control rod panel might not be indicating the true state of the plant and he returned constantly to the same pieces of conflicting information that he could not reconcile. This example illustrates the strength and constraining effect of the operator's representation on his diagnostic reasoning and awareness about an unusual plant event. Even though he appears to be close to the solution, psychologically it is some distance away.

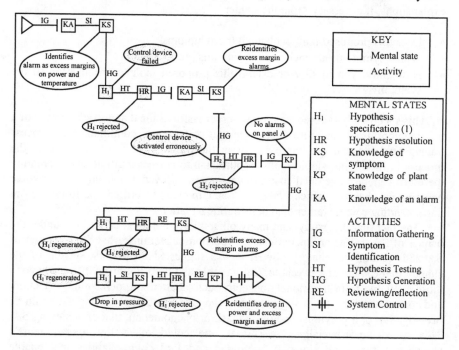

Figure 4.4 MAPS diagram of an operator's awareness during a control rod and instrumentation failure scenario

Two training methods were tested in the attempt to improve operators' comprehension of these unusual events that involved generating multiple hypotheses in the appropriate circumstances. The first training intervention involved making operators aware of these types of fault by reminding them of relevant incidents and asking them to generate examples from their own experience. This training also provided them with a heuristic concerning *when* to consider such unusual possibilities. Unfortunately this awareness training was unsuccessful and therefore a second training intervention was designed that additionally practiced the detailed stages involved in successful hypothesis generation. The goal of this extra training was to enable operators to be aware of the inconsistency between a single fault hypothesis and the available symptoms and to subsequently modify that hypothesis into a consistent multiple fault hypothesis. In order to achieve this, a training videotape was prepared that provided operators with exercises giving opportunities for practicing this. During each individual training session, the operator observed a video recording of a person collecting symptoms during a fault scenario and proposing a hypothesis concerning the nature of the event. At such a point the trainer paused the videotape and asked the operator to record both the symptoms and the proposed fault in a log book. The operator was then required to answer the following three questions, with explanations, if necessary, from the trainer:

- Does this proposed fault explain all the symptoms?
- Which symptoms are inconsistent with this proposed fault?
- How could you modify or extend this proposed fault to account for all the symptoms?

This specifically tailored training was successful as the diagnostic accuracy of a training condition was more than twice that of a control condition. Also process tracing revealed that the improvement in the training condition was due to the process of modifying single fault hypotheses into correct multiple ones. Training therefore can be developed to improve awareness even when this may involve overcoming habits, which facilitate adaptive and skilled performance in understanding routine rather than non-routine situations.

The fact that this study, and many others, have not been carried out under the banner of SA, raises an uncomfortable question concerning what the construct of SA adds to our explanatory power. It was suggested in the first section of the chapter that SA is not a psychological variable and does not bring insights beyond those available from traditional concepts, such as attention, perception, detection, and comprehension. It was suggested that the justification in studying SA could be investigation of a previously neglected task or phenomenon, that of achieving SA. This could be especially powerful if one could reject the operationalist's perspective that each situation is unique and find commonalities that enable solutions to be generalized.

References

Adams, M.J., Tenney, Y.J. and Pew, R.W. (1995), 'Situation Awareness and the Cognitive Management of Complex Systems', *Human Factors*, vol. 37(1), pp. 85-104.

Artman, H. (2000), 'Team Situation Assessment and Information Distribution', *Ergonomics*, vol. 43, pp. 1111-1128.

Bainbridge, L. (1987), 'Ironies of Automation', In J. Rasmussen, K.D. Duncan and J. Leplat (eds), *New Technology and Human Error*, John Wiley and Sons, Chichester.

Baker, S., Gertman, D., Hollnagel, E., Holmstrom, C., Marshall, E. and Owre, F. (1985), 'Experimental Comparison of Three Computer Based Alarm Systems', *OECD Halden Reactor Project, HWR-142*, Halden, Norway.

Becker, G.G. (1990), 'Analysis of Human Behaviour During NPP Incidents: A Case Study', *International Symposium on Balancing Automation and Human Action in Nuclear Power Plants*, Munich, Germany, pp. 9-13.

Bennett, K.B., Woods, D.D., Roth, E.M. and Haley, P.H. (1986), 'Predictor Displays for Complex, Dynamic Tasks: a Preliminary Investigation', In *Proceedings of the Human Factors Society 30th Annual Meeting*, Human Factors Society, Dayton, OH.

Bolman, L. (1979), 'Aviation Accidents and the Theory of the Situation', In G.E. Cooper, M.D. White and J.K. Lauber (eds), *Resource Management on the Flight Deck: Proceedings of a NASA/Industry Workshop*, NASA Ames Research Centre, Moffett Field, CA, pp. 31-58.

Decortis, F. (1992), *'Processus Cognitifs de Résolution d'Incidents Spécifiés et peu Spécifiés en Relation avec un Modèle Théorique'*, Unpublished doctoral dissertation, Faculté de Psychologie et des Sciences de l'Education, Université de Liège, Belgium.

De Keyser, V. and Woods, D.D. (1990), 'Fixation Errors: Failures to Revise Situation Assessment in Dynamic and Risky Systems', In A.G. Colombo, A.S. Bustamanante and A. Saiz (eds), *System Reliability Assessment*, ECSS, EEC, EAEC, Brussels, Belgium, pp. 231-251.

Dominguez, C. (1994), 'Can SA be Defined?' In M. Vidulich, C. Dominguez, E. Vogel and G. McMillan (eds), *Situation Awareness: Papers and Annotated Bibliography. Report AL/CF-TR-1994-0085*, Wright-Patterson Air Force Base, OH: Air Force Systems Command.

Endsley, M.R. (1995), 'Towards a Theory of Situation Awareness in Dynamic Systems', *Human Factors*, vol. 37, pp. 32-64.

Endsley, M.R. (2000), 'Theoretical Underpinning of Situation Awareness: a Critical Review', In M.R. Endsley and D.J. Garland (eds), *Situation Awareness Analysis and Measurement*, Lawrence Erlbaum Associates, Mahwah, NJ, pp. 4-32.

Endsley and Jones, W.M. (2001), 'A Model of Inter- and Intrateam Situation Awareness: Implications for Design, Training, and Measurement', In M. McNeese, E. Salas and M.R. Endsley (eds), *New Trends in Cooperative Activities: Understanding System Dynamics Complex Environments*, Human Factors and Ergonomics Society, Santa Monica, CA, pp. 46-67.

Flach, J.M. (1995), 'Situation Awareness: Proceed with Caution', *Human Factors*, vol. 37(1), pp. 149-157.

Forrester, L. (1978), *Fly for your Life*. (2nd ed.), Bantam Books, New York.

Fowlkes, J.E., Lane, N.E., Salas, E., Franz, T. and Oser, R. (1994), 'Improving the Measurement of Team Performance: The TARGETs Methodology', *Military Psychology*, vol. 6(1), pp. 47-61.

Fracker, M.L. (1988), 'A Theory of Situation Assessment: Implications for Measuring Situation Awareness', In *Proceedings of the Human Factors Society 32nd Annual Meeting*, Human Factors and Ergonomics Society, Santa Monica, CA.

Goodstein, L.P. (1981), 'Discriminative Display Support for Process Operators', In J. Rasmussen and W.B. Rouse (eds), *Human Detection and Diagnosis of System Failures*, Plenum Press, pp. 433-449.

Grime, L.A., Wood, J. and Mominee, D. (1986), 'Root Cause Analysis of the June 9, 1985, Davis-Besse Event', *Transactions of the American Nuclear Society*, vol. 52, pp. 614-615.

Hogg, D.N., Folleso, K., Strand-Volden, F. and Torralba, B. (1995), 'Development of a Situation Awareness Measure to Evaluate Advanced Alarm Systems in Nuclear Power Plant Control Rooms', *Ergonomics*, vol. 38, pp. 2394-2431.

James, W. (1890), *The Principles of Psychology*. Henry Holt, NY.

Kaber, D.B. and Endsley, M.R. (1998), 'Team Situation Awareness for Process Control Safety and Performance', *Process Safety Progress*, vol. 17(1), pp. 43-48.

Kahneman, D., Slovic, P. and Tversky, A. (1982), *Judgement Under Uncertainty: Heuristics and Biases*, Cambridge University Press, Cambridge, UK.

Kishi, S., Nagaoka, Y., Yoneda, Y., Fukuzaki, T., Kiyokowa, K., Serizawa, M. and Nigawara, S. (1976), 'Plant Monitoring by Color CRT Displays for Boiling Water Reactor', *Hitachi Review*, vol. 25(8), pp. 265-270.

Luchins, A.S. (1942), 'Mechanisation in Problem Solving', *Psychological Monographs*, vol. 54, (6, whole No. 248).

Marshall, E.C., Makkonen, L., Kautto, A.M.T. and Rohde, K. (1983), 'An Account of the Methodology Employed in the Experimental Validation of the Critical Function Monitoring System', International Atomic Energy Agency – *Working Group on Nuclear Power Plant Control and Instrumentation Specialist Meeting on Nuclear Power Plant Training Simulation*, Helsinki, Finland.

Miller, R.B. and Slebodnick, E.B. (1958), 'Research for Experimental Investigations of Transferable Skills in Electronic Maintenance', *Technical Report AFPTRC-TR-58-2*, Texas: Air Force Personnel and Training Research Center, Lackland Air Force Base.

Mumaw, R.J., Roth, E.M., Vicente, K.J. and Burns, C.M. (2000), 'There is More to Monitoring a Nuclear Power Plant than Meets the Eye', *Human Factors*, vol. 42(1), pp. 36-55.

Newell, A. and Simon, H.A. (1972), *Human Problem Solving*, Prentice-Hall, Englewood Cliffs, NJ.

NUREG 1154. (1985), *Loss of Main and Auxiliary Feedwater Event at the Davis-Besse Plant on June 9, 1985*, US Nuclear Regulatory Commission, Washington, DC.

Patrick, J., Grainger, L., Gregov, A., Halliday, P., Handley, J., James, N. and O'Reilly, S. (1999), 'Training to Break the Barriers in Reasoning about Unusual Faults', *Journal of Experimental Psychology: Applied*, vol. 5(3), pp. 314-335.

Patrick, J., Gregov, A., Halliday, P., Handley J. and O'Reilly, S. (1999), 'Analysing Operators' Diagnostic Reasoning During Multiple Events', *Ergonomics*, vol. 42(3), pp. 493-515.

Patrick, J. and James, N. (in press), 'Process Tracing of Complex Cognitive Work Tasks'. *Journal of Occupational and Organizational Psychology*.

Patrick, J., James, N. and Ahmed, A. (unpublished), 'Observational Assessment of Situation Awareness and Consistency of Inter- and Intra-Team Differences', Manuscript submitted.

Pawlack, W.S. and Vicente, K.J. (1996), 'Inducing Effective Operator Control through Ecological Interface Design', *International Journal of Human-Computer Studies*, vol. 44, pp. 653-688.

Perrow, C. (1984), *Normal Accidents: Living with High-Risk Technologies*. Basic Books, New York.

Pew, R.W. (1994), 'Situation Awareness: The Buzzword of the 90's', *CSERIAC Gateway*, vol. 5(1), pp. 1-4.

Pew, R.W. (2000), 'The State of Situation Awareness Measurement: Heading Toward the Next Century', In M.R. Endsley and D.J. Garland (eds), *Situation Awareness Analysis and Measurement*, Lawrence Erlbaum Associates, Mahwah, NJ, pp. 33-47.

Pew, R.W., Miller, D.C. and Feeher, C.E. (1981), 'Evaluation of Proposed Control Room Improvements through Analysis of Critical Operator Decisions', *EPRI NP- 1982*, Electric Power Research Institute, Palo Alto, CA.

Pritchett, A.R. and Hansman, R.J. (2000), 'Use of Testable Responses for Performance-based Measurement of Situation Awareness', In M.R. Endsley and D.J. Garland (eds), *Situation Awareness Analysis and Measurement*, Lawrence Erlbaum Associates, Mahwah, NJ, pp. 189-209.

Rasmussen, J. and Vicente, K.J. (1988), 'Coping with Human Errors through System Design: Implications for Ecological Interface Design', *International Journal of Man-Machine Studies*, vol. 31, pp. 517-534.

Reason, J. (1990), *Human Error*, Cambridge University Press, Cambridge, UK.

Salas, E., Prince, C., Baker, D.P. and Shrestha, L. (1995), 'Situation Awareness in Team Performance: Implications for Measurement and Training', *Human Factors*, vol. 37, pp. 123-136.

Salas, E., Cannon-Bowers, J.A., Fiore, S.M. and Stout, R.J. (2001), 'Cue-Recognition Training to Enhance Team Situation Awareness', In M. McNeese, E. Salas and M.R. Endsley (eds), *New Trends in Cooperative Activities: Understanding System Dynamics Complex Environments*, Human Factors and Ergonomics Society, Santa Monica, CA, pp. 169-190.

Sarter, N.B. and Woods, D.D. (1994), 'Pilot Interaction with Cockpit Automation II: An Experimental Study of Pilots' Model and Awareness of the Flight Management System', *International Journal of Medicine*, vol. 4, pp. 1-28.

Sarter, N.B. and Woods, D.D. (1995), 'How in the World did we ever get into that Mode? Mode Error and Awareness in Supervisory Control', *Human Factors*, vol. 37(1), pp. 5-19.

Sebok, A. (2000), 'Team Performance in Process Control: Influences of Interface Design and Staffing Levels', *Ergonomics*, vol. 4, pp. 1210-1236.

Shepherd, A. (2001), *Hierarchical Task Analysis*. Taylor and Francis, London.

Smith, K. and Hancock, P.A. (1995), 'Situation Awareness is Adaptive, Externally Directed Consciousness', *Human Factors*, vol. 37(1), pp. 137-148.

Underwood, B.J. (1957), *Psychological Research*, Prentice Hall, Englewood Cliffs, NJ.

Whitaker, L.A. and Klein, G.A. (1988), 'Situation Awareness in the Virtual World', In *Proceedings of the Eleventh Symposium on Psychology in the Department of Defence (USAFA-TR-88-1)*. USAF Academy.

Wickens, C.D. (2000), 'The Trade-off of Design for Routine and Unexpected Performance: Implications of Situation Awareness', In M.R. Endsley and D.J. Garland (eds), *Situation Awareness Analysis and Measurement*, Lawrence Erlbaum Associates, Mahwah, NJ pp. 211-226.

Woods, D.D. (1988), 'Coping with Complexity: the Psychology of Human Behaviour in Complex Systems', In L.P. Goodstein, H.B. Andersen, and S.E. Olsen (eds), *Tasks, Errors and Mental Models*, Taylor and Francis, London.

Chapter 5

The Role of Awareness in Situation Awareness

Darryl G. Croft, Simon P. Banbury, Laurie T. Butler and Dianne C. Berry

Introduction

In recent years there has been a growing realization of the importance of SA in assessing and predicting operator competence in complex environments, including not only aviation (both flying and air traffic control [ATC], e.g., Endsley, 1993; Durso, Hackworth, Truitt, Crutchfield, Nikolic and Manning, 1998), but also nuclear power plants, refineries and other complex operating systems (e.g., Hogg, Folleso, Strand-Volden and Torralba, 1995), tactical and strategic systems such as fire-fighting, military and police operations (e.g., Kaempf, Wolf and Miller, 1993), driving and operating heavy machinery (e.g., Gugerty, 1997), and medical decision making (e.g., Gaba, Howard and Small, 1995). Since its original conception, numerous definitions of the term 'Situation Awareness' have been proposed, the most widely cited being that by Endsley (1995a) who states that, 'Situation awareness is the perception of the elements in the environment within a volume of time and space, the comprehension of their meaning, and the projection of their status in the near future' (p. 36).

In a seminal paper, Endsley (1995a) also put forward what is still the most widely cited 'theory' of SA to date. In this account, SA is conceptualized as a 'state of knowledge', and Endsley is careful to distinguish this from the processes that are used to achieve the state (which she refers to as Situation Assessment). Other researchers (e.g., Dominguez, 1994; Durso and Gronlund, 1999) have been less committed to the term 'awareness' and have advocated definitions which cover both awareness and assessment, and allow for more 'automatic and veiled processes' (Durso and Gronlund, 1999). However, the emphasis on 'awareness' in Endsley's influential definition and framework has been reflected in the development of measures of SA. Virtually all of the measures used predominantly have been designed to assess operators' explicit conscious knowledge.

In this chapter we argue that existing elicitation techniques will only provide an incomplete picture of SA, given their failure to take account of implicit knowledge. We seek to alert the reader to the importance of the distinction between implicit and explicit processes and the need to assess both. Following this, we describe a variety of approaches available to measure implicit knowledge, selecting those that might be especially useful in measuring SA. Subsequently we guide the transition from the laboratory to the real world by providing recommendations as to how many of these approaches might actually be developed to measure implicit SA. In this context, we provide evidence that suggests that implicit processes may actually play a dominant role in SA in experienced operators working in complex situations.

The 'Implicit' Component and Existing Measures of SA

In light of a number of comprehensive reviews of these measures (e.g., Durso and Gronlund, 1999; Endsley, 1995b; and Endsley and Garland, 2000), our aim is not to assess the relative merits of each SA measure, but rather to highlight a more general limitation which applies to them all. Perhaps the most widely used measure of SA is Endsley's (1990) Situation Awareness Global Assessment Technique (SAGAT) which includes queries relating to operator awareness, system functioning, and relevant features of the external environment. Endsley (2000) herself acknowledges that a limitation of SAGAT is that it is better suited to, and has been primarily used in, part-task simulations rather than in 'real world' control situations. However, we believe that despite its clear utility and applicability in assessing SA in simulations, the technique is subject to a more basic limitation, (see Pew, 1995, and Sarter and Woods, 1991, for other criticisms). As with most of the other methods (see Durso and Gronlund, 1999; Endsley, 1995b; and Endsley and Garland, 2000 for reviews), the technique has been developed to tap operators' explicit (or conscious) knowledge. Yet, we know from a rapidly expanding literature, in the areas of learning and memory, of the existence of implicit (or unconscious) processes and their fundamental role in, amongst other things, the control of complex systems (e.g., Berry and Broadbent, 1984, 1987). SA assessment techniques which are focused solely on eliciting operators' explicit awareness are likely to provide only a partial picture of their knowledge of situation elements and their meaning.

While the suggestion of implicit processes in this context has received little attention to date, Gugerty (1997) published a study which appeared to cast doubt on the role of implicit processes in SA. Briefly, Gugerty showed an apparent absence of implicit knowledge in a simulated driving task. This led Endsley (2000), in an influential and important review, to question altogether the notion of 'implicit situation awareness'. Despite Gugerty's finding, however, we believe that such a view is unwarranted, not least because of the dangers of extrapolating from a single study. More importantly, though, ruling out implicit processes in SA, at this early stage at least, would run counter to almost three decades of research showing the importance of implicit processes in learning and memory. Over the past 30 years, there has been a growing interest in the distinction between implicit and explicit processes in relation to both learning and memory, with a total of over 1000 peer reviewed journal articles being published to date. However, the division between implicit learning and memory is not clear cut (see Berry and Dienes, 1991; Buchner and Wippich, 1998, for a discussion of the relationship between these two phenomena) but, for the purpose of the present discussion, we will describe them separately.

Implicit memory is defined as the non-intentional, non-conscious retrieval of previously acquired information, and is demonstrated by performance on tasks that do not require conscious recollection of past experiences. This form of memory can be contrasted with explicit memory, which refers to the conscious, intentional recollection of past experiences as measured by standard recognition or recall tasks (e.g., Schacter, 1987). A typical paradigm for studying implicit memory requires participants to study a long list of words (including e.g., elephant) and subsequently, after some intervening filler tasks, to complete a test. Traditionally, an explicit memory task would require participants to recall or recognize previously presented words from the study list. Conversely, for implicit memory tasks participants are not asked to think back to the study list but are instead asked to carry out a seemingly unrelated task, which can be completed without reference to the study episode. Thus participants are typically asked to respond with the first word that comes to mind to a series of word stems (e.g., ele-----), fragments (e.g., e-e--a-t), or even sentences (e.g., ---------s live in Africa). In all cases, priming is typically observed; that is a greater proportion of study words are produced relative to non-studied ones. A number of other paradigms have been used to assess implicit memory; non-verbal tasks (e.g., degraded line drawings, Hayes and Hennessey, 1996; picture naming, Cave and Squire, 1992; picture fragment completion, Berry, Banbury and Henry, 1997, and Musen 1991), object judgments (e.g., real/unreal objects, Kroll and Potter, 1984; possible/impossible objects, Schacter, Cooper and Merikle, 1990), affective judgments (e.g., preference, Kunst-Wilson and Zajonc, 1980), and non-affective judgments (e.g., relative brightness or loudness, Mandler, Nakamura and van Zandt 1987). Once again, priming is usually shown by faster naming, or greater selection, of studied objects compared to non-studied ones.

A widely cited definition of implicit learning is provided by Berry and Dienes (1993) who state that 'learning is implicit when we acquire new information without intending to do so, and in such a way that the resulting knowledge is difficult to express'. This can be contrasted with explicit learning, which is a conscious, hypothesis driven process employed when learning how to solve a problem (see Cleeremans, Destrebecqz and Boyer, 1998, and Stadler and Frensch, 1988, for recent reviews). Implicit learning has been explored in several different domains including the learning of conditioned responses (Shanks, Green and Kolodny, 1994), and the acquisition of invariant characteristics (Cock, Berry and Gaffan, 1994). However, the three that have received the most attention are undoubtedly artificial grammar learning (e.g., Reber, 1967; 1993), control of dynamic systems (e.g., Berry and Broadbent, 1984, 1987; Dienes and Fahey, 1995) and sequence learning tasks (e.g., Buchner, Steffens and Rothkegel, 1997; Nissen and Bullemer, 1987; Reed and Johnson, 1994). Typically, such paradigms consist of three components. First, participants are exposed, under incidental learning conditions, to a situation governed by a relatively complex rule. Second, there is some measure that tracks how well participants can express their newly acquired knowledge in task performance, and third, there is a measure of the degree to which any of the knowledge is explicitly available. Typically, participants can perform at above chance level on the tasks but are subsequently unable to report the underlying rules.

The problem of 'contamination' from explicit processes has also been a concern in the area of implicit memory (see Butler and Berry, 2001, for a recent discussion). A range of approaches to minimize or eradicate the problem has been developed (e.g., Jacoby, 1998; Schacter, Bowers and Booker, 1989). Although a full discussion of the problems of 'contamination', and evaluation of the recommended approaches, is beyond the scope of the present chapter, it is worth pointing out that the issue of contamination does need to be considered in relation to assessing SA. Clearly, there would be little point in developing new 'implicit' measures, if these measures are primarily tapping explicit knowledge. Conversely, we suggest that any explicit measures are likely to be 'contaminated' by influence from implicit processes.

Implicit Processing in Complex Task Situations

It is perhaps not altogether surprising that implicit measures have received little attention in applied research domains given that, until recently, 'implicit' research has been rather inwardly focused on theoretical and definitional issues as described above (see e.g., Schacter et al., 1989; Berry, 1997). However, significant progress has been made and we believe that there is now a sufficiently large and varied body of approaches to begin to tackle the measurement of implicit knowledge in the real world. Whilst the majority of research on implicit processing to date has involved very simple and artificial stimuli, a few studies have been carried out which have attempted to use more complex displays and environments. In the following section, we will overview some of this work, first in relation to implicit memory, and then to implicit learning.

Implicit Memory in Complex Displays

In most implicit memory studies, stimuli are presented in isolation at both study and test. As such, the ecologically important issue of whether implicit memory can be obtained for stimuli studied in complex displays has received little attention. However there are a few relevant studies that are reported below.

Words Embedded in Text Studies have examined whether implicit memory can be obtained for words embedded in text (e.g., Nicolas, Carbonnel and Tiberghien, 1994). For example, Wippich and Mecklenbraeker (1995) presented a passage of text at study (on how to make an Italian meal), and participants were required either to read the text or generate mental images of some of the activities contained in the text (e.g., washing the celery). Subsequently, half of the participants completed a word stem completion task (e.g., ce----, for celery), and the other half completed a word association task (e.g., think of something that you can wash).

Both tasks showed significant priming, although only word association was affected by the read / generate manipulation.

Brand Names Embedded in Advertisements A second line of evidence comes from experiments that have examined the extent to which implicit memory can be shown for brand names initially presented as part of adverts. Bock and von Rath (1997), for example, conducted a study whereby attention to a series of magazine articles containing adverts for brands was varied (i.e., participants processed either articles, adverts, or both). Surprisingly, priming (as indexed by an affective ratings task) was greatest when both the advert and article were processed at study. Of interest here, though, is the finding that priming for brand names was also significant when attention was focused on the adverts at study (i.e., advert or advert plus article processing). Although not all evidence is consistent (see, for example, Perfect and Heatherley, 1997), it seems likely that amount of priming will increase as a function of the degree to which the stimulus receives dedicated processing at study.

Implicit Memory for Environmental Sounds

While many implicit memory studies have used spoken words (e.g., see Schacter, 1994, for a review), a few have used more complex sounds. For example, Stuart and Jones (1995, 1996) presented participants with a series of spoken words (e.g., car) and sounds (e.g., the sound of a car starting up and driving away) during a study phase. Subsequently, participants completed an auditory version of a clarification task for a series of sounds. Some of the sounds had been heard earlier, whereas for others only the name of the sound source had been heard. Stuart and Jones found that priming was only obtained when the sounds were heard at study.

Implicit Memory for Location

Musen (1996) examined whether knowledge for object locations can be implicit. Musen showed participants a series of nine letters which were displayed, one at a time, in one of nine locations on a rectangular grid. The performance measure was a location naming task, which required participants to name the location on a grid in which each letter was presented, as quickly as possible. After each letter had been presented nine times in the same location, the positions of the letters changed. Musen reasoned that if knowledge about letter location had been learned then location naming times should increase dramatically following the location change. This was indeed the case. Further testing revealed that participants could not recall which letters appeared in which location, suggesting that the knowledge was implicit. In a subsequent experiment, Musen (1996) showed implicit knowledge for location following only a single study presentation of each letter.

In a study which has direct relevance for assessing SA, Gugerty (1997) also examined the extent to which acquired location knowledge is implicit. Briefly, Gugerty examined SA in a simulated driving task, in which participants watched short animated scenes of a car viewed from the driver's seat. On some trials, participants simply watched the scene and were subsequently asked to recall all of the vehicles, and their positions, on a grid. On other trials, participants could make responses to the incidents (such as a car moving into the driver's lane ahead) by pressing keys to move their own car (i.e., to move left, right, or to accelerate, decelerate). The assumption was that if knowledge (i.e., of the location of other cars) used during maneuvering was primarily explicit, then performance and recall measures should be associated. However, if implicit knowledge was important for maneuvering then the two measures should be uncorrelated. Gugerty found that almost all participants performed above chance on both recall and performance measures and that the two types of test were correlated, suggesting that they accessed a shared explicit knowledge base.

It should be noted that there are a number of features of Gugerty's study which suggest caution when drawing conclusions from his results. First, as Gugerty himself points out, the correlations were only moderate, leaving open the possibility that some participants were using implicit knowledge. Second, the nature of the performance task may have encouraged participants to employ explicit knowledge, making the resulting association with the recall measure unsurprising. Third, given the ease of the performance task, it is plausible that implicit knowledge was simply not required. Overall, then, the Gugerty study might be better viewed as signaling the need for further research on the topic, rather than as strong evidence against the existence of implicit processes in SA.

Implicit Learning of Complex Dynamic Systems

In dynamic control tasks, participants learn to control a computer simulation of an interactive system, such as a sugar production factory (e.g., Berry and Broadbent, 1984, 1987), and their task is to reach and maintain a specified level of sugar output by manipulating one or more input variables (such as the number of workers employed). Typically, participants can achieve a good level of system control without being able to describe the underlying rules of the system. Although the Berry and Broadbent task is more complex than many traditional laboratory tasks, it only involved participants manipulating one or two input variables in order to control the level of one or two output variables. A small number of studies have used much more complex and realistic versions of control tasks (see Frensch and Funke, 1995 for an overview). Doerner, for example, has developed several complex computerized tasks that contain up to 2000 interconnected variables (e.g., Doerner, Kreuzig, Reither and Staudel, 1983; Doerner and Pfeifer, 1990; Doerner and Wearing, 1995). In one version (Doerner et al., 1983) participants had to take on the role of mayor of a computer-simulated town and to look after the social and economic welfare of the inhabitants (for another example of this approach see Staudel, 1987). In general, findings from studies which have used these more complex and ecologically valid tasks are in line with those which have used the relatively less complex versions, in terms of providing clear evidence for the importance of implicit processing in control performance.

Moving from the Laboratory to the Real World: 'Implicit SA'

The following sections of this chapter consider how many of the implicit approaches reviewed here might be adapted to measure implicit processes in SA, or 'implicit SA',[1] in the real world. The first section reviews a number of characteristics of implicit processes which suggest that progress towards this goal is not only well advised, but crucial, if truly comprehensive measures of SA are to be achieved. Having outlined various approaches for assessing implicit knowledge in complex tasks, the following section considers how they might be modified or adapted for SA measurement. Finally, a proof-of-concept study relating to SA in datalink applications is reported.

Characteristics of Implicit Processes and Implications for SA Measurement

There are a number of characteristics of implicit processes that are especially pertinent when considering SA. Indeed, their unique characteristics offer a number of advantages over explicit measures; implicit processes are more robust in the face of competing attentional demands, are extremely durable, are unrelated to meta-cognitive judgments, and are associated with the development of expertise.

Independent of the Locus of Attention

In many aviation-related scenarios, complex information in the environment (e.g., other aircraft in the vicinity, their position and speed etc.) will not always receive full and continuous attention from an operator or pilot. It is therefore of particular interest to note that a key feature of implicit memory (see e.g., Mulligan, 1998 for review), and to some extent, implicit learning (e.g., Berry and Broadbent, 1995; Buchner and Wippich, 1998) is that it is relatively insensitive to divisions of attention, compared to explicit forms of memory and learning. For example, Parkin and Russo (1990) required participants to identify pictures during a study phase with or without a simultaneous tone monitoring task. At test, participants then completed an implicit (picture clarification) or explicit (free recall) memory task. Parkin and Russo found that only explicit memory was significantly impaired when attention was divided at study (see also Mulligan and Hartman, 1996; Kellogg, Newcombe, Kammer and Schmitt, 1996). Furthermore, there is some evidence that implicit memory is preserved under encoding conditions where explicit memory is obliterated altogether. For example, Eich (1984) required

---

[1] We acknowledge that the term 'implicit situation awareness' can be misleading, given that the strict definition of the term 'awareness' excludes any implicit content. The term 'implicit situational knowledge' would therefore be a more accurate description. We also alert the reader to alternative (i.e., unrelated) uses of the term 'implicit' in the Human Factors literature; for example, implicit (i.e., non-verbal) team coordination, (e.g., Entin and Serfaty, 1999) and implicit (i.e., embedded) performance-based measures (e.g., Vidulich, 1995; Wickens, 2000).

participants to shadow a prose passage presented to one ear, while critical word pairs were repeatedly presented to the other ear. Each of the word pairs comprised a homophone and a descriptive word that biased interpretation towards the less common meaning (taxi-FARE). At test, participants displayed no explicit memory for the homophones. Critically though, they were biased towards giving the less common spelling for old over new homophones in an implicit memory spelling test.

That implicit knowledge can be acquired even when attention is reduced would seem to have clear implications for the measurement of SA. In situations of reduced attention, a pilot's or operator's SA is likely to comprise a substantial implicit component (and impaired explicit knowledge), and ignoring this is likely to result in a seriously distorted picture of an operator's SA. This will be discussed later in the context of acquiring explicit and implicit knowledge from datalink information.

Temporal Durability

Many early studies have shown that introducing a delay between study and test phases can produce reliable dissociations between performance on implicit and explicit tasks, with large decrements in performance on the latter task only (Jacoby and Dallas, 1981). For example, Tulving, Schacter and Stark (1982) found very little decline on a word fragment completion task at testing intervals of one hour and one week, despite a substantial decline on an explicit memory task over the same period. While other studies have shown that implicit memory is not completely resistant to forgetting (Komatsu and Ohta, 1984), there is clear evidence that the effect can be long lasting (e.g., Tulving et al., 1991; Roediger, Weldon, Stadler and Riegler, 1992), and that, on occasion, the rate of decay may be more gradual than for explicit memory (e.g., Parkin and Streete, 1988).

In relation to SA, one potential benefit of this is that implicit knowledge could be assessed some time after a trial, avoiding the need to 'freeze' a simulation. Although, interrupting an experimental trial to administer tests may not necessarily be detrimental to task performance (Endsley, 1995b; Snow and Reising, 2000), it may nevertheless affect task strategy (Pew, 1995). For example, pilot participants in a study by Snow and Reising (2000) reported that simulator freezes in which questions were asked about their environment altered their subsequent attentional and cognitive behavior.

Incidental Testing

By its nature, the testing of implicit knowledge must be performed covertly, insofar as explicit memory probes direct participants to consciously retrieve past experiences, whereas implicit memory probes involve the participants carrying out a seemingly unrelated task. As a result, participants are less likely to 'catch on to the fact' that they are being tested on their memory of events in their environment, and are therefore less prone to bias (e.g., Snow and Reising, 2000).

Independent of Subjective Confidence

Several studies (e.g., Chan, 1992; Dienes, Altmann, Kwan and Goode, 1995) have shown that performance on implicit tests is unrelated to subjective confidence, whereas performance on explicit tests tends to be positively correlated with such metacognitive judgments (see Dienes and Berry, 1997 for a review). For example, Dienes et al., (1995) showed that participants were just as likely to be correct in their classification judgments on an artificial grammar learning task when they believed they were guessing as when they were very confident that they were correct. Such findings have implications for the use of self-report tasks to assess SA, as operators may express confidently inaccurate knowledge and fail to report (possibly veridical) knowledge about which they are less confident.

Sensitive to the Phenomenon of Implicit Expertise

It has long been recognized that as individuals master increasing amounts of knowledge in order to carry out a task efficiently, they lose awareness of what they know (see Johnson, 1983). This has clear implications for SA, especially given the need to be able to measure expert knowledge accurately. Specifically, much of an operator's knowledge may be implicit either because their knowledge has never been represented explicitly (implicit learning route) or because their knowledge is no longer consciously accessible. Worryingly, experts often seem to be oblivious to the problem, having been shown to be unaware of the discrepancy between what they think they do and what they do (see Berry, 1987).

Paradigms for Measuring Implicit SA

In this section we offer some guidance to researchers and practitioners, framed in relation to the three levels of SA identified by Endsley (1995a; i.e., perception, comprehension and projection). The following proposals are offered as a guide to the sorts of ways in which implicit SA might be measured using methodologies adapted from the existing literature. The assumption inherent in all of these approaches is that they could be integrated into, or run concurrently with, existing explicit measures of SA such as SAGAT (Endsley, 1987; 1990), and the Situation Awareness Rating Technique (SART; Taylor, 1990).

In order to select and adapt existing implicit knowledge tasks to create SA tests, researchers will need to have a clear understanding of the types of knowledge that they wish to elicit. Therefore, as a general rule, if researchers are interested in the knowledge of SA elements contained in the environment (for examples, see Endsley, 1995b) then methodologies taken from the implicit memory literature should prove to be the most useful. In contrast, it is likely that measures more in line with those used in the implicit learning literature would be needed to measure more complex forms of knowledge (e.g., understanding of the relationships between elements).

Level 1 SA – Perception

Endsley defines Level 1 SA as the ability to 'perceive the status, attributes and dynamics of relevant elements in the environment' (Endsley, 1995a, p.36). For example, in aviation, the relevant SA elements would include the other aircraft in the vicinity, the position and height of the terrain, and the status or parameters of the cockpit instrumentation. From the existing corpus of research, the most conceptually clear way in which implicit knowledge elicitation techniques might be used is at Level 1 SA. As we have already discussed, measuring a participant's memory for elements in the environment using only explicit measures of memory is limited. For example, the exclusive use of explicit memory measures might well lead to the erroneous conclusion that a pilot simply failed to monitor critical aspects of a display, should they not be able to recall the correct heading or altitude when asked directly about these parameters. However, the correct information may have been held as implicit knowledge. Assessing this implicit information is likely to be particularly revealing in situations whereby knowledge that was once held explicitly is no longer available at test due to factors such as poor encoding and forgetting.

Thus, there is a clear role for tests of implicit knowledge in measuring 'awareness' of situational elements. Suitable approaches, for example, might include those that require affective judgments of stimuli, such as those relating to preference (e.g., Kunst-Wilson and Zajonc, 1980) or non-affective ratings of brightness or loudness (e.g., Mandler, Nakamura and van Zandt, 1987). For these tests, implicit knowledge is shown by greater selection of previously studied items over non-studied items, on the basis of preference or as appearing brighter or louder. In reality, of course, all the items are matched on these parameters.

To illustrate the practical application of such paradigms the following example is offered. Following a trial in a flight simulator, pairs of Primary Flight Displays (PFDs) could be presented. The pilot would be required to make an affective judgment about the brightness, luminance or loudness (in the case of auditory stimuli) of pairs of PFDs. These pairs of stimuli would have been matched for these attributes, the only difference between items in a pair being that one would represent the flight parameters that were displayed during the trial (i.e., studied), and the other equally plausible, but non-studied, flight parameters. Thus, implicit SA of these flight parameters would be demonstrated by the tendency to perceive studied PFDs as brighter say, than non-studied ones.

The advantage of using such judgments as a probe of implicit SA is that it is relatively straightforward to hide the true role of the test from the participant as comparisons of brightness and loudness are commonly used in psychophysical ergonomic studies. Given that the test can be administered incidentally it is unlikely to bias the strategies or responses of the participants' post test.

Beyond assessing knowledge for the elements themselves, it is possible to examine their spatial attributes (e.g., location) as well. Firstly, implicit SA for scenes (e.g., out of the cockpit view) encountered during a flight simulator trial could be measured using judgment tasks, in a similar way to that demonstrated by Anooshian and Seibert (1997) who demonstrated implicit knowledge for complex scenes which comprised video clips of routes of travel. For example, participants could be required to make preference judgments between scenes depicting correct (i.e., previously shown in a simulation) and incorrect arrangements of obstacles and objects on the ground (e.g., position of enemy forces, high ground etc.). To probe implicit SA for the location of individual elements, it may be possible to adapt a method devised by Musen (1996) which used a location naming task. The fact that Musen (1996) obtained evidence of implicit location knowledge following a single presentation of a stimulus (e.g., the letter 'I') prior to test, suggests that this task might be fruitfully employed in applied settings. Basically, knowledge of the location of items could be assessed by examining location naming times for elements presented in the same position during the simulation and at test, to ones displayed in different positions. Although subject to empirical confirmation, it seems likely that the location task could be integrated into a more realistic simulation involving the monitoring of complex objects (e.g., other aircraft in the vicinity or objects on the ground) rather than the single letters that have been used to date in the laboratory (see Musen, 1996).

Level 2 SA – Comprehension

Endsley describes Level 2 SA as going 'beyond simply being aware of the elements that are present to include an understanding of the significance of those elements in light of pertinent operator goals' (Endsley, 1995a, p.37). One approach might be to use conceptual implicit knowledge tests, such as general knowledge questions (e.g., Blaxton, 1989) and category verification (e.g., Vaidya et al., 1997). Before describing how these methodologies might be applied to a real world context, we briefly describe how they have been used in laboratory settings. As with other implicit memory tasks, participants are first exposed to a series of stimuli at study (typically words e.g., elephant). Subsequently, after intervening filler tasks, participants might be asked to verify members of a particular category (e.g., whether elephant is an animal or not) or be given general knowledge questions, such as 'What animal did Hannibal use to help him cross the Alps in his attack on Rome?' Evidence of implicit memory is assessed by the speed or accuracy with which studied compared to non studied words are verified or by the percentage or speed with which correct answers are given.

It should be possible to adapt these tasks for measuring an operator's implicit understanding of critical features of their environment in more applied settings. Thus, pilots could be required to answer 'general knowledge' questions about their system or tactical knowledge. For example, tactical questions might be asked about different classes of aircraft (e.g., capabilities, weapon loads) in an effort to gauge the degree to which pilots possessed level 2 implicit SA for particular aircraft present during an earlier simulation. It might be expected that pilots would answer these generic questions faster/more accurately if an aircraft from that class has actually been encountered than for those that have not. Not surprisingly, the way in which the test is administered would be crucial in minimizing the likelihood of explicit contamination (Butler and Berry, 2001). Unlike explicit tests of general knowledge, these questions would be presented without reference to the earlier simulation (i.e., as is the convention with most implicit memory tasks) and would need to appear to be unrelated to, and separate from, the simulation itself. It is also possible that a modified version of category verification could also be designed to measure SA, whereby implicit understanding of individual elements (i.e., level 2 SA) could be inferred from the speed/accuracy with which they were later classified (e.g., particular aircraft as hostile/friendly).

Level 3 SA – Projection

Finally, Level 3 SA is defined as 'the ability to project the future actions of the elements in the environment ... [and] is achieved through knowledge of the status and dynamics of the elements and comprehension of the situation' (Endsley, 1995a, p.37). At present, there seem to be two major ways in which implicit knowledge techniques might be employed to measure Level 3 SA. First, performance-based tasks could be adapted to assess, for example, whether a military pilot possesses knowledge that a threat aircraft in a particular location will attack in a given manner. A simplistic task might involve two enemy aircraft following the participant's aircraft at his/her four and eight o'clock. The pilot is then given the option of having to make a turn to the left or right. In this scenario, the enemy aircraft at the four o'clock position has been designated to attack the participant's aircraft, whereas the enemy aircraft at the eight o'clock position has been designated to attack another aircraft in the vicinity. Thus, the ability to avoid being attacked (i.e., turning to the left) would provide an index of the participant's knowledge about the projected future states of the enemy aircraft (level 3 implicit SA). As with all performance measures, the 'implicitness' of the resulting knowledge would also need to be assessed by means of an explicit knowledge measure. In addition, caution must always be used when inferring SA from performance-based measures given the possibility of good situation knowledge but poor decision making leading to poor performance and vice versa.

Second, a free generation paradigm could also be used to measure future status knowledge (Perruchet and Amorin, 1992; see also, Willingham, Nissen and Bullemer, 1989; Shanks, Green and Kolodny, 1994). This laboratory-based paradigm requires participants to predict the next stimulus position of a repeating sequence. Although originally designed as an explicit measure, Willingham et al., (1989) have used a matched 'implicit' version of this task, which does not make reference to the relationship between study and test phases. To illustrate the application of such a measure, consider a pilot who is told during de-brief (i.e., post trial) the location and other important characteristics (e.g., type, heading and altitude) of a hypothetical enemy aircraft and then asked to predict its probable manner of attack. In fact, unbeknown to the pilot participant, the question is related to the actual behavior of an enemy aircraft, with identical attributes, that were presented during the simulator session. Level 3 SA would be indicated by the ability of the pilot to correctly predict the manner of attack of the aircraft on the basis of the simulator experience. The degree to which this represented implicit or explicit SA would then be assessed through the use of a standard explicit generation task. Note that these prediction tasks can be used to assess SA specifically acquired during the simulation itself (as above) or SA built up through longer term experience. An important consideration of this approach is how to determine whether participants who correctly predict the behavior of the 'hypothetical' aircraft are doing so on the basis of the simulator experience (which would reflect implicit SA) and not on a general knowledge of the aircraft's behavior patterns.

Validation of the Concept of Implicit SA: Experimental Evaluation of Datalink Information as a Source of SA

In the preceding pages we have proposed a number of techniques by which both researchers and practitioners might measure implicit SA. These have been made under the clear understanding that the approaches from which they are adapted are laboratory based. As such, some work remains to be done in terms of their development for real world applications.

The following experiment seeks to adapt laboratory-based techniques to measure implicit SA (i.e., a sentence completion test to measure perceptual implicit memory) in a more realistic context in which participants' attention to items of information was manipulated. An explicit measure (i.e., cued memory test) was also used to serve as a comparison to the implicit measure. The task involved participants tracking an enemy surveillance aircraft across a terrain map. At the same time a number of 'datalink' text messages, comprising intelligence updates, were flashed on the screen next to the icon representing the enemy aircraft. A proportion of this datalink communication was of the utmost importance and was carefully attended to by participants. However, some of the datalink information was not directly relevant to participants and as a result was poorly attended or ignored completely. Although deliberate attention to the datalink information should lead to good explicit (and implicit) knowledge, it is probable that such information will only be represented implicitly when attention is reduced, and as a result explicit knowledge will be impaired. In cases of reduced attention, we would therefore expect that the explicit test will be less sensitive to datalink item knowledge than the implicit test.

Methodology

Participants Fifty-two volunteers, comprising roughly equal numbers of males and females, ranging from 24 to 40 years of age, were recruited. Participants were randomly assigned to one of the two test conditions (explicit or implicit).

Design A 3 (Attention: 'Attended', 'Reduced attention', and 'Baseline') x 2 (Memory Probe: 'Implicit' sentence completion and 'Explicit' cued recall) mixed factorial design. The 'attention' factor was manipulated within-subjects and the 'memory probe' factor was manipulated between-subjects. The dependent variables measured were the number of sentence endings/words retrieved from memory and tracking task performance.

Materials The datalink information used in the experiment consisted of three 30 sentence lists, with all of the sentence-stems offering several possible completions (e.g., 'Enemy fighters have engaged the ...'). These lists were generated by piloting 180 sentence-stems on 20 participants and recording the typical completions for each. Target words (i.e., sentence completions) were selected for the lists if less than two people had completed the sentence stems with a particular word. Additionally, all target words were carefully selected to ensure that they were similar in both length and frequency of use. The order in which the three sentence lists were assigned to the 'attended', 'reduced attention' and 'baseline' conditions was counterbalanced. Each sentence was presented visually within one degree of visual angle from the aircraft symbol participants were tracking and presented for five seconds with a three second delay in between sentence presentations. At the same time as each sentence was being presented, participants were required to perform a manual tracking task using a PC and a joystick. The tracking task involved the use of a control stick to keep a small cross centered on a moving aircraft icon.

Procedure Training was first provided to familiarize participants with the tracking task. During the first phase of the experiment, participants in the 'attended' condition were required to carry out two tasks simultaneously: a tracking task (i.e., tracking the movement of the enemy surveillance aircraft) and a visual monitoring task (i.e., attending to the datalink messages). Participants were informed that both tasks were of equal importance and that they should divide their efforts equally between the two. For the visual monitoring task participants were presented with 30 sentences (i.e., one list at a rate of one sentence every eight seconds) and were required to read the sentence and indicate to the experimenter the number of words it comprised. In contrast, participants in the 'reduced attention' condition were instructed to concentrate all of their attention to the tracking task and ignore any sentences presented on the screen. During this time participants were once again presented with 30 sentences (i.e., one list at a rate of one sentence every eight seconds). Finally, participants in the 'baseline' condition were required to perform the tracking task alone (i.e., no sentences were presented during this time).

The second phase of the experiment comprised a 'filler task' in which participants were required to complete a short (i.e., five minute) questionnaire on the effects of background sound on performance. However, the true nature of this task was to ensure that participants were not able to rehearse in memory any of the items from the previous phase.

The third phase of the experiment consisted of either a cued recall memory test (explicit test condition), or a sentence-stem completion memory test (implicit test condition), depending on the test condition that participants were allocated to. In both cases participants were presented with 90 sentence-stems: 30 stems corresponding to the sentences presented during the 'attended condition; 30 stems corresponding to the sentences presented during the 'reduced attention' condition; and 30 stems corresponding to the sentences unseen during the 'baseline' condition. The presentation order of the stems was randomized and a further 15 stems were presented as practice at the beginning. For those allocated to the 'explicit' cued recall test condition, participants were instructed to recall and complete as many of the sentences that they had seen during the first phase as possible, using the sentence stems to help them. For those allocated to the 'implicit' sentence-stem completion condition, participants were instructed to respond to each stem by writing down the first word that came to mind. They were not instructed to recall the words that they had seen in the first phase of the experiment. When they had completed all of the sentence-stems participants were asked to complete a test awareness questionnaire. The purpose of the questionnaire was to examine whether participants had realized that memory was being tested, and hence had possibly employed intentional retrieval strategies that would contaminate the implicit data. Participants in both conditions were fully debriefed before they left the laboratory.

Results

For the number of target words retrieved correctly, the implicit and explicit data were analyzed separately. The reason for this was that any direct comparison between tests would be misleading, since the 'baseline' condition will produce different baselines for the two types of test. The statistical analyses therefore focused on the effects of manipulating attentional demands on the implicit and explicit tests. Tracking task error data were combined for the implicit and explicit conditions. This was because both groups of participants were engaged in exactly the same task at this point in the experiment. Tracking task data were examined to identify any differences in tracking performance for the three study conditions.

Explicit Test Results The mean number of correct completions for each condition is shown in Figure 5.1. A one-way ANOVA (Attention: 'Attended', 'Reduced attention', and 'Baseline') showed a significant main effect [$F_{(1.13,28.16)}=22.06$; $p<0.001$]. Post-hoc analyses showed that significantly more target words were remembered from both the 'attended' and the 'reduced attention' conditions compared to the 'baseline' condition ($p<0.001$ and $p<0.05$, respectively). In addition, significantly more target words were retrieved in the 'attended' condition compared to the 'reduced attention' condition ($p<0.001$).

Implicit Test Results The mean number of correct completions for each condition is shown in Figure 5.2. A one-way ANOVA (Attention: 'Attended', 'Reduced attention', and 'Baseline') showed a significant main effect [$F_{(2,50)}=13.28$; $p<0.001$]. Post-hoc analyses showed that significantly more target words were remembered from both the 'attended' and the 'reduced attention' conditions compared to the 'baseline' condition ($p<0.001$ in both cases). However, there was no significant difference in the number of target words retrieved in the 'attended' and 'reduced attention' conditions ($p>0.1$).

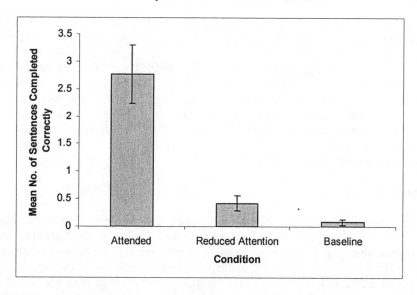

Figure 5.1 Mean number of correct sentence completions for each condition in the explicit (cued-recall) test

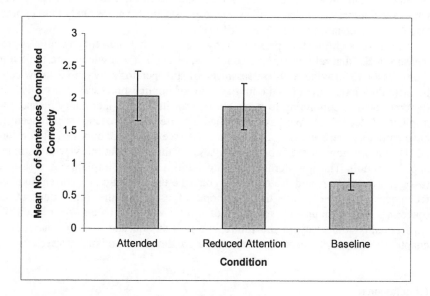

Figure 5.2 Mean number of correct sentence completions for each condition in the implicit (sentence completion) test

Tracking Task Performance A one-way ANOVA (Attention: 'Attended', 'Reduced attention', and 'Baseline') conducted on the RMS tracking error data was significant [$F_{(1.72, 87.75)}=38.13$; $p<0.001$]. Post-hoc analyses showed that RMS tracking error was significantly greater in the 'attended' condition compared to the 'reduced attention' and 'baseline' conditions ($p<0.001$ in both cases). However, there was no significant difference in tracking error between the 'reduced attention' and 'baseline' conditions ($p>0.1$). Given the significant increase in tracking error in the 'attended' condition compared to the 'reduced attention' and 'baseline' conditions, we can be confident that participants were attending to the experimental stimuli as instructed.

Discussion

The findings of this experiment show that, for the implicit test (sentence completion), there was no significant difference between the 'attended' and 'reduced attention' conditions, in terms of the number of target words that were remembered. In contrast, for the explicit test (cued recall), far fewer target words were remembered from the 'reduced attention' condition than from the 'attended' condition. It would seem therefore that information that is not actively attended to will nevertheless be encoded to some degree in a form that can be accessed by implicit measures, but only to a much lesser extent by explicit measures. This finding confirms those of other researchers, such as Merikle and Reingold (1991), who have demonstrated that implicit memory tests are far more likely than explicit tests to show retention of poorly attended stimuli.

The results from the present study suggest that current techniques for measuring SA that rely on tapping conscious, or explicit, knowledge are limited in their ability to provide a full assessment of an operator's available knowledge because they have failed to take into account of implicit processes. Currently, our research team is continuing to work on the transition from laboratory measure to implicit SA technique. We have identified a subset of approaches which seem to have particular merit in measuring implicit SA (see Croft, Banbury and Thompson, 2001) and are now in the process of assessing their compatibility with complex applied stimuli. The long-term goal is to build a suite of implicit SA measures (assessing level 1, 2, and 3 SA) which could be used to augment current explicit techniques, thus increasing the likelihood of assessing the full extent of an operator's SA. Although the existence of a fully validated battery of implicit SA tests remains some way in the future, the information and ideas in the present chapter should provide useful guidance to future developers of such tests.

Conclusions

The aim of SA measures must be to assess as much of what an operator knows as possible. However, current SA techniques only make use of explicit knowledge probes, despite almost three decades of research showing the importance of implicit processes. We have argued that ignoring implicit knowledge is unacceptable, particularly given key characteristics, such as its significance in assessing knowledge of poorly attended material. Therefore, to provide truly comprehensive assessment of SA, future research efforts will need to concentrate on developing implicit techniques to supplement existing measures. In this chapter, we have started this process by outlining a number of potential techniques for measuring implicit SA and examining the utility of one of the measures empirically. Clearly though, much remains to be done to turn these promising, but currently laboratory based techniques, into usable implicit SA probes that are applicable in a range of real world situations.

Acknowledgements

The authors would like to thank Dr Shaun Helman for critical reading of an earlier version of this paper. In addition, we acknowledge that some of the work discussed in this chapter was funded by the Human Sciences Domain of the United Kingdom Ministry of Defence Scientific Research Programme.

References

Anooshian, L.J. and Seibert, P.S. (1997), 'Effects of Emotional Mood States in Recognizing Places: Disentangling Conscious and Unconscious Retrieval', *Environment and Behavior*, vol. 29, pp. 699-733.

Berry, D.C. (1987), 'The Problem of Implicit Knowledge', *Expert Systems*, vol. 4, pp. 144-151.

Berry, D.C. (1997), *How Implicit is Implicit Learning?* Oxford University Press, Oxford.

Berry, D.C., Banbury, S. and Henry, L. (1997), 'Transfer Across Form and Modality in Implicit and Explicit Memory', *Quarterly Journal of Experimental Psychology*, vol. 50A, pp. 1-24.

Berry, D.C. and Broadbent, D.E (1984), 'On the Relationship Between Task Performance and Associated Verbalisable Knowledge', *Quarterly Journal of Experimental Psychology*, vol. 36A, pp. 209-231.

Berry, D.C. and Broadbent, D.E. (1987), 'The Combination of Explicit and Implicit Learning Processes', *Psychological Research*, vol. 49, pp. 7-15.

Berry, D.C. and Broadbent, D.E (1995), 'Implicit Learning in the Control of Complex Systems', In P.A. Frensch and J. Funke (eds), *Complex Problem Solving: The European Perspective*, Lawrence Erlbaum Associates, Hillsdale, NJ.

Berry, D. C. and Dienes, Z. (1993), *Implicit Learning: Theoretical and Empirical Issues*, Erlbaum, Hove.

Blaxton, T.A. (1989), 'Investigating Dissociations Among Memory Measures: Support for a Transfer Appropriate Processing Framework', *Journal of Experimental Psychology: Learning, Memory and Cognition*, vol. 15, pp. 657-668.

Bock, M. and von Rath, W. (1997), 'The Influence of Attention on Advertising Effectiveness', *Swiss Journal of Psychology*, vol. 56, pp. 42-50.

Buchner, A., Steffens, M.C. and Rothkegel, R. (1997), 'A Multinomial Model to Assess Fluency and Recollection in a Sequence Learning Task', *Quarterly Journal of Experimental Psychology*, vol. 51, pp. 251-281.

Buchner, A. and Wippich, W. (1998), 'Differences and Commonalties Between Implicit Learning and Implicit Memory', in M.A. Stadler and P.A. Frensch (eds), *Handbook of Implicit Learning*, Sage, London.

Butler, L.T. and Berry, D.C. (2001), 'Implicit Memory: Intention and Awareness Revisited', *Trends in Cognitive Science*, vol. 5, pp. 192-197.

Cave, C.B. and Squire, L.R. (1992), 'Intact Long-lasting Repetition Priming in Amnesia', *Journal of Experimental Psychology: Learning, Memory and Cognition*, vol. 18, pp. 509-520.

Chan, C. (1992), *Implicit Cognitive Processes: Theoretical Issues and Applications in Computer System Design*, Unpublished D.Phil. thesis, University of Oxford.

Cleeremans, A., Destrebecqz, A. and Boyer, M. (1998), 'Implicit Learning: News from the Front', *Trends in Cognitive Sciences*, vol. 2, pp. 406-416.

Cock, J., Berry, D.C. and Gaffan, E.A. (1994), 'New Strings for Old: The Role of Similarity Processing in an Incidental Learning Task', *Quarterly Journal of Experimental Psychology*, vol. 47, pp. 1015-34.

Croft, D., Banbury, S.P. and Thompson, D. (2001), 'The Development of an Implicit Situation Awareness Toolkit', *Proceedings of the 45th Annual Human Factors and Ergonomics Society Conference*, HFES, Santa Monica.

Dienes, Z., Altmann, G., Kwan, L. and Goode, A. (1995), 'Unconscious Knowledge of Artificial Grammars is Applied Strategically', *Journal of Experimental Psychology: Learning, Memory and Cognition*, vol. 21, pp. 1322-1338.

Dienes, Z. and Berry, D.C. (1997), 'Implicit Learning: Below the Subjective Threshold', *Psychonomic Bulletin and Review*, vol. 4, pp. 3-23.

Dienes, Z. and Fahey, R. (1995), 'The Role of Specific Instances in Controlling a Dynamic System', *Journal of Experimental Psychology: Learning, Memory and Cognition*, vol. 21, pp. 848-862.

Doerner, D., Kreuzig, H.W., Reither, F. and Staudel, T. (1983), *Lohhausen. Vom Umgang mit Unbestimmtheit und Komplexitaet Lohhausen*, [On dealing with uncertainty and complexity], Hans Huber, Bern, Switzerland.

Doerner, D. and Pfeifer, E. (1990), 'Strategisches Denken und Stress [Strategic thinking and stress], *Zeitschrift fur Psychologie* (Supplement), vol. 11, pp. 71-83.

Doerner, D. and Wearing, A.J. (1995), 'Complex Problem Solving: Toward a Computer Simulated Theory', in P.A. Frensch and J. Funke (eds), *Complex Problem Solving: The European Perspective*, Lawrence Erlbaum Associates, Hillsdale, NJ.

Dominquez, C. (1994), 'Can SA be Defined?', in M Vidulich, C. Dominquez, E. Vogl and G. McMillan (eds), *Situation Awareness: Papers and Annotated Bibliography*, Technical Report AL/CF-TR-194-0085, Armstrong Laboratory, Dayton.

Durso, F.T. and Gronlund, S.D. (1999), 'Situation Awareness', in F.T. Durso, R.S. Nickerson, R.W. Schvaneveldt, S.T. Dumais, D.S. Linsay, and M.T.H. Chi (eds), *Handbook of Applied Cognition*, John Wiley and Sons.

Durso, F.T., Hackworth, C., Truitt, T.R., Crutchfield, J., Nickolic, D. and Manning, C.A. (1998), 'Situation Awareness as a Predictor of Performance in en route Air Traffic Controllers', *Air Traffic Control Quarterly*, vol. 6, pp. 1-20.

Eich, E. (1984), 'Memory for Unattended Events: Remembering With and Without Awareness', *Memory and Cognition*, vol. 12, pp. 105-111.

Endsley, M.R. (1987), 'SAGAT: A Methodology for the Measurement of Situation Awareness', Technical Report NOR DOC 87-83, Northrop Corp, Hawthorne, CA.

Endsley, M.R. (1990), 'Situation Awareness Global Assessment Technique (SAGAT): Air-to-Air Tactical Version User Guide', Technical Report, NOR DOC 89-58(A), Northrop Corp, Hawthorne, CA.

Endsley, M.R. (1993), 'A Survey of Situation Awareness Requirements in Air-to-Air Combat Fighters', *International Journal of Aviation Psychology*, vol. 3, pp. 157-168.

Endsley, M.R. (1995a), 'Toward a Theory of Situation Awareness in Dynamic Systems', *Human Factors*, vol. 37, pp. 32-64.

Endsley, M.R. (1995b), 'Measurement of Situation Awareness in Dynamic Systems', *Human Factors*, vol. 37, pp. 65-84.

Endsley, M.R. (2000), 'Direct Measurement of Situation Awareness: Validity and Use of SAGAT', in M.R. Endsley and D.J Garland (eds), *Situation Awareness, Analysis and Measurement*. Lawrence Erlbaum Associates, Mahwah, NJ.

Endsley, M.R. and Garland, D.J. (2000), *Situation Awareness, Analysis and Measurement*. Lawrence Erlbaum Associates, Mahwah, NJ.

Entin, E.E. and Serfaty, D. (1999), 'Adaptive Team Coordination', *Human Factors*, vol. 41, pp. 312-325.

Frensch, P.A. and Funke, J. (1995), *Complex Problem Solving: The European Perspective*. Lawrence Erlbaum Associates, Hillsdale, NJ.

Gaba, D.M. Howard, S.K. and Small, S.D. (1995), 'Situation Awareness in Anaesthesiology', *Human Factors*, vol. 37, pp. 20-31.

Gugerty, L.J. (1997), 'Situation Awareness during Driving: Explicit and Implicit Knowledge in Dynamic Spatial Memory', *Journal of Experimental Psychology: Applied*, vol. 3, 42-66.

Hayes, B.K. and Hennessey, R.L. (1996), 'The Nature and Development of Nonverbal Implicit Memory', *Journal of Child Psychology*, vol. 63, pp. 22-43.

Hogg, D.N., Folleso, K., Strand-Volden, F. and Torralba, B. (1995), 'Development of a Situation Awareness Measure to Evaluate Advanced Alarm Systems in Nuclear Power Plant Control Rooms', *Ergonomics*, vol. 11, pp. 394-413.

Jacoby, L.L. (1998), 'Invariance in Automatic Influences of Memory: Toward a User's Guide for the Process-Dissociation Procedure', *Journal of Experimental Psychology: Learning, Memory and Cognition*, vol. 24, 3-26.

Jacoby, L.L. and Dallas, M. (1981), 'On the Relationship between Autobiographical Memory and Perceptual Learning', *Journal of Experimental Psychology: General*, vol. 110, pp. 306-340.

Johnson, P. (1983), 'What Kind of Expert should a System be?', *Journal of Medicine and Philosophy*, vol. 8, pp. 77-97.

Kaempf, G.L., Wolf, S. and Miller, T.E. (1993), 'Decision making in the AEGIS combat information center', in *Proceedings of the Human Factors and Ergonomics Society Conference*, Santa Moncia, CA.

Kellogg, R.T., Newcombe, C., Kammer, C. and Schmitt, K. (1996), 'Attention and Direct and Indirect Memory Tasks with Short- and Long-term Probes', *American Journal of Psychology*, vol. 109, pp. 205-217.

Komatsu, S.I. and Ohta, N. (1984), 'Priming Effects in Word Fragment Completion for Short and Long Retention Intervals', *Japanese Psychological Research*, vol. 26, pp. 194-200.

Kroll, J.F. and Potter, M.C. (1984), 'Recognising Words, Pictures and Concepts: A Comparison of Lexical, Object, and Reality Decisions', *Journal of Verbal Learning and Verbal Behaviour*, vol. 23, pp. 39-66.

Kunst-Wilson, W.R. and Zajonc, R.B. (1980), 'Affective Discrimination of Stimuli that cannot be Recognized', *Science*, vol. 207, pp. 557-558.

Mandler, G., Nakamura, Y. and Van Zandt, B.J. (1987), 'Nonspecific Effects of Exposure to Stimuli that cannot be Recognized', *Journal of Experimental Psychology: Learning, Memory, and Cognition*, vol. 13, pp. 646-648.

Merikle, P.M. and Reingold, E.M. (1991), 'Comparing Direct (Explicit) and Indirect (Implicit) Measures to Study Unconscious Memory', *Journal of Experimental Psychology: Learning, Memory, and Cognition*, vol. 17, 224-233.

Mulligan, N.W. (1998), 'The Role of Attention during Encoding in Implicit and Explicit Memory', *Journal of Experimental Psychology: Learning, Memory, and Cognition*, vol. 24, pp. 27-47.

Mulligan., N.W. and Hartman., M. (1996), 'Divided Attention and Indirect Memory Tests', *Memory and Cognition*, vol. 24, pp. 453-465.

Musen, G. (1991), 'Effects of Verbal Labelling and Exposure Duration on Implicit Memory for Visual-Patterns', *Journal of Experimental Psychology: Learning, Memory and Cognition*, vol. 17, pp. 954-962.

Musen, G. (1996), 'Effects of Task Demands on Implicit Memory for Object-Location Associations', *Canadian Journal of Experimental Psychology*, vol. 50, pp. 104-113.

Nicolas, S., Carbonnel, S. and Tiberghien, G. (1994), 'Data-driven Processing and Priming Effects in a Word-fragment Completion Task', *International Journal of Psychology*, vol. 29, pp. 233-248.

Nissen, M.J. and Bullemer, P. (1987), 'Attentional Requirements of Learning: Evidence from Performance Measure', *Cognitive Psychology*, vol. 19, pp. 1-32.

Parkin, A.J. and Russo, R. (1990), 'Implicit and Explicit Memory and the Automatic/Effortful Distinction', *European Journal of Cognitive Psychology*, vol. 2, pp. 71-80.

Parkin, A.J. and Streete, S. (1988), 'Implicit and Explicit Memory in Young Children and Adults', *British Journal of Psychology*, vol. 79, pp. 361-369.

Perfect, T.J. and Heatherley, S. (1997), 'Preference for Advertisements, Logos, and Names: Effects of Implicit Memory', *Psychological Reports*, vol. 80, pp. 803-808.

Perruchet, P. and Amorin, M.A. (1992), 'Conscious Knowledge and Changes in Performance in Sequence Learning: Evidence against Dissociation', *Journal of Experimental Psychology: Learning, Memory and Cognition*, vol. 18, pp. 785-800.

Pew R.W. (1995), 'The State of Situation Awareness Measurement: Circa 1995', in *Proceedings of the International Conference on Experimental Analysis and Measurement of Situation Awareness*, Daytona Beach, FL.

Reber, A.S. (1967), 'Implicit Learning of Artificial Grammars', *Journal of Verbal Learning and Verbal Behavior*, vol. 6, pp. 855-863.

Reber, A.S. (1993), *Implicit Learning and Tacit Knowledge*, Oxford University Press, Oxford.

Reed, J. and Johnson, P. (1994), 'Assessing Implicit Learning with Indirect Tests: Determining What is Learned about Sequence Structure', *Journal of Experimental Psychology: Learning, Memory, and Cognition*, vol. 20, pp. 585-594.

Roediger, H.L., Weldon, M.S., Stadler, M.A. and Riegler, G.L. (1992), 'Direct Comparison of Two Implicit Memory Tests: Word Fragment and Word Stem Completion', *Journal of Experimental Psychology: Learning, Memory and Cognition*, vol. 18, pp. 1251-1269.

Sarter, N.B. and Woods, D.D. (1991), 'Situation Awareness: A Critical but Ill-defined Phenomenon', *International Journal of Aviation Psychology*, vol. 1, pp. 45-57.

Schacter, K.L. (1987), 'Implicit Memory: History and Current Status', *Journal of Experimental Psychology: Learning, Memory and Cognition*, vol. 13, pp. 501-518.

Schacter, D.L. (1994), 'Priming and Multiple Memory Systems: Perceptual Mechanisms of Implicit Memory', in D.L. Schacter and E. Tulving (eds), *Memory Systems*, MIT Press, Cambridge, MA.

Schacter, D.L., Bowers, J. and Booker, J. (1989), 'Intention, Awareness and Implicit Memory: The Retrieval Intentionality Criterion', in S. Lewandowsky, J.C. Dunn and K. Kirsner (eds), *Implicit Memory: Theoretical Issues*. Lawrence Erlbaum Associates, Hillsdale, NJ.

Schacter, D.L., Cooper, L.A. and Merikle, E.P. (1990), 'Implicit Memory for Unfamiliar Objects depends on Access to Structural Descriptions', *Journal of Experimental Psychology: General*, vol. 119, pp. 5-24.

Shanks, D., Green, R. and Kolodny, J. (1994), 'A Critical Examination of the Evidence for Nonconscious (Implicit) Learning', in C. Umilta and M. Moscovitch (eds), *Attention and Performance XV*, MIT Press, Cambridge, MA.

Snow, M.P. and Reising, J.M. (2000), 'Comparison of Two Situation Awareness Metrics: SAGAT and SA-SWORD', in *Proceedings of the Human Factors and Ergonomics Society Conference*, HFES, Santa Monica, CA.

Stadler, M. and Frensch, P.A. (1998), *Handbook of Implicit Learning*, Sage, London.

Staudel, T. (1987), *Problemlosen, Emotionen und Kompetenz* [Problem solving, Emotions and Competence], Roderer, Regensberg, Germany.

Stuart, G.P. and Jones, D.M. (1995), 'Priming the Identification of Environmental Sounds', *Quarterly Journal of Experimental Psychology*, vol. 48A, pp. 741-761.

Stuart, G.P. and Jones, D.M. (1996), 'From Auditory Image to Auditory Percept: Facilitation through Common Processes?', *Memory and Cognition*, vol. 24, pp. 296-304.

Taylor, R.M. (1990), 'Situational Awareness Rating Technique (SART): The Development of a Tool for Aircrew Systems Design', in *Situational Awareness in Airspace Operations*, Technical Report AGARD-CP-478(PP.3/1-3/17), NATO-Advisory Group for Aerospace Research and Development, Neuilly-Sur-Seine, France.

Tulving, E., Hayman, C.A.G. and MacDonald, C.A. (1991), 'Long-lasting Perceptual Priming and Semantic Learning in Amnesia: A Case Experiment', *Journal of Experimental Psychology: Learning, Memory, and Cognition*, vol. 17, pp. 595-617.

Tulving, E., Schacter, D.L. and Stark, H.A. (1982), 'Priming Effects in Word Fragment Completion are Independent of Recognition Memory', *Journal of Experimental Psychology: Human Learning and Memory*, vol. 8, pp. 336-342.

Vaidya, C.J., Gabrieli, J.D.E., Keane, M.M., Monti, L.A., Gutiérrez-Rivas, H. and Zarella, M.M. (1997), 'Evidence for Multiple Mechanisms of Conceptual Priming on Implicit Memory Tests', *Journal of Experimental Psychology: Learning, Memory, and Cognition*, vol. 23, pp. 1324-1343.

Vidulich, M.A. (1995), 'The Role of Scope as a Feature of Situation Awareness Metrics', in *Proceedings of the International Conference on Experimental Analysis and Measurement of Situation Awareness*, Daytona Beach, FL.

Wickens, C.D. (2000), 'The Trade-off of Design for Routine and Unexpected Performance: Implications for Situation Awareness', in M.R. Endsley and D.J Garland (eds), *Situation Awareness, Analysis and Measurement*, Lawrence Erlbaum Associates, Mahwah, NJ.

Willingham, D.B., Nissen, M.J. and Bullemer, P. (1989), 'On the Development of Procedural Knowledge', *Journal of Experimental Psychology: Learning, Memory and Cognition*, vol. 15, pp. 1047-1060.

Wippich, W.A. and Mecklenbrauker, S. (1995), 'Implicit Memory for Textual Materials', *Psychological Research*, vol. 57, pp. 131-141.

Chapter 6

Modeling Situation Awareness in an Organizational Context: Military Command and Control

David J. Bryant, Frederick M.J. Lichacz, Justin G. Hollands and Joseph V. Baranski

Introduction

Situation awareness (SA) is a cognitive construct that refers to an awareness and understanding of external events in our immediate and near future surroundings. The concept can be traced back to World War I, when pilots came to understand the 'importance of gaining awareness of the enemy before he gained awareness of one's self...' (Endsley, 1988, p. 97). Since then, researchers and practitioners have come to view SA as critical for accurate decision-making and performance in a variety of work domains such as air traffic control (Endsley and Rogers, 1994), general aviation (Adams, Tenney, and Pew, 1995; Endsley, 1993), nuclear power plant management (Hogg, Felleso, Strand-Volden, and Torralba, 1995), medicine (Gaba, Howard and Small, 1995), and driving (Lee, 1999).

A Model of Situation Awareness

Although recent decades have seen numerous attempts to develop a cognitive model of SA, arguably it has been Endsley's (2000) model that has been most influential, particularly with respect to shaping our understanding of the concept. Like the origins of the SA construct, Endsley's model of SA arose primarily from practical needs associated with military applications; more specifically, the information requirements of US fighter pilots. As shown in Figure 6.1, Endsley's model has the appearance of the general information-processing model portrayed in psychology textbooks (e.g., Wickens and Hollands, 2000). Endsley postulates that SA is derived within an iterative cycle in which information from the external world is processed through three stages of information processing with each level passing information onto the next level. Level I SA involves perceiving the different elements (e.g., aircraft, terrain) in the environment and their characteristics (e.g., color, size and location). Level II SA involves the comprehension and significance associated with the perceived elements in the environment. Level III SA involves the ability to predict future actions of those elements in the environment. The attained level of SA is believed to influence decision-making, which in turn guides action. Indeed, Endsley's model has a great deal of face validity and perhaps because of this has gained prominence as a popular and generally useful descriptive theory of the cognitive issues involved in SA and applied decision-making.

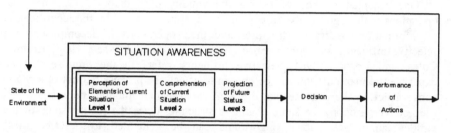

Figure 6.1 Endsley's model of Situation Awareness

Descriptive versus Prescriptive Models of SA

As noted, Endsley's (2000) model represents a descriptive theory of SA and applied decision-making. Within cognitive psychology, descriptive theories attempt to provide a broad overview of the different stages that information passes through before a decision is made or an action engaged. In contrast, prescriptive theories identify the rules and heuristics that guide the operations within and between each stage of processing. Moreover, prescriptive theories inform and guide experimental inquiry into the existence and order of proposed stages of information processing. Thus in contrast to descriptive theories, prescriptive theories specify how information is represented and how information and variables from the external world interact to impact decision-making and potential courses of action. The result of such specificity is the ability to make precise predictions and explanations about behavior across a variety of settings. Rousseau, Tremblay, and Breton (Chapter 1, this volume) offer a more detailed discussion of the issues surrounding the characterization of SA models as descriptive versus prescriptive.

As currently formulated, Endsley's model does not possess this level of specificity and is therefore limited in its predictive and explanatory ability. For example, Endsley's model offers no clear means of delineating the cognitive processes underlying her general SA framework. Moreover, it is unclear whether the proposed stages of Endsley's (2000) model represent independent stages of processing, whether information flows across each stage in a serial manner or all three types of information (perceptual, comprehension, projection) are processed in parallel, or within some intermediate or hybrid process. Knowledge of the processing architecture is essential to understanding how different kinds of information (e.g., perceptual, semantic) are treated and how information is represented in the system (e.g., as patterns of activation or localized representations). Moreover, advances in the psychological and behavioral sciences have identified the important role that 'top-down' cognitive processes have on information processing and decision-making (e.g., Baranski and Petrusic, 2003; Vickers, 1979). Such properties are generally accepted as necessary components of valid prescriptive models of information processing and prerequisites for testing the validity of hypothesized structures and operations, and for predicting performance (Marr, 1982; Newell, Shaw, and Simon, 1958).

One accepted method of testing the validity of a theory's structures and operations is through the use of converging operations, whereby the identification of information-processing structures and their operations is accomplished via selective influence and convergence (Garner, Hake and Eriksen, 1956; Kramer, Coles, and Logan, 1996). Selective influence refers to the premise that an experimental manipulation can be chosen to affect one process but not others and convergence to the premise that different experimental manipulations can affect (i.e., converge upon) the same cognitive structure. Once the relationships of the various stages are known, algorithms can be generated to describe these relationships and the operations that occur within the stages, which will facilitate the generation of clear and empirically testable hypotheses about performance (Newell et al., 1958).

Rather than relying on converging operations to validate her model, Endsley's (2000) framework of SA has to date been supported primarily on the basis of verbal reports of subject matter experts (SMEs) (Endsley, 1993; Endsley and Rogers, 1994). While cognitive psychologists have often used introspective reports to understand the underlying psychological processes of behavior, seldom is this information used as a direct source of data. Rather, this information is typically used to help interpret more objective data (e.g., response times and error rates) within a specific theoretical context (Hintzman, 1978). Moreover, verbal reports about cognitive processes are often limited in their utility because processes may be automatized and therefore inaccessible (Nisbett and Wilson, 1977; Shiffrin and Schneider, 1977), working memory limitations (Baddeley, 1986), and time lags between performance and verbal reports can distort the accuracy and ultimately restrict the utility of these reports (Gopher and Donchin, 1986). Accordingly, conclusions drawn about SA and decision-making based on Endsley's model should be made cautiously.

This critique of Endsley's (2000) model notwithstanding, as a descriptive model of the cognitive processes involved in the development of SA and decision-making, Endsley's model has played an important role in the delineation of the concept of SA and has demonstrated how SA can be applied in many work domains. Moreover, the model provides a recognized and accepted foundation from which to develop tools to enhance and maintain SA for decision-making.

The Value of a Descriptive Model of SA

When viewed as a descriptive rather than prescriptive theory, Endsley's SA model has proven valuable as a framework in which to explore important issues related to human performance. It has, for example, helped researchers identify human and task/system factors that affect SA (e.g., Endsley, 1997). More importantly, Endsley's model has energized and focused interest in determining the relationship between SA (an often vague concept) and task performance. Thus, researchers have found that SA plays an important role in many complex tasks, such as flying, driving, and air traffic control (Endsley, 1995). Air traffic controllers, for example, spend roughly 90 per cent of their time processing information rather than implementing procedures (Kaempf and Orasanu, 1997). Similarly, researchers (e.g., Drillings and Serfaty, 1997; Kaempf, Klein, Thordsen, and Wolf, 1996) have noted the importance of developing good SA in naval warfare.

Although Endsley's model is not of a form that allows detailed specification of the cognitive operations underlying SA, it has delineated classes of cognitive processes linked to errors of performance. Endsley and colleagues (Endsley, 1997; Jones and Endsley, 1996) have even developed a taxonomy of errors that can occur in SA. Their classification system highlights the problems that a person might have in developing a full understanding of the situation. Errors at Level I, for example, centre around failures to perceive information, often due to some inherent lack of detectability or discriminability in sensor data, failure of the human perceptual system, or over-abundance of data that overwhelms the human perceptual capacity. In contrast, errors at Level II center around failures to comprehend the significance of events, perhaps because a system operator lacks sufficient mental models to interpret data. Errors at Level III centre around difficulties in processing the dynamics of the situation.

Endsley's model has contributed to the development of intuitive or 'naturalistic' theories of decision-making. These theories are based not on formal analyses but strategies of experienced decision makers; i.e., an observational/descriptive approach that assumes human strategies are good strategies in situations in which time is limited and data ambiguous (Klein, 1997). Intuitive theories assume that decisions are made by holistic evaluation of potential courses of action. As such, the evaluation process relies heavily on memory of workable solutions and complete and accurate SA of the current situation. Thus, according to this class of theory, a decision maker identifies potential courses of action by first assessing the situation then recognizing past situations that are similar.

The role of SA in decision making has highlighted the importance of seeking ways in which complex systems and their interfaces can be designed to enhance SA (Adelman, 1992). This entails study of the nature of the task to identify what particular display elements are needed. In general, however, there needs to be greater emphasis on data extraction (ability of the user to obtain information in the form needed) than data availability (the amount of data presented). Here, Endsley's model has served as a framework in which to develop practical approaches to supporting SA. Endsley (1995, 1997) and Garner and Assenmacher (1997) offer specific guidelines for interface design.

A Different Framework for Military Command and Control

As discussed, Endsley's model has, to date, been profitably used as a descriptive model that summarizes important concepts for application to military and industrial domains. When considered as a descriptive rather than prescriptive theory, Endsley's model has been valuable but should not be viewed as sacrosanct. The value of a descriptive model derives from its applicability to the domain and types of problems under consideration. For this reason, we argue that Endsley's model, developed originally in the context of single operator or small team task performance, is not the best descriptive model available for decision making in an *organizational* setting. Consider the fratricide incident described by Vidulich, Bolia, and Nelson (Chapter 13, this volume), in which two US Air Force F-15 pilots shot down two US Army Blackhawk helicopters over Iraq. Although the pilots may have had excellent SA with respect to their tactical environment, the interconnectivity of assets across services failed to deliver the knowledge necessary to correctly identify the Blackhawk helicopters as friendly aircraft. Organizations are, in their own way, organic entities that attempt to accomplish multiple objectives through coordinated action. Understanding the dynamics of military organizations is key to describing SA. In particular, military Command and Control (C^2) requires a descriptive model that borrows from cognitive research in areas of constructive perception, mental representation, and critical thinking that aid our understanding of the interaction between operational planning and decision making in the field. In this section, we discuss the Critique, Explore, Compare, and Adapt (CECA) model of C^2 decision making (Bryant, 2003) as a competing framework in which to address issues of situation awareness.

The CECA Loop

The CECA loop, shown in Figure 6.2, begins with planning activities that establish the initial conceptual model of the operation to be conducted (illustrated in the top-most box in Figure 6.2). Throughout an operation, the conceptual model will be a representation or mental model of how the operation is intended to proceed. The conceptual model can be thought of as a working description of the intended states of the battlespace as well as the ultimate desired end-state. Detailed specification of desired battlespace states is crucial for a) devising appropriate actions, b) assessing the effectiveness of actions in achieving desired battlespace states, and c) assessing the relevance and effectiveness of the plan itself (and goals) in meeting higher-level operational aims.

To know when and how to adapt, one must have a situation model (illustrated by the middle box in Figure 6.2), which is a representation of the current state of the battlespace (i.e., 'how it currently is') in a form that can be understood with respect to the conceptual model. The situation model should represent all aspects of the battlespace that affect the validity of the conceptual model. Disconfirming evidence, which can indicate ways in which the conceptual model is not an accurate representation of the situation, is especially valuable because it forces one to be adaptive to the actual conditions of the battlespace.

Because the conceptual model is goal-oriented, information gathering must be directed toward determining the ways in which the current situation is facilitating the achievement of goals and more importantly the ways in which it is thwarting the achievement of goals or putting one's own forces at risk. Thus, information needs are established in the 'Critique' phase of the CECA Loop by questioning the critical aspects of the conceptual model; i.e., those aspects that, if invalidated, would render the plan of operation untenable. Specific kinds of required data types can be identified based on these questions and promulgated down to the sensor level.

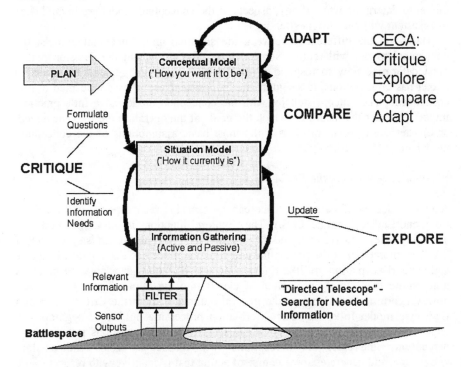

**Figure 6.2 Critique, Explore, Compare, and Adapt (CECA) model of C²
decision making (Bryant, 2003)**

The 'Explore' phase of the CECA Loop comprises the active and passive collection of data from the battlespace. Active collection is guided by the information needs developed in the Critique phase and thus is directed to answering questions concerning the validity of the conceptual model. The directed telescope is a term applied to the various means of focused data collection – electronic, personal, and so on – available to individuals within the C² structure. The directed telescope serves to make optimal use of limited processing capacity to rapidly obtain relevant information. A second means of information gathering involves the continual reception and filtering of sensor data according to intelligently determined criteria. The filter shown in Figure 6.2 actually refers to all the mechanisms in place to block irrelevant information from further processing. Events in the battlespace are monitored by these passive data collection mechanisms, which apply predetermined criteria to determine whether unassessed aspects of the battlespace should receive attention.

Gathered data are used to update the situation model of the battlespace, reflecting changes that have occurred in the battlespace, corrections of errors in the situation model, the addition of missing elements, and the enhancement of relevant detail. In the 'Compare' phase, the situation model is compared to the conceptual model to determine what, if any, aspects of the conceptual model are invalid (i.e., inconsistent with the current situation).

Based on the differences between the situation and conceptual models, the conceptual model will require some degree of revision and the decision maker must determine how to respond in the 'Adapt' phase. In general, the decision maker has three options, to a) ignore the inconsistencies if they are deemed of low consequence (i.e., inconsistencies with the conceptual model have little practical impact), b) alter the means by which the goals of the operation are to be achieved, or c) alter the goals themselves if the most basic assumptions of the conceptual model are invalidated.

Situation Awareness in the CECA Model

A certain degree of correspondence can be seen between aspects of the CECA Loop and Endsley's model of SA. The 'Explore' functions in the CECA Loop are akin to Endsley's Level I SA and the situation model similar to Endsley's Level II SA. The interaction of the conceptual and situation models to discern discrepancies and support adaptation are like Endsley's Level III, although adaptation involves much more than simply projection of events into the future. These similarities, however, are not surprising as the general outlines of both the CECA Loop and Endsley's model follow a basic information processing outline of cognition, in which an organism senses the environment, synthesizes sensations into coherent perceptions, interprets the perceptions with respect to goals and existing knowledge, and generates some course of action that is adaptive with respect to the environment. Such a biological framework has often been cited as an analogy for C^2 (e.g., Coakley, 1992).

The concept of SA in the CECA Loop is based on the constructivist perspective of human perception. The constructivist perspective on perception considers how people bring existing knowledge to direct sensory systems, set attentional thresholds, and assemble gathered sensory data into a coherent and plausible interpretation of the state of the world around us (see Rock, 1993). One important element of this perspective is the integration of bottom-up and top-down processes, which captures the goal-directedness of human cognition. Another key premise is that our experience of the world is not an absolute truth; it is, instead, the mental 'theory' we create to explain the data our senses have gathered and provide a mental model that can be used to plan actions to be taken in that world. We may not be aware of the hypothetical nature of perceptual experience in our daily existence, but when we step into the unnatural and complex world of modern warfare, it is critical to bear in mind that data are simply building blocks and the value of the end product, our understanding, depends also on the concepts and knowledge brought to bear in interpreting the data.

Thus, in the CECA Loop, SA is conceived, in part, as a set of processes – critiquing processes that derive information needs through analysis of the conceptual model, exploration processes that actively seek data that will bear on the validity of the conceptual model, and comparison processes that determine the respects in which the current situation differs from the intended state of the conceptual model. In the CECA Loop, however, there is also a focus on mental representation, which requires that SA be considered in terms of how data and information are integrated in an understanding of the situation and its implications. The concept of the mental model is particularly important as a means to describe complex and rich mental representations used in reasoning (e.g., Fiore, Salas, and Cannon-Bowers, 2001). Moreover, mental models are dynamic and situational representations, continually adjusting to represent the current state of the system (Hatano and Inagaki, 2000; Moray, 1999). If problem solving is viewed as the exercise of control over a complex system, the mental model plays a key role as the indicator of the current state of the system, the 'here and now' (Jansson, 1999).

Thus, in the CECA Loop, SA resides, in part, in the situation model, which is created to describe the state of the battlespace. That precise nature of that representation is determined by the conceptual model and, more specifically, the key elements within the conceptual model that bear most significantly on its validity as a plan of action. It is only through an assessment of the correspondence of situation to conceptual model that the C^2 organization can adapt appropriately to the evolving flow of events. The representation of the current situation can only be conceived with respect to the organizational goals that lie at the heart of the conceptual model.

Like Endsley's model, the CECA Loop can be characterized as predominantly operator-focused (see Rousseau, Tremblay and Breton, Chapter 1, this volume) because it focuses on the representation and transformation processes that are essential to SA. There is, however, an important role of the environment in determining how personnel should assess the situation to build the best situation model. In this respect, the CECA Loop agrees with the premise of the situation-focused approach that to understand perception one must understand the environment. In particular, we view SA processes as adaptive processes that bring the conceptual model in line with the environmentally-defined situation.

Because C^2 is not an individual task but rather an intricate set of organizational procedures, we must finally also consider SA as an organizational framework. That is, as well as being the situational representation of the battlespace, SA exists in the organizational structure used to assign information processing roles, decision making authority, and responsibilities to push information needs down to the sensor level and pull relevant information up to the decision making units.

A key element of the CECA Loop is the shared nature of the conceptual and situation models. Members of the military commonly refer to the notion of a commander's 'vision' for a military operation, which lays out a plan for an operation with contingencies and indicators used to monitor whether the operation proceeds as anticipated (Builder et al., 1999; Shattuck and Woods, 2000). Two key elements that affect the quality of C^2 are the commanders' vision, or conceptual model, and the degree to which that vision is shared among individuals and units who will contribute to accomplishing specified goals (Builder et al., 1999). By reference to a shared conceptual model, subordinate commanders can respond to unfolding events in a manner consistent with the overall commander's vision. Sharing the concept also enables subordinate commanders to select and channel upward only information that relates to the continuing effectiveness of the concept. Pigeau and McCann (2000) have described these processes, collectively, as 'the establishment of common intent to achieve coordinated action,' which is consistent with the notion of a conceptual model.

It is important to distinguish the concept of a model from that of SA. Different levels of command need different views on the underlying situation because they have different responsibilities and functions. The different views represent not just different 'levels' of awareness (cf. the 'cone of awareness' discussed by French, Matthews, and Redden, Chapter 14, this volume). Rather, each view is qualitatively different according to the specific functional requirements of the individual or individuals. Therefore, we must conceive of shared SA in a way that allows individuals with unique functional requirements to access a common situation model but obtain an understanding appropriate in scope and form to their functions.

Value of the CECA Loop Model

As mentioned earlier, both Endsley's SA model and the CECA Loop are descriptive models. Neither model is sufficiently detailed to allow many testable hypotheses to be formulated. Their value stems from the usefulness of the model as a framework for discussion. In this sense both models are applicable to military C^2 but, as we will argue, the CECA Loop has a number of advantages over Endsley's model in this context. These advantages are generally matters of degree or focus but they illustrate how each model may be more profitably used for one purpose than another.

The CECA Loop differs from Endsley's model in three key respects. The first difference, which has already discussed, is that Endsley's model deals more with the individual or small team than a large organization. Although each individual in an organization undoubtedly builds SA with respect to his or her specific tasks and areas of responsibility, the main thrust of the CECA Loop model is to provide a framework for exploring the shared SA within the organization. To that end, the conceptual and situation models are intended to be shared, joint products of all levels within the organization.

A second difference between the models lies in CECA's specification of process and structure. CECA illustrates how a descriptive model can specify general constraints on how prescriptive models can operate, and how and why particular processing stages or sequences of stages are necessary. We argue that a good descriptive model should constrain how a prescriptive model can operate. For example, CECA specifies that the SA process requires a comparison of situation and conceptual models, and that this drives the need to propagate information needs/requests to obtain relevant sensor data.

The CECA Loop offers a discussion of processing steps but puts the conceptual and situation models at the heart of C^2. In this sense, the major issues to explore within the CECA Loop pertain to the nature of the representations of the conceptual and situation models, the format of data requirements pushed down, and the relevance of information pushed up. With its focus on comparing a situation model to one's conceptual model, the CECA Loop correctly recognizes that data and information are relative to the decision maker. This makes clear that the amount of data is not the paramount factor but rather the informativeness of those data in terms of allowing the decision maker to evaluate the validity of his or her mental models.

In considering how to improve and speed up decision making processes within a C^2 organization, it is critical to examine how changes to procedures or technology will affect the representation of the plan. Changes that seem to enhance procedural aspects of decision making may actually impair overall performance if they disrupt the formulation or understanding of the conceptual model. On a more positive note, changes to the planning procedure or communication of the plan throughout the C^2 organization could yield significant benefits to decision making by making it easier for individuals to identify relevant information and use it appropriately.

A third point of departure is the scope and time scales to which the two models apply. Endsley's model, linked as it is to the individual, deals with SA of the immediately perceivable world in more-or-less 'real-time.' The projection of events in the future is limited to the immediate implications of data with respect to the task the individual is currently performing. In contrast, the CECA Loop, because it applies to military C^2, deals with a much less well-defined but undoubtedly larger time scale. Indeed, the conceptual model at the heart of C^2 is a means of representing 'conceptual time' through a series of intended states of the battlespace. Through this representation, the complex planned actions of a military unit are represented and used as the bases for determining relevant data and evaluating the current state of the battlespace. Different levels within the C^2 organization consider different time scales, which become progressively broader as one moves up the organizational structure. Obtaining and processing data in an organization requires time, so the organization's SA cannot refer to the immediate perceivable world; rather, it must represent the situation at a higher level of abstraction. The key element of organizational C^2 is not time per se but the validity of the conceptual model as it unfolds over time.

Conclusions

In summary, we are not arguing against Endsley's model as a descriptive framework. It has, after all, proven useful in a number of situations. That model, however, was not specifically formulated for military C^2 and it is limited in a number of respects. Military C^2 is an important domain that deserves a descriptive framework design specifically to deal with SA issues in the organizational context. The CECA Loop is intended to provide such a new, cognitively relevant descriptive model for C^2.

Correspondence

Address correspondence to David J. Bryant, Judgment and Decision Making Group, Defence Research and Development Canada – Toronto, 1133 Sheppard Ave. West, Toronto, Ontario, Canada, M3M 3B9. Email: david.bryant@drdc-rddc.gc.ca.

References

Adams, M.J., Tenney, Y.J. and Pew, R.W. (1995), 'Situation Awareness and the Cognitive Management of Complex Systems', *Human Factors*, vol. 37, pp. 85-104.

Adelman, L. (1992), *Evaluating Decision Support and Expert Systems*, John Wiley and Sons, New York.

Baddeley, A. (1986), *Working Memory*, Oxford University Press, Oxford.

Baranski, J.V. and Petrusic, W.M. (2003), 'Adaptive Decision Processes in Perceptual Comparisons: Effects of Changes in the Global Difficulty Context', *Journal of Experimental Psychology: Human Perception and Performance*, vol. 29, pp. 658-674.

Bryant, D.J. (2003), *Critique, Explore, Compare, and Adapt (CECA): A New Model for Command Decision Making*, DRDC Toronto Technical Report (TR 2003-105), Defence Research and Development Canada – Toronto, Toronto, Canada.

Builder, C.H., Bankes, S.C. and Nordin, R. (1999), *Command Concepts: A Theory Derived from the Practice of Command and Control*, Rand Corporation, Santa Monica, CA.

Coakley, T.P. (1992), *Command and Control for War and Peace*, National Defense University Press, Washington, DC.

Drillings, M. and Serfaty, D. (1997), 'Naturalistic Decision Making in Command and Control', In G. Klein and C.E. Zsambok (eds), *Naturalistic Decision Making*, Lawrence Erlbaum Associates Inc, Mahwah, NJ, pp. 71-80.

Endsley, M.R. (1988), 'Design and Evaluation for Situation Awareness Enhancement', In Proceedings of the Human Factors Society 32nd Annual Meeting, The Human Factors Society, Santa Monica, CA, pp. 97-101.

Endsley, M.R. (1993), 'A Survey of Situation Awareness Requirements in Air-to-air Combat Fighters', *International Journal of Aviation Psychology*, vol. 3, pp. 157-168.

Endsley, M.R. (1995), 'Toward a Theory of Situation Awareness in Dynamic Systems', *Human Factors*, vol. 37, pp. 32-64.

Endsley, M. (1997), 'The Role of Situation Awareness in Naturalistic Decision Making', In G. Klein and C.E. Zsambok (eds), *Naturalistic Decision Making*, Lawrence Erlbaum Associates, Mahwah, NJ, pp. 269-283.

Endsley, M.R. (2000), 'Theoretical Underpinnings of Situation Awareness: A Critical Review', In M.R. Endsley and D.J. Garland (eds), *Situation Awareness Analysis and Measurement*, Lawrence Erlbaum Associates, Mahwah, NJ, pp. 3-32.

Endsley, M.R. and Rogers, M.D. (1994), 'Situation Awareness Information Requirements for Enroute Air Traffic Control', In Proceedings of the Human Factors Society 38th Annual Meeting, The Human Factors Society and Ergonomics Society, Santa Monica, CA, pp. 71-75.

Fiore, S.M., Salas, E. and Cannon-Bowers, J.A. (2001), 'Group Dynamics and Shared Mental Model Development', In M. London (ed.), *How People Evaluate Others in Organizations*, Lawrence Erlbaum Associates, Mahwah, NJ, pp. 309-331.

Gaba, D.M, Howard, S.K. and Small, S.D. (1995), 'Situation Awareness in Anesthesiology', *Human Factors*, vol. 37, pp. 20-31.

Garner, K.T. and Assenmacher, T.J. (1997), *'Situational Awareness Guidelines'*, Naval Air Systems Command, Washington, DC.

Garner, W.R., Hake, H.W. and Eriksen, C.W. (1956), 'Operationism and the Concept of Perception', *Psychological Review*, vol. 63, pp. 149-159.

Gopher, D. and Donchin, E. (1986), 'Workload – An Examination of the Concept', In K.R. Boff, L. Kaufman, and J.P Thomas (eds), *Handbook of Perception and Performance: Volume II, Cognitive Processes and Performance*, John Wiley and Sons, New York, pp. 41-49.

Hatano, G. and Inagaki, K. (2000), 'Knowledge Acquisition and use in Higher-order Cognition', In K. Pawlik and M.R. Rosenzweig (eds), *International Handbook of Psychology*, Sage Publications, London, England, pp. 167-190.

Hintzman, D. (1978), *The Psychology of Learning*, W. H. Freeman and Company, San Francisco.

Hogg, D.N., Folleso, K., Strand-Volden, F. and Torralba, B. (1995), 'Development of a Situation Awareness Measure to Evaluate Advanced Alarm Systems in Nuclear Power Plant Control Rooms', *Ergonomics*, vol. 38, pp. 2394-2413.

Jansson, A. (1999), 'Goal Achievement and Mental Models in Everyday Decision Making', In P. Juslin and H. Montgomery (eds), *Judgment and Decision Making: Neo-Brunswikian and Process-Tracing Approaches*, Lawrence Erlbaum Associates, Mahwah, NJ, pp. 23-43.

Jones, D.G., Endsley, M.R. (1996), 'Sources of Situation Awareness Errors in Aviation', *Aviation, Space and Environmental Medicine*, vol. 67, pp. 507-512.

Kaempf, G.L., Klein, G., Thordsen, M.L. and Wolf, S. (1996), 'Decision Making in Complex Naval Command-and-control Environments', *Human Factors*, vol. 38, pp. 220-231.

Kaempf, G.L. and Orasanu, J. (1997), 'Current and Future Applications of Naturalistic Decision Making in Aviation', In G. Klein and C.E. Zsambok (eds), *Naturalistic Decision Making*, Lawrence Erlbaum Associates, Mahwah, NJ, pp. 81-90.

Klein, G. (1997), 'An Overview of Naturalistic Decision Making Applications', In G. Klein and C.E. Zsambok (eds), *Naturalistic Decision Making*, Lawrence Erlbaum Associates, Mahwah, NJ, pp. 49-59.

Lee, J.D. (1999), 'Measuring Driver Adaptation to In-vehicle Information Systems: Dissociation of Subjective and Objective Situation Awareness Measures'. In Proceedings of the Human Factors Society 43rd Annual Meeting, The Human Factors Society, Santa Monica, CA, pp. 992-996.

Kramer, A.F., Coles, M.G.H. and Logan, G.D. (1996), *Converging Operations in the Study of Visual Selective Attention*, American Psychological Association, Washington, DC.

Marr, D. (1982), *Vision: A Computational Investigation into the Human Representation and Processing of Visual Information*, W.H. Freeman, San Francisco.

Moray, N. (1999), 'Mental Models in Theory and Practice', In D. Gopher and A. Koriat (eds), *Attention and Performance XVII: Cognitive Regulation of Performance: Interaction of Theory and Application*, The MIT Press, Cambridge, MA, pp. 223-258.

Newell, A., Shaw, J.C. and Simon, H.A. (1958), 'Elements of a Theory of Human Problem Solving', *Psychological Review*, vol. 65, pp. 151-166.

Nisbett, R.E. and Wilson, T.D. (1977), 'Telling more than we can know: Verbal Reports on Mental Processes', *Psychological Review*, vol. 84, pp. 231-259.

Pigeau, R. and McCann, C. (2000), 'Redefining Command and Control', In C. McCann and R. Pigeau (eds), *The Human in Command: Exploring the Modern Military Experience*, Kluwer Academic/Plenum Publishers, New York, pp. 163-184.

Rock, I. (1993), *The Logic of Perception*, The MIT Press, Cambridge, MA.

Shattuck, L.G. and Woods, D.D. (2000), 'Communication of Intent in Military Command and Control Systems'. In C. McCann and R. Pigeau (eds), *The Human in Command: Exploring the Modern Military Experience*, Kluwer Academic/Plenum Publishers, New York, pp. 279-291.

Shiffrin, R.M. and Schneider, W. (1977), 'Controlled and Automatic Human Information Processing: II. Perceptual Learning, Automatic Attending, and a General Theory', *Psychological Review*, vol. 84, pp. 127-190.

Vickers, D. (1979), *Decision Processes in Visual Perception*, Academic Press, New York.

Wickens, C.D. and Hollands, J.G. (2000), *Engineering Psychology and Human Performance* (3rd ed.), Prentice Hall, New Jersey.

Chapter 7

A Cognitive Streaming Account of Situation Awareness

Simon P. Banbury, Darryl G. Croft, William J. Macken and
Dylan M. Jones

Introduction

This chapter will present a recent conceptualization of human cognition which has
been used with some success to explain a number of key phenomena associated
with selective attention and short-term memory[2] (STM). We argue that the
Cognitive Streaming framework developed by Jones (1993; see also Jones,
Beaman and Macken, 1996) also has utility for explaining key observations from
Situation Awareness (SA) research, and in particular the cognitive processes
underlying anticipation. In broad terms, the concept of Cognitive Streaming refers
to ways in which information is organized within the cognitive system, and in
particular within STM. A key concept is that of *transitional probabilities*; the
likelihood that certain types of event will occur following the occurrence of other
events. Although the Cognitive Streaming approach has up until now been applied
to understanding selective attention and STM, we believe that this approach
provides a compelling account of how operators are able to acquire and maintain
an awareness of present and future states of entities in their environment. We will
argue that the use of transitional probabilities is the mechanism by which we are
able to anticipate.

The chapter will first make the case that STM is fundamental to how we
acquire and maintain SA. We will then discuss the limitations of current
conceptualizations of SA based on their inability to encapsulate the dynamic nature
of SA within their frameworks and to describe what cognitive processes are
brought to bear when anticipating the future states of entities. Finally, we will
describe how the Cognitive Streaming account of selective attention and STM can
explain the key phenomena of SA, in the context of a radar operator attempting to
anticipate the movement of tracked aircraft. Specifically, we will describe the
cognitive processes that are utilized when anticipating, the beneficial effects of
previous experience, limits in number of aircraft that an operator can have

---

[2] In this Chapter we refer to short-term memory as the mechanism by which information is
held active for processing and includes the notion of a capacity-limited store. Other
researchers have referred to the former as *working* memory.

awareness of concurrently and the fate of unattended stimuli that nevertheless might contribute to SA.

Short-Term Memory and Situation Awareness

Holding information active for processing is viewed by a number of influential authors as pivotal to performing real-world tasks that require dynamic and complex processing (Durso and Gronlund, 1999; Endsley, 1995). Examples include air traffic control (e.g., Gronlund, Ohrt, Dougherty, Perry and Manning, 1998); driving (e.g., Gugerty, 1997); and flying (e.g., Sohn and Dattel, 2001; Sohn and Doane, 2000). Endsley (1995) argues that real-world tasks conducted in these domains require high levels of SA for successful task performance and that STM is one of the critical factors that limit operators from acquiring and interpreting information to form SA. Furthermore, the active processing of situational information must occur within STM as new information must be combined with existing knowledge and a composite picture of the situation developed. This situational picture, or situation model, includes the projection of future status and is used to generate and evaluate a number of courses of action (Endsley, 1995). These processes also occur in STM. In these circumstances, Endsley argues, a heavy load is imposed on STM as it is required to achieve high levels of SA, formulating and selecting responses, and carrying out subsequent actions. As well as memory for situational information, the order in which this information is manifest over time is also an important factor in the formation of SA. For example, the effective monitoring of displays or system parameters over time requires that the temporal order of this information be kept intact in STM. In doing so, trend information can be inferred. Indeed, Banbury, Fricker, Tremblay and Emery (2003) suggest that memory for order plays a pivotal role in an operator's ability to acquire and maintain SA.

The contention that STM is an important determinant of successfully acquiring and maintaining SA has been supported by a number of empirical studies. For example, Carretta, Perry and Ree (1996) found that verbal and spatial STM were good predictors of 31 supervisory/peer ratings on the United States Air Force's SA battery. Bolstad (1991) also found that STM predicted SA as measured by the Situation Awareness Global Assessment Technique (SAGAT).

However, the link between STM and SA is 'not a ubiquitous one' (Durso and Gronlund, 1999, p.294). A number of studies found little or no evidence for the link between performance, decision making and SA, and STM, prompting Durso and Gronlund to conclude that the correlation between STM and SA is due to the processing of information (i.e., memory skill), rather than the storage of information. Consistent with popular conceptualizations of STM (e.g., Working Memory Model; Baddeley and Hitch, 1974), Durso and Gronlund argue the importance of executive processing (e.g., chunking, gistification, prioritization, and restructuring the environment) to real-world performance in information-intensive domains. Clearly, executive processes such as these take time to acquire, leading Durso and Gronlund to argue that experts do not rely on STM but on Long-Term Working Memory (LTWM; Ericsson and Kintsch, 1995) in which pointers in STM activate information stored in long-term memory, facilitating the rapid and efficient storage and retrieval of situational information. However, in the case of novices, or when the situation is suitably novel, these LTWM structures cannot be brought to bear, necessitating real-time computational processes heavily dependent on STM (Endsley, 1997; Stokes, 1991). For example, Sohn and Doane (2000) found that spatial and verbal memory span (i.e., memory capacity) and performance on reconstructing plausible and implausible cockpit configurations (i.e., memory skill) correlated to performance on predicting future states of the cockpit instrumentation (i.e., SA). However, this effect was a function of the participants' level of expertise; STM capacity was critical for novice pilots, while memory skill was important for expert pilots.

The contention that experts are able to restructure their knowledge (e.g., chunking) and adopt skilled memory strategies (e.g., prioritization) to mitigate the load on their STM when engaging in complex and dynamic tasks seems very plausible and compelling. It is not our intention to argue with this account, but instead to point out this account relies heavily on anecdotal evidence (e.g., skilled memory of waiters) and observations from overly simplistic laboratory-based studies (e.g., reading of text). Critically, there is no discussion and therefore account of the key observation of SA; that of anticipation. It is also not entirely clear how the acquisition of memory skill might enhance (or limit) the quality of anticipation that can be achieved.

Given the importance of SA in everyday complex activities and the pivotal role of STM to the acquisition and maintenance of SA, especially in novel situations, we argue that models of STM have utility for elucidating some of the key phenomena that have emerged from SA research. However, contemporary conceptualizations of memory shed little light on the highest level of SA achievable; that of the accurate projection of future states of an entity (Endsley, 1995), or more simply put, our ability to *anticipate*.

Short-Term Memory and Anticipation

The ability to anticipate, think-ahead or project is arguably the most important component of most, if not all, contemporary conceptualizations of SA (Dominguez, 1994; Endsley, 1995). Endsley argues that this ability is 'the mark of a skilled expert' (Endsley, 2000, p.7); allowing timely decision making in a variety of domains, including aviation, process control and medicine. Wickens (1984, p.201) argues that anticipation imposes a heavy load on STM by requiring the maintenance of present conditions, future conditions, rules used to generate the latter from the former, and actions that are appropriate to future conditions. But what are the psychological processes, particularly those relating to memory, which underlie anticipation? McGowan and Banbury (Chapter 10, this volume) discuss a number of studies of anticipation; however the majority of this research is concerned with psychomotor reactions to relatively simplistic laboratory-based stimuli. What of the literature pertaining to SA?

A number of conceptualizations of SA argue that the acquisition of higher levels of SA (e.g., understanding and anticipation) is achieved through a process of 'pattern-matching' with previous experience (e.g., Endsley, 1995; 2000). Long-term memory structures (i.e., mental models) are utilized to construct a situation model of the environment; the situation model being equivalent to SA (Endsley, 2000). Mental models allow operators to 'generate descriptions of system purpose and form, explanations of system functioning and observed system states, and predictions of future states' (Rouse and Morris, 1985, p.7). Similarly, Durso and Gronlund (1999) argue that situation models are the momentary instantiation of long-term working memory (LTWM) that allow, amongst other things, predictions into the near future (p.298). Endsley argues that a major advantage of pattern-matching between a representation of the situation and past experience is that the match does not have to be exact. In other words, the present situation and the situation retrieved from memory need not be identical. However, it is not clear what exactly constitutes a match and what the impact of an approximate match has on how good anticipation can be. Crucially there is also no explanation of *how* the situation model is constructed to facilitate anticipation, what information it might contain, and what cognitive processes might be applied to it. Without such insights, we are not able to make any a priori predictions about the quality of anticipation given our knowledge of the operator's situation model, nor about what the effects of interruption, workload and interference on anticipation might be.

Endsley (1995) states that projection relies on 'many underlying cognitive processes' (Endsley, 1995, p.37) and in a framework conceptually similar to models used to explain human information processing (for a recent version see Wickens and Hollands, 2000, pp.10-14), projection is described as a process within STM that follows from perception and leads to decision making (Endsley, 1995, p. 41). Successful projection is derived from an accurate match between the mental model (i.e., knowledge of a particular system derived from previous experience) and the situation model (i.e., an understanding of the current situation; SA); providing:

> A mechanism for projecting future states of the system based on its current state and an understanding of its dynamics. (Endsley, 1995, p. 44)

What this 'mechanism' might be is not elucidated. Indeed, the use of information-processing based accounts of SA is problematic because the psychological constructs that they are based on (e.g., attention and memory) were not conceived to account for anticipation. In addition, Ulharik and Comerford (2002) argue that when couched in terms of the information-processing model, the process of acquiring SA appears to be relatively static. This is rather unfortunate given that the temporal nature of SA is one of its defining characteristics.

Adams, Tenney and Pew's (1995) conceptualization of SA emphasizes its dynamic nature by describing it as the current state of Neisser's (1976) perception-action cycle. The dynamism of SA is expressed by a cyclical and adaptive process: the environment shapes the agent by modifying its knowledge; this knowledge in turn directs the agent's activity in the environment; and this activity samples, alters or anticipates the environment, which then informs the agent (and so on). Adams et al. argue that anticipation is central to the discussion of SA and that 'managing the attentional and conceptual processes that permit cogent SA involves significant cognitive resources' (p. 87):

> At the cognitive level, anticipation follows from the consideration of alternative implications and interpretations of perceived events and may include such knowledge-intensive activities as fault diagnosis and contingency planning. (Adams, Tenney and Pew, 1995, pp. 89-90)

However, similar to Endsley's information-processing based account, Adams et al.,'s account based on the perceptual-cycle also lacks precision. Although their account captures the dynamic essence of SA, a number of constructs used in their account (e.g., memory) are not able to explain the processes and structures underlying anticipation. Indeed, both Endsley's and Adams et al.,'s accounts describe only higher-order psychological processes, and offer little insight into the lower-order processes that are brought to bear when engaging in higher-order activities such as anticipation. Indeed, this is a reflection of SA research in general. Lichacz (2001) conducted a brief overview of the research conducted on SA to date and concluded that SA research has concentrated on higher-order psychological processes (e.g., mental models, reasoning and goals, to name but a few), at the expense of studying lower-order processes (e.g., perceptual and encoding processes). He believes that this narrow focus is a limiting factor of SA research in general, and in particular, to efforts to develop a theoretical model of SA (see Fracker, 1988).

Lichacz notes that the information-processing approach has not been wholly embraced by the SA community, even though it offers a consideration of both the higher and lower-order processes utilized when humans interact with systems. Lichacz cites Flach's (1996) explanation as to why SA researchers have shied away from research into the lower-order processes using information-processing inspired approaches from cognitive psychology. Flach (1996) is critical of the information-processing approach, arguing that it has little application for understanding performance in real-world situations. Presumably, this is due to the propensity of experimental cognitive psychology to study phenomena in highly-controlled laboratory settings. However, Lichacz argues that current conceptualizations of SA rely too heavily on anecdotal reports and questionnaire data which do not constitute strong empirical support. As a result, Lichacz argues that the development of a theory of SA would be best served through an understanding of both lower- and higher-order psychological processes; the former through augmenting current SA research with basic cognitive psychological research. The benefits of such an endeavor are two-fold:

> Such a theory would lead to a less ambiguous account of the psychological processes involved in SA as well as a forum for a more empirical testing of hypotheses about various aspects of SA. (Lichacz, 2001, p. 308)

Although, we might have a reasonably clear idea which higher-level processes are required to acquire and maintain high levels of SA (e.g., projection of future states based on an understanding of the situation), we are still unclear about which lower-order cognitive processes and structures are utilized to achieve such goals. Crucially, such a theory should help to explain the effects of distraction, interruption, workload, stress and dual-task combinations on anticipation, as well as differences between novices and experts.

In the next section, we will introduce an information-processing based account of selective attention and STM. We argue that this framework; the Cognitive Streaming account of STM (Jones, 1993; Jones, Beaman and Macken, 1996), has utility for also explaining key observations from Situation Awareness research; in particular the cognitive processes underlying anticipation. We hope to bring together these seemingly contradictory notions; that a model originating from basic laboratory-based research on selective attention and STM can be extended to explain real-world phenomena, particularly the psychological processes and structures underlying anticipation.

A Cognitive Streaming Account of Situation Awareness

Introduction

Cognitive Streaming was developed by Jones and colleagues (Jones, 1993; Jones, Beaman and Macken, 1996; Macken, Tremblay, Alford and Jones, 1999) to account for the deleterious effects of extraneous sound on cognitive processing (for a review see Banbury, Macken, Tremblay and Jones, 2001). Disruption to cognitive processing by background sound is observed, particularly in tasks that are heavily reliant on serial memory, even though individuals are instructed to ignore the sound (for example, Beaman and Jones, 1997, 1998). The Cognitive Streaming account of these effects differs from theories based on specialized mental resources (e.g., Wickens, 1992); the Cognitive Streaming account predicts that interference between tasks occurs when they draw upon the same mental process (e.g., memory for order) rather than when their content is similar (e.g., both are spatial tasks) (Macken et al., 1999; Tremblay and Jones, 2001). The pattern of disruption to cognitive processing by extraneous sound has led to reappraisal of the classic notion of STM; that of a faculty distinct from others such as perception. Based on an analogy with computer storage drawn upon extensively in the 1950s, it was argued that memory was based upon the notion of 'modularity' (e.g., Baddeley and Hitch, 1974; Baddeley, 1990). Indeed, these models postulate that human cognition is divided into distinct modules based on the nature (e.g. modality) of the information being processed.

The Role of Transitional Probabilities

Jones and his colleagues argue that STM can be conceptualized in an alternative way. The Cognitive Streaming approach suggests that 'memory storage' phenomena represent one region of a continuum of behavior. Rather than suppose

STM is a store, the Cognitive Streaming approach suggests that it is one of a range of skilled behaviors. To reiterate, a key concept of Cognitive Streaming is that of transitional probabilities; the likelihood that certain types of event will occur following the occurrence of other events. To-be-remembered items in STM can therefore be characterized as sequences with low transitional probabilities to which habits of language processing (e.g., rehearsal using our 'inner voice') are applied. For example, in a sequence of random numbers, each digit gives no inherent information about the next in the sequence; however, the individual may apply a number of strategies, from mere repetition to complex association with previously stored knowledge to assist in the retention of the sequence. Thus, transitional probabilities are low because the materials that typically have to be retained are in an unfamiliar order (e.g., a new telephone number or unfamiliar driving directions), with weak or non-existent linkages between them. Alternatively, the transitional information normally present in familiar sequences (e.g., 'the cat sat on the ...') leads to a high transitional probability for the word 'mat'. In fact, transitional probabilities are not static and can change over time. For this example, transitional probabilities between the word 'the' to the word 'cat' are relatively low because there are a countless number of words that could follow 'the'. However, the transitional probability that the word following the second instance of 'the' will be the word 'mat' is much higher due to preceding succession of words; there is only one expression that starts with the words 'the cat sat on the'.

In terms of SA, transitional probabilities capture the temporal nature of SA well. SA is not necessarily acquired instantaneously; indeed it is hard to think of circumstances in which it would be. Rather, operators must take into account the dynamics of the situation, which are acquirable only over time, in order to be able to anticipate the future state of entities (Endsley, 1995). The notion of transitional probabilities also resonates well with how we view the world in probabilistic terms. Shepard (1981) argues that a crucial mechanism for how humans become attuned to an uncertain world is their ability to learn about, and exploit, the statistical regularities of events that occur in the environment. For example, we rely on assessments of likelihood, such as there is 40 per cent chance that it will rain tomorrow, to assist decision making under conditions of uncertainty in business, finance and medicine (Karelitz and Budescu, 2004). Objects whose movements over time exhibit high transitional probabilities (e.g., the movement of a train locomotive along a track) are easy to understand and predict. Objects whose transitional probabilities are not inherently high (e.g., the movement of an enemy aircraft) are not easy to predict and require deliberate effort to maintain so that the cognitive processes required to achieve SA (e.g., problem solving and hypothesis testing to enable comprehension) can be brought to bear. However, even an object with low transitional probabilities can be understood and anticipated more readily by 'grafting' transitional probabilities onto it through 'pattern matching' from long-term memory structures, or *schema* (e.g., previous experience of the aircraft's capabilities and likely tactics).

From these examples, we argue that deliberate and effortful behavior belongs to one end of a continuum and effortless and fluent skilled behavior belongs to the other end. 'Short-term memory' phenomena occur when stimuli are imperfectly related to skill; effort has to be expended in applying a range of linguistic skills to support the retention of information in memory. When perfectly matched, automaticity of performance can be achieved. This has the advantage of releasing resources to deal with other streams of information. Notions related to *skill*, rather than to storage, are therefore appropriate (e.g., Neumann, 1996).

The Functional Architecture of Cognitive Streaming

The Cognitive Steaming account is underpinned by a more general model of STM called the Object-Oriented Episodic Record (O-OER) model (Jones, 1993; Jones, Beaman and Macken, 1996). A central feature of this model is the formation of *objects* on an episodic surface, or *blackboard*. The blackboard contains a record of the events that have occurred, and knowledge structures that have been constructed or activated as a consequence, over the course of a task.

Objects from a visual source are usually formed on the blackboard by deliberate conscious control, while objects of auditory origin can be formed with or without conscious control (Jones, Madden and Miles, 1992). Object formation is achieved by a process of *segmentation*. For example, a stream of non-speech sounds might be segmented into objects if interspersed with silence, or an unbroken signal might be perceived as being segmented by sufficiently sharp changes in pitch and intensity (Jones, 1993). Similarly, a stream of information from a visual display might be segmented into objects each and every time one of its parameters (e.g., the spatial location of a radar track) changes significantly.[3]

Objects are organized into *cognitive streams* on the episodic blackboard. Although each object exists as a separate entity on the blackboard surface, Jones (1993) argues that perceptual factors organize and link them (such as those documented by the work on auditory streaming; Bregman, 1990). If the stream contains repetition of the same item, then no such links, or *pointers*, will be formed. For auditory material, pointers are formed automatically by auditory streaming; however for material of visual origin, pointers and objects are organized into streams either automatically (if related to familiar entities) or by deliberate rehearsal (if related to unfamiliar entities). The model supposes that the pointers between the objects are subject to decay, rather than the objects themselves. In contrast to other models of STM (e.g., Baddeley and Hitch, 1974), the objects are assumed to have relatively prolonged lives, but the short existence of the pointers governs the success of information retrieval. The strength of a pointer, and its robustness to decay, is determined by the transitional probability between the objects it is linking; high transitional probabilities will create robust pointers necessitating little or no rehearsal to maintain the associations, whereas low transitional probabilities will create weak pointers necessitating constant and deliberate rehearsal to maintain the associations. Rehearsal is by the use of *threads*

---

[3] Although it is less clear what constitutes 'significant' change for visual material, there are a number of well-established parameters for auditory material (see Banbury et al., 2001, for a review).

to trace back through the pointers and objects (i.e., the cognitive stream). By retracing the cognitive stream, the pointers between the objects are rehearsed and not the objects themselves.

Cognitive Streams Form the Basis of Situation Awareness

We believe that the Cognitive Streaming account overcomes some of the basic limitations of previous accounts of SA; in particular their inability to elucidate the cognitive processes and structures underlying anticipation in detail, and to capture the dynamic nature of SA. We will contextualize the theoretical account outlined above by describing how an experienced radar operator is able to track the movement of an unknown aircraft on his or her radar screen and to anticipate the aircraft's likely trajectory. Let us assume that the operator has experience of monitoring many types of aircraft, including this one, but has not been monitoring this particular aircraft prior to its appearance on the radar screen and as a result is unsure of the aircraft's type. The operator's goal is to anticipate the likely trajectory of the unidentified aircraft track so that he or she is more able to coordinate air defenses against the potential threat. Before the operator is able to anticipate the likely trajectory of the unknown aircraft, he or she must first attempt to identify what type of aircraft it is likely to be (e.g., military jet, commercial airliner and so on) by observing its movement over time (i.e., track history). Identifying that the unknown aircraft is of a certain type will then give the operator a better indication of how it is likely to behave in the future.

The process of acquiring SA begins when the aircraft first appears on the radar screen and is represented on the episodic blackboard as an object (see Figure 7.1). Consistent with Logan's (1988) theory of automaticity, the formation and retrieval of instances associated with that object is unavoidable as a consequence of attention; 'attention to an object is sufficient to cause retrieval of whatever information has been associated with it in the past' (Logan, 1988, p. 587). Therefore, inherent in the representation of the aircraft as an object on the blackboard (e.g., its position in time and space) is the activation of any other information from long-term memory associated with this type of aircraft; such as its properties (e.g., flight characteristics), operations (e.g., flight capabilities), constraints (e.g., rules of interaction with other aircraft in the vicinity) and contingencies (e.g., transitional probabilities; the likelihood that certain types of event will occur following the occurrence of other events). With the inclusion of transitional probabilities, the retrieval of information from long-term memory covers all aspects of the current and potential future states of the aircraft. We argue therefore, that the acquisition of SA is automatically primed for familiar entities; once the object is perceived, understanding and anticipation will follow intuitively (for similar arguments about the non-hierarchical nature of SA, see Durso and Gronlund, 1999; Horswill and McKenna, Chapter 9, this volume; McGowan and Banbury, Chapter 10, this volume).

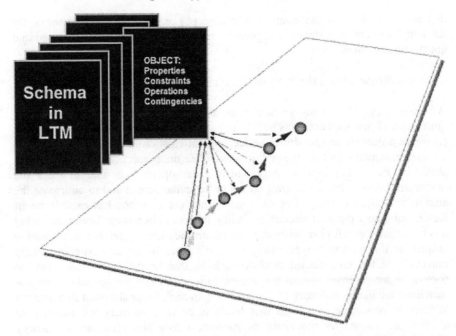

Figure 7.1 Formation of a Cognitive Stream on the episodic surface (or 'blackboard') for a single entity (e.g., the movement of a single aircraft across a radar screen). Each significant change of the entity is represented as an object (as depicted by the circles). As the number of objects increase, the strength of the pointers (i.e., transitional probabilities) between each object (as depicted by shaded arrows between objects) also increase as a function of more accurate matches with previous experience (Schema in Long-Term Memory)

There is an attempt to match the object with representations in long-term memory but as there is little information about the aircraft, other than its current position and altitude, it is possible the aircraft can be one of many different types. Crucially, in terms of anticipation, the activation of information in long-term memory includes transitional probability information. But given that there is only one representation, or object, of the aircraft on the blackboard, the transitional probability information is low and making its next future trajectory difficult to determine.

Significant changes in the aircraft's parameters (e.g., height, heading, speed or location) will also be represented by objects on the blackboard and organized into a single cognitive stream as all objects are associated with the same entity (see Figure 7.2). The strength of association (i.e., transitional probabilities) between the objects now start to increase; similar to the earlier example of 'the cat sat on the mat', the operator recalls from past experience how the pattern of movement of the unknown aircraft is indicative of a narrower class of aircraft (e.g., a military jet fighter). As the aircraft's track history builds up, previous experience narrows down the flight patterns the aircraft is likely to make, resulting in an increase in the transitional probabilities between these objects, allowing the future trajectory of the aircraft to become easier to anticipate correctly (see Figure 7.2). However, the amount of anticipation is also dependent on the strength of the transitional probabilities; the further ahead in time, the less accurate the predictions are likely to be.

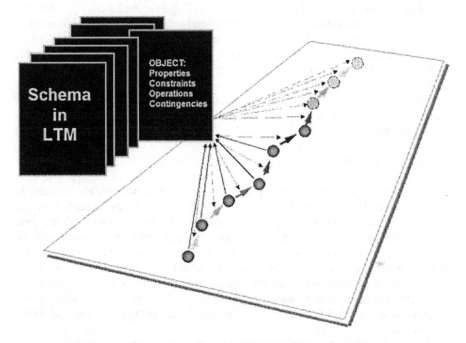

Figure 7.2 Anticipation: Using Transitional Probability information to predict likely future states of entity. The further ahead in time, the weaker the associations (i.e., transitional probabilities) between the pointers leading to less accurate predictions about the future state of the entity

High levels of SA are therefore not achieved straight away; high transitional probabilities are acquired over time and facilitate anticipation by indicating the most likely future states of an entity. As previously discussed, the increase in the transitional probabilities between the objects on the blackboard serves to strengthen the pointers between them; requiring fewer resources to maintain the cognitive streams. With less processing being required to maintain the streams, resources are released to deal with other streams of information. The strengthening of the association between pointers serves to make them more resilient to interference from other cognitive activities, such as ignoring extraneous radio chatter (Banbury, Jones and Emery, 1999) or irrelevant auditory warnings (Banbury, Fricker, Tremblay and Emery, 2001). The disruption to cognitive streams is explained by the co-existence of objects from deliberate rehearsal of the visual material and objects derived from the irrelevant stream on the blackboard. Jones assumes that auditory material, even when ignored, has obligatory access to the blackboard (Jones, Madden and Miles, 1992). Disruption occurs as a result of a conflict in organization of two sets of pointers, one from the material that is deliberately rehearsed and the other from the irrelevant stream.

Parallels can therefore be made between a Cognitive Stream and a Situation Model. Both are transitory representations assembled in an ad hoc way in order to meet the particular demands of a particular set of circumstances (see Flach, Mulder and van Paassen, Chapter 3, this volume; Patrick and James, Chapter 4; this volume). However, the Cognitive Streaming account, with its notion of transitional probabilities, makes explicit what processes might be brought to bear to anticipate the future states of an entity. Cognitive Streaming can also be used to explain how, and to what extent, we are able to acquire and maintain SA for multiple entities in the environment.

Maintaining Multiple Cognitive Streams

The appearance of more aircraft on the radar screen now requires the operator to monitor several aircraft tracks at once. In the same way as described in the previous section, separate cognitive streams are formed for each of the new aircraft. The number of streams that can be maintained concurrently will be dependent not on storage capacity (as the traditional accounts of memory imply) but on processing capacity; the operator must continually rehearse each stream to prevent its decay and the resultant loss of SA for that entity. As previously discussed, the amount of rehearsal required for each stream is dependent on the strength of association (i.e., transitional probabilities) between the objects within the stream.

Figure 7.3 illustrates two cognitive streams representing an aircraft that the operator has prior experience of (left stream) and an aircraft that the operator has no experience of (right stream). As the familiar aircraft's track history builds up, previous experience narrows down the flight patterns the aircraft is likely to make (i.e., increase in the transitional probabilities between objects in the stream), enabling the future trajectory of the aircraft to be anticipated and requiring fewer cognitive resources to maintain its cognitive stream. However, this is not the case for the unfamiliar aircraft. With no previous experience to utilize, the operator is forced to impose transitional probabilities on to the objects through deliberate and effortful rehearsal in order to maintain the stream in STM and allow other cognitive processes required to achieve SA (e.g., problem solving and hypothesis testing) to be brought to bear. Although there is no upper limit to the number of streams than can be maintained concurrently, the number of streams that can be maintained is related to the finite amount of processing resources available and how much effort it takes to maintain each cognitive stream. Capacity can therefore be described in terms of an interaction between the number of streams maintained concurrently and the processing requirements of maintaining information within each stream. For example, the operator will be able to maintain far more cognitive streams for familiar aircraft, than for unfamiliar aircraft, as cognitive streams for familiar aircraft require less cognitive resources to maintain because the strength of association (i.e., transitional probabilities) between objects within each stream are higher.

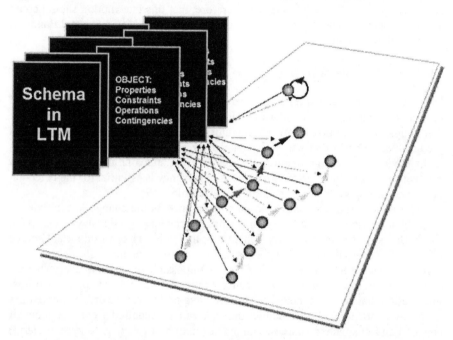

Figure 7.3 Multiple Streams: Cognitive Streams are formed for all perceived entities in the environment, irrespective of whether they are attended to or not

The quality of SA that an operator is able to achieve will be related to the number of streams that an operator is able to maintain, which in turn is a function of expertise. We can therefore elucidate Endsley's (2001) contention that 'the deployment of attention in the perception process acts to present certain constraints on the operator's ability to accurately perceive multiple items in parallel, and, as such, is a major limit to SA' (p.5) and Fracker's (1987) hypothesis that STM constitutes the main bottleneck for SA; particularly, for novices or those dealing with novel situations. In addition to being less able to maintain multiple cognitive streams (and a limit on the quality of SA that this implies), novices are less able to apply high transitional probabilities to objects in the cognitive stream and as a result have difficulty in anticipating the future state of an entity.

Finally, the accuracy and unobtrusiveness of how operator SA is measured will depend on how well the operator is able to maintain multiple cognitive streams.

Measures of SA that are based on asking questions about particular entities in the environment during the experimental session (e.g., SAGAT, Endsley, 1990) require participants to deliberately retrace the cognitive stream that has been formed for that entity so that information from it can be retrieved to answer the SA probe. We argue that the deliberate retracing of a cognitive stream requires processing resources that would have been otherwise deployed to maintain other cognitive streams. We would predict, therefore, that this interruption should come at some cost to the operator's overall level of SA (see also McGowan and Banbury, Chapter 10, this volume).

The Fate of Unattended Stimuli

We have argued that experienced operators are able to process, anticipate and respond to environmental regularities. However, there must be another mechanism that counters the propensity of the operator to be biased towards the normal and predictable, such that they can be interrupted by novel and unexpected occurrences in the environment (Hughes and Jones, 2003). From an evolutionary perspective, a mechanism that is sensitive to violations of expectancy is essential for the detection of danger, or opportunity, for the individual (Sokolov, 1963).

Information from an unattended parameter, such as the change in pitch of the noise of an engine, is cited by a number of researchers (e.g., Endsley, 1995, p.46; Croft, Banbury, Butler and Berry, Chapter 5, this volume) as an important source of SA. However, the selectivity of attention poses a number of problems for current models of SA. Given that it is clearly impossible to attend to every channel of information in our environment, conceptualizations of SA cannot explain how information that is unattended (i.e., that we have no awareness of) can sometimes capture our attention. It is assumed that SA can be acquired from a number of attended and unattended sources; 'some cues may be overt (e.g., a system alarm) and some so subtle that they are registered only subconsciously (e.g., the slight change in the hum of an engine)' (Endsley, 2000, p.10). However, explanations based on an executive function that switches attention between information sources cannot fully explain why, and under what circumstances, information is selectively attended to.

Cowan (1988) argues that there are both voluntary and involuntary shifts of attention. For example, although it is easy to selectively attend to specific physical characteristics of an input, it is also easy to detect a physical change in an unattended channel, such as a change from male to female voice. Cowan argues that a physical description of the unattended stimuli is developed in memory, which results in habituation to that stimulus and would inhibit further processing of any stimulus fitting that description. In this example, the cognitive system develops a description of a particular male voice entering from an unattended channel. Cowan's model is based on the Orienting Response (OR) which was first introduced by Pavlov to describe the reflex that brings about an immediate response to the slightest change in the environment. Pavlov defined OR as the reflex which 'brings about the immediate response in man and animals to the slightest changes in the world around them' (Pavlov, 1960, p. 12). According to

Sokolov (1963) repeated presentations of a given stimulus result in an internal representation of that stimulus input. This representation, which Sokolov termed the neuronal model, contains the parameters of the stimulus. All input information is compared with existing neuronal models; a mismatch between stimulus input and the models will result in an orientation reaction. If the input matches the existing models, the orienting response (OR) will be inhibited. Cowan argues that the important features of the OR are its tendency to direct the selective-attention mechanism to a stimulus modality or location in which the stimulus has recently changed, and habituation to stimuli that remain constant and do not prove to be of significance to the operator. Similarly, Öhman (1979) has suggested a number of refinements of the neural-model concept; we appear to form a set of implicit expectations about stimuli and orienting occurs when these expectations are violated. For example, the noise of an aircraft's engine will not orientate the pilot's attention to it unless it unexpectedly changes in pitch; such a change indicating that the engine is not operating normally.

These concepts fit well with the Cognitive Streaming framework in that the 'changeability' of visual or verbal stimuli, regardless of modality or code (i.e. verbal or spatial), will determine how they are represented on the blackboard, rather than whether they are attended to or not. For example, it is argued that auditory information is represented on the blackboard automatically (Jones, 1993; Hughes and Jones, 2003) to account for disruption to cognitive processing by background irrelevant sound even though individuals are instructed to ignore it (for a review see Banbury, Macken, Tremblay and Jones, 2001). It is highly probable, therefore, that such unconscious, or *implicit*, memory contributes to the operators overall knowledge of the situation (Hughes and Jones, 2003; for a discussion about the role of 'awareness' in SA, see Croft, Banbury, Butler and Berry, Chapter 5, this volume). As previously discussed, the degree of change is also important; for example a constant sound, such as the hum of an engine, would be represented as a single object and the pointer self-referential (see Figure 7.3). However, if any parameters of that object change significantly (e.g., a change in pitch), these changes will be automatically represented as new objects, even without deliberate attention. We argue that opportunities and objects that have high transitional probabilities are easy to understand and predict. Those that are not, alert our attention; unexpected changes to entities that we are familiar with (e.g., a change in the pitch of the noise of an engine) will therefore re-orient our attention to them.

Conclusions

We have attempted to apply the Cognitive Streaming account of selective attention and STM to explain key phenomena in SA and in doing so have tried to avoid treating SA as 'yet another box in our information processing diagram' (Flach, 1995, p. 153). Although speculative, there is a substantial weight of evidence to suggest that we use existing statistical regularities (i.e., transitional probabilities) of entities in our environment to inform and guide our behavior.

Our goal now will be to build upon this promising account and test more detailed predictions about how anticipation is affected by a number of factors, such as interference from concurrent tasks and interruptions, which have been observed to affect SA. In doing so, we hope to realize the aim of achieving a more substantive theoretical account of the cognitive processes and structures underlying SA.

Acknowledgements

The authors would like to thank Dr Robert Hughes, Dr Alastair Nicholls and Dr Sébastien Tremblay for critical reading of an earlier version of this paper. In addition, we acknowledge that some of the work discussed in this chapter was funded by the Human Sciences Domain of the United Kingdom Ministry of Defence Scientific Research Programme.

References

Adams, M.J., Tenney, Y.J. and Pew, R.W. (1995), 'Situation Awareness and the Cognitive Management of Complex Systems', *Human Factors*, vol. 37, pp. 85-104.

Baddeley, A.D. (1990), *Human Memory*, Erlbaum, Hove, East Sussex.

Baddeley, A.D. and Hitch, G. (1974), 'Working Memory', in G. Bower (ed.), *Recent Advances in Learning and Motivation 8*, Academic Press, New York, pp. 47-89.

Banbury, S., Fricker, L., Tremblay, S. and Emery, L. (2003), 'Using Auditory Streaming to Reduce Disruption of Serial Memory by Extraneous Auditory Warnings', *Journal of Experimental Psychology: Applied*, vol. 9, pp. 12-22.

Banbury, S., Jones, D.M. and Emery, L. (1998), 'Extending the Irrelevant Sound Effect: The Effects of Extraneous Sounds on Aircrew Performance', in D. Harris (ed.), *Engineering Psychology and Cognitive Ergonomics: Vol. 3. Transportation Systems, Medical Ergonomics and Training*, Ashgate and Town, Aldershot, UK.

Banbury, S., Macken, W.J., Tremblay, S. and Jones, D.M. (2001), 'Auditory Distraction: Phenomena and Practical Implications', *Human Factors*, vol. 43, pp. 12-29.

Beaman, C.P. and Jones, D.M. (1997), 'The Role of Serial Order in the Irrelevant Speech Effect: Tests of the Changing State Hypothesis', *Journal of Experimental Psychology: Learning, Memory and Cognition*, vol. 23, pp. 459-471.

Beaman, C.P. and Jones, D.M. (1998), 'Irrelevant Sound Disrupts Order Information in Free as in Serial Recall', *Quarterly Journal of Experimental Psychology: Human Experimental Psychology*, vol. 51A, pp. 615-636.

Bolstad, C.A. (1991). 'Individual Pilot Differences Related to Situation Awareness', in *Proceedings of the Human Factors and Ergonomics Society*, HFES, Santa Monica, CA.

Bregman, A.S. (1990), *Auditory Scene Analysis: The Perceptual Organization of Sound*, MIT Press, Cambridge, MA.

Carretta, T.R., Perry, D.C. and Ree, M.J. (1996), 'Prediction of Situational Awareness in F-15 Pilots', *International Journal of Aviation Psychology*, vol. 6, pp. 21-41.

Cowan, N. (1988), 'Evolving Conceptions of Memory Storage, Selective Attention and their Mutual Constraints within the Human Information-Processing System', *Psychological Bulletin*, vol. 104, pp. 163-191.

Dominguez, C. (1994), 'Can SA Be Defined?', in M. Vidulich, C. Dominguez, E. Vogel and G. McMillan (eds), Situation *Awareness: Papers and Annotated Bibliography*, United States Air Force Armstrong Laboratory, Brooks Air Force Base.

Durso, F.T. and Gronlund, S.D. (1999), 'Situation Awareness', in F.T. Durso, R. Nickerson, R. Schvaneveldt, S. Dumais, S. Lindsay and M. Chi (eds), *The Handbook of Applied Cognition*, Wiley, New York.

Endsley, M.R. (1990), 'Predictive Utility of an Objective Measure of Situation Awareness', in *Proceedings of the Human Factors and Ergonomics Society*, HFES, Santa Monica, CA.

Endsley, M.R. (1994), 'Situation Awareness in Dynamic Decision Making', in R.D. Gilson, D.J. Garland and J.M. Koonce (eds), *Situational Awareness in Complex Systems: Proceedings of a CAHFA Conference*, Embry-Riddle Aeronautical University Press, Daytona Beach, FL, pp. 139-167.

Endsley, M.R. (1995), 'Toward a Theory of Situation Awareness in Dynamic Systems', *Human Factors*, vol. 37, pp. 32-64.

Endsley, M.R. (1997), 'The Role of Situation Awareness in Naturalistic Decision Making', in G.K. Caroline and E. Zsambok (eds), *Naturalistic Decision Making Expertise: Research and Applications*, Lawrence Erlbaum Associates Inc, Mahwah, NJ., pp. 269-283.

Endsley, M.R. (2000), 'Theoretical Underpinnings of Situation Awareness: A Critical Review', in M.R. Endsley and D.J. Garland (eds), *Situation Awareness Analysis and Measurement*, Lawrence Erlbaum Associates Inc, Mahwah, NJ.

Endsley, M.R. (2001), 'Designing for Situation Awareness in Complex Systems', in *Proceedings of the Second International Workshop on Symbiosis of Humans, Artifacts and Environment*, Kyoto, Japan.

Ericsson, K.A. and Kintsch, W. (1995), 'Long-term Working Memory', *Psychological Review*, vol. 102, pp. 211-245.

Flach, J. M. (1995), 'Situation Awareness: Proceed with Caution', *Human Factors*, vol. 37, pp. 149-157.

Flach, J.M. (1996), 'Situation Awareness: In Search of Meaning', *CSERIAC Gateway*, vol. 6, pp. 1-4.

Fracker, M.L. (1987), *Situation Awareness: A Decision Model*, Unpublished manuscript, Dayton, Ohio.

Fracker, M.L. (1988), 'A Theory of Situation Assessment: Implications for Measuring Situation Awareness', in *Proceedings of the Human Factors and Ergonomics Society Meeting*, HFES, Santa Monica, CA.

Gronlund, S.D., Ohrt, D.D., Dougherty, M.R.P., Perry, J.L. and Manning, C.A. (1998), 'Role of Memory in Air Traffic Control', *Journal of Experimental Psychology: Applied*, vol. 4, pp. 263-280.

Gugerty, L.J. (1997) 'Situation Awareness during Driving: Explicit and Implicit Knowledge in Dynamic Spatial Memory', *Journal of Experimental Psychology: Applied*, vol. 3, pp. 42-66.

Hughes, R.W. and Jones, D.M. (2003), 'Indispensable Benefits and Unavoidable Costs of Unattended Sound for Cognitive Functioning', *Noise and Health*, vol. 6, pp. 63-76.

Jones, D.M. (1993), 'Objects, Streams, and Threads of Auditory Attention', in A.D. Baddeley and L.Weiskrantz (eds), *Attention: Selection, Awareness and Control*, Clarendon Press, Oxford.

Jones, D.M., Beaman, C.P. and Macken, W.J. (1996), 'The Object-Oriented Episodic Record Model', in S. Gathercole (eds.), *Models of Short-term Memory*, Lawrence Erlbaum Associates, London.

Jones, D.M., Madden, C. and Miles, C. (1992). 'Privileged Access by Irrelevant Speech to Short-term Memory: The Role of Changing State', *The Quarterly Journal of Experimental Psychology*, vol. 44A, pp. 645-669.

Karelitz, T.M. and Budescu, D.V. (2004), 'You Say Probable and I Say Likely: Improving Interpersonal Communication with Verbal Probability Phrases', *Journal of Experimental Psychology: Applied*, vol. 10, pp. 13-24.

Lichacz, F.M.J. (2001), 'The Missing Cognitive Link in Situation Awareness Research', in D. Harris (ed.), *Engineering Psychology and Cognitive Ergonomics, Vol 5: Aerospace and Transportation Systems*, Ashgate, Aldershot.

Logan, G.D. (1988), 'Automaticity, Resources, and Memory: Theoretical Controversies and Practical Implications', *Human Factors*, vol. 30, pp. 583-598.

Macken, W.J., Tremblay, S., Alford, D. and Jones, D.M. (1999), 'Attentional Selectivity in Short-Term Memory: Similarity of Process, Not Similarity of Content, Determines Disruption', *International Journal of Psychology*, vol. 34, pp. 322-327.

Neisser, U. (1976), *Cognition and Reality*, W.H. Freeman and Co, San Francisco.

Neumann, O. (1996), 'Theories of Attention', in O. Neumann and A.F. Sanders, *Handbook of Perception and Action*, Academic Press, London, pp. 389-446.

Öhman, A. (1979), 'The Orienting Response, Attention and Learning: An Information-Processing Perspective', in H.D. Kimmel, E.H. van Olst and J.F. Orlebeke (eds) *The Orienting Reflex in Humans*, Lawrence Erlbaum Associates Inc, Mahwah, NJ.

Pavlov, I.P. (1960), *Conditioned Reflexes*, Dover, New York.

Rouse, W.B. and Morris, N.M. (1985), *On Looking into the Black Box: Prospects and Limits in the Search for the Mental Models*, DTIC AD-A159080, Georgia Institute of Technology, Center for Man-Machine Systems Research, Atlanta, GA.

Shepard, R.N. (1981), 'Psychophysical Complementarity', in M. Kubovy and J.R. Pomerantz (eds), *Perceptual Organization*, Lawrence Erlbaum Associates Inc, Mahwah, NJ, pp. 279-341.

Sohn, Y.W. and Dattel, A.R. (2001), 'Expertise Effects in Situation Memory and Awareness', in *Proceedings of the Human Factors and Ergonomics Society*, HFES, CA.

Sohn, Y.W. and Doane, S.M. (2000), 'Predicting Individual Differences in Situation Awareness: The Role of Working Memory Capacity and Memory Skill', in *Proceedings of the Human Performance, Situation Awareness and Automation Conference*, Savannah, GA.

Sokolov, E.N. (1963), *Perception and the Conditioned Reflex*, Pergamon Press, New York.

Stokes, A.F. (1991), 'Flight Management Training and Research Using a Micro-Computer Flight Decision Simulator', in R. Sadlowe (ed.), *PC-Based Instrument Flight Simulation – A First Collection of Papers*, American Society of Mechanical Engineers, New York, pp. 47-52.

Tremblay, S. and Jones, D. M. (2001), 'Beyond the Matrix: A Study of Interference', in D. Harris (ed.), *Engineering Psychology and Cognitive Ergonomics: Industrial Ergonomics, HCI and Applied Cognitive Psychology*, Ashgate, Aldershot, pp. 255-263.

Ulharik, J. and Comerford, D.A. (2002), *A Review of Situation Awareness Literature Relevant to Pilot Surveillance Functions*, Technical Report DOT/FAA/AM-02/3, Office of Aerospace Medicine, Washington.

Wickens, C.D. (1984). *Engineering Psychology and Human Performance*, Merrill, Columbus, OH.

Wickens, C.D. (1992), 'Workload and Situation Awareness: An Analogy of History and Implication', *Insight: The Visual Performance Technical Group Newsletter*, vol. 14, pp. 1-3.

Wickens, C.D. and Hollands, J.G. (2000), *Engineering Psychology and Human Performance*, Prentice Hall, Upper Saddle.

PART II
APPLICATION

Chapter 8

SPAM:
The Real-Time Assessment of SA

Frank T. Durso and Andrew R. Dattel

What is SA?

As we enter a new century, the cognitive demands of the industrial tasks we ask operators to perform are dramatically higher than the cognitive demands of workers entering the last century. Durso and Hall (in press) note that only 51 per cent of the work force in the early 1900s were skilled or semiskilled, whereas all of the fastest growing occupations in 2000, from computer engineers to physician assistants, are primarily cognitive jobs.

If today's work is largely cognitive, then it makes sense for ergonomists to focus on cognitive issues. This focus often is discussed under the rubric of situation awareness (SA). Although SA can be thought of as something quite specific, in our view we consider it synonymous with situation comprehension. The term *comprehension* carries less baggage for us than does the term *awareness*. It also allows clear connections to the intellectual roots of SA found in the reading comprehension literature: notions such as mental model, situation model, and long-term working memory (Durso and Gronlund, 1999) are examples of the concepts from the reading literature that have found their way into discussions of SA. This comprehension framework also helps us remember that seductively similar terms are not the same as SA. So, for us, knowledge is a part of comprehension (Bransford and Johnson, 1972) not synonymous with it. Other parallels can be found as well, such as the levels of SA (Jones and Endsley, 1996) and levels of comprehension, task structure and story grammar, and so on (Just and Carpenter, 1980). The comprehension framework also makes worthy the study of those comprehension processes and implicit representations about which the operator is unaware. It remains to be seen when this analogy to reading comprehension will break down. We suspect it will be in the dynamic nature of the input that occurs in industrial tasks, a lesson ecologically-minded researchers have been trying to teach. Until then, however, thinking of SA as something like reading comprehension, but in a dynamic environment, will serve as an effective analogy (see Oppenheimer, 1956).

Why is it important that we assess the SA of an operator? In most studies that investigate SA, it would be considerably easier simply to assess performance directly, rather than add the extra procedures or events needed to assess SA. And

137

isn't it performance, after all, that matters? The counterarguments to this position have been two-fold. First, the right SA measure can be more sensitive than performance measures, thus allowing more efficient comparisons of two displays or two people. Therefore, it is important that the measure of SA actually be more sensitive than performance. Second, faulty SA has been argued to be a harbinger of performance problems, even when no particular problem was apparent in current performance. Therefore, the measure of SA should have some predictive value. The measure we discuss in this chapter meets these criteria.

What is SPAM?

In this chapter, we discuss a procedure developed in our lab in 1995 to assess SA that we hoped would be a sensitive measure and one that had predictive value (Durso et al., 1995). Briefly, operators are presented with queries about the situation while the situation remains present and while they continue to perform the primary task. Response time, in addition to accuracy, is recorded. Response time should vary with the level of SA. Illustratively, if an operator has the answer to the query in active memory, response times should be short. If the operator knows where to find the answer, in either memory or the environment, but must search for the particular value, then response time should be slower. Still slower would be an operator who did not know where to look for the answer.

We have referred to the procedure as the Situation Present Assessment Method or SPAM. The name reflects the important contribution of the procedure: the techniques needed to measure comprehension when the situation remains present. The unusual acronym also serves to remind us that we are making unsolicited requests of the operator, and that like most SA procedures, and all query techniques, the assessment of SA could affect the manner in which the primary task is performed. As we will discuss, SPAM has been used primarily to study air traffic controllers, but we will also review recent data looking at flying, driving, and playing chess. SPAM has been investigated in both the Federal Aviation Administration (FAA) and Eurocontrol. In addition, SPAM has been used as a foundation for the development of other query procedures both in our lab and elsewhere (e.g., Jeannot, Kelly, and Thompson's SASHA, 2003; Willems and Heiney's SAVANT, 2002). We will discuss these developments at the end of the chapter.

We believe that there are a number of reasons that SPAM should have a place in the researcher's toolbox of SA methods. First, SPAM's use of response time promises to provide a more statistically sensitive measure than accuracy, as is usually the case when both accuracy and speed are recorded in the same cognitive task. On occasion, the effects may be dramatic enough to be reflected in accuracy of response to the on-line queries (e.g., Cooke, Kiekel, and Helm, 2001), but we have often found effects with response time that were not reliable with accuracy alone.

Second, SPAM's use of response time allows researchers to assess SA when it succeeds, rather than only when it fails. Historically, research on mental processes evolved from accuracy as a dependent measure to response time. For example, earlier studies of memory used the number of items recalled or recognized as a measure of memory. Researchers noted that with accuracy measures, assessment of memory depended on when memory failed; with response time, we were measuring memory when it succeeded. This change not only allowed tests that were more sensitive, but also allowed the study of memories heretofore inscrutable (see Lachman, Lachman, and Butterfield, 1979, for a review of the cognitive revolution). Notably, response time opened the area of semantic memory, and epistemological questions could now be addressed empirically. Thus, with accuracy, we learn about SA only when a mistake is made, that is only when SA fails. However, if we measure response time, an operator using two different displays can make no error on either one, yet be considerably slower to answer SPAM queries with one of the displays. Ironically, the logic used against performance measures – that there will be an SA difference even when there is no performance difference – can also be applied against accuracy measures of SA. Of course, if both accuracy and latency reveal similar effects, the researcher has additional reason to trust the outcome.

Third, SPAM is consistent with the pretheoretical position that understanding of a situation is best accomplished when the situation is present and the operator is engaged. One may have had quite good situation awareness a moment ago when she stopped at the red light, but now has no recollection of whether she stopped or not. A corollary to this pretheoretical position is the presumption that knowing where to find a piece of information is an important part of SA. For operators like air traffic controllers, it may be more efficient to know where to find a call sign or an altitude, than it would be to use limited cognitive resources to remember it.

Fourth, researchers have rightly expressed concern with the ability of query methods to be exported to the field (e.g., Jeannot et al., 2003; Militello, Quill, Vinson, and Gorman, 2003). Theoretically, however, because the environment is not removed in SPAM, the procedure can be used in the field. Later in this chapter, we discuss a preliminary use of SPAM in an on-the-road driving study that produced some interesting results. And although it is true that the details of the SPAM procedure when used in the field are only beginning to be developed, the procedure does, in principle, have the ability to address SA in environments that are difficult to simulate, like command and control (Militello et al., 2003).

Our goals in this chapter are to present data reflecting on the validity and sensitivity of SPAM as a measure of SA and to provide guidelines for the use of SPAM and its variants. We begin by discussing the logic of SPAM.

Logic of SPAM

SPAM is an example of a query technique. The logic of query techniques is that SA is reflected in the ability of operators to answer questions about the situation that they are, or have been, controlling or managing. With off-line measures, the assumption is that the ability to retrieve the correct answer from memory reflects SA. Of course, memory is influenced by a number of factors, not all of which influence comprehension. The obvious way to eliminate memory factors is to assess SA on-line.

SPAM is an example of an on-line technique. Implicit performance techniques (e.g., Croft, Banbury, Butler, and Berry, Chapter 5, this volume; McGowan and Banbury, Chapter 10, this volume) are also on-line; but they assess SA by measuring operators' responses to task relevant events embedded in a scenario rather than by using direct queries. For example, in air traffic control (ATC), a flight might veer off-course. The experimenter might be interested in how quickly, or if, the controller corrects the problem. Clever experimenters can do this without affecting the task, and perhaps without even being noticed by the operator. Another on-line approach, the one captured by SPAM, is to ask questions, as in other query procedures, but to do so while the situation is present and while the operator is performing the task.

Response time is a critical part of on-line queries given that the correct answers are available to the operator, making it less likely that errors will occur with any frequency. Consistent with our expectations, when we work with professionals, like air traffic controllers, accuracy is typically near ceiling making analysis of the accuracy insensitive to our manipulations. Surprisingly, however, we have found that when working with less than expert populations, like undergraduates performing low-fidelity air traffic control, accuracy to on-line queries in addition to response time can be a sensitive dependent variable. Cooke et al. (2001) using Air Force ROTC cadets also found that accuracy to on-line queries could be revealing.

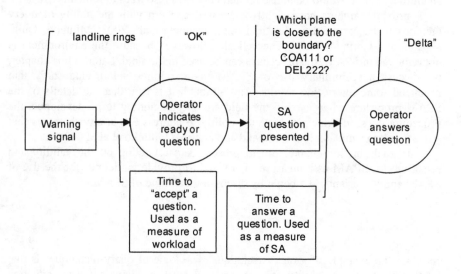

Figure 8.1 A depiction of the prototypical SPAM procedure. Examples are given across the top

In the prototypical SPAM procedure depicted in Figure 8.1, the operator is given the opportunity to indicate willingness to accept a question, a question is then presented, and the operator responds as accurately and quickly as possible. The questions have typically been constructed with the aid of an expert (e.g., ATC instructor, chess master) to probe a particular, important part of the scenario. This will be the case even in the on-the-road driving test of SPAM described later. In that case, the experimenters studied the routes for query opportunities prior to asking participants to drive the route. Variants of SPAM are possible, yielding what could be considered a family of SPAM measures. We will consider two variants here. Some variations come from treatment of the 'warning signal' used to assess operator readiness. Other variations come from construction of the queries.

Separating Workload and SA

Although mental workload and SA are related, they are not identical constructs (e.g., Vidulich, 2003). The constructs have been distinguished both in arguments (e.g., Wickens, 1992) and experimentation (e.g., Endsley, 1993). For example, Durso et al., (1998) used multiple regression to predict performance with both SPAM and workload measures as predictors. Although the constructs were correlated, some performance models included both workload and SA measures indicating that the measures account for different parts of the variance in performance.

In an effort to separate workload from SA, query methods must be constructed so that the workload when the SA query is presented is not a factor. SAGAT (Endsley, 1995) accomplishes this as a matter of course when the display is removed and the operator no longer performs the task. If the environment is dynamic, and the operator is asked an SA question on-line, the possibility exists that the question will arrive when the operator is unusually busy, or unusually idle. Of concern is the possibility that the latency to respond to the SA question will reflect workload as well as SA. This would present fundamental methodological and statistical problems that we, of course, want to avoid.

SPAM distinguishes workload from SA in dynamic environments by warning the operator that a query is in the queue and waiting until the operator is willing to attempt the question. Only the time from the presentation of the SA question until response reflects situation awareness. The time from the warning until the agreement to take the question is a measure of workload. Thus, SPAM allows the separation of workload from SA, and yields independent measures of both. As we report below, it is sometimes the case that a variable affects, not SA, but the management of resources (Durso Crutchfield, and Batsakes, 2001). Finally, we should mention that this warning procedure seems unnecessary when the environment is not dynamic. For example, when Durso et al. (1995) studied chess players, the board was static until after the player made a move, making the warning procedure less important.

Binary versus Open Responses

We sometimes use closed-response queries and sometimes open-response queries. For example, in a closed, binary response query, the operator is asked a question that could be answered with a 'yes' or 'no,' or, with a choice between experimenter-supplied possibilities, 'Which aircraft will leave the sector first? COA112 or DEL222?' Binary response queries have the advantage of producing cleaner latency data, and therefore yielding a more sensitive measure. The disadvantage is that the questions are sometimes difficult to construct, restricting the experimenter's ability to probe all aspects of the situation. This would be especially difficult in the field. Another possible disadvantage is that the responses themselves, often call signs in our ATC research for example, may not have a simple, automatic connection to the target. The controller may, for example, know that aircraft X will leave the sector before aircraft Y but not know which one is COA112. In ATC, the problem does not appear to be great because the controller uses call signs to communicate verbally with the aircraft and knowing, or knowing where to find, call signs can be argued to be part of good SA. In other domains, however, it may not be the case that the binary choice given the participant is important to SA.

With free responses, the experimenter is unconstrained in the construction of queries, but the response phase of such queries adds noise to the latency distribution. An experiment is currently underway in our lab to compare binary and free responses.

Research Using SPAM

Comparing SA for Master and Novice Chess Players

SPAM was initially tested with chess (Durso, et al., 1995), a domain that has been called the Drosophila of cognitive psychology (Charness, 1989). In that study, an expert, intermediate, and novice chess player were instructed to monitor computer simulated chess games and make judgments of imminent material loss. The participant pulled back on a joystick if a chess piece would be taken 'in the near future' or pushed forward on the joystick if no chess piece was expected to be taken in the near future.

Eighteen questions were asked of each participant. Six of the questions were based on perceptual characteristics ('where is the white queen?'), six of the questions were based on the present but asked about conceptual relations ('what piece is the white bishop attacking?'), and six of the questions were about the future ('what piece can white move to pin black's rook?'). Of course, questions were asked of the participant while the situation remained present.

Response times for answering the questions were shortest for the expert and longest for the novice. A main effect for type of question was found with future relation questions taking longer to answer than either the perceptual characteristic or present conceptual type questions. Questions about the future most easily discriminated among levels of expertise.

SPAM seemed able to distinguish among levels of expertise (other measures did not). Of importance was the fact that asking the questions during the experiment did not appear to disrupt the task: Participants were as able to project material loss during SPAM trials as during other parts of the experiment. Thus, the initial use of SPAM was successful enough to continue exploring in other situations. Chess was a valuable initial domain to explore given the extensive understanding of the task that had accumulated over the years, however it was not a fully dynamic domain typical of most industrial tasks.

Using SA to Predict Performance of Air-Traffic Controllers

Unlike chess, air traffic control is a fully dynamic cognitive task. Planes continue across the sky whether or not the controller takes an action. Controllers influence this flow by issuing commands to pilots. The controllers keep the planes a safe distance apart and attempt to move them to their destination as efficiently as possible.

In a study comparing SA and workload as predictors of air-traffic control performance (Durso et al., 1997), 12 air-traffic controllers directed traffic during 30-minute scenarios. SA was measured using SPAM, workload was measured using the NASA TLX (Hart and Staveland, 1988), and performance was measured in two ways. A subjective measure of performance used ratings administered by subject matter experts (SME). A more objective measure of performance was the remaining actions count (RAC). RAC is the total number of actions required to move all remaining airplanes out of the controller's sector. A low RAC is regarded as more efficient controller performance. Finally, errors (e.g., deviating flight) were also embedded into some scenarios.

In the SPAM procedure, six forced-choice questions were asked during each scenario. Questions were asked at approximately five-minute intervals. Half of the questions asked were present-oriented (e.g., 'which has the lower altitude, TWA799 or AAL957?') and half of the questions asked were future-oriented (e.g., 'will DAL423 and FDX279 be traffic for each other, yes or no?'). Questions were always binary.

To simulate real world operations during SPAM, a landline (telephone) was activated when a question was to be asked. Controllers frequently answer a landline when another controller has a question or information to pass on to other controllers. The time it takes a controller to answer a landline is an indication of workload at that particular time. The time it takes a controller to answer the question is an indication of SA.

Mental demand from the TLX subscale together with SPAM queries about the present predicted the SME evaluation. Thus, both workload and SA had some independent ability to predict the evaluations from expert judges. SPAM also predicted the RAC. The time to answer future oriented questions predicted the number of control actions remaining at the end of the scenario. Those controllers who answered future-oriented queries faster had better RAC scores than did controllers who answered these questions more slowly. Together with additional analyses, this result led Durso et al. to distinguish between future-oriented controllers and present-oriented controllers. There was evidence that suggested that those controllers who professed a greater understanding of the particular situation did so at the expense of the future.

It was also found that the longer the controller took to answer the landline, the more errors that had been embedded in the scenario were detected and corrected. If a controller is detecting and correcting for errors, the higher the workload and the longer it should take to answer the landline. Here, and elsewhere, we have found that both the latency to indicate readiness and the latency to answer the query can be informative about the processes involved in performing a task.

SA During Monitoring and Active Control

Willems and Truitt (1999) asked air-traffic controllers to monitor scenarios or to control them. The monitored scenarios simulated the potential role that air-traffic controllers will play in the proposed 'free flight' National Route Program expansion. During free flight, the pilots will have more freedom to select routes and flight plans. Using more sophisticated traffic-management systems equipped in the cockpit, pilots will be able to make route decisions that are presently decided by a ground-based air-traffic controller.

Sixteen air-traffic controllers each participated in four 30-minutes scenarios. In half the scenarios, the participant actively controlled the air traffic; in the other half of the scenarios, the participant monitored the air traffic. The scenarios were equally divided between high load traffic with an airplane entering the sector on average once per minute, and low load traffic with an airplane entering the sector on average once every two minutes.

During the scenarios, participants were presented with six forced-choice questions in the SPAM format. Half the questions were present-oriented and half the questions were future-oriented. Questions appeared at an average rate of one every five minutes. In addition to the SPAM questions, the participants rated their workload perception on a scale of 1 (low workload) to 10 (high workload) by responding to the air traffic workload input technique (ATWIT; Stein, 1985). The ATWIT was presented every five minutes throughout each scenario. Each rating request was preceded by a tone, and the participant had 20 seconds to respond.

Participants indicated that their perceived workload was greater during the high-load active scenarios than during the low-load active scenarios. Perceived workload was rated as being greater during the active scenarios than during the monitored scenarios. Participants also indicated perceived workload increased over time. Response time to accept a SPAM question was consistent with the participants' perceived workload. Participants took longer to answer the landline (accept a question) while engaged in the high-load active scenarios than while engaged in the low-load active scenarios. Participants took longer to answer the landline during high-load scenarios than they did to answer the landline during low-load scenarios.

Response times to answer SPAM questions were analyzed separately for present-oriented and future-oriented questions. No differences in response time were found between active or monitored scenarios when participants answered future-oriented questions. Whether the controller actively controlled the scenario or monitored it, understanding of the future was comparable. Either the monitoring controllers were able to develop plans and anticipate events as well as the active controllers, or the active controllers did not do a lot of preplanning, instead interacting with the aircraft tactically; what Durso et al (1998), called present-oriented controllers.

However, during present-oriented questions, participants took twice as long to answer questions during high-load scenarios they were monitoring than in any of the other three conditions (see Figure 8.2). At first blush, one might expect responding to be faster when the controller is doing less on the primary task, as with monitoring, than when the controller is doing more, as with active control. However, because SPAM removed workload time, Figure 8.2 presents evidence that monitoring a complex situation does not allow the development of situation awareness that actively controlling the situation does.

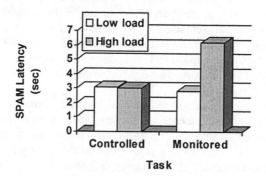

Figure 8.2 Time to answer present-oriented SPAM SA questions (in seconds) as a function of traffic load and whether the controller actively controlled the traffic or merely monitored it. After Willems and Truitt (1999)

SA when Automation Fails

Related to issues of monitoring versus active control has been the concern that automation can take operators out of the loop. If Willems and Truitt (1999) are correct (see also Metzger and Parasuraman, 2001) then human factors specialists are right to be concerned about automation that relegates the human operator to one of monitor. In addition, there are concerns with what might happen should the automation fail and the operator is thrust into an active control situation that he or she had only been monitoring up until then.

SA was measured using SPAM during an air-traffic control simulation in which automation was normal or there was an automation failure (Durso, Crutchfield, and Batsakes, 2001). The expectation was that automation failure would negatively affect SA.

In addition to the automation manipulation, Durso et al., looked at an individual difference variable that they thought would also affect SA, working memory span. To measure working memory span, participants were given the Operation Span (OSPAN; LaPointe and Engle, 1990); those who scored in the lowest quartile were placed in the low working memory span group, and those who scored in the highest quartile were placed in the high working memory span group.

Thus, automation failure and working memory span were varied. The participants worked with the air traffic scenarios test (ATST). The ATST is a low fidelity simulation that is part of a battery of tests for selecting air traffic controllers. The ATST simulates a radar screen with flights that can vary in three levels of speed, four levels of altitude, eight directions, and six destinations. Periodically, new aircraft appear on the screen representing additional air traffic entering the operator's sector. The operator 'clears' the airplane by clicking on the radar blip of the new aircraft. When the operator accepts the aircraft, it then becomes activated and becomes part of the air traffic the controller is responsible for managing. An aircraft remains on the screen until it reaches it destination or crashes. In addition to the radar screen, participants were provided with paper flight progress strips during the ATST simulation. The flight progress strips served as a backup to the radar display. These paper strips included the same information as on the aircraft datablocks of the ATST.

After the participants completed several practice scenarios, they controlled traffic in two 16-minute test scenarios. Performance was measured by delay in the time to clear aircraft and number of traffic errors. One test scenario was normal automation in that all information was provided on the radar screen datablock. The other test scenario contained an automation failure in that the aircraft destination information was absent from the datablock. Therefore, during automation failure the participant had to rely on the paper flight progress strips to determine the destination for those aircraft. Both working memory span and automation status affected performance: Time to accept an aircraft was longer in the scenario that had automation failures. Traffic errors were greater with low span participants.

Of interest in this chapter was the relationship between SPAM measures and these performance measures. Initially, one might be tempted to believe that both the automation failure and the memory span variables had their effect on performance through SA. The literature is replete with claims that SA mediates some manipulation's effect on performance although SA is never directly measured. A main effect of automation was found for SPAM errors and for the time to answer the SPAM questions, with longer times for the automation failure scenario than for the normal automation scenario. This effect suggests the involvement of SA in the automation failure effect. However, no differences in errors or time to answer the SA questions were found between working-memory-span groups. Thus, both the high and low working memory span operators had comparable SA.

Interestingly, however, high span and low span individuals differed in how quickly they accepted a query. High span individuals in the automation failure scenario modified their strategies and took longer to accept a question (time to indicate they were ready for the question) than they had when the automation was working. Low span individuals made no such adjustment when the automation failed. This suggests that high span and low span individuals differ in their management of resources. Perhaps lower working memory span operators were less able to evaluate their workload or were less flexible in the resource allocation than were high spans.

You Need Intelligence for SA and SA for Performance

More recently, we (Durso, Dattel, Bleckley, Norris, Perez, Hall, and Cardenas 2004) have been conducting experiments trying to understand what makes a good candidate for air traffic control training. In one experiment, 51 participants were tested on several cognitive variables, including crystallized and fluid intelligence, cognitive style, short-term memory, and working memory, and several personality and cognitive-style variables, including the Big Five, need-for-cognition, and field-dependence. The participants were then trained on ten 30-minute ATST scenarios followed by eight 20-minute ATST test scenarios. SPAM as well as SAGAT and modified versions of SPAM were administered as SA measures. For the purpose of this chapter, we restrict our discussion to traditional SPAM. Six questions were asked during each scenario. Two of the questions were past-oriented, two of the questions were present-oriented, and two of the questions were future-oriented. The participant clicked an empty flashing text box to indicate he or she was ready for a question. A text display of the question then appeared in the box. (For an audio group, when the participant heard the tone and was ready to answer the question, she said, 'yes' aloud. The participant heard the question over a pair of headsets.)

No difference in performance was found between SPAM and control scenarios, indicating that querying the participants did not interfere with normal performance. SA seemed to be good for the past and present, but relatively poor for the future: Past-oriented questions were answered in a significantly shorter time than present or future-oriented questions and present-oriented questions were answered in a significantly shorter time than future-oriented questions.

Cognitive, personality, and traditional SPAM variables were used to predict performance. Clearance delays, en route delays, traffic errors and crashes were scored as performance variables. En route delay is the total time the airplanes are activated (until the airplane reaches its destination or crashes). Regression models were run with and without SPAM as predictor variables. In all models SPAM added to the explained variance. Briefly, performance depended on a host of factors, including SA, intelligence, memory capacity, workload, gender, and some personality factors (e.g., conscientiousness). For example, preliminary results suggest that anxious, young, smart people with a better understanding of the present situation crashed fewer aircraft.

Also of interest is the possibility that SA itself is predictable from such factors. For example, high cognitive abilities (e.g., IQ, short-term memory) and conscientiousness seem relevant to good SA in ATST, a finding reminiscent of earlier work by Carretta, Perry, and Ree (1996) with F-15 pilots.

Training SA

Improving SA through training has been of interest for a number of years (e.g., Endsley, 1989) and continues today (e.g., Strater and Endsley, 2003). We recently collected preliminary data comparing two different types of flight training methods. Participants who had no official flight training, but had at least eight hours of recent experience with Microsoft Flight Simulator 2002 were randomly assigned to one of two training groups. The cognitive training group watched 40 short (less than one minute) animated flight videos. The videos were dynamic representations of seven basic flight instruments of a fixed-wing aircraft. While watching the flight videos, the participants were given tasks to increase their understanding of various flight situations.

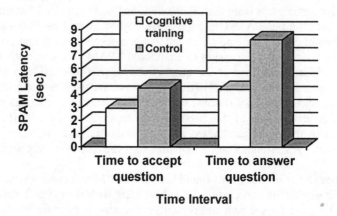

Figure 8.3 Time to indicate readiness to accept a question (workload) and time to answer a question about the situation (SA) as a function of type of training received

The control group instead practiced for one hour on Microsoft Flight Simulator 2002. They were shown how to modify weather features on the simulator such as adding rain, increasing cloud coverage, and limiting visibility. They then spent one hour flying the simulator.

After the training sessions, participants were tested on a 15-minute flight on the Microsoft Flight Simulator. The test flight required participants to maintain specified heading assignments, altitude levels, and airspeed. Visibility was set at 1/16 of mile and 80 per cent of the flight prevented the participant from having a visual reference to the horizon. Therefore the flight required the participants to rely on the flight instruments for navigation and coordinated flight. During the test flight, five questions were asked using the traditional SPAM format.

Performance measures were heading, altitude, and airspeed deviations. No differences between the two groups were found for any of the performance variables, consistent with the claim that performance variables are often insensitive. However, a significant SA difference was found between the training groups. The cognitive training group answered the questions in a shorter time than the control group. Although not significant, there was a trend for the cognitive training group to accept a question in a shorter time than the control group (See Figure 8.3).

SA while Driving in Familiar and Unfamiliar Locations

We end this section on research uses of SPAM with a study begun at the University of Oklahoma as an undergraduate project supervised by Todd Truitt that continues today in our lab at Texas Tech. This study is particularly interesting for two reasons. First, it is a demonstration that SPAM is a measure that can be used effectively in the field. Second, it addresses an interesting question about familiarity and SA. When comparing SA in familiar versus unfamiliar situations, it is possible that SA will be poorer in the unfamiliar situation because there is less knowledge available to aid in maintaining an understanding of the situation. On the other hand, when in familiar territory, the driver may spend less effort constructing the understanding of a situation that he or she has experienced on multiple occasions. Horswill and McKenna (Chapter 9, this volume) consider a number of SA relevant aspects of driving.

In the Oklahoma study, undergraduates drove their cars along predetermined routes. Sometimes the predetermined route was familiar to the driver and occurred in town (Norman), and sometimes it was unfamiliar and occurred in a neighboring town (Moore). One experimenter sat in the front passenger seat with a laptop computer that indicated the appropriate question to ask and the appropriate point along the route at which to ask it. The question could be about the present situation or the immediate future. The experimenter asked the participant if he or she were ready for a question, waited for an affirmation, and then asked the question while pressing a button on the laptop. When the participant answered the question, the experimenter pressed another button, interrupting a timing routine that stored the latency. The experimenter then typed in the participant's answer. In the meanwhile, a second experimenter, who also knew what the upcoming question was, checked the environment for the correct answer.

As Figure 8.4 indicates, questions about the future were more difficult than questions about the present. Understanding the present seemed relatively unaffected by familiarity, but understanding the near future was greatly affected by it. This pattern is consistent with the notion that the future has its roots in the present, and experienced operators – experts or those familiar with the situation – have easy access to the immediate future. This is similar to positions like that underlying recognition primed decision making (Klein, 1997).

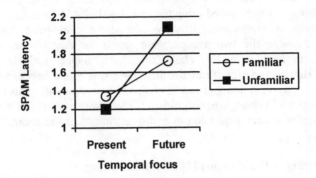

Figure 8.4 Time to answer a SPAM SA question as a function of the driver's familiarity with the route and whether the question was about the present situation or the immediate future

Guidelines

This section describes the stipulations and fundamentals for developing a battery of questions in the SPAM format. It is strongly encouraged that researchers work with subject matter experts to develop questions. Such a team effort will ensure that the questions are relevant to that specific environment and enhance sensitivity to SA differences.

Brevity and simplicity should be considered when developing questions for SPAM. Little effort should be needed to understand the question itself. Questions that are ambiguous or equivocal should be avoided. Additionally, for methodological purposes, efforts should be made to ensure that the questions are comparable in length.

Researchers should decide if the questions are queried for binary (e.g., yes, or no; A or B), forced-choice (e.g., which of the three levels is the target currently), or open-ended responses. The researchers should also decide if the queries are about the past, present, or future. Much of the research regarding SPAM has focused on either present or future-oriented questions. If past-oriented questions are desired, the researcher should ensure that the questions are relevant to the current situation. For example, asking a driver how many cars were passed during the last three minutes may be relevant to the current situation. This information is important to the driver because in all probability the cars that had recently been passed are not far behind. Therefore, with the awareness of the position of the other vehicles to that of the driver's position, he or she will know what kind of corrective actions need to be taken if a sudden stop is required. Additionally, if the driver passed the cars because the other cars noticeably decelerated, then the driver should consider that the other drivers might be aware of some restrictions or limitations to the environment (e.g., roadwork around the next bend). In contrast, probing a participant about the number of red cars that have been passed during the drive may not have any importance to the current situation. Therefore, questions should be developed that are components of the participant's current or future situation rather than a solely a test of memory that is not relevant to the situation.

Because SPAM is predicated on how quickly a participant can retrieve information, latency of responding to a question is the dependent measure. Additionally, accuracy should be recorded to compare with the latencies and because even on-line accuracy has proven useful (e.g., Cooke, et al., 2001; Durso, et al., 2004). However, response times for incorrectly answered questions are typically discarded from the analyses.

When developing a SPAM measure, the researcher needs to consider whether to implement the warning (workload) measure. We recommend the warning measure for all dynamic environments. This part of SPAM accomplishes two things: First, it measures a participant's workload. There is a positive relationship with how busy one is to how long it takes one to respond to a warning. Second, a cleverly contextualized warning signal can attenuate the interference of the task.

Questions should be developed that can transfer to all participants. We typically query participants at pre-determined times or based on predetermined triggers throughout the scenario. The situation 10 minutes into the scenario for one participant may be quite different from the situation of another. If the questions will be presented automatically, they should be flexible enough to accommodate the variances in situations across participants. Inspired by criticisms from Jeannot et al., (2003), we are currently testing the viability of having subject matter experts deliver the questions by following a pre-determined protocol (see Future directions). For example, when a question is due, the subject matter expert can choose from a set of questions that will be most relevant to the participant at that particular time in the scenario.

Future Directions

Overall, this review has suggested that on-line query techniques like SPAM can be effective measures of SA. SPAM has been used in domains from chess to air traffic control. It has been used in the lab and in the wild. It has revealed interesting characteristics of SA, including how factors affect SA and how SA affects performance.

Other on-line query techniques have attempted to improve on SPAM. For an excellent review of a variety of SA measures, the reader is directed to Jeannot et al (2003). Jeannot et al. report a number of advantages of using SPAM, including its unobtrusiveness, its on-line nature, and its face validity, ultimately arguing, 'it [SPAM] offers perhaps the most promising approach to measuring SA' (p 42). However, they raise reasonable concerns that center on the selection of the SA queries. In SPAM, the questions are scripted and targeted at aspects of the situation that are deemed important, either by a subject-matter expert or the experimenter. This makes using SPAM in unscripted situations difficult or impossible. SASHA, the adaptation of SPAM proposed by Jeannot et al., proposes to solve this problem by 1) having the SME rate the queries as to their operational importance, 2) having the SME formulate the queries in real-time. SASHA differs from SPAM in other ways with which we disagree (e.g., changing measured interval-scaled latency to judged ordinal-scaled classifications of speed), but we will not elaborate on this difference.

We do agree, however, that more precise consideration of the queries would be useful in gaining a better understanding of SA. Rating the queries for importance strikes us as a good idea. However, we believe that giving SMEs free rein over the type of queries asked and time those queries are asked may be too extreme. We suspect that such freedom in the hands of system users, even highly skilled hands, would lead to confoundings, personal bias, and a general lack of control. However, a modification of SPAM could be made that is informed by the SASHA procedure. If SMEs are given freedom to ask questions, but within constraints, the concerns of Jeannot et al., might be minimized. For example, it may be possible for a laptop computer to suggest a type of question 'Ask a question about the immediate future. Or, 'ask about the future of a flight that will be leaving the sector in 2 minutes.' In a related vein, a SME can be presented with a cluster of specific questions and his or her task is to ask one of them. This allows control over the questions by the experimenter, but acknowledges the dynamic nature of the task and reduces the prescribed nature of SPAM questions. Obviously, we do not know how to best characterize this tradeoff between constraint and freedom, but once this is determined such a procedure could be used effectively in the lab and in *prescribed* situations in the field. Although many of the studies reviewed here also compared SPAM to SAGAT, to date, there is little empirical data comparing on-line procedures like SAVANT (Willems, and Heiney, 2002) and SASHA (Jeannot et al., 2003) with each other or with SPAM.

Regardless of the ultimate characterization of on-line query methods, it seems to be the case that there is a need for an effective on-line measure. SPAM, the on-line measure reviewed in this chapter, seems to be a sensitive measure that leads to valid, interpretable conclusions about how operators understand the situations they manage. SPAM and its variants can make a useful addition to the SA researcher's toolkit.

References

Bransford, J.D. and Johnson, M.K. (1972), 'Contextual Prerequisites for Understanding: Some Investigation of Comprehension and Recall', *Journal of Verbal Learning and Verbal Behavior,* Vol. 11, pp. 717-726.

Carretta, T.R., Perry, D.C. and Ree, M.J. (1996), 'Prediction of Situational Awareness in F-15 Pilots', *International Journal of Aviation Psychology*, vol. 6, pp. 21-41.

Charness, N. (1989), 'Expertise in Chess and Bridge', in D. Klahr and K. Kotovsky (eds), *Complex Information Processing: The Impact of Herbert A. Simon*, Erlbaum, Hillsdale, NJ, pp. 183-208.

Cooke, N.J., Kiekel, P.A. and Helm, E.E. (2001), 'Measuring Team Knowledge during Skill Acquisition of a Complex Task', *International Journal of Cognitive Ergonomics,* vol. 5, pp. 297-315.

Durso, F.T., Crutchfield, J.M. and Batsakes, P.J. (2001), 'Cognition in a Dynamic Environment', in M.J. Smith, G. Salvendy, D. Harris, and R.J. Koubek (eds), *Usability Evaluation and Interface Design*, Erlbaum, Hillsdale, NJ, pp. 1373-1377.

Durso, F.T., Dattel, A.R., Bleckley, M.K., Norris, J.D., Perez, A.M., Hall, C.F. and Cardenas, D.D. (2004), 'SA Queries during the Air Traffic Scenarios Test: Keep the Situation Present', *Seventy-fifth Annual Aerospace Medical Association Scientific Meeting*, Anchorage, AK.

Durso, F.T. and Gronlund, S. (1999), 'Situation Awareness', in F.T. Durso (ed.), *The Handbook of Applied Cognition*, John Wiley, Chichester, pp. 284-314.

Durso, F.T., Hackworth, C.A., Truitt, T.R., Crutchfield, J., Nikolic, D. and Manning, C.A. (1998), 'Situation Awareness as a Predictor of Performance for En Route Air Traffic Controllers', *Air Traffic Control Quarterly*, vol. 6, pp. 1-20.

Durso, F.T. and Hall, C.F. (in press), 'Technology and the Real World: Should Cognitive Psychologists Pick the Red Pill?', in W.R. Walker and D. Hermann (eds), (in preparation) *Cognitive Technology: Transforming Thought and Society*, Mayfield.

Durso, F.T., Truitt, T.R, Hackworth, C.A., Crutchfield, J.M. and Manning, C.A. (1997), 'En Route Operational Errors and Situation Awareness', *The International Journal of Aviation Psychology*, vol. 82, pp. 177-194.

Durso, F.T., Truitt, T.R., Hackworth, C.A., Crutchfield, J.M., Nikolic, D., Moertl, P.M., Ohrt, D. and Manning, C.A. (1995), 'Expertise and Chess: A Pilot Study Comparing Situation Awareness Methodologies', in D.J. Garland, and M.R. Endsley (eds), *Experimental Analysis and Measurement of Situation Awareness*, Embry-Riddle Aeronautical University Press, Daytona Beach, pp. 295-304.

Endsley, M.R. (1989), 'Pilot Situation Awareness: The Challenge for the Training Community', *Proceedings of the Interservice/Industry Training Systems Conference (I/ITSC)*, American Defense Preparedness Association, Ft. Worth, pp. 111-117.

Endsley, M.R. (1993), 'Situation Awareness and Workload: Flip Sides of the Same Coin', *Proceedings of the Seventh International Symposium on Aviation Psychology*, vol. 2, Columbus, pp. 906-911.

Endsley, M.R. (1995), 'Toward a Theory of Situation Awareness in Dynamic Systems', *Human Factors*, vol. 37, pp. 32-64.

Hart, S.G. and Staveland, L.E. (1998), 'Development of NASA-TLX (Task Load Index): Results of Empirical and Theoretical Research', in P.A. Hancock, and M. Najmedin (eds), *Human Mental Workload: Advances in Psychology*, North-Holland, Oxford, pp. 139-183.

Jeannot, E., Kelly, C. and Thompson, D. (2003), '*The Development of Situation Awareness Measures in ATM Systems'*, (HRS/HSP-005-REP-01), EUROCONTROL Experimental Centre, Bretigny-sur-Orge, France.

Jones, D.G. and Endsley, M.R. (1996), 'Sources of Situation Awareness Errors in Aviation', *Aviation, Space, and Environmental Medicine*, vol. 67, pp. 507-512.

Just, M. and Carpenter, P. (1980), 'A Theory of Reading: From Eye Fixations to Comprehension', *Psychological Review*, vol. 87, pp. 329-354.

Klein, G. (1997), 'The Recognition-primed Decision (RPD) Model: Looking Back, Looking Forward', in C.E. Zsambok (eds), *Naturalistic Decision Making*, Erlbaum, Hillsdale, NJ, pp. 285-292.

Lachman, R., Lachman, J.L. and Butterfield, E.C. (1979), *Cognitive Psychology and Information Processing: An Introduction*, Erlbaum, Hillsdale, NJ.

LaPointe, L.B. and Engle, R.W. (1990), 'Simple and Complex Word Spans as Measures of Working Memory Capacity', *Journal of Experimental Psychology: Learning, Memory, and Cognition*, vol. 16, pp. 1118-1133.

Metzger, U. and Parasuraman, R. (2001), 'The Role of the Air Traffic Controller in Future Air Traffic Management: An Empirical Study of Active Control Versus Passive Monitoring', *Human Factors*, vol. 43, pp. 519-528.

Militello, L.G., Quill, L.L., Vinson, K.M. and Gorman, M.E. (2003), 'Toward Developing Situation Awareness Evaluation Strategies for Command and Control Environments', *Proceeding of the Human Factors and Ergonomics Society 47th Annual Meeting*, Denver, CO, pp. 434-438.

Oppenheimer, T. (1956), 'Analogy in Science', *American Psychologist*, vol. 11, pp. 127-135.

Strater, L. and Endsley, M.R. (2003), 'Training Situation Awareness for Improved Performance', *Proceedings of the XVth Triennial Congress of the International Ergonomics Association*, Seoul, Korea.

Stein, E.S. (1985), *'Air Traffic Controller Workload: An Examination of Workload Probe'*, (DOT/FAA/CT-TN84/24), William J. Hughes Technical Center, Atlantic City International Airport, NJ.

Vidulich, M.A. (2003), 'Mental Workload and Situation Awareness: Essential Concepts for Aviation Psychology Practice', in P.S. Tsang and M.A. Vidulich, (eds), *Principles and Practice of Aviation Psychology*, Erlbaum, Mahwah, NJ, pp. 115-146.

Wickens, C.D. (1992), 'Workload and Situation Awareness: An Analogy of History and Implication', *Insight: The Visual Performance Technical Group Newsletter*, vol. 14, pp. 1-3.

Willems, B. and Heiney, M. (2002), *'Decision Support Automation Research in En Route Air Traffic Control Environment'*, (DOT/FAA/CT-TN02/10), William J. Hughes Technical Center, Atlantic City International Airport, NJ.

Willems, B. and Truitt, T.R. (1999, *'Implications of Reduced Involvement in En Route Air Traffic Control'*, (DOT/FAA/CT-TN99/22), William J. Hughes Technical Center, Atlantic City International Airport, NJ.

Chapter 9

Drivers' Hazard Perception Ability: Situation Awareness on the Road

Mark S. Horswill and Frank P. McKenna

Introduction

Of all the different components of driving skill, only hazard perception has been found to relate to accident involvement across a number of studies. Hazard perception can be considered to be situation awareness for dangerous situations in the traffic environment. There is a long history of research into hazard perception testing in which drivers are required to detect potential dangers, usually in filmed road scenes.

One key question for road safety researchers is whether there is some quantifiable component of driving skill that can explain why some drivers are more likely to crash than other drivers. The identification of such of a skill would have important implications for reducing accident involvement in terms of driver assessment and training.

In the early seventies there was a prevailing assumption that superior driving skill per se led to reduced accident liability. However, this assumption was not supported by the empirical evidence. Williams and O'Neill (1974) found, contrary to prediction, that highly skilled drivers (a sample of licensed race drivers) had more accidents on public roads than a control group matched for exposure. Subsequent research has failed to yield any substantial safety benefits for what most people would consider to be driver skill. For example, McPherson and McKnight (1976) developed a Motorcycle Operator Skills Test, which focused on vehicle control skills, but this failed to discriminate between accident-involved and accident-free motorcyclists (Jonah, Dawson, and Bragg, 1981). Compulsory skid training in Finland was found to have no overall effect on subsequent accident involvement after controlling for exposure (Katila, Keskinen, Hatakka, and Laapotti, 1996) despite considerable statistical power ($n = 30,616$).

One possibility is that accident liability has more to do with other factors such as driver style (for example, propensity to speed) rather than driver skill. Indeed, speeding has consistently been found to be an important predictor of accident liability (for example Horswill and McKenna, 1999; Quimby, Maycock, Carter, Dixon, and Wall, 1986; Wasielewski, 1984). One might argue that beyond the basic skills needed to control the vehicle, driver skill is simply not an important discriminatory variable for road safety.

There is, however, one component of drivers' skill that does not fit this pattern. Of the many domain-specific skills involved in driving a car, only one has been found to correlate with drivers' accident records across a number of studies. This is drivers' hazard perception: the ability to detect dangerous traffic situations. Hazard perception in driving has been the subject of research for decades (the first article we are aware of was by Spicer in 1964, cited in Pelz and Krupat, 1974). Hazard perception can be viewed as drivers' situation awareness for potentially dangerous incidents in the traffic environment.

In Spicer's (1964) study, participants viewed a number of filmed traffic situations. After each traffic situation, they selected features from a checklist that they considered to be important. They found young, accident-involved drivers to be less accurate in perceiving essential features of the situations than accident-free drivers (see Pelz and Krupat, 1974). Pelz and Krupat (1974) asked participants to move a handle while viewing traffic sequences filmed from the driver's perspective to indicate how safe or unsafe they felt as the sequences unfolded. The point at which participants' noticed each of six hazards was operationalized as the point that the y bega n to mo ve the lever to wards the ' unsafe' position. Those drivers who had no history of accidents or convictions for moving traffic offences responded 500 milliseconds before those with accidents but no convictions and 1200 milliseconds before those with accidents and convictions. These differences were statistically significant.

Watts and Quimby (1979) developed a hazard perception simulator based on the same principles as Pelz and Krupat, though participants sat in a car body to view the filmed scenes. They found a significant correlation (*Spearman's Rho* = .28) between drivers' reaction time to hazards and their road accident frequency over the previous three years (Transport and Road Research Laboratory, 1979). Smaller, though still significant, correlations (between .11 and .13) were found in a later replication (Quimby et al., 1986) in which age and mileage were controlled for.

McKenna and Crick (1991) developed an alternative version of the hazard perception test based on the idea that it may not be necessary to simulate all parts of the driving task in order to measure hazard perception. They argued that the critical part of the hazard perception task was processing the visual scene and therefore other elements of previous si mulators, such as sitting participants in mock-up cars, might not be critical for measurement. In McKenna and Crick's test, participants simply sat in front of a television monitor and pressed a response button as quickly as possible whenever they detected a traffic hazard in a video of traffic scenes. This test was cheap and simple to implement, opening the possibility of mass testing and inclusion in driving licensing tests. Using data from McKenna's laboratory, we have found those with a greater number of accidents over the previous two years are worse at the McKenna and Crick hazard perception test, after partialling out the effects of age and mileage ($r = .11$, $n = 398$, $p = .03$). Hull and Christie (1992) developed a test in which participants watched video of road scenes and touched the screen when they considered it safe to commence a maneuver. There was a significant difference (.4 of a standard deviation) between accident-involved and accident-free drivers.

One weakness of the findings reported so far is that they rely on retrospective reports of accident involvement. However, a large scale prospective study using the test described by Hull and Christie (1992) was conducted by the Australian Council of Educational Research (ACER) in 1999 and was described by Drummond (2000). They used data from around 100,000 probationary drivers who completed the touch-screen hazard perception test and analyzed their subsequent involvement in police-reported casualty accidents. Using multiple regression techniques, they found that poor hazard perception was associated with increased risk of fatal or serious accidents but not minor accidents or accidents overall (the magnitude of this effect varied with age at licensing). Those who scored low in the hazard perception test had double the likelihood of being involved in a fatal accident in the first year post-test.

In this chapter, we will review some of the key methodological and theoretical issues involving hazard perception. First, we shall discuss potential criticisms of the relationship between accident involvement and hazard perception. Second, we shall look at hazard perception tests and their psychometric properties. Third, we shall contrast some alternative theoretical accounts of hazard perception. Finally, we shall look at practical applications of hazard perception knowledge such as driving training and assessment.

Methodological Issues Involving the Relationship between Accident Involvement and Hazard Perception

It is possible to criticize the relationship between accident involvement and hazard perception abilit y o n t wo fronts. F irst, t he size o f so me of t he e ffects, while statistically significant, may be considered by some to be trivially small. Second, Groeger (2000) described some failures to replicate the relationship between accident involvement and hazard perception though these have not been reported in the literature. A skeptic could argue that given non-significant findings are less likely to be published, the accident-hazard perception relationship may be less substantial than has been portrayed.

While relationships with accident involvement are often regarded by policy makers and researchers as a key benchmark for road safety research, they are a psychometric nightmare. Elander, West, and French (1993) reviewed correlations between accident rates over consecutive time periods. These correlations could be considered a measure of test-retest reliability of the accident variable and they are typically small. For example, McKenna, Duncan, and Brown (1986) found a correlation of .31 between accidents over two one-year periods, controlling for mileage. French, West, Elander, and Wilding (1993) also found a correlation of .31 between accidents over a three year period and accidents in the subsequent year. Poor reliability is likely to result in the underestimation of any relationship with another variable.

There are a number of reasons why accident involvement is likely to be an unreliable measure of an individual's accident liability. First, accidents are not homogeneous. To start with, they may or may not be the fault of the driver being assessed. For example, a driver who is struck from behind while stationery at traffic lights would be described as accident-involved but it is unlikely that assessing this driver's abilities would have any predictive value. Even when drivers are to blame for their accidents, this may be caused by temporary states such as fatigue rather than enduring traits like driver skill.

Second, accidents are caused by the interaction of multiple factors. This makes the chance of finding a substantial relationship with a single psychological trait, such as hazard perception, remote. Third, accidents are rare events for the individual driver. Evans (1991) estimated that the average driver has one accident in every ten years of driving so if we examine accident frequencies during one year in a typical sample of drivers, 90 per cent will be accident-free. Without prior screening, this indicates that we would require a very large sample of drivers to obtain even a modest number of accident-involved drivers.

There are also numerous biases in the measurement of accident involvement itself. For example, self-reported accident history has been shown to be affected by forgetting (about 30 per cent per year), while police records tend to exclude minor crashes (see Elander et al., 1993). There are many problems with controlling for exposure to accident situations. Drivers who travel further have more accidents (Maycock and Lockwood, 1993) but this does not necessarily mean that they are more dangerous drivers. Even if we control for mileage, other problems remain. For example, some traffic situations, such as driving on urban roads or driving at night, are more risky than other situations, such as driving on motorways (see Elander et al., 1993; Brown, 1982; or Evans, 1991, for further discussion of these problems).

In the light of these problems, we should be suspicious if any relationship between accident involvement and any single behavioral variable was not small. When designing studies to search for accident relationships, large sample sizes or the use of pre-selected samples that increase the likely effect size (such as comparing accident-free individuals with individuals with two or more accidents) are needed.

Some would argue that the question of whether the relationship between hazard perception and accidents is statistically significant or not is irrelevant as this is just a fu nction of sa mple size (Hunter, 1997) . What really matters i s whether t he magnitude of the effect size itself is trivial or not in the context of road safety. According to Cohen's (1992) effect size classifications, the correlations fou nd between hazard perception (and indeed any behavioral variable) and accident involvement would be considered small but are they important? The traditional method of evaluating correlation coefficients is to square them to obtain the proportion of variance shared between the two variables. However, this estimate usually gives a misleading picture as it assumes that any lack of reliability in the variables has been accounted for (Ozer, 1985). In the case of accident involvement, the lack of reliability is considerable and has not been accounted for in the reported studies. A number of authors have suggested that it is more appropriate to use the correlation coefficient itself as a direct measure of how much one variable is affected by another (Rosenthal, 1990). That is, if the correlation between hazard perception and accidents is .11 then this indicates that those people better than average at hazard perception are 11 per cent less likely to have an accident than those worse than average. To put it another way, this suggests that if we could train those below average at hazard perception to be equivalent to those above average at hazard perception, we could expect to prevent 11 accidents in every 100. Given the undoubted impact of road accidents on life and health, how does this size compare w ith w hat are considered important effects in the m edical literature? Rosenthal (1990) described two typical examples of medical studies in which the effects were considered uncontroversially important. In one, the influence of aspirin on heart attack frequency was measured and, in the second, the effect of the drug Propranodol was examined. Both studies were stopped prematurely because the effects obtained were considered so substantial that it would have been unethical to withhold treatment from the control groups. The correlation coefficients between treatment/control group and outcome in these studies were .03 and .04 respectively.

Why are such small correlations considered important? If we present the data as odds ratios we obtain a different perspective (Howell, 1992). For the aspirin study, 0.94 per cent of those in the aspirin group and 1.71 per cent of those in the control group had heart attacks. This gives an odds ratio of 1.83. That is, those without aspirin are 1.83 times more likely to suffer a heart attack. It was argued that this is an important effect.

In summary, a number of studies have found a significant relationship between hazard perception and accident involvement and this relationship, though small, in part due to psychometric problems with accident involvement, could be argued to be important when compared with other variables, such as medical interventions, that are considered substantial. This is in contrast to other aspects of vehicle skills such as vehicle control. However, one possibility is that skills like vehicle control have beneficial effects that are too small to be detected in the studies reported earlier but might, nevertheless, be considered important. Evidence to indicate that this is unlikely comes from examining the non-significant relationships between motorcyclists' vehicle control and their subsequent accident involvement reported by Jonah et al., (1981). The direction of all the effects was opposite to what we would expect if improved vehicle control reduced accident liability. Those who were better at vehicle control appeared to have more accidents.

The Validity of Hazard Perception Tests

There are a number of studies examining the validity of hazard perception tests. Measures taken during hazard perception tests have been found to equate well with similar measures taken during actual driving. There are learner / novice / experienced / expert driver differences in hazard perception skill that map onto what would be expected if hazard perception is a skill that improved with experience and training. As previously noted, hazard perception can predict individuals' accident involvement.

The study of any behavioral variable relies on our ability to measure it. Some of the different approaches to measuring hazard perception have already been illustrated. Most of these involve the use of filmed traffic sequences to which drivers respond either by manipulating a lever to indicate the level of perceived risk or by pressing a response button to indicate when a hazard has been detected. Groeger (2000) has questioned the extent to which these tests map onto what individuals actually do when driving a car. That is, are these types of test valid?

One test of validity is to determine the extent to which peoples' behavior in the hazard perception tests reflects their real-world driving behavior. A few studies have involved measuring drivers' behavior in a real-world drive and comparing it with their performance in a hazard perception test. Watts and Quimby (1979) found that participants' ratings of risk in a hazard perception test were similar to their ratings during actual driving. Also, they reported that skin conductance changes in the simulated and real settings were equivalent. The authors interpreted this to indicate that participants' emotional responses to the test were similar to those they experienced during real driving. Participants rated the face validity of their test as good. Mills et al., (1998) found that driving instructors' on-road ratings of novice drivers correlated well with both reaction time and number of hazards missed in a hazard perception test. Grayson (1998, cited in Groeger, 2000) found that drivers who were rated by driving examiners 'as being attentive, safe, and skilful drivers, and as having good anticipation and good speed setting abilities' (p. 11) on the road tended to have faster response times in a hazard perception test. However, Groeger (2000) noted that age is a possible confound in this case. That is, examiners might assess older drivers more positively due to stereotypes and older drivers also tend to be faster at responding in hazard perception tests. Salter, Carthy, Packham, and Rhodes-Defty (1993, cited by Haworth et al., 2000) found a .94 correlation between risk ratings of real w orld driving and fil med footage. Hughes and Cole (1986) asked one group of participants to drive a set route while giving a commentary on what attracted their attention. A second group of individuals gave a commentary while viewing video footage obtained during the real-world drives. The authors reported a 'satisfying parity' (p. 382) between the real world and the video-based commentaries.

A second line of evidence that has been used to test validity is to examine differences between novice and experienced drivers. As with any skill, it is reasonable to assume that people become better with practice. Accident liability decreases sharply during the first few years of driving and one possible explanation is that drivers become better at hazard perception. McKenna and Crick (1991) found that experienced drivers (more than ten years experience) reacted significantly faster to hazards than novice drivers (up to three years experience). Raikos (2003) recently replicated this finding using alternative stimuli. In addition, Sexton (2000) found that learner drivers were slower than novices (less than two years experience) who in turn were slower than experienced drivers (greater than ten years driving). Experienced drivers have also been found to detect a greater number of hazards than novices (McKenna and Crick, 1991; Renge, 1998).

Not all studies ha ve fo und novice/experienced driver dif ferences in hazard perception tests (Chapman and Underwood, 1998; Crundall, Underwood, and Chapman, 1999; Underwood, 2000). Crundall, Chapman, Phelps and Underwood (2003) suggested that these discrepancies could be due to differences between hazard perception tests. Specifically they suggest that the hazards used in tests that find novice/experienced differences may be more likely to be staged events and might be preselected for their ability to demonstrate group differences. However, in a test developed in Horswill's laboratory (Raikos, 2003), novice/experienced driver differences were found even though all of the hazards presented were genuine incidents and none were pre-selected. An alternative explanation is the definitions of experienced and novice drivers used in these studies. In all the studies cited in which no experienced/novice difference was found, experienced drivers tended to have had between five and ten years of post-test experience. However, in all the studies in which a difference has been found, the experienced drivers had more than nine or ten years experience. The greater difference in experience between the groups may have increased the effect size beyond that necessary to be detected as statistically significant given similar sample sizes.

One problem with many studies comparing novice and experienced drivers is that age is often confounded with experience (Groeger and Chapman, 1996). Maycock and Lockwood (1993) have demonstrated that both age and experience have separate effects on accident involvement independent of mileage. However, Ahopalo (1987, cited in Groeger and Chapman, 1996) found that drivers with a median age of 24 years responded more quickly in a hazard perception test if they had more than 40,000 km of experience and more slowly if they had less than 10,000 km of experience and that both groups were faster than people of the same age who did not drive. This indicates that experience is likely to be a key influence on hazard perception independent of age.

Finally, the relationships found between accident involvement and hazard perception test latencies also suggest that the tests reflect real world driving to some extent.

The Reliability of Hazard Perception Tests

The psychometric reliability of hazard perception tests is variable. This is likely to be due to the wide variety of hazard perception tests. We hypothesize that some tests with low internal consistency may be using a broader definition of what constitutes a hazard, which may be inappropriate given findings from Principal Component Analysis.

A number of hazard perception tests have poor reliability, which could limit their predictive power and place a ceiling on estimates of relationships with other measures. The internal consistency of Pelz and Krupat's hazard perception test was low (Cronbach's alpha = .48) and Deery and Love (1996) reported alphas between .39 and .82. Hull and Christie (1992) report the internal consistency of their hazard perception test as 'relatively low' (Catchpole, Congdon, and Leadbeatter, 2001, report the overall reliability of the Hull and Christie test as .27).

However, this is not true of all hazard perception tests. The internal consistency of a ten item version of the hazard perception test developed at McKenna's laboratory was .68 (reported in Horswill and Helman, 2003) and a hazard perception test developed at Horswill's laboratory, using the same response mode as McKenna's test but with 41 hazards, was .93 (Raikos, 2003). Also, McGowan and Banbury (Chapter 10, this volume) report an alpha of .72 for their hazard perception test.

One reason for the variation in internal consistency could be due to the different criteria used to define a hazardous scene in different tests. Broader definitions of what constitutes a hazard may lead to more heterogeneous measures of hazard perception, hence limiting internal consistency. For example, Deery and Love's (1996) test included what were described as 'active hazards', such as the camera car tailgating. Hull and Christie (1992) included the gap acceptance behavior of the driver of the camera car as a potential hazard to be detected. In contrast, none of the hazards in McKenna and Crick's (1991) test were a direct result of the driver of the camera car's risk-taking behavior. It is possible to argue that all these elements might reflect a single dimension of risk perception. However, McKenna and Horswill (1997) re ported res ults from a Principal Co mponent Analysis, which indicated that items from McKenna's hazard perception test loaded onto a separate component from video-based measures of tailgating propensity, gap acceptance behavior, overtaking behavior, and speed choice. That is, drivers' risk-taking propensity correlates poorly with hazard perception ability. This distinction maps onto the driving skill and driving style differentiation noted by a number of authors (for exa mple, Elander et al., 199 3) and c ould indicate that aspects of drivi ng behavior that reflect drivers' risk-taking propensity should be measured independently from skill-based elements such as hazard perception. Any test that includes elements of risk-taking propensity as hazards to be detected may be more heterogeneous and thus have lower internal consistency.

It is worth noting that a redeveloped version of the test described by Hull and Christie (1992) was found to improve reliability from .27 to .68 (Catchpole, Congdon, and Leadbeatter, 2001). This increase was attributed partly to increasing the number of items (from 12 to 28) as well as rejecting items which correlated poorly with the others. Other changes that may have influenced reliability in this case include an increase in the number of practice scenes and the redesign of instructions and user interfaces.

Response Bias and Hazard Perception Tests

Individual differences in hazard perception could be linked to differing thresholds for classifying an incident as a hazard rather than drivers' ability to detect that incident. There is data to suggest that drivers' hazard perception scores can be improved by asking participants to adopt a more liberal criterion for what they class as a hazard. However, there is little relationship between drivers' ratings of risk and their hazard perception score and novice/experienced driver differences in eye scanning indicate different search strategies are being used by these groups. This suggests that while response bias may influence an individual's hazard perception score, this account cannot provide a complete explanation.

One potential theoretical account of hazard perception is that it is a reflection of different drivers using different decision thresholds at which to classify an incident as a hazard. This account implies that their ability to detect the incident may not necessarily vary much. For instance, individuals who consider driving to be generally a more risky activity than others may be more inclined to label incidents as hazardous. That is to say that they have a lower response threshold for hazards. As most hazardous situations tend to develop (in the sense of becoming more risky over time), those participants with a lower response threshold would be more likely to achieve faster latencies as well as identifying greater numbers of hazards in a typical hazard perception test.

Novice/experienced differences may occur because experienced drivers are more likely than novices to label a traffic situation as hazardous even though both groups have detected the situation. The strong version of this account would predict that there are few individual differences in what drivers notice in a traffic scene. Individual differences measured in hazard perception tests are a function of response bias and not ability to detect hazardous situations. There is some evidence to indicate that response bias does influence hazard perception scores. Farrand and McKenna (2004) found that changing the response bias of drivers by using alternative instructions did alter response latencies in a hazard perception test. The question is whether individual differences in response bias can account for all variation in hazard perception scores or does drivers' ability to detect hazards also play a role?

The traditional method of unpacking the confounded effects of response bias and sensitivity in detection tasks is to use signal detection theory (Green and Swets, 1966; Stanislaw and Todorov, 1999). This procedure takes into account both the number of correct detections of a stimuli and the number of false positive responses to generate separate measures of sensitivity and response bias. Would it be possible to apply this technique to hazard perception tests in order to determine how much of the variance in scores could be accounted for response bias and how much by sensitivity? Unfortunately there is a practical problem. The identification of traffic sequences with unarguably no hazard present has not proved to be trivial. For example, during development of McKenna and Crick's hazard perception test (1991), some e xpert police drivers responded in sce nes where t he researchers believed there to be no hazard. On questioning, the experts reported that they were responding to the possible presence of oil on the road which, in their view, could present a braking hazard.

While it has so far not been possible to address response bias directly due to the problem of applying signal detection theory, there is nevertheless indirect evidence indicating that response bias is unlikely to give a full account of hazard perception.

First, if novice and experienced drivers perceive driving scenes in the same way (that is, there is no difference in detection ability just response bias) then we would not expect drivers' eye-scanning movements to change with experience. Mourant and Rockwell (1972) found that novice drivers tended to look closer to the front of their veh icle, used their m irrors less fre quently, and fi xated in a smaller area compared with more experienced drivers. They argued that these differences reflected novices' lack of skill and increased accident liability in driving. While more recent studies have failed to replicate these specific findings, the general notion that experienced drivers have different scanning patterns from novices has been supported. Crundall and Underwood (1998) found that experienced drivers' scanning patterns appeared to adapt to differe nt road sit uations while no vices tended to use the same scanning pattern for all road types. Also, novices fixated for longer durations than experienced drivers. This was interpreted as indicating that novices took longer to process events. These findings are consistent with the idea that experienced drivers are conducting a more efficient and effective search for hazards rather than simply lowering their criterion for what constitutes a hazard.

Second, if hazard perception is entirely a result of differences in perceived risk (such that those w ho perceived more risk in driving would be more likely to classify incidents as hazards) then we would expect significant relationships between drivers' ratings of the level of risk in a scene and their hazard perception score. That is, those drivers who perceived hazards sooner should also rate the scene overall and driving in general as more risky. Farrand and McKenna (2001) found no correlation (for example, $r = -.08$, n. s.) between drivers' ratings of risk (both for driving in general and for individual scenes presented in the hazard perception test) and their hazard perception response latencies. In addition, Deery (1999) re ported that d rivers' subjective ratin gs o f risk a nd even p hysiological measures of stress did not map onto actual road conditions (though note that this appears at odds with Watts and Quimby's (1979) findings that galvanic skin response did appear to correspond to road conditions). The previously described Principal Component Analysis carried out by McKenna and Horswill (1997) on a battery of video-based driving measures suggested that hazard perception is independent of risk-based measures of driving behavior.

Third, if drivers who obtained faster hazard perception latencies were not more aware of hazards then we might predict that their incidental memory for the hazards would be no greater than individuals with slower latencies. One characteristic of expertise in a wide range of domains is enhanced incidental recall of stimuli structured according the domain. For example, chess experts can recall chess game positions better than chess novices (Chase and Simon, 1973). Rowe (1997) found that experienced drivers exhibited this memory advantage for hazardous road situations over novice drivers. This was found to be a very specific advantage. Experienced drivers showed no advantage in memory not related to everyday driving hazards (for example, advertisements or filmed accidents on a race track).

Finally, McGowan and Banbury (Chapter 10, this volume) report no significant correlation between number of responses and anticipation scores in their hazard perception test. This indicates that those drivers with faster anticipation scores were not gaining this advantage by responding more often.

In conclusion, while response bias appears to be one factor that can influence hazard perception latencies, it is unlikely to be the central mechanism that determines drivers' hazard perception skill. However, it should be noted that it should not necessarily be considered a problem in the context of road safety if some differences in hazard perception ability are due to response bias. Drivers who are more ready to label an incident as hazardous may well make safer drivers independent of their perceptual skill. Quimby (1988, cited in Deery, 1999) found that drivers who rated risk as lower in given traffic scenes tended to have been involved in more accidents.

Is Hazard Perception a Skill that Becomes More Automated with Practice?

One view is that as drivers gain experience, they require less cognitive resources to perform hazard perception effectively. This is compatible with the process of hazard perception being one of memory retrieval in which drivers identify hazards by either matching them w ith previous incidents they have encountered or by noticing the incident is novel in some way. One prediction that arises from this account is that experienced drivers should be less subject to interference by a secondary task when performing a hazard perception test. As described below (McKenna and Farrand, 1999), the opposite has been found to be the case, suggesting that experienced drivers may actually require more attentional resources to achieve their superior level of hazard perception and does not appear to become more automated with practice.

Many theories of skill acquisition predict that, as a skill is developed, it requires fewer cognitive resources to perform (Fitts and Posner, 1967). One example is Anderson's (1982) influential ACT* theory in which problem-solving is represented as if-then production rules. Skill acquisition is viewed as a process in which increasingly sophisticated conditions are encoded into production rules, allowing experts in a domain to respond more quickly and accurately to situations they have previously encountered. For example, Rowe and McKenna (2001) found that the ability of expert tennis players to anticipate the direction of an opponent's shot was less impaired by a demanding secondary task than novices. This implies that this ability becomes more automated with increasing expertise. Using Logan's (1988) account of automaticity, hazard perception could be viewed as a pattern-matching task (Groeger, 2000). Experienced drivers have an array of hazardous traffic situations in memory. Whenever they encounter one of these hazardous traffic situations they can recognize it swiftly with minimum processing. In contrast, novices would be less familiar with hazardous situations and so would be required to deduce the danger in an effortful manner instead of simply recognizing it. An alternative, though not incompatible, view is that hazardous traffic situations are out of the ordinary. Experienced drivers are familiar with a wider range of ordinary non-hazardous traffic situations and so are faster to recognize dangerous situations by virtue of their distinctiveness (Groeger, 2000). Both these alternatives imply that hazard perception is cued retrieval from memory in experienced drivers but is a more effortful process in novices. Hence, experienced drivers are faster at responding to hazards than novices. This account maps onto Fitzgerald and Harrison's (1999, cited in Ha worth e t al., 2000) ap plication of a recog nition-primed decision-making model developed by Klein (1989, 1993) to drivers' hazard perception. They describe hazard perception as the recognition of an incident as familiar or unfamiliar leading to a serial option evaluation of what to do.

If hazard perception does become more automated with practice then we would expect experienced drivers to suffer less interference than novices when they perform a second task simultaneously with a hazard perception test because experienced drivers should require fewer cognitive resources to carry out the task. McKenna and Farrand (1999) tested this prediction by asking experienced and novice drivers to complete a random letter generation task while undergoing a hazard perception test. The prediction was not supported. They found that experienced drivers suffered greater interference on the hazard perception task under dual task conditions when compared with novices. Rowe (1997) also carried out this study using a letter detection task. Though the experience by dual task interaction was significant for the letter detection task scores and not the hazard perception scores, the findings still indicated that the experienced drivers required proportionally more atte ntional resources to   maintain t heir performa nce i n the hazard perception task. While the experienced drivers were older than the novice drivers in both these studies, Rowe (1997) demonstrated that the dual task interaction was unlikely to be due to the divided attention problems reported among older people. He compared the performance of younger experienced drivers with older experienced drivers and found no significant differences in dual task performance (trends indicated that older drivers were actually less impaired). Also, the experienced drivers in both studies were much younger (in Rowe's study, the mean age was 41 years and maximum age was 50 years) than the age at which divided attention deficits are typically reported.

Hazard Perception as an Effortful Proactive Process

Given that experienced drivers appear to devote more attentional resources to obtain their superior performance in hazard perception, it is proposed that good hazard perception is better conceived as an effortful, proactive process. Those drivers w ho are best at haz ard perception actively search for hazards using a dynamic mental model of the traffic environment. Using the working memory framework, evidence suggests that hazard perception, as performed by expert and experienced drivers, is a ce ntral e xecutive tas k. Whe n experienced drivers no longer apply these central resources, their hazard perception ability appears to be reduced to the level of novices. This maps onto epidemiological evidence that the use of mobile telephones when driving (even hands-free sets) leads to a four-fold increase in crash risk.

One alternative to the passive pattern-recognition account of hazard perception is one in which drivers generate an active mental model of the driving environment and use that mental model as the basis for actively predicting dangerous situations. This account is more in line with theoretical accounts used for situation awareness in general. Endsley (2000) remarks that, 'people under automaticity tend to be unreceptive to novel events...' (p.15) and argues that the proactive requirements of situation awareness are incompatible with the automaticity account. In the context of general expertise, Ericsson and Lehmann (1996) argued that experts should not be characterized as automatons and that verbal protocols from experts across a range of domains indicate that they are more likely to be engaging in effortful prediction and monitoring of their situation than novices.

We argue that effective hazard perception is cognitively demanding and does not possess the requisite properties of an automatic task. One of the requirements of an automatic task is that the stimuli must have a direct consistent mapping onto a response (Shiffrin and Schneider, 1977). This condition is unlikely in hazard perception due to the complex and infrequent nature of traffic hazards (Groeger, 2000). Experienced drivers have a more sophisticated and accurate mental model of driving than novices but this mental model demands more cognitive resources to implement.

Crundall and Underwood (1998) found, when recording eye movements during real drivin g, tha t no vices ap pear to search the road way less t han experienced drivers in certain demanding traffic conditions. One possible explanation for this was that novices have fewer mental resources to devote to searching because they must assign more mental resources to deal with basic vehicle control than experienced drivers. A second possibility is that novice drivers have an impoverished mental model of the road environment in these conditions. Their searches were restricted because they had less expectation of where potential sources of danger might arise. Underwood, Chapman, Bowden, and Crundall (2002) recorded the eye movements of experienced and novice drivers watching filmed footage of the type of demanding traffic conditions found to generate differences in visual scan. They found that even in the simulator, where novice drivers did not have to control the vehicle, the horizontal width of their search patterns was less than experienced drivers. They argued that experienced drivers have a more sophisticated mental model of the traffic environment rather than novices' search being restricted by vehicle control requirements. However, they also argue that the knowledge associated with this mental model is implicit and automated, though this assumption is not tested.

The studies by McKenna and Farrand (1999) and Rowe (1997) described in the previous section, in which experienced drivers suffered greater interference under dual-task conditions than novices, suggest that experienced drivers may indeed have a more sophisticated mental model of the traffic environment but that this model i s subject to interference and there fore is not aut omated. Ro we (1997) conceptualized hazard perception in terms of Baddeley and Hitch's (1974) working memory model. He carried out a series of dual-task experiments using secondary tasks that were designed to engage the different components of working memory (visuospatial sketchpad, articulatory loop, and central executive) independently. He found no interference between hazard perception performance and the visuospatial sketchpad and articulatory loop secondary tasks, suggesting that the hazard perception did appear to be more of a central executive task for the experienced drivers. Another property of automatic tasks, according to Schneider, Dumais, and Shiffrin (1984), is that specific stimuli are less likely to be remembered. If hazard perception becomes more automated with practice then we might therefore expect memory recall of specific hazards to decrease rather than increase. However, as reported earlier, Rowe (1997) found that experienced drivers had better recall than novices for hazards that they were presented.

Groeger (2000) noted that the evidence regarding mental workload and hazard perception has invariably been acquired in test-like conditions, mainly with video-based hazard perception tests. While experienced drivers may indeed devote more cognitive resources to hazard perception than novices under test conditions, he suggests that this is unlikely to transfer into real-world everyday driving in which experienced drivers are more likely to be daydreaming or route-finding than conducting extensive and effortful searches for infrequent traffic hazards. That is, experienced drivers in hazard perception tests may indeed be engaged in an effortful, intention-driven search but this is not what they do in the real world. He argued that it is unclear where the bottleneck lies in dual-task experiments involving hazard perception. That is, the interference could come at the detection level but it could also come at a response level, w hich is artificial in hazard perception tests (typically a button press). However, Rowe's (1997) failure to find dual-task interference between non-central-executive tasks and hazard perception suggests that the interference found with central executive tasks is less likely to be a simple consequence of response mode. Also, it is worth noting that a connection between performance in hazard perception tests and real world driving has been demonstrated via transfer of training evidence. As will be described in the next section, specific real-world training in hazard perception on the road has been found to transfer to superior performance in video-based hazard perception tests (McKenna and Crick, 1991; Mills et al., 1998) and video-based training has been found to transfer to superior performance in real-world assessments (Mills et al., 1998).

Evidence to suggest that driving is not resource-free in the real world when drivers are not under test conditions comes from epidemiological studies on mobile telephones. Redelmeier and Tibshirani (1997) studied accident-involved drivers with mobile telephones and analyzed call patterns over a 14 month period. They found that the risk of a collision increased four-fold when a mobile telephone was in use, whether or not it was a hands-free set. While it may be possible that experienced drivers sometimes spare little attention for hazard perception in the real road, as suggested by Groeger (2000), we would argue that when they do so, they are likely to lose much of their hazard perception advantage. In fact, the magnitude of the dual task effect found by McKenna and Farrand (1999) suggests that, when the attentional resources of experienced drivers are diverted to other tasks, their hazard perception ability is reduced to the level of novice drivers.

Driver Training

There are indications that hazard perception can be trained using a number of low cost techniques (though not all techniques are effective). This raises one possibility for reducing the accident liability of drivers though the impact of such training on accident involvement has yet to be empirically tested.

If hazard perception ability is important to safe driving and it appears to improve with experience then can this improvement be accelerated with training? Is it necessary for novice drivers to live with elevated risk for their first few years of driving while they acquire hazard perception skills?

McKenna and Crick (1991) compared an experienced group of drivers with a group of drivers with the same level of driving experience but who had been through an ad vanced dri ving course t hat i ncluded hazard perception as a key ability. This expert group were Class One police drivers in the UK. They found that the expert group did have significantly superior hazard perception scores to their untrained counterparts.

One problem with these comparisons is that effects could be the result of self-selection. McKenna and Crick (1991) addressed this criticism by testing a group of civilian drivers before and after they either took part, or did not take part, in an advanced driving course containing on-road hazard perception training. They found that the training had both a significant within-subject and between-subject effect, where self-selection was unlikely to account for the within-subject effect. Experimental studies, in which novice drivers are randomly assigned to either a trained or an untrained group, also demonstrate significant benefits for hazard perception training. McPherson and Kenel (1968) found that an instructional film improved participants' ability to perceive potential hazards in a slide-based hazard perception test, in which traffic scenes were rated for level of danger. More recently, McKenna and Crick (1994) developed a training package based on the account of hazard perception as drivers constructing a mental model of the road environment and making predictions based on that model. Training involved participants watching video-based scenes of traffic situations and being encouraged to look further ahead down the road. At various points, the video was paused and drivers were asked to generate possibilities for what might happen next. McKenna and Crick (1994) compared training schedules with and without this prediction task and found significant improvements only when the prediction task was included. Sexton (2000) reported a replication of this finding, in which advanced training (three hours long) was found to be superior to basic training (one hour long) which in turn was superior to no training (both in comparison with an untrained group and with a pre-training test).

Another training schedule that has been found to be effective is asking novices to generate verbal commentaries as they either drive or view filmed road scenes (McKenna and Farrand, 2004; Marek and Sten, 1977; Gregersen, 1993; Spolander, 1990, the latter three cited by Deery, 1999). Novice drivers indicate where they are looking and what they are looking out for, including other road users and potential hazards. The aim is to force the novice to proactively engage the traffic environment and encourage elaboration of their mental model of driving. McKenna and Farrand (2004) found the effect of this type of training was still apparent a week after the initial session.

A similar technique was used by McKenna, Horswill, and Alexander (under review) who presented drivers with a video of traffic scenes accompanied by a pre-recorded verbal co mmentary b y a n e xpert driver. Thi s was found to i mprove hazard perception ability as measured by McKenna's latency-based video test. The effect was replicated using different stimuli in Horswill's laboratory (Raikos, 2003). McKenna, Horswill, and Alexander (under review) found that this training also had the effect of reducing drivers' risk-taking propensity. In a video simulation, trained drivers slowed up to a greater extent than the untrained drivers when a hazard was present (there was no difference in speed intentions when a hazard was not present). This pattern of results was replicated with expert and novice police drivers (where experts were taught hazard perception as part of their training) indicating some generalizability.

Mills et al. (1998) used a combination of classroom and on-road training. In the classroom technique, a driving instructor told participants how to identify hazards using filmed traffic scenes. The instructor placed emphasis on looking ahead, using critical scanning areas, and anticipating hazards. The on-road technique involved one-on-one instruction from an advanced driving instructor and participants produced a running commentary while they drove. Both these techniques significantly reduced latencies in a video-based hazard perception test, with the greater reduction for drivers who underwent both techniques. The training also improved driving instructors' ratings of participants' on-road driving skill, though these findings were less unequivocal.

Regan, Deery, and Triggs (1998b, cited by Deery, 1999) developed a computer-based training package using photographs and video clips of traffic scenes, in which participants were given training in visual scanning, hazard prediction, and safe decision-making. These skills were then applied in a driving simulator and participants were required to criticize their own performance. This training was found to improve hazard perception performance in the driving simulator.

Another approach taken by Regan, Deery, and Triggs (1998a, cited by Deery, 1999) was to design a training regime to improve the attentional control of younger drivers. Participants practiced performi ng a drivin g-related task (maintaining a certain headway to the vehicle in front) concurrently with a numerical calculation task. The amount of attention participants were told to assign to each task was varied over 20 trials and feedback on performance was given. Deery (1999) reported that this Variable Priority Training improved subsequent dual task performance and hazard perception ability. It was suggested that ability to divide attention could be an important component of risk perception.

It should be noted that not all types of hazard perception training have been successful. For example, Underwood (2000) describes training that was designed to develop novices' visual search for hazards. While this had the effect of extending the search patterns of drivers both in the laboratory and on the road, no difference in reaction time between trained and untrained novices was found in a hazard perception test. However, Underwood notes that the version of the test being used failed to discriminate between novices and experienced drivers, so that the apparent lack of a training effect could be due to insensitivity of that particular hazard perception test.

Groeger (2000) questioned the generalizability of this type of hazard perception training to real driving and noted that it remains unclear precisely what drivers are learning from such training. For example, could such training simply be changing the response bias of drivers (that is, m aking them m ore likely to describe an incident as hazardous) without actually developing hazard detection skills that they use in the real world driving? The findings of McKenna et al., (under review) suggest this explanation is unlikely to account for differences, given that individuals trained in hazard perception only reduced their speed more than untrained individuals when a hazard was present (that is, the training did not render them slow in all situations). McGowan and Banbury (Chapter 10, this volume) report a hazard perception training program in which hazard perception is conceptualized in terms of Endsley's three tier model of situation awareness. This program improved anticipation time without affecting response rate, indicating that the training was unlikely to be simply changing response bias.

Driver Assessment

Hazard perception tests are now part of driver licensing in the UK and Australia. There is some evidence that separate hazard perception tests for different road user groups such as motorcyclists could be of use.

Hazard perception tests have a number of practical uses in driver assessment outside the research domain. Hazard perception tests are already a compulsory part of the official driving test in the UK (as of November 2002) and in most states in Australia. Given the relationships found with accident involvement and the effectiveness of certain training schedules, it is the hope that these inclusions will impact road safety, especially given that the ability of traditional driving tests to predict accident liability is known to be limited (Sheppard, Henry, and Mackie, 1973). One issue to be addressed is whether different types of hazard perception test need to be developed for different types of road user. Haworth, Symmons, and Kowadlo (2000) put the case for a need for a special test for motorcyclists as some of the hazards they face may differ from car drivers. This is supported by the findings of a study by Horswill and Helman (2003), which found that motorcyclists were faster in a hazard perception test than a matched group of car drivers, but only when the motorcyclists performed the hazard perception test as if they were driving a car. When asked to respond to hazards as if they were riding a motorcycle, their advantage disappeared. Horswill and Helman (2003) suggested that this was likely to be due to their hazard perception test having been designed for cars and some of the hazards (for example, those involving the camera car fitting through a narrow gap) could be considered less of a risk for motorcycles.

Conclusions

Some have questioned whether enough research in hazard perception has been done to justify the inclusion of hazard perception assessments in driving tests (Ferguson, 2003; Groeger , 2 000; Groeger and Chapman, 1996) . Ho wever, t he evidence presented in this chapter gives grounds for optimism. In contrast to other aspects of driver skill, hazard perception can predict (in the real sense of the word) accidents. Reliable measures of hazard perception have been achieved and these hazard perception tests also appear to have some degree of validity. Hazard perception can be improved through relatively quick and cheap training techniques and this training has been demonstrated to transfer to real driving. However, it should be noted that one aspect that has not yet been tested is whether hazard perception training directly impacts drivers' accident liability.

Why are some drivers better than others at hazard perception? While differences in response bias might account for some of the variance, they are unlikely to provide a full account. In terms of novice/experienced driver differences, the evidence appears to indicate that hazard perception is an effortful, central executive task, such that when experienced drivers are distracted, their advantage over novices is eradicated. This has practical implications for situations that may distract drivers, such as when using mobile telephones (whether hands-free or not).

In conclusion, we argue that hazard perception is an important component of driving that impact a number of theoretical and practical issues. The case of drivers' hazard perception demonstrates how situation awareness research can have far-reaching policy implications for a key public health issue like traffic safety and could lead to significant reductions in deaths and injuries.

References

Anderson, J.R. (1982), 'Acquisition of Cognitive Skill', *Psychological Bulletin*, vol. 89(4), pp. 369-406.

Baddeley, A.D. and Hitch, G.J. (1974), 'Working Memory', In G.H. Bower (ed.), *The Psychology of Learning and Motivation* (vol. 8), Academic Press, New York, pp. 47-89.

Brown, I.D. (1982), 'Exposure and Experience are a Confounded Nuisance in Research on Driver Behaviour', *Accident Analysis and Prevention*, vol. 14(5), pp. 345-352.

Catchpole, J., Congdon, P. and Leadbeatter, C. (2001), 'Implementation of Victoria's new Hazard Perception Test', in *Proceedings of the Road Safety Research: Policing and Education Conference 2001* (19th to 20th November), Melbourne. Available at: http://www.monash.edu.au/oce/roadsafety.

Chapman, P. and Underwood, G. (1998), 'Visual Search of Driving Situations: Danger and Experience', *Perception*, vol. 27, pp. 951-964.

Chase, W.G. and Simon, H.A. (1973), 'The Mind's Eye in Chess', In W.G. Chase (ed.), *Visual Information Processing*, Academic Press, New York.

Cohen, J. (1992), 'A Power Primer', *Psychological Bulletin*, vol. 112(1), pp. 155-159.

Crundall, D., Chapman, P., Phelps, N. and Underwood, G. (2003), 'Eye Movements and Hazard Perception in Police Pursuit and Emergency Response Driving', *Journal of Experiment Psychology: Applied*, vol. 9(3), pp. 163-174.

Crundall, D., Underwood, G. and Chapman, P. (1999), 'Driving Experience and the Functional Field of View', *Perception*, vol. 28, pp. 1075-1087.

Crundall, D.E. and Underwood, G. (1998), 'Effects of Experience and Processing Demands on Visual Information Acquisition in Drivers', *Ergonomics*, vol. 41(4), pp. 448-458.

Deery, H.A. (1999), 'Hazard and Risk Perception among Young Novice Drivers', *Journal of Safety Research*, vol. 30(4), pp. 225-236.

Deery, H.A. and Love, A.W. (1996), 'The Effect of a Moderate Dose of Alcohol on the Hazard Perception Profile of Young Drink Drivers', *Addiction*, vol. 91, pp. 815-827.

Drummond, A.E. (2000), 'Paradigm Lost! Paradigm Gained? An Australian's Perspective on the Novice Driver Problem', In *Proceedings of the Novice Driver Conference* (1st–2nd June), Bristol, Available at: http://www.dft.gov.uk.

Elander, J., West, R. and French, D. (1993), 'Behavioural Correlates of Individual Differences in Road Traffic Crash Risk: An Examination of Methods and Findings', *Psychological Bulletin*, vol. 113(2), pp. 279-294.

Endsley, M.R. (2000), 'Theoretical Underpinnings of Situation Awareness: A Critical Review', In M.R. Endsley and D.J. Garland (eds), *Situation Awareness Analysis and Measurement*, Erlbaum, Mahwah, NJ.

Ericsson, K.A. and Lehmann, A.C. (1996), 'Expert and Exceptional Performance: Evidence of Maximal Adaptation to Task Constraints', *Annual Review of Psychology*, vol. 46, pp. 273-305.

Evans, L. (1991), *Traffic Safety and the Driver*, Van Nostrand Reinhold, New York. Available online at: http://www.scienceservingsociety.com/book.

Farrand, P. and McKenna, F.P. (2001), 'Risk Perception in Novice Drivers: The Relationship between Questionnaire Measures and Response Latency', *Transportation Research Part F*, vol. 4, pp. 201-212.

Farrand, P. and McKenna, F.P. (2004). 'Effect of Varying Instruction Set on Applied Task Performance', unpublished report, School of Psychology, University of Reading, UK.

Ferguson, S.A. (2003), 'Other High-risk Factors for Young Drivers – How Graduated Licensing Does, Doesn't, or Dould Address Them', *Journal of Safety Research*, vol. 34, pp. 71-77.

Fitts, P.M. and Posner, M. I. (1967), *Human Performance*, Brooks/Cole, Belmont, CA.

French, D.J., West, R.J., Elander, J. and Wilding, J.M. (1993), 'Decision-making Style, Driving Style, and Self-reported Involvement in Road Traffic Accidents', *Ergonomics*, vol. 36(6), pp. 627-644.

Green, D. and Swets, J. (1966), *Signal Detection Theory and Psychophysics*, John Wiley, New York.

Groeger, J.A. (2000), *Understanding Driving*, Psychology Press, Hove.

Groeger, J.A. and Chapman, P.R. (1996), 'Judgement of Traffic Scenes: The Role of Danger and Difficulty', *Applied Cognitive Psychology*, vol. 10, pp. 349-364.

Haworth, N., Symmons, M. and Kowadlo, N. (2000), 'Hazard Perception by Inexperienced Motorcyclists', Research Report, Monash University Accident Research Centre. Available at: http://www.monash.edu.au/oce/roadsafety.

Horswill, M.S. and Helman, S. (2003), 'A Behavioral Comparison between Motorcyclists and a Matched Group of Non Motorcycling Car Drivers: Factors Influencing Accident Risk', *Accident Analysis and Prevention*, vol. 35(4), pp. 589-597.

Horswill, M.S. and McKenna, F.P. (1999), 'The Development, Validation, and Application of a Video-based Technique for Measuring an Everyday Risk-taking Behaviour: Drivers' Speed Choice', *Journal of Applied Psychology*, vol. 84(6), pp. 977-985.

Howell, D.C. (1992), *Statistical Methods for Psychology* (3rd ed.), PWS-Kent, Boston.

Hughes, P.K. and Cole, B.L. (1986), 'What Attracts Attention when Driving?' *Ergonomics*, vol. 29(3), pp. 377-391.

Hull, M. and Christie, R. (1992), 'Hazard Perception Test: The Geelong Trial and Future Development', In *Proceedings of the National Road Safety Seminar*, Wellington, New Zealand.

Hunter, J.E. (1997), 'Needed: a Ban on the Significance Test', *Psychological Science*, vol. 8(1), pp. 3-7.

Jonah, B.A., Dawson, N.E. and Bragg, B.W.E. (1981), 'Predicting Accident Involvement with the Motorcycle Operator Skill Test', *Accident Analysis and Prevention*, vol. 13, pp. 307-318.

Katila, A., Keskinen, E., Hatakka, M. and Laapotti, S. (1996), 'Skid Training for Novice Drivers-Benefit for Adults, Pitfall for Youngsters', Paper presented at the International Conference of Traffic and Transport Psychology, Valencia, Spain.

Klein, G.A. (1989), 'Recognition Primed Decisions', In W.B. Rouse (ed.), *Advances in Man-Machine Research*, (vol. 5), JAI Press, Greenwich, CT, pp. 47-92.

Klein G.A. (1993), 'A Recognition-primed-decision (RDP) Model of Rapid Decision Making', In G.A. Klein, J. Orasanu, R. Calderwood, and C.E. Zsambok (eds), *Decision Making in Action: Models and Methods*, Ablex, Norwood, NJ, pp. 138-147.

Logan, G.D. (1988), 'Towards an Instance Theory of Automatization', *Psychological Review*, vol. 95, 492-527.

Maycock, G. and Lockwood, C.R. (1993), 'The Accident Liability of British Car Drivers', *Transport Reviews*, vol. 13(3), pp. 231-245.

McKenna, F.P. and Crick, J.L. (1991), 'Hazard Perception in Drivers: a Methodology for Testing and Training', Final Report. Behavioural Studies Unit, Transport and Road Research Laboratory, Crowthorne, UK.

McKenna, F.P. and Crick, J.L. (1994), 'Developments in Hazard Perception', Final Report. Department of Transport, UK.

McKenna, F.P., Duncan, J. and Brown, I.D. (1986), 'Cognitive Abilities and Safety on the Road: a Re-examination of Individual Differences in Dichotic Listening and Search for Embedded Figures', *Ergonomics*, vol. 29(5), pp. 649-663.

McKenna, F.P. and Farrand, P. (1999), 'The Role of Automaticity in Driving', In G.B. Grayson (ed.), *Behavioural Research in Road Safety IX*, Transport Research Laboratory, Crowthorne, UK.

McKenna, F.P. and Farrand, P. (2004), 'Drivers' Hazard Perception and Training', Paper in preparation. School of Psychology, University of Reading, UK.

McKenna, F.P. and Horswill, M.S. (1997), 'Differing Conceptions of Hazard Perception', In G.B. Grayson (ed.), *Behavioural Research in Road Safety VII*, Crowthorne: Transport Research Laboratory, pp. 74-81.

McKenna, F.P., Horswill, M.S. and Alexander, J. (under review), 'Does Anticipation Training Affect Drivers' Risk Taking?' Submitted to the *Journal of Experimental Psychology: Applied*.

McPherson, K. and Kenel, F.C. (1968), 'Perception of Traffic Hazards: A Comparative Study', *Human Factors*, vol. 17(5), pp. 488-501.

McPherson, K. and McKnight, A.J. (1976), 'A Task Analytic Approach to Development of a Motorcycle Operator License Skill Test', *Human Factors*, vol. 18, pp. 351-360.

Mills, K.L., Hall, R.D., McDonald, M. and Rolls, G.W.P. (1998), 'The Effects of Hazard Perception Training on the Development of Novice Driver Skills', Research Report. London: Department for Transport, UK. Available at: http://www.dft.gov.uk.

Mourant, R.R. and Rockwell, T.H. (1972), 'Strategies of Visual Search by Novice and Experienced Drivers', *Human Factors*, vol. 14(4), pp. 325-335.

Ozer, D.J. (1985), 'Correlation and the Coefficient of Determination', *Psychological Bulletin*, vol. 97(2), pp. 307-315.

Pelz, D.C. and Krupat, E. (1974), 'Caution Profile and Driving Record of Undergraduate Males', *Accident Analysis and Prevention*, vol. 6, pp. 45-58.

Quimby, A.R., Maycock, G., Carter, I.D., Dixon, R. and Wall, J.G. (1986), 'Perceptual Abilities of Accident Involved Drivers', Research Report 27, Transport and Road Research Laboratory, Crowthorne, UK.

Raikos, M.K. (2003), 'Improving Speed in Skilled Anticipation: The Case of Hazard Perception in Driving', Unpublished honours thesis. School of Psychology, University of Queensland. Contact: m.horswill@psy.uq.edu.au.

Redelmeier, D.A. and Tibshirani, R.J. (1997), 'Association between Cellular-telephone Calls and Motor Vehicle Collisions', *The New England Journal of Medicine*, vol. 336(7), pp. 453-502.

Renge, K. (1998), 'Drivers' Hazard and Risk Perception, Confidence in Safe Driving, and Choice of Speed', *Journal of the International Association of Traffic and Safety Sciences*, vol. 22(2), pp. 103-110.

Rosenthal, R. (1990), 'How are we doing in Soft Psychology?', *Psychological Science*, vol. 45, pp. 775-777.

Rowe, R.M. (1997), 'Anticipation in Skilled Performance', Unpublished PhD thesis. University of Reading, Reading, UK.

Rowe, R.M. and McKenna, F.P. (2001), 'Skilled Anticipation in Real-world Tasks: Measurement of Attentional Demands in the Domain of Tennis', *Journal of Experimental Psychology: Applied*, vol. 7(1), pp. 60-67.

Schneider, W., Dumais, S.T. and Shiffrin, R.M. (1984), 'Automatic and Control Processing and Attention', In R. Parasuraman and D.R. Davies (eds), *Varieties of Attention*, Academic Press, Inc, London, pp. 1-27.

Sexton, B. (2000), 'Development of Hazard Perception Testing', in *Proceedings of the DETR Novice Drivers Conference*, Bristol. Available at: http://www.dft.gov.uk.

Sheppard, D., Henry, J.P. and Mackie, A.M. (1973), 'Faults in the Driving Test and their Relationship with Subsequent Accidents', Report 782, Crowthorne, UK: Transport and Road Research Laboratory.

Shiffrin, R.M. and Schneider, W. (1977), 'Controlled and Automatic Human Information Processing: Perceptual Learning, Automatic Attending, and a General Theory', *Psychological Review*, vol. 84, pp. 127-190.

Stanislaw, H. and Todorov, N. (1999), 'Calculation of Signal Detection Theory Measures', *Behavioral Research Methods, Instruments, and Computers*, vol. 31(1), pp. 137-149.

Transport and Road Research Laboratory. (1979), 'A Hazard Perception Test for Drivers', Leaflet, Transport and Road Research Laboratory, Crowthorne, UK.

Underwood, G. (2000, 1-2 June), 'In-depth Study of Young Novice Drivers', in *Proceedings of the Novice Driver Conference*, Bristol. Available at: http://www.dft.gov.uk.

Underwood, G., Chapman, P., Bowden, K. and Crundall, D. (2002), 'Visual search while driving: skill and awareness during inspection of the scene', Transportation Research Part F, Vol. 5, pp. 87-97.

Wasielewski, P. (1984), 'Speed as a Measure of Driver Risk: Observed Speeds Versus Driver and Vehicle Characteristics', *Accident Analysis and Prevention*, vol. 16(2), pp. 89-103.

Watts, G.R. and Quimby, A.R. (1979), 'Design and Validation of a Driving Simulator', Report LR 907. Transport and Road Research Laboratory, Crowthorne, UK.

Williams, A.F. and O'Neill, B. (1974), 'On-the-road Driving Records of Licensed Race Drivers', *Accident Analysis and Prevention*, vol. 6, pp. 263-270.

Chapter 10

Evaluating Interruption-Based Techniques using Embedded Measures of Driver Anticipation

Alastair M. McGowan and Simon P. Banbury

Introduction

> It's only when you look at an ant through a magnifying glass on a sunny day that you realize how often they burst into flames. (Harry Hill, 1992)

A crucial concern in research is the interdependence between an act of measuring and the data the measure produces. In other words, it is important that we avoid influencing a phenomenon while it is being measured. For example, a method that requires a participant to interact with the experimenter, or questionnaire material, may be more susceptible to these extraneous effects than one based on passive measurement, such as that afforded by embedded metrics. Many researchers have questioned the utility of interruption-based measures of situation awareness (SA) in terms of both the necessity for interrupting the simulation and the possibility of reorienting the participant (and therefore the task) to future SA probes. To this end, McKenna and Crick's (1994) driving hazard perception test was adapted to measure SA using embedded measures of anticipation alongside interruption-based SA probes. The interruption-based measures were manipulated so that the effects of task interruption could be differentiated from the effects of task reorientation in terms of their effects on the embedded measures of anticipation.

This chapter first describes earlier assessment of the hazard perception measure where SA strategies were trained, and then an experiment is reported in which both the interruption effects and reorientation effects of SA queries were investigated. The hazard perception method uses a version of the driving hazard perception test discussed by Horswill and McKenna (Chapter 9, this volume). This measure can be considered a hybrid between a performance measure and a measure of SA through its dependence on projection, or the output level, of SA. As hazard perception is a synonym for SA, so hazard perception anticipation is a likely overall measure of SA.

The hazard perception test provides a measure of anticipatory responding, and it is a high-fidelity non-invasive tool. This objective-performance method is sensitive to training (McKenna and Crick, 1993) and SA training (McGowan and

Banbury, 2004) and its resolution extends to the measurement of interruption effects and demand effects such as reorientation to the task. It provides an embedded measure with which to investigate SA metrics and theory, and may therefore also be useful as an SA assessment method. Embedded measures are known to be '...comparatively unbiased, non-intrusive and objective' (Pritchett and Hansman, 2000, p. 207) and because the hazard perception test provides a scale of anticipation it is therefore directly accessing the product of SA – projection.

Although the hazard perception test only offers a rating of the projection component of SA, this can be used to infer the overall level of SA. Furthermore, as an adjunct to other measures of SA the anticipation test seems to have sufficient resolution for it to provide an independent measure during assessment of SA metrics, and to be used as a tool for investigating SA theory. The most widely cited SA measure is the interruption-based Situation Awareness Global Assessment Technique (SAGAT; Endsley, 1995b, 2000). This method interrupts the operator of a simulator with queries about aspects of the task that are relevant to SA. Endsley (2000) has found no effects of interruption, and this raises the question of how SA – a complex phenomenon that is likely to involve a sophisticated pattern of processes – can be resistant to the effects of interruption. Interruption-based SA measures question the operator about aspects of a simulated task during pauses in performance, and when the query has ended the operator resumes the same task. Therefore it is important to discover the extent to which information imparted to the operator during the query affects their performance on the task, and whether there are effects on further query responses. An attempt to investigate this issue is reported using the hazard perception test as a dependent measure of anticipation.

Anticipation

Anticipation is an important factor in the skilled performance of dynamic tasks; accurate anticipatory decisions and actions increase performance. A model which can be used to explain anticipation is that of SA (Endsley, 1995a). Situation awareness describes a three-level process of perception supporting comprehension which enables a projection of events in space and time. This model describes a framework of processes leading to anticipation, and its use extends from an individual to team performance within a wide range of complex dynamic situations.

Anticipation is also a function of SA; a synonym for Endsley's (1995a) SA level three – projection. Therefore it would be useful to test a measure of anticipation for correlation with measures of SA. Although anticipation can be considered a performance variable, in the case of SA where anticipation is level three SA, a test of anticipation would also be a test of this level of SA. Furthermore, because anticipation is a macro-level product of SA it follows that a measure of anticipation should correlate with overall SA. If this is correct then cognitive factors underlying anticipation skills should resemble the same structure as those in SA (e.g., Endsley, 1995a, 2000). However, we argue that although anticipation has been studied for some time from a cognitive perspective so far there is little indication of such a pattern emerging.

Ericsson and Kintsch's (1995) theory of long term working memory (LT-WM) indicates that skilled performance is characterized by task related long-term memory structures made immediately available to short-term memory retrieval cues. LT-WM develops when its processes are required in order to subsume mental models and routines, implying a system which is involved in skilled performance (Chase and Ericsson, 1982). It follows that the management of changing goals and context-cue associations could be mediated by a process such as LT-WM. It has been argued by Altmann and Trafton (2002) that goal-directed cognition does not require support from specialized processes such as the goal stack that has been a standard model (Newell, 1990). The goal stack model states that the goals and sub-goals of a task drive the behavior in a sequential process. Altmann and Trafton (2002) argue that this is not necessary and that a simpler explanation also describes goal-directed behavior; the overall goal of the task is sufficient alone to invoke activation and associative priming related to the lowest level task elements. This generally accords with the idea of LT-WM in skilled performance, skilled mental simulation, and context driven anticipatory behavior.

Therefore the investigation of anticipation and how it relates to ecological and process oriented approaches is an imperative if we are to understand the cognitive factors leading to projection, and to SA. Early research indicated that anticipation could be classified into two types of behavior; apprehensiveness and searching (Lindner, 1938). Lindner also found that in some cases the resulting advanced action was not preceded by apprehensiveness or searching; there appeared to be a route directly to action. Engstroem, Kelso, and Holroyd (1996) argue that reaction and anticipation are two parts of one pattern recognition system. In an experiment where participants tried to match finger movement to a metronome in different patterns participants displayed a transition from reaction to anticipation and from anticipation to reaction. These transitions imply that dual processes may support anticipation.

It has also been suggested that context is important in anticipation. Kay and Poulton (1951) used a complex motor learning task to show how anticipation about the context in which recall will take place affects the way in which the participant integrates information about the task. Peterson, Brewer, and Bertucco (1963), found that early in a paired-associate word task participants had been using the context of the previous trial to guide probabilistic responses, suggesting that context is fundamental to anticipation. Cavallo, Brun Dei, Laya, and Neboit (1988) found that novice drivers use a rudimentary control process while negotiating curves and experienced drivers use a more sophisticated anticipation process based on general knowledge *about* curves. Expert anticipation therefore seems to involve using contextual knowledge in order to reduce uncertainty, and this involvement of context is consistent with the ecological approach, and with the idea that awareness is task specific (Patrick and James, Chapter 4 this volume).

It is also likely that mental simulation is involved in anticipation, reflecting Endsley's (1995a) model of SA as a process combining perception, comprehension, and projection. However, this simulation may be automatic.

Chaminade, Meary, Orliaguet, and Decety (2001) found that when a moving dot was used to show motion similar to mechanical movements, movements showing pointing action, and movements simulating handwriting patterns, anticipation of the mechanical motion activated the right intraparietal suculus and the left prefrontal cortex (relating to spatial awareness and prediction). However, the left frontal operculum and superior parietal lobule (motor areas) were activated when handwriting was being anticipated. This is interpreted by Chaminade et al. as showing that anticipation of motion in skilled tasks involves a degree of simulation in the motor areas; there appears to be a motor input to the calculation even when there is no action. This simulation may be a way in which experts can test a hypothesis about future action using their motor experience without the need for trial and error action, and such a process could be an important part of skilled spatial anticipation. This accords with Elsner and Hommel's (2001) two-phase model of action control, in which during early skill acquisition an association is learned between contingencies of motor patterns and spatial movements. Only after this level of skill has been achieved can the associations be used for higher level learning and goal-directed, and therefore contextually-driven, associations.

Hazard Perception

Recently research has focused on the role of skilled anticipation in real-world tasks such as the use of video in sports activity (Rowe and McKenna, 2001) and driving hazard perception. In the driving hazard perception task McKenna and Crick (1994) presented video scenes of dynamic events to which participants respond when they first see the hazard developing. An earlier hazard perception test was developed by Pelz and Krupat (1974), who presented video recorded from the forward view of a vehicle to which drivers responded by moving a lever when they perceived an increase in hazards. Pelz and Krupat's method was refined by Quimby and Watts (1981) and Quimby, Maycock, Carter, Dixon, and Wall (1986) who found that hazard perception test performance is related to driving record and accident involvement. It was also found that response times on the hazard perception test are positively correlated with experience (Quimby and Watts, 1981), and McKenna and Crick (1993) found that the hazard perception test differentiated between novice and expert drivers.

Rowe and McKenna (2001) sought to validate a video-based measure of anticipation skills in a sports setting. Video of tennis rallies was presented to participants from the point of view of a player. The participants were set the task of anticipating the onset of the opponent's final stroke. Their experiment showed that this method, like the hazard perception test, was also able to discriminate between experts and experienced players, and between levels of expertise and levels of experience. The results from the separate tasks of sports and driving indicate that the method of using video to present a monitoring task, to which participants respond by anticipating events, is likely to be a valid method of measuring anticipation levels.

The basis of the hazard perception method is that it presents video of road scenes filmed from the driver's position of a moving vehicle. The scenes include road hazards to which the participant responds with a button press when they perceive a hazard developing. With a button press the response can be utilized either categorically as a hit or a miss, or it can be subtracted from the moment of maximum hazard to give scale data representing anticipation. This feature makes the hazard perception test ideally suited to assessing task performance in terms of anticipation and SA. The development of the hazard perception test is described in detail by Horswill and McKenna (Chapter 9, this volume).

The hazard perception test has also been developed by McGowan and Banbury (2004). In this version additional data is collected by recording spatial data from mouse-clicks as well as the temporal data. This provides information about the response in relation to the parts of the image involved in the hazard. In driving hazard perception the events are based on a visually identifiable cue, and this identification of the target compared to the on-screen response location provides data that may be used in signal detection analyses. It is anticipated that the mouse response data may also be used together with eye tracking data to determine the degree of correspondence between the mouse-tracking of events and eye movements.

A further alteration to the method was to use a wide range of video collected for the purpose of police road patrols and then to select the hazardous events using a panel of expert drivers. This, along with the avoidance of staged events, enables a critical incident approach, ensuring that the hazards relate to real road skill criteria. In addition, the pre-selected video footage was provided by experienced police patrol drivers, whose policing duty while collecting the film was to actively monitor roads for hazardous events. This provided footage that ranged from safe clear roads to highly hazardous situations, and included both static and dynamic items. Therefore we propose that the relatively high internal consistency of the hazard perception based anticipation test (McGowan and Banbury, 2004) is due to a close matching of the items to the task. The instruction to the participants was to look for and respond to events that would cause them to take some action if they had been driving.

The expert drivers provided the earliest time from which the event is predictable, and its moment of maximum hazard, as well as identifying the visual cue related to that hazard on the screen. This defines the parameters of the anticipation latency period $t x -t0$, where 0 is the moment of maximum hazard and a high score represents earlier (i.e., better) anticipation, and the spatial frame x_1-x_2 and y_1-y_2. Figure 10.1 shows the location of these hidden spatial criteria for a correct response. The vehicle directly ahead is at its moment of maximum hazard, after decelerating significantly during the preceding three seconds. This frame follows the item as it moves within the screen. If the participant had clicked within the spatial frame during those three seconds then an anticipation score would be calculated ahead of the moment of maximum hazard. In this case the vehicle that has decelerated, and which the participant appears to be approaching rapidly, will now begin to accelerate and the distance between it and the participant's position will begin to increase, therefore the hazard diminishes. Other parts of the scene may have attracted a response and these responses would not be included as an anticipation score because they did not meet the experts' criteria for hazards. The events in which there is no correct response are scored as zero, thereby reducing the mean anticipation score as though a correct response had fallen on the moment of maximum hazard. In Figure 10.1 for example, the white vehicle to the right of the correct target is a police patrol car and this may have attracted an incorrect response. The same applies to any response outside the correct spatial frame.

Therefore the rationale for event selection may help to provide signal detection analyses; by the expert drivers' criteria the most relevant hazard for the task is always one which occurs within the spatial frame. This, combined with the finding that the anticipation scores do not correlate with the total number of mouse clicks (McGowan and Banbury, 2004) indicates that the method is not susceptible to changes in the overall response rate and that its resolution is likely to be high.

Figure 10.1 Hazard perception video scene at a moment of maximum hazard

Training Situation Awareness

The goal of this stage was to assess the level of resolution that can be achieved using the hazard perception test as an anticipation scale. McGowan and Banbury (2004) measured the effects of training drivers in hazard perception techniques, basing the SA training on three discrete categories designed to convey strategies at the SA levels of perception, comprehension, and projection, using the hazard perception test as a dependent measure of anticipation. The SA training conditions in this experiment used combinations of the SA training components, control training using the same basic materials but conveying a strategy for lateral distance perception, and a no-training control.

The SA training conditions were full SA, perception, comprehension, projection, and perception plus comprehension conditions. The latter condition was included in order to assess whether a cumulative effect of training the first two levels of Endsley's (1995a) model of SA would show effects using the hazard perception test as an independent measure of anticipation. The training material was designed by isolating the main structure of Endsley's SA model, with the aim of manipulating SA enhancing strategies. The material was therefore developed using Endsley's definition of SA in place of a task analysis. The SA model shows that it is clearly a cognitive or metacognitive skill. It therefore requires a capability to be trained in the category that Gagne (1985) defines as a cognitive strategy. The training material was aimed at the likely level of understanding of the participants, undergraduate psychology students. The training material consisted of four components. Firstly, a pre-training section in which the participants are invited to think about their driving experiences, how they had learned to drive, and whether they have continued to learn driving skills. Secondly, SA is introduced within the context of enhancing driving skills and road safety, giving the participants an opportunity to connect this with their own experiences. This pre-conceptual framework sets the context for the following training. Thirdly, the behavior and knowledge required for each of the three levels of SA are trained separately. Finally, the context of SA is returned to, and explored as a complete process. This SA training was used in the full SA condition. For the other four SA training conditions, perception, comprehension, projection, and perception plus comprehension, the material was divided into its constituent parts and delivered without reference to any of the concepts in the other conditions. For example, in the projection condition there was only reference to projection and anticipation, and in the comprehension condition the terms used were comprehension and understanding, while the perception condition used looking and perceiving.

The distance perception condition was a training control, and it used material that was as close as possible in format to that of the training condition. It used the same screen images as the training condition, but the task was not related to road awareness, or SA anticipation skills. This control training material was titled distance perception test and the exercises based around the images required the participants to estimate distances between objects in the videos laterally and longitudinally. The aim was not to train any skill related to SA but to encourage the participants to engage as fully as possible with the same pictures as those in the training condition, in a task that did not involve monitoring dynamic events over time. Arrows on the images indicated the items between which to estimate distance in either metric or imperial measurements. The remaining condition was a control training control, consisting of a screen break. This mixed design experiment was carried out with 214 participants.

It was predicted that following the training of SA strategies anticipation scores would improve significantly; McKenna and Crick (1993) found an effect of training hazard perception, equivalent to the difference found between novices and experts. Another prediction that can be derived from Endsley's (1995a) model of SA would be that training elements of SA relating to the three proposed SA component levels of (1) perception, (2) comprehension, and (3) projection, would show a pattern of differences as follows. Training perception alone would show some improvement in anticipation scores and then combining perception with comprehension would lead to a further improvement in anticipation scores. However, training comprehension and projection alone should not lead to anticipation scores higher than the level achieved by combined training of perception and comprehension, because each of the levels of SA is dependent on the preceding components.

The results of this experiment (Figure 10.2) suggest that the 120 items comprising the two counterbalanced videos have high homoegeniety (Cronbach's α = 0.72), and are therefore comparable to the original hazard perception test described by Horswill and McKenna (Chapter 9, this volume). The high reliability between the 120 items suggests that they are measuring the same effect. This is likely to be due to the consistency with which a panel of expert drivers was able to assess hazards together with any pre-selection that may have occurred due to experienced police drivers of the camera vehicle actively seeking hazards. A repeated measures analysis of variance showed a significant interaction between training conditions on pre and post training anticipation scores $[F(6,1)=3.54, MSE=16.62, p=0.002]$. Training also showed a significant effect $[F(1,212)=56.28, MSE=264.32, p=0.001]$. Tukey's HSD post hoc test showed that the training effect on anticipation scores of the SA group was significantly greater than both the no training group ($p<0.05$) and the distance perception training group ($p<0.05$). The training effect on anticipation scores of the perception group was significantly greater than both the no training group ($p<0.05$) and the distance perception training group ($p<0.05$). Finally, the training effect on anticipation scores of the perception plus comprehension group was significantly greater than the no training group ($p<0.05$). This shows that training SA and training its perception component seems to improve anticipation ability above both a no training control and a distance perception control. Training SA perception and comprehension components together seem to improve anticipation ability above that of a no training control but no more than that of the distance perception control.

To assess the degree to which these results may have been due to a difference in overall response rates an analysis of covariance was computed with participants' difference in response rates between pre and post intervention as a covariate. This showed no significant effect of change in response rate $[F(1,212)=1.27, MSE=3.30, p=0.263]$ on pre and post training measures between the training conditions. In addition, no significant correlation was found Pearson (r=-0.051, p=0.639) between the overall response rate per participant and the mean score per participant. Therefore it appears that the measure discriminates between overall response rates and relevant anticipation scores.

These results imply that the hazard perception test of anticipation can discriminate the effects of training hazard perception in the form of SA training. The level of resolution seems to measure the differences between training perception, comprehension, and projection. Interestingly, a prediction about these results that may have been drawn from Endsley's (1995a) model of SA is that training perception and comprehension together would show a greater effect than training either of them individually. This pattern does not appear in the results. In addition, it would also be predicted that training comprehension and projection alone would have been ineffective without training the foundation level of SA, perception. There is no indication of this pattern either. Therefore the further investigation of changes to the individual levels of SA, in ways other than through training, while using an independent anticipation measure may provide useful data with which to gain insight into the theoretical basis of SA.

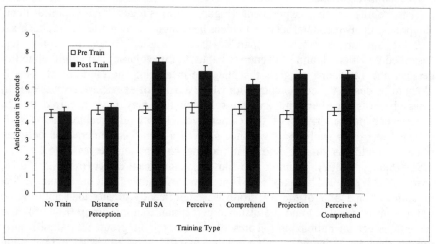

Figure 10.2 Effects of situation awareness training on hazard perception test anticipation scores

The results of the training experiment are encouraging, indicating that this method which has been a valuable tool for the investigation of cognitive factors in driving may prove a useful adjunct to current methods of SA measurement. The results are consistent with McKenna and Crick (1993), and it appears that the current method using expert rating of a priori events, together with a combined spatial identification and time filter on the responses is sufficient to distinguish effects of training, and sufficient to distinguish between overall responses and relevant anticipation responses. The effect of training SA was that the anticipation scores increased in all the conditions where SA strategies were provided, in comparison to a no-training control and a training condition that did not involve SA or hazard perception. This supports the proposition that hazard perception and anticipation are the same processes. Similar to McKenna and Crick's (1993) findings in hazard perception training, this experiment showed a large increase in scores after training of approximately two seconds greater anticipation than a baseline mean anticipation latency of less than five seconds.

It was also predicted that when training the components of SA separately there would be a certain pattern of changes in anticipation scores; comprehension and projection would show better scores than combined perception and comprehension, because comprehension and projection depend on input from earlier levels. This prediction was not supported, there was an improvement in anticipation in all the training conditions and the perception, projection, and perception plus comprehension conditions did not differ from each other. Although the semantics used to divide the training material into three conditions were very carefully controlled to ensure that the categories related to each of the three SA levels, it is accepted that this pattern of results may be due to the way in which the participants conceptualize the information. For example, to engage the participant in an exercise to increase their projection ability without any reference to perception may nevertheless still imply that they should first consider the current situation in order to develop a projection. Therefore it may be that by attempting to train one level of SA the other levels may be automatically expressed. However, this does not explain why the anticipation scores of the comprehension level were worse than in the other SA conditions.

Alternatively, if an automaticity account of hazard perception is invoked, then causing the participants to engage in the hazard perception task at any level may result in a full implementation of their hazard perception abilities. An interesting interpretation of the results is that the perception training condition anticipation scores increased as much as those in the full SA training condition. This may have been due to the particular task or its constituent items being more dependent upon perceiving relevant information and recognizing it as a possible – rather than likely – hazard. Such a process could support an anticipatory response before any synthesis (comprehension) or projection of the likely consequences had occurred. An automatic process is possible when consistent mapping (Shiffrin and Sneider, 1977) is conceptualized within a probabilistic account (Banbury, Croft, Macken, and Jones, Chapter 7, this volume) of anticipation. Therefore, we would contend that the results of this experiment tend to support the involvement of an automatic process in anticipation and hence SA also.

An explanation of the effect of training the components of SA separately may also be derived from the theory of LT-WM (Ericsson and Kintsch, 1995). The basis of this theory is that task-component cues are encoded in long-term memory structures which are then made available when an association is made during short-term memory processing. If a task has been encoded into cues that can activate an automatic skilled response when their need is recognized, then the most important part of a skilled task would be to monitor performance in order to compare it with cues. In other words, the bottom-up scanning for performance-related cues is likely to be the most important part of a hazard perception process and explains why the perception training shows the same effect as full SA training. It is likely that it is the correct use of attention in relation to the task that causes this apparently large increase in anticipation across the training conditions, an idea reflected by the importance of attentional processes in SA individual differences (Gugerty, Brooks, and Treadway, Chapter 11, this volume). Effective scanning and searching may account for a significant part of SA abilities.

The training effects are also consistent with Altmann and Trafton's (2002) goal activation model, in that the driving monitoring context of the anticipation task would be sufficient to increase performance if that context could be maintained in working memory, and the perception condition with its scanning strategy may have provided this context maintenance. The other two conditions may not have been sufficient, nor necessary, in order to maintain the context-goal trace. This is of particular relevance because context is known to be important in anticipation (Kay and Poulton, 1951; Peterson et al., 1963). The pattern of results, showing the apparent importance of the perception training condition, is also generally in line with Engstroem et al's (1996) argument that reaction and anticipation are part of the same system. From this point of view anticipation may be less dependent on real-time working memory synthesis and projection processing, and more dependent on pattern recognition between performance and long-term memory stores. The mechanism of LT-WM (Ericsson and Kintsch, 1995) explains how this could work. An alternative account of anticipation of motion (Elsner and Hommel, 2001) is also not dependent on working memory synthesis and projection, and is consistent with an automaticity account.

Therefore, although driving itself involves many complex factors (Groeger, 2000) its hazard perception component could be constrained to the mapping of probable threats and visual cues. The training experiment suggests that further development of the driving hazard perception task would be useful to investigate the effects of levels of expertise and experience on SA, and the use of full control driving simulation.

Effects of Interruption and Reorientation

Having shown that the hazard perception test can measure the effects of training manipulations and obtained results showing it to have a useful level of resolution, another experiment investigated interruption and reorientation effects. This experiment used an interruption-based SA measure alongside the hazard perception test while varying the content of the queries and involving conditions with and without interruption.

The most widely cited SA measure is the SA global assessment technique (SAGAT; Endsley, 1995b; 2000). This method aims to directly and objectively measure SA during a simulator task. The basis of this type of measure is that the system is frozen at random times and the operator is then queried using question items relating to aspects of SA derived from a requirements analysis (Endsley, 1995a; 2000). Another widely used method, the Situation Present Assessment Method (SPAM, described by Durso and Dattel, Chapter 8, this volume), probes the operator in a similar way to SAGAT but continues to present the context during the queries, and uses question acceptance and response latency times as a measure of SA, thereby aiming to ameliorate the effects of interruption. While there is no indication of interruption effects in interruption-based SA probes, (e.g., Endsley, 2000) the possibility remains for the interruption to affect cognitive processing (Sarter and Woods, 1991), and for the measure to be involved in circular reasoning about SA processes (Flach, 1995). Interruption is known to limit performance at task resumption across a broad range of domains (Miyata and Norman, 1986; McFarlane and Latorella, 2002) and the continuous and dynamic nature of SA would appear to make it vulnerable to disruption.

In another investigation of interruption-based methods, Snow and Reising (2000) found no negative effects using an interruption-based SA probe, but they noted that '...pilot comments also indicated that their attentional or cognitive behavior may have been altered by the fact that the questions were asked.' (Snow and Reising, 2000, p.52). This implies that asking questions can have an effect on task performance by highlighting the relevancy of the questions to the task. Such a reorientation could affect performance and help to offset the effects of the interruption. So far, there has been no investigation of interruption effects on SA using a non-interrupting and independent measure. Therefore, we set out to further investigate the effects of orienting and interruption, using the hazard perception test as an embedded measure of anticipation while manipulating the query content of an interruption-based SA probe.

In this experiment it was therefore predicted that because anticipation is a product of SA there would be a correlation between hazard perception test scores and SA probe scores (SA queries). Secondly, interruption effects are common in cognitive tasks, and because the hazard perception test task is complex and dynamic there would be a negative effect of query interruption on anticipation scores. Finally, as it is likely that the queries may reorient the operator to the task, it was predicted that the content of the queries would be associated with an improvement in anticipation scores.

The anticipation measure was combined with an interruption-based SA probe. The mixed design experiment was undertaken with 152 participants. A subset of 70 of the 120 items used in the training experiment were selected for use in an interruption-based format (i.e., these items were temporally separated by at least 3 seconds, and the maximum item latency was greater than 3 seconds to enable some encoding before interruption occurs). Of the 70 continuously presented hazard perception events in the video 32 were interrupted at evenly distributed points along the span of anticipation latency as defined by the driving instructors. These 32 interrupted events were balanced with the 38 non-interrupted events according to anticipation latency and other criteria (McGowan and Banbury, 2004). During each of the 32 pauses the probe inserted a query. There were four probe types: The SA Query condition presented multiple choice queries based on perception, comprehension, and projection (e.g., 'where will the car in the outside be in five seconds?'). The Orienting Query condition was not a test of SA but instead oriented the attention of participants to the same objects that the SA Query was probing (e.g., 'it is important to pay attention to vehicles in the outside lane that might move into your lane'). The Irrelevant Query condition used questions unrelated to road hazards but congruent with the video (e.g., 'would you buy a car based on its color?'). The dependent measure of the SA probe was the accuracy of participants' responses. The video-based hazard perception test task was presented using a Visual Basic program. This program ran an automated interruption-based SA probe which paused the video during the anticipation latency period of each of the 32 interrupted events and presented a query. The length of the interruption was 10 seconds; irrespective of when a response was made. Figure 10.3 represents the design of the experiment. The anticipation measure was taken at the 32 interrupted and 38 non-interrupted events in all four conditions. Therefore the interrupted events were compared between participants in four conditions and the interrupted events were compared with the non-interrupted events within participants. The No Query condition was not interrupted and provided a control comparison for both the interrupted and non-interrupted events.

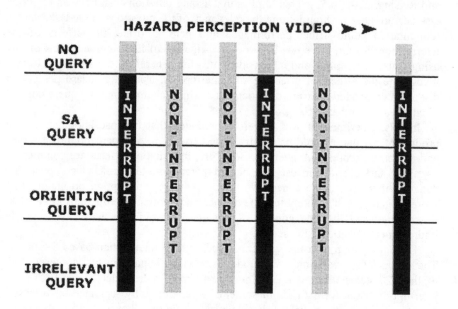

Figure 10.3 Interruption Design: Hazard events are depicted by the vertical bars, some of which (black bars) are interrupted by one of four Query types (depending on between-subjects condition)

The result of this experiment (Figure 10.4) was a highly significant positive correlation ($r=0.557$, $p=0.001$) between the SA probe accuracy scores in the SA queries condition and hazard perception test scores. There was a significant interaction between SA probe type and interruption on hazard perception test scores [$F(3,1)=2.972$, $p=0.032$]. There was a significant effect of interruption on the hazard perception test scores [$F(1)=21.41$, $p=0.001$] and a Tukey HSD post hoc test showed the hazard perception test scores of the non-queried events were significantly better than the queried events ($p<0.01$). There was also a significant effect of query type on hazard perception test scores [$F(3)=184.53$, $p=0.001$], and a Tukey HSD post hoc test showed that the hazard perception test scores of the query types all differed from each other ($p<0.01$). The anticipation scores of the probe types improved in the SA query and orienting query conditions but worsened in the irrelevant query condition.

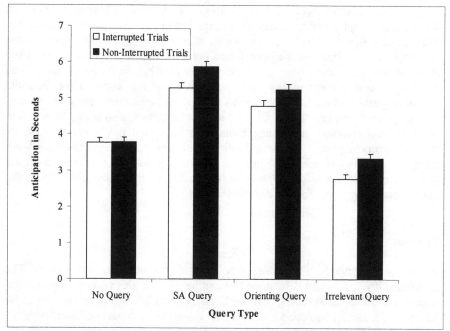

Figure 10.4 Effects of interruption and query type on anticipation scores

Firstly, these results supported the prediction that there would be a correlation between the hazard perception test and the interruption-based SA probe scores. This strongly suggests that the interruption-based SA probe and the hazard perception test measure the same factor.

Secondly, there was a negative effect of interruption on hazard perception test scores. This was expected in accordance with Miyata and Norman (1986) and McFarlane and Latorella (2002). Interruption almost always has a cost in terms of task resumption, and it would appear that the hazard perception test task is affected by the interruption-based SA probe. The hazard perception test scores of the non-interrupted trials in the irrelevant query condition worsened below those of the no-query condition. This may be because the negative interruption effect is encroaching on the non-interrupted intervening trials. Interruption is known to affect performance on task resumption, and some of the events follow each other immediately or within a few seconds. It is likely then that a deficit caused by interruption in one event may carry over into subsequent events if there is no opportunity for recovery. Given the influence of context in anticipation it can be seen that if interruption occurs serially then reestablishment of the context from the road environment would be impaired. Furthermore, this deficit in both the interrupted and non-interrupted trials of the irrelevant query condition, below that of the non-query control condition, indicates that where there is no reorientation to the task the effect of interruption is greatest. The inference is that a reorientation effect of the queries compensated for interruption effects.

Thirdly, the hazard perception test scores of interrupted trials improved in both the SA query and orienting query conditions but not in the irrelevant condition. This supports the idea that SA probes which interrupt the task to query the operator will also serve to reorient the operator to the task, and therefore also affect the measure that is produced from the same queries. In this case the SA probe queries and the hazard perception test task are measuring the same factor, and the reorienting effect of the SA probe seems to increase hazard perception test scores. This positive effect, like the negative effect of interruption, also seems to encroach on the non-interrupted intervening trials. It is important that a measure of SA should be unobtrusive, yet these findings indicate that interruption-based SA measures do affect performance through interruption and the reason such effects have not been found before appears to be because reorientation effects from the queries can compensate for the interruption effects.

Summary

A way to objectively assess SA is to measure its product, anticipation. The embedded driving hazard perception test can be used for this purpose, providing a measure of anticipation during real-world task of monitoring the driving scene for hazards. The hazard perception method was shown to be capable of measuring the effects of training SA and the effects of interruption. The resolution of the hazard perception test was shown when analyzing the effects of interruption and the effects of reorientation. Therefore, embedded measures of anticipation appear to offer a means of accurately assessing the performance of task-critical items while at the same time providing a scale representing SA. This makes the hazard perception test a useful objective and non-invasive adjunct to other methods of SA measurement. The interruption experiment suggests that interruption-based measures of SA do impact on performance. The results of the interruption-based measure experiment showed that hazard perception scores decrease when participants are interrupted, and that these effects carry over onto adjacent items. Conversely, while interruption was found to reduce hazard perception scores there also appears to be an effect of reorientation which increases hazard perception scores. This reorientation effect also seems to carry over onto adjacent items. This evidence indicates that we need to be careful how we interpret the results of SA assessments derived from interruption-based measures. Furthermore, the development of theory based on the results of studies using interruption-based measures also requires greater scrutiny due to the possibility that the measure may reorient the operator to the task and produce results that are dependent on the constructs used to generate the queries. In this way interruption-based measures could give an overly optimistic picture of SA, and may lead to circular reasoning about the structure of SA processes. It is anticipated that the use of anticipation measures such as the hazard perception test will provide an objective and high-fidelity means to assess the level of interruption and reorientation effects of interruption-based measures of SA, facilitating their adjustment for such effects, providing an objective comparison measure, and thereby further informing SA measurement and theory.

References

Altmann, E.M. and Trafton, J.G. (2002), 'Memory for Goals: An Activation-based Model', *Cognitive Science*, vol. 26(1), pp. 39-83.

Cavallo, V., Brun Dei, M., Laya, O. and Neboit, M. (1988), 'Perception and Anticipation in Negotiating Curves: The Role of Driving Experience', In A.G. Gale (ed.) *Vision in Vehicles II*. Oxford, England, North-Holland, pp. 365-374.

Chaminade, T., Meary, D., Orliaguet, J.P. and Decety, J. (2001), 'Is Perceptual Anticipation a Motor Simulation? A PET Study', *Neuroreport: For Rapid Communication of Neuroscience Research*, vol. 12(17), pp. 3669-3674.

Chase, W.G. and Ericsson, K.A. (1982), 'Skill and Working Memory.' In G.H. Bower (ed.) *The Psychology of Learning and Motivation*, vol. 16, Academic Press, New York, pp. 1-58.

Durso, F.T. (1999), 'Situation Awareness', In F.T. Durso (ed.), *Handbook of Applied Cognition*, John Wiley and Sons Ltd, New York.

Elsner, B. and Hommel, B. (2001), 'Effect Anticipation and Action Control', *Journal of Experimental Psychology: Human Perception and Performance*, vol. 27(1), pp. 229-240.

Endsley, M.R. (1995a), 'Toward a Theory of Situation Awareness', *Human Factors*, vol. 37 (1), pp. 32-64.

Endsley, M.R. (1995b), 'Measurement of Situation Awareness in Dynamic Systems', *Human Factors*, vol. 37(1), pp. 65-84.

Endsley, M.R. (2000), 'Direct Measurement of Situation Awareness: Validity and Use of SAGAT', In M.R. Endsley and D.J. Garland (eds), *Situation Awareness Analysis and Measurement*, Erlbaum, NJ.

Engstroem, D.A., Kelso, J.A.S. and Holroyd, T. (1996), 'Reaction-anticipation transitions in human perception-action patterns', *Human Movement Science*, vol. 15(6), pp. 809-832.

Ericsson, K.A. and Kintsch, W. (1995), 'Long-Term Working Memory', *Psychological Review*, vol. 102(2), pp. 211-245.

Flach, J.M. (1995), 'Situation Awareness: Proceed with Caution', *Human Factors*, vol. 37(1), pp. 149-157.

Gagne, R.M. (1985), '*The Conditions of Learning and Theory of Instruction*', CBS College Publishing, New York.

Groeger, J.A. (2000), '*Understanding Driving: Applying Cognitive Psychology to a Complex Everyday Task*', Psychology Press, Philadelphia, PA.

Hill, H. (1992), *Flies* [Live performance], Edinburgh Festival, Edinburgh.

Kay, H. and Poulton, E.C. (1951), 'Anticipation in Memorizing', *British Journal of Psychology*, Vol. 42, pp. 34-41.

Lindner, R.M. (1938), 'An Experimental Study of Anticipation', *American Journal of Psychology*, Vol. 51, pp. 253-260.

McFarlane, D.C. and Latorella, K.A. (2002), 'The Scope and Importance of Human Interruption in Human-Computer Interaction Design', *Human Computer Interaction*, vol. 17(1) pp. 1-61.

McGowan, A. and Banbury, S. (2004), 'Hazard Perception Test as a Measure of Situation Awareness Training', *Manuscript submitted for publication*.

McKenna, F.P. and Crick, J.L. (1993), 'A Cognitive Psychological Approach to Driver Training: The Use of Video Technology in Developing the Hazard Perception Skills of Novice Drivers', *Behavioral Research in Road Safety III*, TRL article pa3004/93, Crowthorne, UK.

McKenna, F.P. and Crick, J.L. (1994), '*Hazard Perception in Drivers: a Methodology for Testing and Training*', TRL report CR313, Crowthorne, Berkshire.

Miyata, Y. and Norman, D.A. (1986), 'Psychological Issues in Support of Multiple Activities', In D.A. Norman, and S.W. Draper (eds), *User Centered System Design*, Erlbaum, NJ, pp. 265-284.

Newell, A. (1990), '*Unified Theories of Cognition*', Harvard University Press, Cambridge, MA.

Pelz, D. and Krupat, E. (1974), 'Caution Profile and Driving Record of Undergraduate Males', *Accident Analysis and Prevention*, vol. 6(1), pp. 45-58.

Peterson, L.R., Brewer, C.L. and Bertucco, R.A. (1963), 'Guessing Strategy with the Anticipation Technique', *Journal of Experimental Psychology*, Vol. 65(3), pp. 258-264.

Pritchett, A.P. and Hansman, R.J. (2000), 'Use of Testable Responses for Performance-based Measurement of Situation Awareness', In M.R. Endsley, and D.J. Garland (eds), '*Situation Awareness Analysis and Measurement*', Erlbaum, NJ.

Quimby, A.R. and Watts, G.R. (1981), 'Human Factors and Driving Performance', TRL, Report 107, Crowthorne, Berkshire.

Quimby, A.R., Maycock, G., Carter, I.D., Dixon, R. and Wall, J.G. (1986), 'Perceptual Abilities of Accident Involved Drivers', TRL Report 27, Crowthorne, Berkshire.

Rowe, R.M. and F.P. McKenna (2001), 'Skilled Anticipation in Real-World Tasks: Measurement of Attentional Demands in the Domain of Tennis', *Journal of Experimental Psychology: Applied*, vol. 7(1), pp. 60-67.

Sarter, N.B. and Woods, D.D. (1991), 'Situation Awareness: A Critical but Ill-Defined Phenomenon', *The International Journal of Aviation Psychology*, vol. 1(1), pp. 45-57.

Shiffrin, R.M. and Sneider, W. (1977), 'Controlled and Automatic Human Information Processing: II. Perceptual Learning, Automatic Attending, and a General Theory', *Psychological Review*, vol. 84, pp. 127-190.

Snow, M.P and Reising, J.M. (2000), 'Comparison of two Situation Awareness Metrics: SAGAT and SA-SWORD', *Proceedings of the IEA / HFES 2000 Congress*.

Chapter 11

Individual Differences in Situation Awareness for Transportation Tasks

Leo Gugerty, Johnell O. Brooks and Craig A. Treadaway

Introduction

This chapter focuses on individual differences in operators' ability to perform transportation tasks, such as driving and flying. Most people are familiar with these individual differences from performing the common task of driving a motor vehicle. Individual differences in driving ability can be seen by looking at driving style (e.g., speeding) and the outcomes of driving performance (e.g., crash involvement). Matthews et al. (1998) have documented individual differences in attitudes towards driving and driving style. Also, individual differences in driving performance are associated with group differences, such as gender and age. Thus, fatal crashes by United States drivers in 2002 were highest for males and younger drivers; and males and younger drivers were more likely to be speeding at the time of these crashes (NHTSA, 2004). Similarly, middle-aged aircraft pilots (age 35-55) in the United States had lower accident rates from 1988-1997 than younger or older pilots (Broach, Joseph and Schroeder, 2003).

Individual and group differences in performing transportation tasks are probably due to many factors, including experience-level, perceptual and cognitive abilities, and attitudes towards the task. For example, researchers have shown that crash involvement among older drivers is related to perceptual and cognitive abilities such as the ability to divide visual attention over a wide area, as measured by the Useful Field of View (UFOV) test (Ball, Owsley, Sloane, Roenker and Bruni, 1993; Owsley, Ball, Sloane, Roenker and Bruni, 1991). Matthews et al., (1998) found that aggressive attitudes towards driving were related to driving behaviors such as speeding and overtaking, cautious attitudes were related to behaviors such as driving slowly and poor steering, and attitudes favoring alertness were related to faster reactions to hazards. This study also showed that older drivers and women had more cautious attitudes towards driving. In Chapter 8 of this volume, Durso and Dattel suggest that differences in the ability to maintain situation awareness during an air-traffic control task are related to differences in intelligence, short-term memory ability, and personality (i.e., conscientiousness).

This chapter focuses on how individual differences in perceptual and cognitive abilities are related to the performance of specific transportation subtasks and to the ability to maintain situation awareness while performing transportation tasks.

We define situation awareness as a high-level attentional skill that involves updating and maintaining knowledge of a real-time situation that is changing unpredictably.

We take a componential approach to our investigation, first dividing the complex task of operating a vehicle into three main subtasks: navigation, maneuvering (e.g., awareness and avoidance of local hazards), and tracking (e.g., heading and speed control). We then look for cognitive correlates of the ability to maintain situation awareness during two of these subtasks, navigation and maneuvering.

Cognitive Correlates of Navigation Ability

We first point out that maintaining navigation-related knowledge while performing a transportation task does involve situation awareness. During a transportation task, operators must update and maintain knowledge of their own location, the relative location of route landmarks, and environmental constraints on navigation (e.g., traffic, weather). Much of this navigation information is changing during the task, and some of it is changing unpredictably. Thus, navigation knowledge is one part of the knowledge comprising a driver's or pilot's situation awareness, as this term has been defined above.

Researchers have identified individual differences in navigation ability that are associated with factors such as gender and age. Lawton, Charleston and Zieles (1996) found that males were better than females at accurately pointing to their initial position after following a complex path. Sholl, Acacio, Makar and Leon (2000) found that males were better than females at pointing to cardinal directions after being oriented to the cardinal directions and then following a complex path. Dabbs, Chang, Strong and Milun (1998) found what could be called differences in navigational style among age and gender groups, with females and younger people tending to use egocentric terms (e.g., right-left) and landmarks when giving route directions and males and older people using cardinal directions and Euclidian distances (e.g., two miles) more frequently.

The task of navigation can also be broken down into subtasks. Researchers have suggested that the three main subtasks of navigation are: identifying one's current location, identifying the locations of other objects in the environment (e.g., a destination), and finding a route from the current location to the destination (Wickens, 1999). In this chapter, we used a cardinal-direction judgment task as a criterion task representing some aspects of navigational performance. In this task, participants determined their current heading from a map and then judged the bearing between two objects seen in a three-dimensional (3D) perspective display. For example, they determined whether an object in the 3D display was north, south, east, or west of another object.

This cardinal-direction task taps into the navigational subtask of identifying the locations of environmental objects. Gugerty and Brooks (2001, in press) have shown that the task is a difficult one that requires participants to coordinate information in a map and a forward, 3D view, and to coordinate information in the egocentric, body-centered reference frame with information in the exocentric, world-centered reference frame. No single task can represent the entire range of navigational tasks. However, we feel that the cardinal-direction task represents some of the complexity of navigation in its requirement to coordinate 3D and map information, as well as egocentric and exocentric information. Thus, we use it in this investigation as a criterion task that partially represents the overall task of navigation, with the expectation that later research will focus on tasks representing other aspects of navigation.

Navigation Study 1

In our first navigation study, we investigated cognitive correlates of the cardinal direction task using primarily the Armed Services Vocational Aptitude Battery (ASVAB), the selection and classification test given to members of the United States' military. The ASVAB was designed for selection and classification, and has been validated in terms of predicting performance during training and on the job (Carretta, 1999). However, the ASVAB also measures some basic aspects of knowledge and cognitive ability, in particular: fluid intelligence, crystallized intelligence, clerical speed, and technical knowledge (Roberts et al, 2000; Tirre and Field, 2002). The ASVAB does not focus on spatial ability, as the only ASVAB test with significant spatial content is the Mechanical Comprehension test. Thus, we supplemented the ASVAB battery with a mental rotation test. In the data analysis, we created ability factors from the ASVAB tests and the mental-rotation test and regressed the criterion variable from the cardinal-direction test on these factors.

For half of the participants in the current study (those in the enhanced feedback condition that is described below) some of the cardinal-direction performance data were presented in Gugerty and Brooks (in press). However, the ASVAB data and the regression analysis of cognitive correlates were not included in that study.

Participants The 207 participants, 150 males and 57 females, were United States Air Force recruits at Lackland Air Force Base, TX, from 17 to 27 years old ($M =$ 19.0), who participated in the study as part of their basic training. The number of aircraft flight hours for the group ranged from 0 to 200 ($M = 2.5$, median $= 0$). ASVAB scores were available for 202 of these participants, so the reported analyses are based on this sample size.

Materials and Tasks The cardinal direction task was presented using personal computers with CRT monitors. On each trial, participants pressed the '5' key on the number pad and then saw a problem with the map (Figure 11.1) on the right and the forward (camera) display on the left (Figure 11.2). The map showed the location and heading of an aircraft, and the forward display showed the 3D, ground view that would be seen from a camera facing forward from the aircraft. The actual displays were in color and were 10.2 cm on a side. Below these displays the text message 'Which parking lot has vehicles in it?' was shown. Participants used the number pad on the right of the keyboard to respond, pressing 8 for north, 2 for south, 6 for east and 4 for west. After responding, the text message below the camera and map displays was replaced with feedback. Half of the participants ($n = 103$) received simple feedback displayed for one second including: 1) the camera and map displays; 2) 'CORRECT' or 'WRONG'; and 3) the response time, e.g., '4.59 seconds.' Half of the participants ($n = 104$) received enhanced feedback which remained visible until the participant pressed 5 to start the next trial, including: 1) the camera and map displays; 2) 'CORRECT' or 'WRONG'; 3) the response time; 4) the participant's answer; and 5) if an incorrect response was made, the correct answer. This feedback manipulation was designed to test whether the more extensive feedback would improve performance.

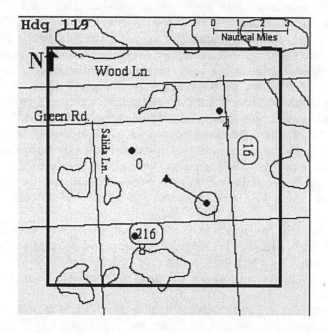

Figure 11.1 Map display used in the cardinal direction task. The triangle icon shows the aircraft. The line from the aircraft shows the heading of a camera mounted on the front of the aircraft and always facing forward. The circle shows where the camera is pointing on the ground. The aircraft is facing southeast in this map. All maps were north-up maps

Twelve camera (i.e., aircraft) headings were presented across trials, from 0° (facing north) to 330°, in 30° increments. For each heading, there were problems with the vehicles in each of the four parking lots (north, south, east and west). This yielded 48 trials in a block; these were presented in random order for every block. All of the map displays showed north as up. The instructions for the cardinal direction task were presented via computer. These clearly explained that the camera display always pointed ahead of the aircraft and showed the forward view from the aircraft, and explained how to read the information about the aircraft and camera heading on the map.

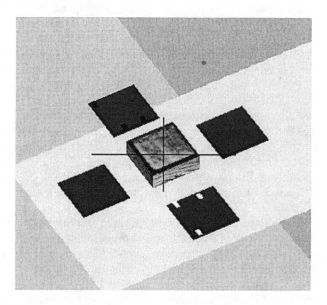

Figure 11.2 Three-dimensional display showing the forward view from the aircraft, as used in the cardinal direction task. Given the map in Figure 10.1, the parking lot with the three white cars is west of the central building

On each trial of the mental rotation task, participants saw a map indicating a target and an aircraft location and heading (using the same icons as in the cardinal direction task), and then used the keyboard to indicate the direction (right or left) in which the aircraft had to turn to reach the target. The heading of the aircraft varied randomly across trials in 45° increments. This task is described as a mental rotation task because response times normally decrease as the aircraft heading changes from facing the top of the map to the bottom. Shepard and Hurwitz (1984) and Aretz (1991) have used this task and have interpreted the response-time decrease with heading change as evidence that participants use mental rotation to perform this task. Although the mental rotation task used the same map as the cardinal-direction task, there are a number of differences between these two tasks. The mental rotation task is much easier. Individual differences are reflected mainly in response time in the mental rotation task, and in accuracy in the cardinal direction task. Finally, the mental rotation task uses no 3D display and involves egocentric but no exocentric information; so it does not require coordination of map and 3D information, or of egocentric and exocentric information, as the cardinal direction task does.

Participants' ASVAB scores were also obtained for this study. The ASVAB is a multiple-aptitude battery consisting of 10 tests: General Science, Auto and Shop Information, Mechanical Comprehension, Electronics Information, Arithmetic Reasoning, Mathematics Knowledge, Word Knowledge, Paragraph Comprehension, Numerical Operations, and Coding Speed.

Procedure Participants were tested in groups of about 50, but worked at individual workstations. Participants completed 144 trials in the mental-rotation task, which took about 20 minutes. Following this, participants read the instructions and performed 144 trials in the cardinal direction task, which took about 25 minutes.

Results and Discussion The enhanced feedback seemed to provide little benefit in performing the cardinal direction task, since participants with the enhanced feedback (M = 55.9 per cent correct, SE = 2.3) were slightly less accurate than those with the simple feedback (M = 57.7 per cent, SE = 2.5). These means were not significantly different, $t(205)$ = 0.52, p = .60, and the SE of the difference between the means, 3.5, was small. Thus, the two feedback groups were collapsed for further analysis.

Figure 10.3 shows the distribution of accuracy scores on the cardinal direction task for the entire sample. The difficulty of the cardinal direction task is suggested by its low mean accuracy of 57 per cent correct (SE = 0.3). However, a number of participants found the task particularly difficult, as is shown by the bimodal distribution of task accuracy scores displayed in Figure 11.3. This bimodal distribution, coupled with the distribution's negative kurtosis of -1.5, indicate wide individual differences within this group for this task. This bimodal distribution is not driven by gender differences, as both the males and females distributions are bimodal when plotted separately. The response time distribution for the cardinal direction task was unimodal and positively skewed, with a mean of 6.6 s (SE = 0.3) and a median of 5.8 s.

In order to create a criterion variable for the regression analysis describing overall performance on the cardinal direction task, we created a single variable by first correcting the accuracy scores for chance (i.e., proportion above chance = (proportion correct − 0.25) x (1.0 / 0.75)) and then calculating the number of above-chance responses per minute (i.e., proportion above chance / average response time). This combined variable, which will be called 'accuracy per minute', gives a more complete picture of overall performance on the cardinal direction than the separate accuracy and response time variables because it reflects participants' speed-accuracy tradeoffs. The accuracy-per-minute variable was distributed normally and showed no outliers.

To obtain factors describing participants' cognitive abilities from the ASVAB, we used three factor analytic studies of the ASVAB with sample sizes of 346, 349, and 6751 from Roberts et al. (2000) and Tirre and Field (2002). These studies all found four ability factors represented in the ASVAB: fluid intelligence, i.e., abstract and logical reasoning (based on Arithmetic Reasoning, Mathematics Knowledge); crystallized intelligence, i.e., reasoning and knowledge based on acculturation and learning (Word Knowledge, Paragraph Comprehension, General

Science); clerical speed, i.e., speed at completing simple visual and cognitive tasks (Numerical Operations, Coding Speed); and technical knowledge (Auto and Shop Information, Mechanical Comprehension, Electronics Information). Fluid and crystallized intelligence and clerical speed are basic factors in Carroll's (1993) influential model of the structure of human cognitive abilities. The fourth ASVAB factor, technical knowledge, is described in the model of Roberts et al., (2000) as a sub-factor related to Carroll's broad-visual factor, which focuses on spatial ability. Thus, the four ASVAB ability factors can be mapped onto well-accepted factors representing human cognitive abilities.

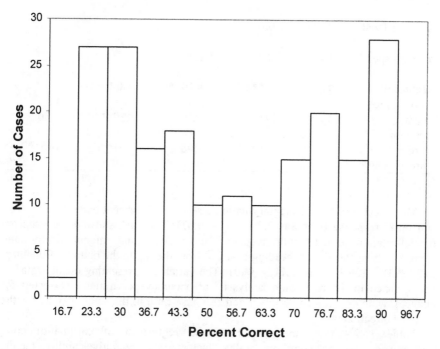

Figure 11.3 Distribution of accuracy scores for the cardinal direction task

Although the ASVAB technical knowledge factor can be related to visual-spatial ability, only one of the three tests comprising this factor, Mechanical Comprehension, has significant spatial content. To improve our ability to assess the contribution of spatial abilities to cardinal-direction performance, we added the mental-rotation test, another visual-spatial test, to our set of predictors. The correlation within our sample between mental-rotation performance and the technical-knowledge factor, .29, was not high enough to combine these into a single spatial factor. Therefore, we used fluid intelligence, crystallized intelligence, clerical speed, technical knowledge, and mental-rotation ability as predictors of cardinal-direction performance. Standardized ASVAB scores for individual tests were combined into factor scores using unit weighting. Table 11.1 shows the intercorrelations of these factors and their correlation with cardinal-direction performance. The factors were weakly inter-correlated, with a median r of .21 and a maximum r of .37.

Table 11.1 Factor intercorrelations and correlations with cardinal-direction performance

	g fluid	g crystallized	clerical speed	technical knowledge	mental rotation
g fluid	1.00				
g crystallized	.29**	1.00			
clerical speed	.18**	-.01	1.00		
technical knowledge	.24**	.37**	-.19**	1.00	
mental rotation	.32**	.17*	.09	.29**	1.00
cardinal direction task	.37**	.35**	-.08	.51**	.46**

*$p < .05$, **$p < .01$

Mean accuracy for the mental rotation task was 95 per cent correct ($SE = 0.6$), and mean response time was 2.2 s ($SE = 0.07$). This task showed the expected mental-rotation effect, with response time decreasing monotonically and significantly as the aircraft heading changed from the top to the bottom of the map, $F(7,1393) = 129.3$, $MSE = .71$, $p < .01$. The variable representing mental-rotation performance in the regression analysis was accuracy per minute (corrected for chance), which combined accuracy and response time in the same way as for the cardinal direction task.

Table 11.2 shows the results of the regression of cardinal-direction performance on the cognitive ability factors. The cognitive ability factors accounted for 42 per cent of the variance in cardinal-direction performance. The two factors theoretically related to visual-spatial cognition, mental rotation and technical knowledge were the two best predictors. Each of these factors accounted for 7.6 per cent of the unique variance in cardinal-direction performance. Within the technical knowledge factor, the Mechanical Comprehension test had the highest correlation with cardinal direction performance, .52; as would be expected from the relatively high spatial content of this test. Fluid and crystallized intelligence also accounted for significant variance in cardinal-direction performance.

To summarize, the bimodal distribution of accuracy scores on the cardinal direction task suggests wide individual differences in this particular navigation task, with a large group of 106 participants performing poorly on the task (35 per cent correct) and another large group of 101 doing fairly well (80 per cent). These wide individual differences have been replicated in another sample of Air Force recruits (Gugerty and Brooks, 2001). The cognitive correlates analysis presented here suggests that performance on the cardinal direction task depends primarily on spatial abilities and knowledge, including mental-rotation ability and knowledge of mechanical relationships. Abstract reasoning ability (fluid intelligence) and acculturated learning (crystallized intelligence) also contribute to performance in this navigation task.

Table 11.2 Regression of cardinal direction performance on ASVAB and mental-rotation predictor variables ($N = 202$)

Variable	Beta	Part r	Partial r	t
g fluid	.173	.20	.16	2.84**
g crystallized	.134	.16	.12	2.23*
clerical speed	-.076	-.09	-.07	-1.32
technical knowledge	.317	.34	.27	5.04**
mental rotation	.300	.34	.28	5.04**

Note: $R = .65$, $R_{adj} = .63$, $F(5, 196) = 28.0$, $p < .01$
*$p < .05$, **$p < .01$

Navigation Study 2

Our second navigation study was motivated by the wide individual differences we found in performing the cardinal direction task in the first study and in Gugerty and Brooks (2001), and by the fact that some participants have considerable difficulty with this task. In Gugerty and Brooks (in press), novice navigators' accuracy on the cardinal direction task was distributed bimodally, with poor-performing novices averaging 25 per cent correct and better-performing novices 75 per cent, while expert pilots' accuracy was about 95 per cent. Given this poor performance by many participants, we felt that understanding the strategies used on this difficult task would help in developing training and interfaces to improve performance on the task. Therefore, our second navigation study focused on understanding and describing the strategies used by experienced navigators on the cardinal direction task. Many problems that arise during navigation are difficult enough to require the application of problem-solving strategies. An example is when our forward heading is towards the bottom of a map and we must decide whether to turn right or left in order to reach a specific destination shown on the map. In this situation, many people use a strategy of rotating the map so their heading is towards the top of the map. When people cannot physically rotate the map in this situation, evidence suggests that they use a mental rotation strategy (Aretz, 1991; Hintzman, O'Dell, and Arndt, 1981; Shepard and Hurwitz, 1984).

By focusing on strategies, our second study used a very different method than the first study. Instead of using a psychometric approach to identify basic cognitive abilities associated with poor and good cardinal direction performance, we collected verbal protocols in order to describe participants' strategies in detail. Verbal protocols are a useful source of information about cognitive processes and have been used successfully to investigate cognitive processes during navigation tasks (e.g., Gunzelmann and Anderson, 2002).

The current study examines the strategies used by experienced navigators, licensed pilots. Their strategies will be compared to less-experienced navigators, college students, which were reported in Gugerty and Brooks (2001). The 12 less-experienced navigators (seven female) completed two blocks of the cardinal direction task before giving verbal protocols on their third block. After each cardinal direction trial, they received the simple feedback described in the previous navigation study (correctness and response time for one second).

Participants Ten male licensed pilots were paid for their participation. They ranged in age from 20 to 44 years ($M = 31.7$), in flight hours from 80 to 3300 ($M = 1055$), and in flying experience from two to 24 years ($M = 7.6$).

Materials and Tasks The cardinal direction task was the same as in the Navigation Study 1 (described above). After each cardinal direction trial, participants received the enhanced feedback described in the Study 1 (correctness, participant's answer, correct answer, and response time until the participant initiates the next trial). The cardinal direction task data were collected as part of a larger three-day study on the effects of uncoupled motion on cognitive and psychomotor performance. The data for these tasks are not presented in this chapter and are not described further.

Procedure On Day One of the study, participants were trained on all tasks and completed three blocks of 48 trials of the cardinal direction task. On Day Two, the participants completed six blocks; each block was separated by a minimum of one hour. The participants returned for two additional blocks on Day Three and verbal protocols were given during the second of the two blocks. Thus, the participants completed 11 blocks: three on Day One, six on Day Two, and two on Day Three.

Results and Discussion The strategies inferred from the verbal protocols are presented below for the ten pilots in the current study and for six of the 12 less-experienced navigators in Gugerty and Brooks (2001). One less-experienced navigator asked to stop participating during the first two blocks of the cardinal direction task, prior to the protocol, and was dropped. Five other less-experience navigators repeatedly requested help from the experimenter on the cardinal direction task while giving the protocol, and did receive some help. The protocols of these participants did not reflect their own strategies, and so were not analyzed.

The ten pilots averaged 83 per cent correct ($SE = 3.6$) for the cardinal direction problems during their first two blocks. In comparison, the six less-experienced navigators whose protocols were analyzed averaged 74 per cent correct ($SE = 11.1$) during their first two blocks; and the five less-experienced navigators whose protocols were not analyzed averaged 55 per cent correct ($SE = 8.4$). Thus, the less-experienced navigators whose protocols were analyzed represented the better performing members of the novice group.

To analyze the verbal protocol data, we developed definitions of strategies for the cardinal direction task that were based on analysis of the novices' verbal protocols from Gugerty and Brooks (2001), and from some of the pilots in the current study. Two experimenters used the strategy definitions to code the protocols for each problem for three participants. The inter-rater agreement for the coding was 95.8 per cent. One experimenter coded the remainder of the protocols.

The strategy definitions will be described using the cardinal direction problem shown in Figures 11.1 and 11.2, in which the aircraft is headed to the southeast and the vehicles are in the west parking lot. One version of the mental rotation strategy involved rotating the aircraft heading on the map counter-clockwise until it reached north, and then rotating the 3D scene by the same amount in the opposite direction. Then the canonical exocentric reference frame – in which north, east, south, and west correspond to top, right, bottom, and left, respectively – is applied to the rotated 3D scene. While this strategy simulates rotating the aircraft, another mental rotation strategy simulates rotating the environment. However, there was usually not enough detail in the protocols to differentiate between these two types of mental rotation. Therefore, they were both treated as examples of the same strategy. Since these strategies involved looking first at the map to determine how much to rotate, we called them *map-first mental rotation*.

Participants sometimes used a noticeably different kind of mental rotation, where they first looked at the 3D view. In this strategy, the first step is to use the 3D view and the egocentric reference frame to describe the bearing from the building to the parking lot with the cars (e.g., for Figure 11.2, before the building and to the right). The second step integrates the egocentric description of this bearing into the reference frame of the map. This is done by imagining where the parking lot with the cars would be located on the map if one were viewing the target building from the perspective of the aircraft. This step seems to involve mental rotation of the 3D configuration until it is aligned with the aircraft heading on the map. The third step involves using the map to determine the exocentric bearing from the target building to the imagined lot with the cars, and reporting this bearing. We called this strategy *3D-first mental rotation*.

Another potential strategy was the *heading referencing* strategy. Step one is to identify the aircraft heading from the map and give it a verbal label (e.g., for Figure 11.1, southeast). Step two involves coordinating exocentric and egocentric reference frames by mentally aligning the current heading (expressed as an exocentric-cardinal direction) with egocentric forward in the 3D view (e.g., towards the top of the 3D view is southeast). Once the current exocentric heading has been integrated into the 3D view, it acts as a reference direction and other directions (or bearings) in the 3D view can be inferred from it. Thus, in the third step, the bearings of the parking lot(s) at the top of the 3D scene (e.g., the south and east lots) are identified. Finally, in the fourth step, the bearings of other lots (e.g., the north and west lots) are inferred based on the bearings identified in Step 3 and the spatial arrangement of the objects in the 3D view. We called this strategy *heading referencing* because it involves using an exocentric heading as a reference within the 3D view.

Each of the ten pilots was very consistent in the primary strategies he used during the protocol session. The participants showed four patterns of strategy use, as shown in Table 11.3. One pilot used map-first mental rotation, two pilots used the 3D-first mental rotation, and six pilots used heading referencing. The other pattern, shown by the remaining participant, involved mixed use of heading referencing and map-first mental rotation. In this pattern, when the aircraft was facing a cardinal direction, heading referencing was always used and mental rotation was never used. Conversely, when the aircraft was not facing a cardinal direction, map-first mental rotation was always used and heading referencing was never used. Thus, the strategy was systematically based on the heading of the aircraft.

For comparison, Table 11.3 also shows the primary strategies used by six of the less-experienced navigators, college students, in Gugerty and Brooks (2001). As mentioned earlier, because participants who had trouble on the cardinal direction task tended to give unusable protocols, the strategy data for the less-experienced group represents the better performing members of this group. Like the pilots, each of these less-experienced navigators was also very consistent in his or her primary strategy use. One novices used map-first mental rotation, two used heading referencing, and three used a mixture of heading referencing and map-first mental rotation in the same manner as the pilot described above.

Table 11.3 The number and percentage of pilots ($N = 10$) and less-experienced navigators ($N=6$) using particular strategies as their primary strategy on the cardinal direction task

	Pilots		Less-experienced	
	Number	%	Number	%
Map-1st mental rotation	1	10	1	17
3D-1st mental rotation	2	20	0	0
Heading referencing	6	60	2	33
Heading referencing and map-1st mental rotation	1	10	3	50

Table 11.3 does not show strong differences in the strategies used by the pilots and the less-experienced navigators. To some extent, this may be due to the fact that the less-experienced group contained only the better performing members of that group. About 70 per cent of the pilots and 83 per cent of the less-experienced navigators showed consistent use of the heading referencing strategy on some or all cardinal direction problems. About 30 per cent of the pilots and 17 per cent of the novices used only strategies involving mental rotation.

Our protocol evidence for the heading referencing strategy suggests a new strategy that involves minimal mental rotation. This finding is important because most prior research on strategy use in navigation tasks other than cardinal direction judgments has concluded that mental rotation is the primary strategy used for these tasks (Aretz 1991; Hintzman et al., 1981; Shepard and Hurwitz, 1984). The verbal protocol data from this study and from Gugerty and Brooks (2001) provides evidence that navigators of varying experience levels commonly use a strategy for making cardinal-direction judgments that minimizes the use of mental rotation. To complicate this picture somewhat, in Gugerty and Brooks (in press), we found evidence that one of the four steps of heading referencing seems to involve some use of mental rotation. However, heading referencing is a more analytic strategy than the purer mental rotation strategies described here (i.e., map first and 3D first mental rotation), and it avoids some of the difficulties involved in rotating the relatively complex images used in this cardinal direction task.

Cognitive Correlates of Maneuvering Ability

Another important transportation sub-task is that of maneuvering, or hazard avoidance. That is, while achieving the goal of navigating to a destination, operators have the goal of maneuvering their vehicle around local hazards. In order to avoid hazards, operators must perceive and comprehend them. Thus, maintaining situation awareness for these local hazards is an important part of maneuvering.

In a preliminary study in the aviation domain, Sohn and Doane (2000) measured situation awareness by a task in which 40 pilots saw two successive views of an instrument panel and judged whether a certain maneuver would be completed in the next five seconds. For student pilots, the accuracy in performing this situation-awareness task was predicted by working memory (WM) capacity but not by long-term-WM skill. For experienced pilots, accuracy was predicted by long-term-WM skill, but not WM capacity. Sohn and Doane's test of long-term-WM skill assessed domain-specific piloting knowledge by measuring the extent to which participants' memory for meaningful flight-instrument configurations exceeded their memory for impossible instrument configurations. By assessing the learning of domain knowledge, the long-term-WM measure seems similar to the measures of acculturated learning captured in measures of crystallized intelligence.

In previous research in our laboratory, we have measured situation awareness related to maneuvering in a driving-related task (Gugerty, 1997). In this task, participants watch animated 3D scenarios simulating highway situations on a personal computer (PC) monitor. The scenarios are shown from the driver's point of view, and the participant must use the forward view and the rear-view and two side-view mirrors to keep track of traffic vehicles ahead and behind (see Figure 11.4). The participant also must respond to hazards (e.g., cars about to hit his or her car), and must respond to queries about the locations of traffic vehicles, especially of vehicles that have been driving in a hazardous manner. This driving task thus assesses a variety of abilities related to maintaining situation awareness during driving, including the ability to identify traffic-vehicle locations and more distant hazards, and to detect and respond to nearby hazards while monitoring a changing roadway scenario.

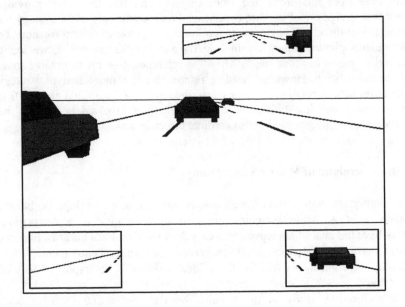

Figure 11.4 Scene from PC-driving task showing forward view and three mirrors from the driver's viewpoint. The actual scenes were moving and in color

In a prior series of studies on individual differences in maneuvering ability, we investigated whether situation awareness ability as measured by this PC-based driving task was correlated with general cognitive ability as measured by the ASVAB, with WM capacity as measured by the Cognitive Abilities Measurement test, and with tests of visual and temporal-processing abilities (Gugerty and Tirre, 2000). Some have suggested that WM capacity is virtually identical to general cognitive ability (Kyllonen and Christal, 1990). In Study 1 of this series (with N = 34), correlations between general ability/WM and the driving-task measures of hazard detection and recalling vehicle locations ranged from .39 to .76 (median = .67). In Study 3 of the series, overall ability to maintain situation awareness, as measured by the driving task, was significantly related to general cognitive ability (as measured by a multi-limb tracking test requiring timesharing ability), to dynamic and static visual ability, and to temporal-processing ability (as measured by tests of duration discrimination and rate extrapolation).

Driving is an attention demanding task, and the task of maneuvering during driving probably requires drivers to use the two major types of attentional processes, serial, top-down processes and parallel, stimulus-driven processes. Serial processes used in driving likely include scanning a complex and changing environment and focusing briefly on important information. The parallel processes probably include attentional capture by peripheral stimuli such as abruptly looming vehicles. It seems likely that these serial and parallel attentional abilities are related to the ability to maintain situation awareness during driving. Washburn, Putney, Tirre, Gugerty and Robbins (1997) provided evidence for this using the PC-based driving task described above. They tested 135 US Air Force recruits on the driving task and a battery of 16 attentional tests. Ability to maintain situation awareness in the driving task was predicted by attentional tests measuring the ability to scan and focus attention and to use peripheral cues to direct scanning, and also by psychomotor ability.

A test that assesses parallel attentional processes is the UFOV test. As mentioned earlier, the UFOV test has been shown to predict crash involvement in older drivers (Ball et al., 1993; Owsley et al., 1991). This test consist of three sub-tests that measure the ability to perform a central visual identification task, to divide attention between a central and a peripheral task, and to select a peripheral stimuli from among distracters. In the rest of this section, we describe a study in which we assessed whether performance on the UFOV test was correlated with ability to maintain situation awareness in the PC-based driving task. This study was previously reported in Chaparro, Groff, Tabor, Sifrit and Gugerty (1999).

Maneuvering Study 1

Participants The 25 participants were licensed drivers ranging in age from 18 to 82.

Materials and Tasks The PC-based driving task described above was used to assess a variety of aspects of situation awareness. In this task, participants view animated scenarios lasting from 18 to 35 seconds. The scenarios are shown from the driver's point of view, and participants can use the forward view and three mirrors to monitor traffic vehicles in front of and behind their simulated vehicle (see Figure 11.4). During each scenario, participants' knowledge of the situation was assessed using a number of probes, which required the participant to recall vehicle locations; identify traffic vehicles that were driving hazardously but not immediately threatening the driver (e.g., tailgating); and detect and respond to nearby hazards that did threaten the driver. Participants did not actively control their vehicle's speed or lane position (i.e., simulated autopilot). They used the computer mouse to indicate vehicle locations and identify distant hazards on a top-down view of the road that appeared at the end of some scenarios. They used the keyboard arrow keys (↑ for accelerate, ↓ for decelerate, → for right, and ← for left) to indicate how they would avoid nearby hazards. Participants completed 60 scenarios.

The UFOV test used was the UFOV ® Visual Attention Analyzer, Model 3000 (Visual Resources, Inc., Bowling Green, KY). This version of the UFOV consists of three tests presented on a PC. In the first test, on each trial the participant identifies one of two shapes presented briefly at a central fixation point. In the second test, the participant sees the central shape along with a peripheral stimuli at one of 24 locations defined by eight radial directions and three retinal eccentricities (10, 20 and 30°) and responds by identifying the central shape and the radial direction of the peripheral stimuli. In the third test, the participant sees the same stimuli as in the second test, except that the peripheral stimuli are shown among distracter shapes, and makes the same responses. For each test, the participant sees a number of briefly presented stimulus trials (less than 240 ms), and the presentation duration is decreased over trials until the participant's accuracy falls below 75 per cent correct for the focused attention test and 50 per cent correct for the other two tests. Participants' score for a test is based on the minimum stimulus duration shown and accuracy at localizing the peripheral stimuli.

Results and Discussion Owsley et al. (1991) describe the first UFOV test, with only a central stimuli, as assessing information processing speed, and the second test, with central and peripheral stimuli, as assessing divided attention. The third UFOV test, with central and peripheral targets among distracters, has been described as assessing selective attention and the ability to ignore visual distracters (Owsley et al., 1991; Chaparro et al., 1999). The second and third UFOV tests are likely to involve parallel attentional processes since they both involve attentional search for a peripheral target that is distinguished from nearby objects by a single feature. This type of search has been shown to involve parallel processing (Treisman and Gelade, 1980).

The analysis focused on the correlations between variables assessing situation awareness in the PC-based driving task and the second and third UFOV tests, the tests assessing divided and selective attention. These correlations are shown in Table 11.4.

Table 11.4 Correlations (*r*) between situation awareness variables measured in the PC driving task and attentional variables measured in the UFOV

Situation awareness variable	UVOF divided attention performance	UFOV selective attention performance
Crash avoidance	.52**	.83**
Hazard detection	.33**	.66**
Location recall	.71**	.62**

**p < .01

The first driving-task variable, crash avoidance, assessed the frequency with which participants could use the arrow keys to avoid nearby hazards in a timely manner without hitting other traffic vehicles. This variable showed high correlations with the divided and selective attention tests. The second driving-task variable measured participants' ability to detect nearby hazards. Hazard detection ability was correlated with the UFOV's divided and selective attention scores. The third driving-task variable was the ability to recall car locations accurately; this was also highly correlated with divided and selective attention. Thus, situation awareness skills needed for maneuvering while driving, including knowledge of traffic car locations and the ability to detect and avoid hazards, were strongly related to attentional abilities related to dividing attention between central and peripheral stimuli (the divided attention test), and to selecting critical information from among distracters (the selective attention test). As mentioned previously, both of these attentional sub-processes likely involve parallel processing.

Conclusions

In this chapter, we investigated the cognitive abilities and strategies associated with individual differences in two transportation sub-tasks, navigation and maneuvering to avoid local hazards. We focused on one particular navigation task, that of making cardinal direction judgments. During navigation, cardinal direction judgments are sometimes used to identify where a navigator is headed or to identify the relative direction (or bearing) between two objects in the environment. The cardinal direction task we used revealed wide individual differences in a population of US Air Force recruits, with about half the participants averaging 35 per cent correct and the other half averaging 80 per cent correct. Our first navigation study used a psychometric approach and found that overall performance on the cardinal direction task was best predicted by visual-spatial abilities and knowledge, including mental rotation ability and technical knowledge. In addition, fluid and crystallized intelligence, that is, abstract reasoning ability and acculturated learning, were predictive of cardinal direction performance.

In our second navigation study, we used a very different methodology – verbal protocol analysis – to investigate the detailed strategies used by less-experienced and more-experienced navigators. In accordance with the first study's finding regarding the importance of mental rotation ability, participants in the second study reported regular use of mental rotation strategies. Two different kinds of mental rotation strategy were identified for the cardinal direction task, which differed in terms of whether the map or the 3D view was attended first. However, the protocols of both novice and expert navigators suggested that another strategy was used more frequently than mental rotation. This strategy, heading referencing, is a more analytic, step-by-step strategy than mental rotation. It involves identifying the navigator's heading from the map and then using this heading as a reference in the 3D view.

It should be noted that these two studies are only the beginning of understanding the cognitive correlates of navigation, as a complex task such as this cannot be adequately represented by a single navigational subtask. Further research on this topic should concentrate on assessing a variety of navigational subtasks, in addition to cardinal direction judgments. One candidate is the path integration task studied by many researchers (e.g., Lawton et al., 1996; Sholl et al., 2000), in which participants are led along a turning path from a start point and then, without the use of landmarks, point back to the start point. Another is the localization task, in which a navigator matches two or more reference points on a map and in the 3D view and then infers his or her position and heading on the map.

In addition to a better variety of criterion tasks representing navigation abilities, future cognitive-correlates research in this area should include better coverage of some of the basic cognitive abilities identified by Carroll (1993). Roberts et al., (2000) point out that the ASVAB tests do not optimally represent abilities such as fluid intelligence, as they are too quantitatively oriented, and visual-spatial ability. Given the findings from our cognitive-correlates study, the most important predictor tests for future studies would be visual-spatial tests, including spatially-loaded tests of technical knowledge. Given the predictive ability of fluid intelligence in our cognitive-correlates study and the inferential reasoning needed in the heading referencing strategy from the protocol study, tests of abstract and inferential reasoning should also be included in a battery intended to predict cardinal-direction judgment ability.

We also investigated the cognitive correlates of the ability to maintain situation awareness during another transportation subtask, maneuvering. Our maneuvering studies used a PC-based driving task that assessed a variety of aspects of situation awareness. Our prior study on individual differences in situation awareness during maneuvering (Gugerty and Tirre, 2000) suggested that general-cognitive ability and WM capacity are good predictors of situation awareness, as are visual and temporal processing abilities. The importance of WM capacity in this study fits with the findings of Durso and Dattel (Chapter 8, this volume), who found that situation awareness during an air traffic control task was related to short-term-memory ability, and with the findings of Sohn and Doane (2000), who found that novice pilots' situation awareness was best predicted by WM capacity. However, Sohn and Doane also found that for expert pilots, WM capacity was not a good predictor of situation awareness. Instead, long-term-WM skill was the best predictor. Sohn and Doane's findings fit with Ackerman's (1988, 1992) theory of how predictors of complex-task performance change as expertise develops. In this theory, WM capacity is expected to predict well during the early phases of learning a complex task. However, in later stages, other abilities such as perceptual speed and psychomotor ability are better predictors. Ackerman's theory, and Sohn and Doane's findings, suggest that researchers investigating cognitive correlates should be careful to study participants with varying levels of expertise.

The other cognitive abilities we found to be correlated with situation awareness during maneuvering involved attentional abilities. In Washburn et al. (1997), serial attentional processes such as scanning and focusing were predictive of performance on the driving situation awareness test. In the maneuvering study presented in detail here (from Chaparro et al., 1999), we documented that parallel attentional processes measured by the UFOV test – including divided and selective attention – are highly correlated with driving situation awareness. These findings fit with the common perception that driving is an attention demanding skill. They also fit with the conclusion by Horswill and McKenna (Chapter 9, this volume) that hazard perception during driving is an attention demanding task even for, and perhaps especially for, experienced drivers. The current findings also begin to identify some of the particular attentional abilities needed for this complex task.

Acknowledgments

We wish to thank Bill Tirre and DeWayne Moore for helpful comments regarding the data analyses in this article.

References

Ackerman, P.L. (1988), 'Determinants of Individual Differences During Skill Acquisition: Cognitive Abilities and Information Processing', *Journal of Experimental Psychology: General*, vol. 117, pp. 288-318.

Ackerman, P.L. (1992), 'Predicting Individual Differences in Complex Skill Acquisition: Dynamics of Ability Determinants', *Journal of Applied Psychology*, vol. 77(5), pp. 598-614.

Aretz, A. (1991), 'The Design of Electronic Map Displays', *Human Factors*, vol. 33, pp. 85-101.

Ball, K., Owsley, C., Sloane, M.E., Roenker, D.L. and Bruni, J.R. (1993), 'Visual Attention Problems as a Predictor of Vehicle Crashes in Older Adults', *Investigative Ophthalmology and Visual Science*, vol. 34, pp. 3110-3123.

Broach, D., Joseph, K.M. and Schroeder, D.J. (2003), 'Pilot Age and Accident Rates Report 4 : An Analysis of Professional ATP and Commercial Pilot Accident Rates by Age', US Federal Aviation Administration, Civil Aeronautical Institute, Oklahoma City, Oklahoma, USA.

Carretta, T.R (1999), 'Determinants of US Air Force Enlisted Air Traffic Controller Success', *Proceedings of the Tenth International Symposium on Aviation Psychology*, pp. 581-586.

Carroll, J.B. (1993), *Human Cognitive Abilities: A Survey of Factor Analytic Studies*, Cambridge University Press, New York.

Chaparro, A., Groff, L., Tabor, K., Sifrit, K. and Gugerty, L. (1999), 'Maintaining Situational Awareness: The Role of Visual Attention'. In *Proceedings of the 43rd Annual Meeting of the Human Factors and Ergonomics Society* (pp. 1343-1347), Human Factors and Ergonomics Society, Santa Monica, CA.

Dabbs, J., Chang, E-L., Strong, R. and Milun, R. (1998), 'Spatial Ability, Navigation Strategy, and Geographic Knowledge Among Men and Women', *Evolution and Human Behavior*, vol. 19, pp. 89-98.

Gugerty, L.J. (1997), 'Situation Awareness during Driving: Explicit and Implicit Knowledge in Dynamic Spatial Memory', *Journal of Experimental Psychology: Applied*, vol. 3, 42-66.

Gugerty L. and Brooks, J. (2001), 'Seeing where you are heading: Integrating Environmental and Egocentric Reference Frames in Cardinal Direction Judgments', *Journal of Experimental Psychology: Applied*, vol. 7, pp. 251-266.

Gugerty, L. and Brooks, J. (in press), 'Reference Frame Misalignment and Cardinal Direction Judgments: Group Differences and Strategies', *Journal of Experimental Psychology: Applied.*

Gugerty, L. and Tirre, W. (2000), 'Individual Differences in Situation Awareness'. In D. Garland and M. Endsley (eds), *Situation Awareness Analysis and Measurement*, Erlbaum, Mahwah, NJ, pp. 249-276.

Gunzelmann, G. and Anderson, J. (2002), 'Strategic Differences in the Coordination of Different Views of Space', In *Proceedings of the 24th Annual Meeting of the Cognitive Science Society*, Cognitive Science Society, Cincinnati, OH.

Hintzman, D., O'Dell, C. and Arndt, D. (1981), 'Orientation in Cognitive Maps', *Cognitive Psychology*, vol. 13, pp. 149-206.

Kyllonen, P. and Christal, R. (1990), 'Reasoning Ability is (little more than) Working Memory Capacity?', *Intelligence*, vol. 14, pp. 398-433.

Lawton, C.A., Charleston, S.I, Zieles, A.S. (1996), 'Individual and Gender-Related Differences in Indoor Wayfinding', *Environment and Behavior*, vol. 28(2), pp. 204-219.

Matthews, G., Dorn, L., Hoyes, T.W., Davies, D.R., Glendon, A.I. and Taylor, R.G. (1998), 'Driver Stress and Performance on a Driving Simulator', *Human Factors*, vol. 40(1), pp. 136-149.

National Highway Traffic Safety Administration. (2004), 'Traffic Safety Facts 2002: Overview', Washington, D.C.: US Department of Transportation. Available: www-nrd.nhtsa.dot.gov/pdf/nrd-30/NCSA/TSF2002/2002ovrfacts.pdf

Owsley, C., Ball, K., Sloane, M., Roenker, D and Bruni, J.R. (1991), 'Visual/Cognitive Correlates of Vehicle Accidents in Older Drivers', *Psychology and Aging*, vol. 6(3), pp. 403-415.

Roberts, R.D., Goff, G.N., Anjoul, F., Kyllonen, P.C., Pallier, G. and Stankov, L. (2000), 'The Armed Services Vocational Aptitude Battery (ASVAB) Little more than Acculturated Learning (Gc)!?', *Learning and Individual Differences*, vol. 12, pp. 81-103.

Sohn, Y.W. and Doane, S.M. (October, 2000), 'Predicting Individual Differences in Situation Awareness: The Role of Working Memory Capacity and Memory Skill'. In *Proceedings of the Human Performance, Situation Awareness and Automation Conference*, Savannah, GA, pp. 220-225.

Sholl, M.J., Acacio, J.C., Makar, R.O, and Leon, C. (2000), 'The Relation of Sex and Sense of Direction to Spatial Orientation in an Unfamiliar Environment', *Journal of Experimental Psychology*, vol. 20, pp. 17-28.

Shepard, R. and Hurwitz, S. (1984), 'Upward Direction, Mental Rotation, and Discrimination of Left and Right Turns on Maps', *Cognition*, vol. 18, pp. 161-193.

Tirre, W.C, and Field, K.A. (2002), 'Structural Models of Abilities Measured by the Ball Aptitude Battery', *Educational and Psychological Measurement*, vol. 62, pp. 830-856.

Treisman, A.M. and Gelade, G. (1980), 'A Feature-Integration Theory of Attention', *Cognitive Psychology*, vol. 12, pp. 97-136.

Washburn, D.A., Putney, R.T., Tirre, W., Gugerty, L. and Robbins, R.D. (October, 1997), 'Individual Differences in Attention and Situation Awareness in Driving'. Poster presented at the University of Minnesota Conference on the Future of Learning and Individual Differences Research, Minneapolis, MN.

Wickens, C. (1999), 'Frames of Reference for Navigation', in D. Gopher and A. Koriat (eds), *Attention and Performance XVII, Cognitive Regulation of Performance: Interaction of Theory and Application*, MIT Press, Cambridge, MA.

Chapter 12

Effects of Situation Awareness Training on Flight Crew Performance

Hans-Jürgen Hörmann, Simon P. Banbury, Helen J. Dudfield,
Mike Lodge and Henning Soll

Introduction

In modern aircraft operation flight crews are dealing with increasingly complex environmental conditions, which impose amplified cognitive demands on the pilots. Technological developments such as highly automated cockpit systems, along with an increasing traffic density and flying under marginal weather conditions, have influenced the job profile of flight crewmembers. In addition to more technical competencies like traditional stick-and-rudder skills, so-called non-technical skills of pilots like decision-making, crew-cooperation, leadership, or general systems management have become more important (Flin et al., 2003). For a long time, pilot training programs have proved effective for the acquisition of the necessary technical knowledge and manual flying skills, which are certainly still essential factors for the safe handling of an aircraft. However, the training of non-technical skills lacks sufficient empirical evidence through systematic research studies that demonstrate its impact on pilot performance. This chapter is focused on the evaluation of new training concepts for training Situation Awareness (SA) and Threat Management (TM) of pilots, two concepts which have received considerable attention in the available literature of the past ten or fifteen years (e.g., Endsley, 1995; Helmreich, Klinect and Wilhelm, 1999). A European research consortium, called ESSAI (Enhanced Safety through Situation Awareness Integration in training) has recently developed a comprehensive training solution for SA and TM, which went through a full-scale evaluation program in a training experiment (ESSAI, 2003).

It is currently widely believed that flight crewmembers' competencies related to SA and TM play an important role in the prevention of accidents and incidents, such as controlled flight into terrain (CFIT), taxiway/runway incursions, or traffic conflictions (Endsley, 1995; O'Leary, 2003). According to the understanding of the ESSAI consortium, SA and TM have to go hand in hand to keep a given flight operation well within its safety envelope. While a certain threat potential is part of any flight, higher SA can contribute to general threat avoidance and reduction of related risks. SA is commonly defined as the 'perception of the elements in the environment within a volume of time and space, the comprehension of their meaning, and the projection of their status in the near future' (Endsley, 1995, pp. 36). Endsley stresses furthermore that the safe operation of an aircraft is highly dependent on the correct assessment of a number of situational factors, including the aircraft's operational parameters, external conditions, navigational information and other aircraft. Therefore, crewmembers with good SA will certainly do better in anticipating and recognizing operational threats in good time. Nevertheless, maximum SA is not always required as it can cost mental resources needed for other vital tasks. According to the model of *Situation Control* (SC) (Amalberti, Masson, Merritt, and Pariés, 2000; Amalberti, in press), it is rather *the dynamic balance of mental resources between action and reflection in accordance with the situational demands,* which keeps the operation away from the 'danger zone'. However, threats are events, not fully under control of the crew. They increase operational complexity and can embrace additional risk (e.g., terrain, weather, system malfunctions, automation anomalies, cabin events or external errors). As threats occur without the direct influence of the flight crew and without proximity to any present activities they can be accompanied by 'effects of surprise' creating temporary uncertainty of action. For a moment the crew will be driven 'behind the aircraft' and needs to update its mental picture for the event to fully restore SA. TM, defined as: *the effective management of complexity and risk in order to prevent or recover from (crew) errors and to increase safety,* has become a popular concept in aviation through the work of the Human Factors Research Project Group within their model of Threat and Error Management (Helmreich et al., 1999). ESSAI produced a tailored training solution built around the three concepts of SA, SC, and TM.

Safety issues related to SA and TM have also been addressed in aircraft design. Many technological improvements in the past decades have contributed significantly to increased aviation safety. However, the reduction of accident rates in the last two decades is rather modest compared to figures of the 1960s and 70s where airline flying became three to four times safer in line with improved aircraft structures, better jet engines and the introduction of Ground Proximity Warning Systems (GPWS). A justifiable question is how more reliable aircraft systems and advanced on-board information and support systems in current and future aircraft have already or will reduce human error in flight operation. O'Leary (2003) has argued that accelerated technological development has been accompanied by increased information integration, digitalization and complexity of the modern flight deck, which might have reduced error potential, but eventually at the cost of transparency and reduced human activity on the flight deck. This is certainly not a new discussion, as Wiener and Curry (1980) made a case already decades ago that automation benefits are primarily visible in increased systems reliability and economy while the most adequate balance between human capabilities and automation support deserves more consideration in research and development. These concerns have triggered a series of human-factors oriented design studies in the US, for example on the crew-centeredness of fly-by-wire concepts (Kelly, Graeber and Fadden, 1992; Graeber and Weener, 1997) or on error rates with electronic checklists (Boorman, 2000). In case of new equipment generally training efforts will be required for the related changes of flight procedures and the system interfaces with the flight crew.

Review of Training Needs

Within the European Commission's 5th Framework program the project called ESSAI (Enhanced Safety through Situation Awareness Integration in training) investigated the role of crewmembers' competencies concerning SA and TM as well as the trainability of these factors. The goal of this project was to provide practicable training methods and media to improve SA and TM of crews on modern aircraft flight decks as well as to validate the effectiveness of these methods in a high fidelity simulation environment. Part of the solution was found in integrating SA and TM into regular training footprints of the airlines in order to:

- provide strategies for adequate Situation Control during flight operations;
- minimize (or recover from) loss of Situation Awareness that could result in hazardous situations;
- provide strategies for effective Threat Management during normal and non-normal flight operations.

In 1997 the US White House Commission put up an ambitious goal for aviation safety: to reduce the fatal accident rate by the factor five by 2008. Ongoing industry and FAA Safer Skies initiatives were combined into the Commercial Aviation Safety Team (CAST). With an accident data-driven, consensus-based, integrated safety strategy, CAST has generated 46 Safety Enhancements and ten research and development projects and studies which received global recognition. With the strong support of different international aviation authorities and aviation organizations as well as the aircraft manufacturers, CAST's safety priorities have influenced worldwide safety initiatives.

In order to identify the most suitable training needs and objectives for SA and TM, ESSAI systematically reviewed the standard problem statements formulated by the Joint Safety Analysis Teams (JSAT). JSAT had been chartered by CAST to review the most common types of aviation accidents of which three could be considered in ESSAI during the time of the project execution: Controlled Flight into Terrain (CFIT), Approach and Landing Accidents (ALA), Loss of Control (LOC). The problem statements described the most dominant contributing factors of each of the analyzed accidents and subsequently specified the most effective intervention strategies that would mitigate the related safety problems. As the problem statements incorporate a large number of non-human factors issues, the first step of the study consisted of selecting the most relevant for the ESSAI Project. This aggregated list contained 300 problem statements. To further de-select problem statements that were not relevant to the project, safety analysts, aviation experts and flight crewmembers of current generation aircraft types were asked to weight the statements according to the levels of SA and TM they would contain. The main issues identified from the JSAT problem statements relating to SA and TM were (ESSAI, 2001):

- crew preoccupation and complacency with modern flight deck automation;
- crews' lack of system situation awareness and mode awareness;
- crews' inappropriate level of automation skill and knowledge;
- crews' inability to handle information being displayed to them and to respond to warnings or alerts;
- crews' workload and workload increase under time constraint;
- inadequate crew training and procedures;
- inappropriate crew co-ordination.

Based on the same list of problem statements one recent JSAT report by Russell and Pardee arrived at a list of 10 highly significant topics requiring immediate activity of aviation safety teams. Situation Awareness and related matters are represented prominently in this list (Russell and Pardee, 2001, p. 8-9):

- Air Traffic Services – impact on pilot workload;
- automation – usage;
- crew failure to follow Standard Operating Procedures (SOPs);
- design – warnings and alerts;
- crew resources management;
- Situation Awareness – airplane energy state (e.g., speed, power setting);
- Situation Awareness – airplane system status assessment;
- Situation Awareness – decision making process;
- training – program design;
- training – conduct.

Taking into account these recommendations, the ESSAI project pursued with a systematic approach the development of its training program for SA and TM. After the initial literature review of factors affecting SA and TM in various operational scenarios like those described above (ESSAI, 2001), several workshops and cognitive interviews were held with flight crews from different airlines and different levels of experience. Through in-depth exploration of crew elicited self-reports of authentic safety critical events, it was possible to determine the criticality and trainability of a comprehensive set of underlying factors and processes. The most relevant and trainable factors were then organized into a competency structure for SA and TM as shown in Figures 12.1 and 12.2 (ESSAI, 2002a).

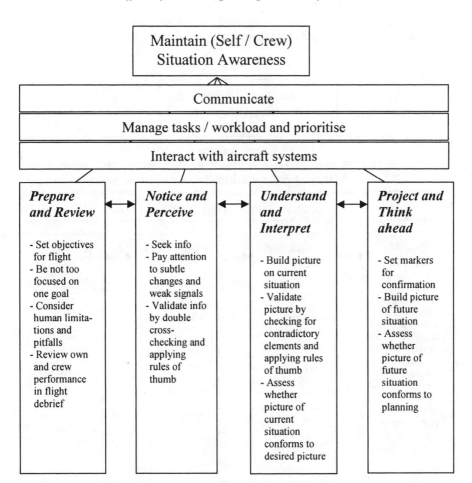

Figure 12.1 ESSAI competency structure for Situation Awareness

According to this analysis of training needs, potential objectives and key learning points were defined for example as:

- to think ahead into the future phases of the flight in order to maintain SA, instead of simply noticing events;
- to avoid threats instead of waiting to trap or mitigate their potential consequences (TM);
- to become vigilant for 'weak signals', indicative of potential threats including loss of SA, both ones own and in others, and to act on that knowledge;
- to re-evaluate critically decisions by seeking data to disprove rather than confirm the current course of action;

- to balance workload (mental as well as manual) between crew-members effectively, depending on the situation (Situation Control).

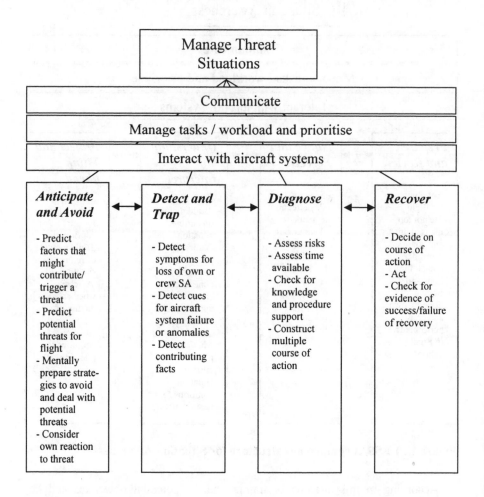

Figure 12. 2 ESSAI competency structure for Threat Management

Following the development of the ESSAI training solution its real effectiveness was evaluated in an experimental study. According to Endsley and Robertson (2000), relatively little research activities have been spent on evaluating the outcomes of similar training methods with aircrews. This is a surprising fact, as training evaluation is the only way to ensure that training programs will have the desired effects and are worth the investment for an organization. The ESSAI project adopted a multi-level approach to the evaluation of its suggested training solution, which is described in more detail in Banbury, Dudfield, Hörmann and

Soll (under review) and in the published project report (ESSAI, 2003). For the measurement of crew performance before and after the training, the results reported here focus on objective performance measures and observational data in realistic flight scenarios rather than on self-reports or questionnaires. Before the empirical study is discussed, the training modules are described in detail in the following section.

Training Design and Media Considerations

The development of the different modules of the ESSAI training solution is described in detail in a project report (ESSAI, 2002b). It has been the basic idea of ESSAI to include a variety of available training media and methods, to accommodate for individually different learning styles of the trainees. In this way relevant skills, behavior patterns, and attitudes, as illustrated in the competency structure, will be addressed in multiple ways throughout the training. Based on incident/accident case examples attention is raised for basic principles and behavioral strategies of SA and TM. In a so-called Low-tech skill-transfer exercise opportunity is given to try out these strategies in a tactical decision scenario. With the practice and self-experience during this exercise, trainees can already build up the first traces of newly acquired skills in a very economic way. These skills will then be transferred into specifically designed flight scenarios in a high-fidelity simulation environment. Afterwards the trained instructor gives feedback based on his behavior observations to further reinforce appropriate skill development. The complete ESSAI training solution consists mainly of four components: 1) a computer based introduction (DVD), 2) a Tactical Decision Game ('Low-tech exercise'), 3) two LOFT-type simulator sessions, and 4) a Train-the-trainer package. Provided that trained trainers are available, one regular training day is needed to conduct the whole course.

Computer-based Introduction (DVD)

Though CBT technology is widely in use by aviation training organizations as the norm for efficient training in the technical arena, the training of non-technical skills such as TM and related cognitive activities such as SA has thus far been treated largely as a classroom-based exercise facilitated by instructors with varying degrees of expertise. The effective use of a computer-based training aid in this field requires a carefully structured approach to the content and methodology of the program. Then this medium will have the advantages of clear standardization, multi-lingual soundtracks, interactivity, and ability to customize modules and subroutines. The ESSAI-DVD is aiming at delivering the required knowledge in a compact, interactive manner, enabling the participants to understand clearly the methodology, concepts and vocabulary that they would encounter during the ESSAI simulator training phase. A great deal of work for the realization of the

DVD was accomplished by the British Airways Human Factors department. In 50 minutes the following points are covered:

- introduction;
- planning;
- operating;
- reviewing;
- summary;
- key learning points.

The Low-tech exercise described in the next section was intended to assist the transfer of these concepts into applied basic skills before further higher level skill development would commence in the simulator.

Low-tech Exercise – A Tactical Decision Game

A short Tactical Decision Game that is undertaken by two interacting pilots in a limited space formed the basis for the Low-tech exercise. It provides the possibility of exploring and reinforcing the messages of the DVD under facilitation of the trainer. The decision to add a Tactical Decision Game for initial skill acquisition to the ESSAI training solution was made for both pragmatic and pedagogical reasons. Such tools are known to be cost-effective and relatively simple to design and execute. The opportunity to reinforce the messages of the DVD could be taken in a low-key environment whilst also demanding some degree of physical activity prior to the simulator phase. The game is embedded in a dynamic, multi-tasking flight coordination scenario with distributed roles for two crewmembers. It requires mainly communication, planning, anticipation, management of ambiguous information, workload management, and updating one's mental picture and strategy under moderate time-pressure. Lessons derived from the DVD would then be facilitated from the pilots by the instructor during the short debrief.

Simulator Training Scripts (Line Oriented Flight Training – LOFT)

Three LOFT-type simulator scenarios were designed for the training purposes in a real-world environment. Since the ESSAI training focuses on non-technical skills related to the competency structures for SA and TM (see Figures 12.1 and 12.2), it was considered essential not to add a high technical content to the scenarios. Furthermore, as all crews were licensed only for the simulated aircraft series but not for the specific type, complicated technical failures unfamiliar to the pilots were effectively precluded. Therefore, the ESSAI training tool is not 'type-specific' but rather generic in its potential applications. However, the development of more type-specific scenarios is still an important pending task in order to implement threats like automation anomalies. Line Oriented Flight Training

(LOFT) has been the preferred vehicle for pilot simulator training for more than two decades and it has shown itself to be particularly suited to exploring human factors issues. For the ESSAI training gate-to-gate scenario types were designed, which were closely aligned with the DVD messages and allowed for instructor intervention when appropriate. Examples of expected and unexpected threats introduced by the instructor in the different exercises were:

Expected threats:
- aircraft dispatched with open items in the minimum equipment list;
- weather (low visibility forecast at arrival airport);
- high terrain in airport vicinity.

Unexpected threats:
- last minute change in Air Traffic Control (ATC) clearance before takeoff;
- intermittent equipment malfunction (e.g., radio-communication or altimeter failure);
- weather deterioration, turbulences;
- ATC delay;
- restricted options for diversion;
- distractions and task interruptions through cabin events and ATC errors.

Train-the-Trainer

Would-be ESSAI trainers were chosen from current type-rated instructors (SFI/TRI) with CRM experience and good working knowledge of non-technical skills and facilitation techniques. A preferred language for the training was determined before the instructors went through an in-depth ESSAI course themselves. ESSAI is presently available in English, Italian, and partly in German. Sufficient time was provided to give the participants the opportunity of exploring different constellations of the scenarios and solutions for the exercises. Wherever necessary proper intervention strategies were discussed and prepared. Additionally, the emphasis was put on practicing and improving debriefing and facilitation techniques which are required for such kind of integrated human factors training of SA and TM. The instructors are supposed to gently guide the trainees through a self-analysis process to enhance their learning progress.

The ESSAI Training Experiment

The effectiveness of the training for desired behavioral changes was evaluated in an experimental study using a high fidelity (level D) training/research simulator of an advanced technology aircraft at the Technical University in Berlin. Two groups of fully qualified airline pilots took part in the experiment, which was arranged as a mixed-model design with one between group factor (Experimental versus Control

Group effects) and one within group factor (pre- versus post-training effects) (see Figure 12.3). In the *Experimental Group (EG)*, eight crews with 16 pilots received the ESSAI training as described above and in the *Control Group (CG)*, a further eight crews with 16 pilots received a normal Line Oriented Flight Training session (LOFT). The subjects were left blind against the experimental conditions and hypotheses of the project. All 32 (31 male and 1 female) subjects were licensed on the specific aircraft type of the simulator. Both groups were comparable in terms of age (mean age 37.1 years), nationality, flying experience (averages of 6306 flight hours total time and 1938 flight hours on type), as well as prior experience with training of Crew Resource Management (CRM) or Human Factors.

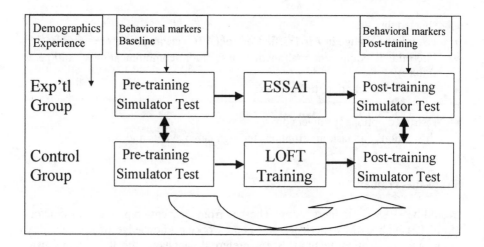

Figure 12.3 Test plan for the ESSAI training experiment

Depending on the time-table for the simulator missions, crews had to stay two or three days for the whole procedure. Different methods were chosen to tap SA and TM for evaluating potential training effects, like questionnaires, self- and peer-ratings or behavior observation techniques. In this chapter the results of observational data on crew performance related to SA and TM are described. All measures were collected either prior to or after the ESSAI/LOFT training. No evaluations took place during the training itself. Two special simulator sessions were designed to collect baseline information and to assess post-training effects for both groups. The *Benchmark Scenario (BS)* was designed to capture the baseline of all measures prior to the training; the *Assessment Scenario (AS)* was designed to evaluate expected gains in regard to SA and TM subsequent to the training. The performance markers for the observation were adopted and modified from previous approaches for the observation and assessment of crew SA and TM. Based on methods like the Line/Los Checklist (Helmreich, Butler, Taggert and Wilhelm, 1997), NOTECHS (Flin et al., 2003), or TARGET (Fowlkes, Lane, Salas, Franz and Oser, 1994) a performance marker system was devised to rate participants' SA and TM behavior during pre-determined scenario test-events. Eighteen test-events were rated in the Benchmark Scenario and 21 in the Assessment Scenario. These events were distributed over all phases of the flight. For the purposes of the statistical analyses observations were aggregated according to the following five phases: pre-flight briefing, departure and climb, descent briefing, approach and landing, and intermittent distractions from cabin or ATC. Additionally two total scores, one for SA and one for TM were calculated. All SA- and TM-performance markers were rated by trained observers on three-point scales, corresponding to *Notice, Understand,* and *Think Ahead* for ratings of SA, and *Ineffective, Partially Effective* and *Effective* for ratings of TM.

With respect to the sample sizes, the statistical analyses for testing training effects reported here were conducted using conservative non-parametric methods. For each of the seven crew-performance measures (five flight phases plus two total scores) four tests were calculated: the differences between the groups (EG vs. CG) before and after the training (Mann-Whitney U-tests; SPSS, 2001) and the differences within each group from before to after the training (Wilcoxon Signed Ranks Tests; SPSS, 2001). According to the experimental hypotheses it was expected to see no significant differences between EG and CG prior to the training and also no significant gain of performance from before to after the training within CG. If ESSAI had a significant impact on flight crews' performance, then within EG the scores are expected to rise from before to after the training and after the training EG should demonstrate superior performance compared to CG. Table 12.1 shows the results for the corresponding statistical tests. Graphical illustrations of the effects are provided in Figure 12.4 to Figure 12.10.

Table 12.1 Results of non-parametric statistical tests for the between-groups and within-group effects

Preflight Briefing			
Source of Variation	**N**	**Test Parameter**	**Significance (one-tailed)**
Between groups:			
pre: EG vs. CG	8;8	Z = -1.376	n.s.
post: EG vs. CG	8;8	Z = -2.319	1 %
Within groups:			
CG: pre vs. post	8;8	Z = -2.383	1 %
EG: pre vs. post	8;8	Z = -.560	n.s.

Departure and Climb

Between groups:			
pre: EG vs. CG	8;8	$Z = -.697$	n.s.
post: EG vs. CG	8;8	$Z = -1.437$	n.s.
Within groups:			
CG: pre vs. post	8;8	$Z = -.491$	n.s.
EG: pre vs. post	8;8	$Z = -.210$	n.s.

Descent Briefing

Source of Variation	N	Test Parameter	Significance (one-tailed)
Between groups:			
pre: EG vs. CG	8;8	$Z = -.161$	n.s.
post: EG vs. CG	8;8	$Z = -2.177$	1 %
Within groups:			
CG: pre vs. post	8;8	$Z = -.351$	n.s.
EG: pre vs. post	8;8	$Z = -1.960$	5 %

Approach and Landing

Between groups:			
pre: EG vs. CG	8;8	$Z = -.588$	n.s.
post: EG vs. CG	8;8	$Z = -1.633$	n.s.
Within groups:			
CG: pre vs. post	8;8	$Z = -2.527$	1 %
EG: pre vs. post	8;8	$Z = -2.371$	1 %

Management of Distractions

Between groups:			
pre: EG vs. CG	8;8	$Z = -1.395$	n.s.
post: EG vs. CG	8;8	$Z = -.616$	n.s.
Within groups:			
CG: pre vs. post	8;8	$Z = -.730$	n.s.
EG: pre vs. post	8;8	$Z = -2.214$	1 %

SA Total score

Between groups:			
pre: EG vs. CG	8;8	$Z = -.158$	n.s.
post: EG vs. CG	8;8	$Z = -2.579$	0.1 %
Within groups:			
CG: pre vs. post	8;8	$Z = -.980$	n.s.
EG: pre vs. post	8;8	$Z = -1.960$	5 %

TM Total score

Between groups:			
pre: EG vs. CG	8;8	$Z = -.368$	n.s.
post: EG vs. CG	8;8	$Z = -1.895$	5 %
Within groups:			
CG: pre vs. post	8;8	$Z = -.560$	n.s.
EG: pre vs. post	8;8	$Z = -1.960$	5 %

The results in Table 12.1 prove firstly that the two groups (EG and CG) showed equivalent performance prior to the training. None of the between-groups tests for the pre-training stage resulted in any significant differences. This finding confirms that the randomization of subjects to experimental conditions was done adequately. For the further interpretation of effects the reader should compare the respective section in Table 12.1 with the corresponding graphical illustration. The Figures 12.4 to 12.10 show vertical box-plots for pre- and post-training score of each group. The boundaries of the boxes correspond to the quartiles of the variable's distribution. Fifty per cent of the values fall into the box. The whiskers are lines that extend from the box to the highest and lowest values, excluding outliers. A line across the box indicates the median.

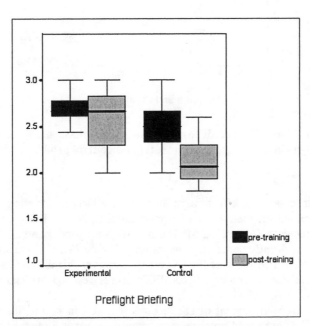

Figure 12.4 Scores for the preflight briefing phase before and after the training for the experimental and control group

EG crews demonstrate superior performance during the Preflight Briefing phase before and after the training, while CG crews' performance decreased (Figure 12.4). This finding corresponds to the observation that all crews were highly alert at the beginning of the experiment because the situation was new and they did not know what exactly they had to expect. While the EG crews could maintain the same high level of awareness until after the training the CG crews showed signs of decreasing attention and routine behavior. A similar pattern was found during Departure and Climb, though not significant (Figure 12.5).

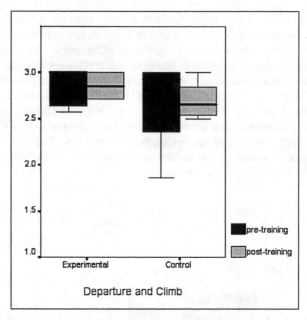

Figure 12.5 Scores for the departure and climb phase before and after the training for the experimental and control group

The most remarkable effects were found for the Descent Briefing were the CG crews maintained on their level of performance while the EG crews showed a substantial increase (Figure 12.6). During Approach and Landing both groups performed significantly better after the training (Figure 12.7). The scores of the EG crews are higher than those of the CG crews, however this differential increase is not significant due to ceiling effects. EG's scores reached the end of the scale (median score = 3).

In regard to Management of Distractions (e.g., cabin events, interruptions by ATC) the EG crews could improve significantly, however Figure 12.8 shows that also the CG crews performed very well before and after the training. Broad-spectrum training effects can best be summarized by Figure 12.9 and 12.10, which contain total scores for SA and TM representing the overall crew performance throughout the scenario. SA increased significantly from before to after the training within the EG but not in the CG. For the ESSAI-trained crews SA-scores progressed from the level of understanding (=2) up to the level of projection (=3), while the CG crews remained on the level of understanding (=2). Similarly the EG crews demonstrated superior performance in regard to TM after the ESSAI training. CG crews had some improvement in TM, but not significant.

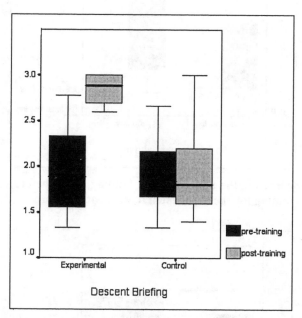

Figure 12.6 Scores for the descent briefing Phase before and after the training for the experimental and control group

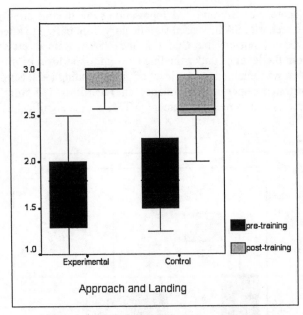

Figure 12.7 Scores for the approach and landing phase before and after the training for the experimental and control group

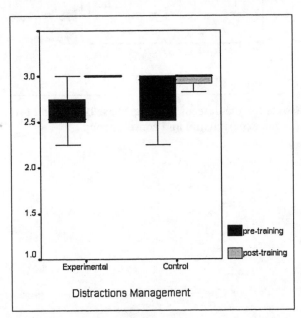

Figure 12.8 Scores for distraction management before and after the training for the experimental and control group

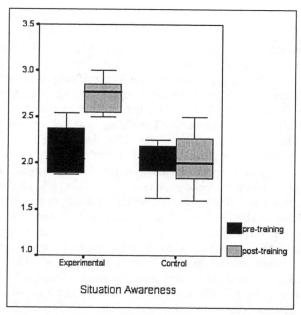

Figure 12.9 Scores for situation management before and after the training for the experimental and control group

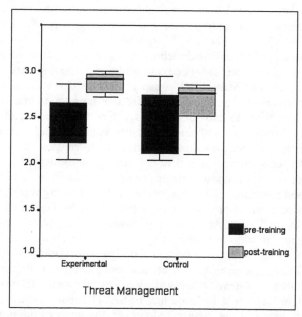

Figure 12.10 Scores for threat management before and after the training for the experimental and control group

Conclusions

The results provided significant empirical evidence for the effectiveness of the ESSAI methods to train flight crews' SA and TM. Positive training effects could be demonstrated on flight crew performance in specifically designed assessment scenarios. Additionally, the ESSAI research report (ESSAI, 2003; Hörmann, Soll, Banbury, and Dudfield, 2003) has described significant training effects across further modalities of measurement, like knowledge tests, self-ratings, peer-ratings, and general questionnaires. Scores for Situation Awareness and Threat Management were increasing as a result of the training throughout all different methods. According to a series of data analyses, it was demonstrated that the ESSAI training solution especially enhances SA. The SA total-score of the observational data was defined with three levels according to the above mentioned definition of Endsley (1995): 'Perception', 'Understanding' and 'Projection'. From before to after the training the majority of ESSAI-trained crews could progress from an SA-level of 'Understanding' to the highest level of 'Projection', while the Control crews remained on the level of 'Understanding'. On the level of 'Projection' ESSAI-trained crews were mentally more 'ahead of the aircraft' than the Control crews. The effectiveness of observed TM strategies did also increase significantly; however, the incremental gain of the ESSAI training compared to a 'normal' LOFT-mission was limited by ceiling effects. As fully qualified experienced airline pilots the crews were all doing well in trapping and mitigating threats. However, the ESSAI-trained crews were superior in avoiding threats. The observational data reported here revealed that especially the briefing quality as well as the approach and landing phase and the management of distractions were significantly enhanced by the ESSAI-training tools DVD, Low-tech exercise, simulator sessions and facilitated debriefing. The advantages of an 'ESSAI-enriched' training concept compared to 'traditional training' are seen in the consistent integration of human factors aspects into regular training events in the real-world environment. To achieve this, effective train-the-trainer courses are a necessary precondition to provide the instructors with the required skills of observation, evaluation and facilitation of desired behaviors and competencies that go beyond the technical stick-and-rudder skills of flight crews.

The ESSAI tools promulgated here are already implemented in the training syllabi of three major European airlines. The proven feasibility and the value of ESSAI tools and principles in different phases of pilot training is rewarding for the three years of research efforts which were funded by the European Commission and carried out by the ESSAI consortium. Systematic operational validation has begun and came up with very promising initial results (Hörmann, Blokzijl and Polo, 2004). Along with crew-centered design considerations (Graeber and Weener, 1997) and the introduction of new equipment, like Enhanced Ground Proximity Warning Systems (EGPWS), Vertical Situation Displays (VSI), or Electronic Flight Bags, it is believed that ESSAI efficiently contributes to fulfill essential safety needs of the industry. Moreover, the goals of the project and the development of its training solution are fully in line with worldwide safety enhancement initiatives kicked-off by the CAST and the JSAT teams. Among other intervention strategies, like the dissemination of the *Approach-and-Landing-Accident-Reduction* (ALAR) Toolkit led by the Flight Safety Foundation (1999), and further enhancements of cockpit design by the manufacturers, ESSAI could contribute to a significant risk reduction of Approach-and-Landing accidents or Controlled Flight into/towards terrain.

Acknowledgements

The ESSAI project was funded by the European Commission DG-TREN under the 'Competitive and Sustainable Growth' Program. We would like to acknowledge the contributions of all consortium partners throughout the project: Aero Lloyd (G), Alitalia (I), British Airways (UK), Dedale (F), German Aerospace Center (DLR) (G), National Aerospace Laboratory (NLR) (NL), QinetiQ (UK), Technical University Berlin (G), and Thales (F). The authors especially thank the aircrews who participated voluntarily in this study and the invaluable support of the trainers in the conduct of the experiment. Further information about the ESSAI project is available at www.essai.net.

References

Amalberti, R. (in press), 'The Cognitive Control of Dynamic Situations', in P. Barach (ed.), *Clambake Seminar on Human Error*, Chicago.
Amalberti, R., Masson, M., Merritt, A. and Pariès, J. (2000), *Briefings. A Human Factors Course for Pilots and Aviation Professionals*, Dedale S.A., Paris, France.
Banbury, S.P., Dudfield, H., Hörmann, H.-J. and Soll, H. (under review), 'FASA: Development and Validation of Novel Measures to Assess the Effectiveness of Commercial Airline Pilot Situation Awareness Training', *International Journal of Aviation Psychology*.
Boorman, D.J. (2000), 'Reducing Flight Crew Errors and Minimizing New Error Modes with Electronic Checklists', in *Proceedings of the International Conference on Human-Computer Interaction in Aeronautics*, Cepadues-Editions, Toulouse, pp. 57-63.
Endsley, M.R. (1995), 'Toward a Theory of Situation Awareness in Dynamic Systems', *Human Factors*, vol. 37, pp. 32-64.
Endsley, M.R. and Robertson, M.M. (2000), 'Training for Situation Awareness in Individuals and Teams', in M.R. Endsley and D.J. Garland (eds), *Situation Awareness: Analysis and Measurement*, Lawrence Erlbaum Associates, Mahwah, NJ, pp. 349-365.
ESSAI (2001), *WP2 Identification of factors affecting situation awareness and crisis management on the flight deck work-package report*, ESSAI/QINETIQ/WPR/WP2/3.0, EC DG-TREN, Contract No.: 2000-GRD1-10450.
ESSAI (2002a), *WP3 Training analysis work-package report*, ESSAI/DLR/WPR/WP3/, EC DG-TREN, Contract No.: 2000-GRD1-10450.
ESSAI (2002b), *WP4 work-package report*, ESSAI/BA/WPR/WP4/1.09, EC DG-TREN, Contract No.: 2000-GRD1-10450.
ESSAI (2003), *WP5 Experimental validation work-package report*, ESSAI/DLR&Q_Q /WPR/WP5/2.0, EC DG-TREN, Contract No.: 2000-GRD1-10450.

Flight Safety Foundation (1999), 'Killers in aviation. FSF taskforce presents facts about Approach-and-landing and Controlled-flight-into-terrain accidents', *Flight Safety Digest* (Special FSF Report), pp. 17-18.

Flin, R., Martin, L., Goeters, K.-M., Hörmann, H.-J., Amalberti, R., Valot, C. and Nijhuis, H. (2003), 'Development of the NOTECHS (non-technical skills) System for Assessing Pilots' CRM skills', *Human Factors in Aerospace Safety*, vol. 3, pp. 97-119.

Fowlkes, J., Lane, N., Salas, E., Franz, T. and Oser, R. (1994), 'Improving the Measurement of Team Performance: The TARGETs Methodology', *Military Psychology*, vol. 6, pp. 47-61.

Graeber, R.C. and Weener, E.F. (1997), '*Integrated Safety Systems Centered Design and Human Factors Considerations for Jet Transport Airplanes*', presented at Technology and Flight Deck Symposium, August 5-6, 1997, Vancouver, BC, Canada.

Helmreich, R., Klinect, J.R. and Wilhelm, J.A. (1999), 'Models of Threat, Error, and CRM in Flight Operations', in *Proceedings of the Tenth International Symposium on Aviation Psychology*, May 3-6, 1999, Columbus, OH.

Helmreich, R., Butler, R., Taggert, W. and Wilhelm, J. (1997), *The NASA/University of Texas/Federal Aviation Administration Line/LOS Checklist: A Behavioural-based Checklist for CRM Skills Assessment (Version 4.4)*, NASA, University of Texas, Federal Aviation Administration Aerospace Group, Austin, Tx.

Hörmann, H.-J., Blokzijl, C. and Polo, L. (2004), 'ESSAI – A European Training Solution for Enhancing Situation Awareness and Threat Management on Modern Aircraft Flight Decks', in *Proceedings of the 16th annual European Aviation Safety Seminar (EASS)*, Barcelona, Spain, March 15-17, 2004, pp. 181-192.

Hörmann, H.-J., Soll, H., Banbury, S.P. and Dudfield, H. (2003), 'ESSAI - Training of Situation Awareness and Threat Management Techniques: Results of an Evaluation Study', in *Proceedings of The Twelfth International Symposium on Aviation Psychology*, April 14-17, 2003, vol. 1, Wright State University, Dayton, OH, pp. 570-575.

Kelly, B.D., Graeber, R.C. and Fadden, D.M. (1992), 'Applying Crew-Centered Concepts to Flight Deck Technology: The Boeing 777', *Flight Safety Foundation 45th IASS and IFA 22nd International Conference*, 1992.

O'Leary, M. (2003), 'Human factors reporting and situation awareness', in G. Edkins and P. Pfister (eds) *Innovation and Consolidation in Aviation*, Ashgate, Aldershot, UK, pp. 89-98.

Russell, P. and Pardee, J. (2001), *Problem Statement Analysis Process Report. CAST – Joint Safety Analysis Team (JSAT)*, Commercial Aviation Safety Team (CAST), Rev. 8, June 9, 2003.

SPSS (2001), *SPSS User Guide*, SPSS Inc, Chicago, USA.

Wiener, E.L. and Curry, R.E. (1980), 'Flight-deck automation: Promises and Problems', *Ergonomics*, vol. 23, pp. 995-1011.

Disclaimer

The views expressed in this paper are the personal opinions of the authors and do not necessarily reflect those of their employing organizations.

Chapter 13

Technology, Organization, and Collaborative Situation Awareness in Air Battle Management: Historical and Theoretical Perspectives

Michael A. Vidulich, Robert S. Bolia and W. Todd Nelson

Introduction

Situation Awareness (SA) has generally been considered as an attribute of an individual performing a set of tasks. For example, in a 1994 bibliography of SA research compiled by Vidulich, Dominguez, Vogel, and McMillan, only 19 of 233 citations were associated with team SA. Despite this trend, there has been some recognition that SA should be considered as a team research issue, although there has also been controversy as to the benefits of research in the area of Team SA (e.g., Stout, Endsley, Vidulich, Orasanu, and Flach, 1997). The purpose of this chapter is to examine the utility of SA as a concept for understanding and improving performance in a very demanding real-world team environment: air battle management. In addition to being a challenging environment due to its intrinsic time pressure and the potentially grave consequences of errors, air battle management is an excellent arena for consideration of team SA issues because it is presently experiencing a level of technological change that will offer many human factors challenges.

Due to the complexity of air battle management and its relative unfamiliarity to many readers, the next section of the chapter will review the air battle management environment. A historical perspective is adopted to demonstrate the importance of effective air battle management by considering its coevolution with fighter combat and strategic bombing. Historical examples will be followed by a description of some current systems, and a discussion of the future of air battle management in the context of network-centric warfare. This will be followed by a review of selected SA and Team SA concepts as they pertain to the task domain, along with an analysis of the implications of projected technological changes to the air battle management environment. The chapter will conclude with a discussion of research needed to maximize SA in future air battle management systems.

The Evolution of Air Battle Management

Air battle management is one aspect of the command and control (C^2) of military forces. In US Air Force doctrine C^2 is defined as:

> The exercise of authority and direction by a properly designated commander over assigned and attached forces in the accomplishment of the mission. Command and control functions are performed through an arrangement of personnel, equipment, communications, facilities, and procedures employed by a commander in planning, directing, coordinating, and controlling forces and operations in the accomplishment of the mission. (United States Air Force, Air Force Doctrine Document 1, 1997, pp. 79-80)

In the current context, one limitation of this definition of C^2 is that it does not distinguish between the strategic and tactical levels of war. According to Air Force Doctrine Document 1 (United States Air Force, 1997), military strategy is 'The art and science of employing the armed forces of a nation to secure the objectives of national policy by the application of force or the threat of force' (p. 84), whereas tactics are 'The employment of units in combat' (p. 86). Air battle management is the tactical C^2 of air combat assets.

In other words, air battle management refers to the part of an air force's C^2 structure that provides real-time control of air assets engaged in combat. The importance of well-integrated and timely air battle management appears obvious now, though historically it was surprisingly slow to develop.

World War I Air Defense

The first major war with an appreciable air combat component was World War I. Many of the air combat functions that are familiar today first appeared during that war. Examples include aerial reconnaissance, strategic and tactical bombing, and air-to-air fighting. The limited communications technology of the early twentieth century severely constrained the air battle management of aircraft in flight. According to Franks (2003), the most common missions for fighter aircraft were the Offensive Patrol and Line Patrol. The former was a mission *across* the front lines into enemy territory, the latter a mission *along* the front line. In either case, the pilots participating in the mission simply looked for enemy aircraft to attack. Less common were Hostile Aircraft or Wireless Interception patrols that were initiated in response to specific reports of enemy aircraft. Since radios were extremely rare in aircraft – especially fighter aircraft – during World War I, there was little opportunity for air battle management by anyone other than the pilots participating in the patrols. Crude attempts were made to direct the aircraft by using anti-aircraft artillery explosions to mark the altitude and sometimes the course of intruding aircraft, or by placing large markers on the ground, but these were rare and not especially effective (Franks, 2003; Fredette, 1976).

Perhaps the most notable harbinger of future air battle management was the response of the British military to air attacks on the United Kingdom, especially London. Germany prosecuted the first large-scale strategic bombing campaign against Britain during World War I using both Zeppelins and fixed-wing, multi-engine bombers (Fredette, 1976). Although the level of damage inflicted by the raids was miniscule compared to the levels that would be inflicted a generation later during World War II, the unexpected novelty generated considerable public unrest and even encouraged the government to create the Royal Air Force as an independent military service.

Another important response of the British military to the German air raids was the creation of a dedicated air defense system (Ashmore, 1929; Fredette, 1976). Brigadier General Edward 'Splash' Ashmore was appointed to command the London Air Defence Area (LADA) on 8 August 1917 (Zimmerman, 2001). Ashmore was an energetic proponent of developing a complete air defense system, including the best sensors and weapons available. At the time, sensors were limited to ground observers, sound amplifiers, and searchlights; weapons included ground-based artillery, barrage balloons, and fighter aircraft. While these tools seem primitive by today's standards, they were conceptually novel at the time, and novel tactics and doctrine for their use had yet to be developed. Ashmore realized that the maximum effectiveness could only be realized if there was a central, guiding intelligence that tied together the information from all of the sensors to the weapons. Toward this end, he encouraged the building of additional telephone communications and established priorities for the use of telephone equipment to facilitate quick reporting of enemy air activity and coordination of appropriate responses. Individual observing stations, searchlight or anti-aircraft artillery positions, and fighter control towers were connected to one of 25 sub-control stations. The sub-controls were connected to Ashmore's central control. Ashmore (1929) described the operation of the system as follows:

> When aircraft flew over the country, their position was reported every half-minute or so to the sub-control, where the course was plotted with counters on a large scale map. These positions were immediately read off by a 'teller' in the sub-control to the plotter in the central control, where the course was again marked out with counters. An ingenious system of colored counters, removed at intervals, prevented the map from becoming congested during a prolonged raid.
>
> I sat overlooking the map from a raised gallery; in effect, I could follow the course of all aircraft flying over the country, as the counters crept across the map. The system worked very rapidly. From the time when an observer at one of the stations in the country saw a machine over him, to the time when the counter representing it appeared on my map , was not, as a rule, more than half a minute.
>
> In front of me a row of switches enabled me to cut into the plotter's line, and talk to any of my subordinate commanders at the sub-controls.
>
> The central control, in addition to receiving information from outside, constantly passed it out to the sub-controls concerned; so that the commander, say, of an anti-aircraft brigade, would know, from moment to moment, where and when hostile aircraft would approach his line of guns. (Ashmore, 1929, pp. 93-94)

Limited though it was, Ashmore's description of the operation of LADA's central control is clearly identifiable as an air battle management system.

Furthermore, the system was successful. As Ashmore noted in his assessment of the last major raid on London during World War I:

> For the defences, this night was a success – six enemy machines shot down; and a failure – thirteen enemy machines over London, a typical example of what a hard-hitting defence organization can accomplish. No scale of defence, however great, can secure complete immunity from bombing; but by suitable arrangements the attacker can be made to suffer such casualties that his efforts will die out.... After the losses of the 19th of May, the German aeroplanes no longer attacked us, and London was free of further trouble. (Ashmore, 1929, p. 89)

During the war and in the years leading up to World War II, Ashmore was a strong advocate for improving the air defense system by continuing the development of the telephone communications system, increasing the size and training of the ground observers, and endorsing the development of real-time communications with airborne aircraft.

World War II Air Defense

Given the utility of the LADA system, it might seem likely that any nation preparing for war prior to World War II would give careful consideration to air defense planning and the creation of integrated sensors, air battle management capabilities, and air defense weapons. Such was not the case.

During the interwar years, air power theorists such as Giulio Douhet postulated that the most effective way to secure command of the air would be by bombing the enemy's airfields. Following that, an independent air force would destroy the enemy's transportation lines and population centers to force the enemy to capitulate. Attempting to stop air attacks by an air defense system was expected to be impractical at best (Douhet, 1927; Futrell, 1989).

In the United States, a debate erupted in the Air Corps Tactical School regarding the relative merits of bomber-based offense and fighter-based defense (Severs, 1997). Several officers (e.g., Ken Walker, Harold George, and Haywood Hansell) that would later become prominent in organizing the United States bomber offensives against Germany and Japan became outspoken advocates of bombardment aviation. A central belief of the time was that the altitude and speed of modern bombers would make any interception by fighter aircraft exceedingly difficult and that the defensive armament carried by the bombers would be able to successfully fend off the few fighters that did manage to intercept them. The bombardment advocates were countered for a time by Claire Chennault, who argued that fighter aircraft combined with an effective warning network of ground observers would be able to reliably intercept attack bombers and render such attacks prohibitively expensive. The Air Corps conducted several exercises in the 1930s to test the relative merits of bomber attacks and fighter defense. Although the results showed potential value for both bombers and fighters, this evidence was generally discounted or ignored by the bomber advocates, who increasingly gained control of Air Force doctrine and procurement.

Even in Britain, despite the first-hand experience in creating an integrated air defense system, the bomber advocates were visible and influential. This was well-illustrated in the 10 November 1932 speech by former Prime Minister Stanley Baldwin containing the lines:

> I think it is well also for the man in the street to realize that there is no power on earth that can protect him from being bombed. Whatever people may tell him, the bomber will always get through. The only defence is offence, which means that you have to kill more women and children more quickly than the enemy if you want to save yourselves. (Quoted in Zimmerman, 2001, p. 36)

Within the Royal Air Force, there was a strong contingent of bomber advocates that agreed with Baldwin's analysis, but the potential role of air defense was not completely overlooked. In particular, the role of Air Chief Marshall Hugh Dowding was crucial in preparing the Royal Air Force for its greatest test. In the early 1930s, Dowding was in charge of developing much of the infrastructure that the Royal Air Force would possess at the outbreak of World War II. This included the development of modern monoplane fighters (i.e., the Hurricane and the Spitfire) and radar.

As important as the development of radar was, it has probably garnered too much of the credit for the Royal Air Force's successful defense against invasion by Germany during the Battle of Britain. Several nations, including Germany, had developed radar capabilities. In fact, Britain's radar was not even the most advanced in the world at the time of the Battle of Britain (Deighton, 1979). The Germans were well aware of the United Kingdom's radar capabilities, but underestimated the importance of the technology by misunderstanding how the Royal Air Force was using the information from radar. The Germans believed that individual radar stations were connected only to local air defense assets and that this system could be relatively easily overwhelmed by concentrated attacks (Deighton, 1979). In fact, Dowding had incorporated radar into a larger version of Ashmore's LADA system with all of the information being filtered and transmitted to his central control office at Bentley Priory. Relevant information was then distributed to the appropriate parts of the air defense system. Most notably for the Battle of Britain, information from Bentley Priory was transmitted to Group 11 Headquarters at Uxbridge where Air Vice Marshall Keith Park would decide on the appropriate response. Just as in Ashmore's control system, the air situation was conveyed to the operators (including Air Vice Marshall Park) by colored counters on a large map (see Figure 13.1) and orders were transmitted throughout the air defense system by telephone. The system was reasonably effective. Although some bombers did indeed get through to bomb their targets, the damage was not sufficient to weaken Britain enough to allow Germany to launch an attack across the English Channel, or to compel a British surrender.

Figure 13.1 The RAF Museum at Hendon's replica of the control room used by Air Vice Marshal Park to direct the actions of 11 Group during the Battle of Britain

While radar did allow the Royal Air Force to respond more quickly and efficiently to incipient German air attacks, the mere possession of radar technology provided no assurance that appropriate air battle management would occur. A good example of this is the American experience with radar during the attack on Pearl Harbor. Radar stations were operational in Hawaii prior to the Pearl Harbor attack and a radar station at Opana Point successfully tracked the incoming attack and reported it to headquarters. Unfortunately, the information was received by an operator who had no proper training or authority to use it (Prange, 1981; Tyler, 1944).

World War II Air Offense

In order to fully appreciate the value of air battle management in World War II, it is also instructive to examine how air forces performed offensive missions when outside of an air battle management system. Given the technological limitations of radar and communications systems during World War II, offensive bomber attacks were executed with little or no real-time air battle management capability. As described above, the German Luftwaffe failed to defeat the integrated air defense system in the Battle of Britain. As the war progressed, the offense shifted to the

Allies and it was the Germans who used a radar-guided integrated defense system to try to fend off bomber offensives by the Royal Air Force and the United States Army Air Force.

For the bomber offensive, C^2 was largely limited to the extensive preparation required to plan, set-up, and launch hundreds of aircraft along carefully planned routes to strike a selected set of targets (Freeman, 1984). Once the mission was launched, only very limited changes to the plan could be accomplished, such as recalling the entire force due to changing weather conditions.

Given such limited capability for adaptation by air battle management, it is not surprising that when some part of the plan was incorrect or poorly executed, deleterious consequences could ensue. As a case in point, consider the experiences of the United States bombers during the 2nd major raid on Schweinfurt on 14 October 1943 (Kuhl, 1993). As part of the 1st Division of attacking bombers, Major Charles Normand, leading the 305th Bomb Group, failed to execute his part in the formation plan for the attack and did not join the 305th aircraft with the aircraft of the 92nd and 306th Bomb Groups, led by Colonel Peaslee. Consequently, Colonel Budd Peaslee elected to execute a turning maneuver to place his groups behind what he expected to be a complete set of 3 groups and hand over the lead position in the Combat Wing to them. In the course of these maneuvers, the planned-for cohesion among bomber groups was lost and the aircraft were distributed over too much space leaving them more vulnerable to fighter attack. Recognizing the vulnerability, the Luftwaffe concentrated its attack on the 1st Division. The result was that the 1st Division lost 45 of its 60 B-17 Bombers during that single mission.

While the events of the 2nd Schweinfurt raid may be an extreme example, they are illustrative of what can happen to an air force operating without an active air battle management system against an enemy that possesses one. Had the technology of the day permitted radar monitoring of the bomber stream moving towards Germany to appear on an air battle management display and secure communications with sufficient bandwidth been available, it is likely that the initial failure of Major Normand's group to meet Colonel Peaslee's Wing could have been compensated for and most likely casualties would have been greatly reduced. As it was, none of the important participants of the day (e.g., Major Normand, Colonel Peaslee) possessed sufficient accurate information to adapt appropriately to unexpected events.

The Vietnam War and the Birth of Airborne Air Battle Management

As United States Air Force and Navy aircraft attempted to wage an air campaign against North Vietnam in the mid-1960s, they once again found themselves at an air battle management disadvantage relative to their enemy (Michel, 1997). The North Vietnamese Ground Control Intercept (GCI) system was capable of detecting US raids early and tracking them continuously to help guide fighter aircraft or surface-to-air missiles (SAMs) against them. As in the World War II attacks against Germany, this pitted relatively brittle and nonadaptive preplanned attacks against an air defense system that possessed air battle management capabilities to react adaptively to real-time events.

Fortunately for US pilots, the US Air Force possessed aircraft that could help to remedy this situation. The EC-121D was a military version of the Lockheed Super Constellation airliner. It was modified to carry two large radar systems and a number of radar operators, plotters, and communications specialists. The original mission for this aircraft was to fill gaps in the warning net against Soviet nuclear attack for the United States. However, in conjunction with radar-equipped US Navy ships the EC-121 aircraft flew patrols that monitored enemy air activity over North Vietnam and provided the information in real-time to US strike aircraft over North Vietnam. The EC-121's radar systems were not accurate enough to provide close control to US fighters in combat, but the warnings of North Vietnamese MiG fighter activity helped US pilots take timely evasive action on many occasions (Michel, 1997). The actions of the EC-121s, other radar-equipped aircraft, and the Navy radar ships to guide offensive strikes over Vietnam can be considered the first large-scale attempt to bring air management capabilities to offensive air strikes over an enemy's territory.

Current Air Battle Management Systems

As a C^2 activity, air battle management can be performed at ground stations or on several types of fixed- and rotary-wing aircraft; however, for the purposes of illustration, only fixed-wing airborne air battle management platforms will be discussed. The E-3 Sentry Airborne Warning and Control System (AWACS) aircraft exemplifies current airborne air battle management capabilities. Originally built for the United States Air Force, the E-3 has also been acquired by NATO, the United Kingdom, France, and Saudi Arabia. Several other countries, including Japan and Australia, have developed or are acquiring similar aircraft.

The E-3 AWACS carries a rotating radar mounted atop its fuselage that is much improved compared to the radar systems of the EC-121 (Armistead, 2002; Hirst, 1983). The AWACS is capable of tracking many airborne targets out to distant ranges and displaying all of the information on operator consoles in the back of the aircraft (see Figure 13.2). The exact number of operators varies across AWACS models and missions, but typically there are several operators working surveillance and several weapons directors. The surveillance team processes unidentified radar returns to classify their identity, and the weapons director teams monitor and control friendly aircraft performing missions. On its own, any AWACS aircraft can provide a potent air battle management asset, but AWACS aircraft usually do not operate alone. In a combat environment, there may be several AWACS operating simultaneously and usually in conjunction with other C^2 aircraft and ground stations.

The US Navy's equivalent of AWACS is the carrier-launched E-2C Hawkeye (Armistead, 2002). This aircraft, much smaller than its Air Force cousin – the Hawkeye has three consoles compared with nineteen on US AWACS models – is used to provide a tactical situational picture for fleet defense, close air support, interdiction, and a variety of other missions. In the United States it is used only by the Navy, but it serves as the principal air battle management platform for the air forces of several nations, such as Egypt and Israel.

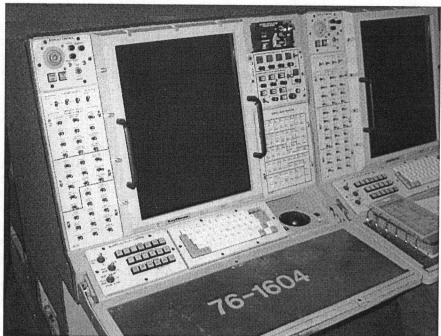

Figure 13.2 Typical air battle manager's console on current AWACS aircraft. The large central display area typically accommodates a map of the operator's AOR with superimposed icons representing aircraft

An interesting variant of an air battle management system is the US Air Force's E-8 Joint Surveillance Target Attack Radar System (JSTARS), whose radar is used for tracking ground targets such as wheeled and tracked vehicles. Its function as an air battle management platform involves directing strike assets against enemy land forces. This system first saw combat in Operation Desert Storm, when the picture it provided allowed coalition air assets to prevent Iraqi armored divisions from escaping the battlefield (Hallion, 1992). This represents a fundamental expansion of the role of air battle management systems, which previously had the capacity to direct air assets against enemy air assets or map-centric coordinates, but lacked the ability to identify and track individual ground targets. The air battle manager's interface in the JSTARS looks very similar to that in the AWACS, but instead of portraying the information relevant to air-to-air combat, the JSTARS radar detects, and the displays depict, friendly and enemy ground forces.

Despite the many technological changes, much of the task of an air battle manager remains the same since Ashmore's development of the LADA central control. The air battle manager uses a geo-spatial display of air activity to maintain SA of the current air combat environment. Based on that SA, the air battle manager decides whether the current plan must be adapted to achieve its goals and issues orders or provides information across communications links to other assets in the air combat system to accomplish the tactical missions. Today's air battle manager deals with much more information throughput, more air assets and enemies, and much faster speeds than those with which Ashmore was confronted. On the other hand, today's air battle manager has better sensors, computer aiding, and better communications than Ashmore probably could have imagined.

Technology and the Future of Air Battle Management

The future of air battle management will likely be guided by developments in the doctrine of network-centric warfare (NCW), a concept of operations that advocates the use of dense networks of geographically distributed sensors, the fusion of data collected from multiple independent sensor platforms, and the integration of collaborative technologies to enhance SA, decision speed and self-synchronization of forces (Cebrowski and Garstka, 1998). This vision of future operations is contrasted with a platform-centric view, in which linkages between sensors and shooters are based on analog systems and situation awareness is built up by means of two-way communications rather than a shared awareness grounded in a common operational picture. While touted as conceptually innovative and frequently referred to as a Revolution in Military Affairs, the novelty of NCW resides primarily in the fact that the digital technology exists that makes it possible. Its historical roots go back at least as far as Moltke, who in the mid nineteenth century was able to leverage developments in communications technology, transportation, and weapon systems to defeat forces that were often numerically, if not doctrinally, superior (van Creveld, 1985).

It can certainly be argued that network-centric air battle management is not new to navies. The carrier battle group sent by the United Kingdom to recapture the Falkland Islands in 1982 had a networked air defense system. Although it did not employ the type of sensor netting commonly talked about by today's advocates of NCW, it did allow the Air Picture Supervisor in the Ops Room of one ship to send track information to the Ops Room of another ship using a tactical data link (Woodward and Robinson, 1997). This allowed for expansion of the situational picture available to a given operator, and for some measure of shared SA within the fleet.

On the other hand, to a large extent this system still reflected a platform-centric view of warfare. In the event of an attack, it would be a particular destroyer or frigate that would engage the incoming missile or aircraft, based on the returns of its own onboard sensor suite. While the shared picture contributed to the SA of the fleet, it did not represent true data fusion, and the rules of engagement (ROE) required that a particular vessel could not fire its weapons at a target unless it had acquired that target with its own organic sensors. At the time this was a reasonable requirement, since the failure to fuse the data in real time could result in duplicate or dropped tracks, and hence *reduced* SA, potentially leading to fratricide.

The United States Navy has responded to this issue by developing its Cooperative Engagement Capability (CEC), a revolutionary approach to fleet defense and the Navy's principal investment in NCW. CEC has addressed some of the problems associated with earlier network-centric concepts by changing the way in which Ops Rooms are connected to the sensors and to each other. CEC uses the concept of sensor netting, by which a processor – the Cooperative Engagement Processor (CEP) – onboard each CEC-equipped fleet element receives the raw radar returns of *all* of the sensors in the fleet. These returns are then correlated by the CEP to produce a single integrated air picture consisting of composite fire-control quality tracks that can be used by all participating platforms (Kerno, 1999; Busch and Grant, 2001). This is possible because the CEP on each platform is running the same software, which means that each operator in the fleet sees the same situational picture with the same track numbers. The implications of this for fleet defense are important: a platform can now engage an airborne threat even if its own radar cannot detect it, leading to significantly earlier interception or engagement of enemy aircraft or missiles (Kerno, 1999). The result, according to one operator who used CEC in a fleet exercise, is 'an incredible level of situational awareness' (Vergun, 2000).

While the US Navy has taken the lead in the development of network-centric concepts, the other services are also heavily engaged (Scott and Hughes, 2003; Toomey, 2003). In addition, many of the United States' major allies, including the United Kingdom, Canada, and Australia, are aggressively pursuing the development of network-centric systems (Squire. 2003; Garnett, 2001; Kruzins and Scholz, 2001). As a result, network-centric or network-enabled operations will play a major role in all future coalition actions.

The NCW concept has numerous implications for the air battle management team. On the one hand, the integration of automated sensor fusion should reduce the workload of individual surveillance operators, potentially resulting in a decrease in the size of the surveillance component of the air battle management team. On the other, increases in bandwidth will translate into more effective use of data link technology as well as a more complete situational picture being available for pilots, diminishing the workload of the weapons team. While the need for these positions will not vanish, the roles played by the operators and the ways in which they interoperate with each other and with fighter and bomber crews will change.

One manifestation of these changes is the development of a new air battle management platform, the US Air Force's Multi-Sensor Command and Control Aircraft (MC2A; Fulghum, 2002). When it becomes fully operational, the MC2A will bring together the functions of AWACS and JSTARS on a single wide-body jet, providing operators with an integrated air-land-sea picture. This will require a re-evaluation of the structure of current air battle management teams and the development of novel workflows. It should also be noted that the importance of air battle management to the US Air Force is indicated not only by the fact that it is acquiring a new platform to perform the mission, but also by the fact that the MC2A was identified as one of the Air Force's 10 most important modernization programs (Wall, 2002).

It is tempting to believe the claims of NCW advocates who argue that increases in bandwidth and sensor netting will automatically provide enhancements in SA. However, it is important to note, as some researchers have done, that technology advancement alone is not enough (Bolia, Vidulich, Nelson, and Cook, in press). Military history has yielded numerous examples of technological innovation, employed in the absence of appropriate tactics and doctrine, leading to accidents, fratricide, or defeat. This suggests that, despite good intentions, a cavalier approach to the introduction of new technology may actually engender decreases in SA.

SA and Team SA in Air Battle Management

Military C^2 functions are often explained using an analogy that likens military forces to a human body (Coakley, 1992). Within this analogy, information sources are considered to be the military's sensory apparatus. So, just as the human body senses the environment through its eyes, ears, nose, *et cetera*, the military senses its environment through radar, human observation, uninhabited aerial vehicle (UAV) reconnaissance, and so forth. Further, whereas the human acts through his or her muscles, the military system acts through its effectors, typically weapon systems (e.g., guns, bombs, missiles). The military C^2 system is the nervous system that links the sensory apparatus to the effectors. Clearly, one important aspect of the C^2 system is to make decisions, just as the human brain chooses the individual's course of action. But to support effective decision making another vital component must be present within the C^2 system. Specifically, a good C^2 system must possess good system-wide situation awareness (SA).

The most obvious component of an air battle management system's SA is the situation display that has been a part of systems ever since the first map with moving counters was constructed in Ashmore's LADA system. Today, the information is likely to be much more dense, more current, and changing more rapidly; but it is still typically presented to the air battle manager in the form of a map with superimposed symbols representing the relevant actors in the air battle manager's area of responsibility (AOR). The individual air battle manager must process the information presented, perhaps integrating it with information from other types of displays or communications, in order to create a mental 'tactical picture' of what is happening. This tactical picture will be the basis for decisions based on the current situation, preexisting plans, known doctrine, and current ROE, and also to monitor the progress of active missions and help them to achieve their goals as circumstances change.

In modern air battle management systems such as AWACS there are likely to be numerous air battle managers with their own, possibly overlapping, AORs to monitor and manage. Although the quality of any individual air battle manger's SA (i.e., his or her 'tactical picture') is a valid and important consideration, it is not sufficient to characterize the state of an air battle management system. The fact that information is present in the air battle management system does not imply that it will be appropriately used to guide the actions of the air combat assets. For example, in April 1994 two US Air Force F-15s patrolling the northern no-fly zone over Iraq mistakenly shot down two US Army Blackhawk helicopters on a United Nations mission over the Kurdish region of Iraq (ABC News Primetime Live, 1995). Although there were many elements involved with this fratricide event, it is appropriate to highlight in the current context that the event was monitored by air battle managers on a United States Air Force AWACS. Although several air battle managers were aware that friendly helicopters were active in the F-15's area, none of them advised the F-15 pilots of that fact (Snook, 2000). When asked why nothing was said to the F-15 pilots, the AWACS Mission Crew Commander explicitly acknowledged that a lack of SA was involved when he replied, 'What a great call that would have been, you know, if somebody had had the situational awareness, I guess, to make that call, but unfortunately, they didn't' (ABC News Primetime Live, 1995, p. 5). In an air battle management environment, good SA consists not only of individuals possessing a good tactical picture of their own, but also of sharing that tactical picture appropriately throughout the system. Such team SA is a common requirement in military environments. For example, French, Matthews, and Redden (Chapter 14, this volume) discussed the vital role of team SA in the context of infantry operations. At a more general level, Endsley (1995) considered the nature of team SA:

> Overall team SA can be conceived as the degree to which every team member possesses the SA required for his or her responsibilities. This is independent of any overlaps in SA requirements that may be present. If each of two team members needs to know a piece of information, it is not sufficient that one knows perfectly but the other not at all. *Every* team member must have SA for all of his or her own requirements or become the proverbial chain's weakest link. (Endsley, 1995, p. 39)

Endsley's concept of team SA is useful in that it clarifies an important aspect of defining team SA and aids in the specification of adequate team SA measurement techniques. It may be expected that many of the same tools used to assess individual SA would also be required for assessing team SA, with the additional requirement that the measurement be extended to all relevant members of the team. Salas, Prince, Baker, and Shrestha (1995) concurred with Endsley that the individual SA of the various team members was an essential component of team SA, but added the requirement that team SA would also have to consider the impact of team processes. Coordination of action, information sharing, and sharing of interpretations of information were activities included in within team processes.

Dominguez (1994) distinguished between two main approaches for defining SA: product and process. Product interpretations of SA focused on a snapshot of the picture possessed by an individual engaged in a task. Process definitions emphasized the extraction, integration, and use of the mental picture. This is a useful distinction for integrating Endsley's concept of SA with the focus on team processes of Salas and his colleagues. Endsley's description describes the SA product that an effective team must possess. Salas et al. (1995) augment that description with a concern for identifying an effective team based on its procedures for performing its mission. Both aspects, product and process, are important considerations in trying to use the SA concept in the air battle management environment.

SA Measurement in Air Battle Management Research

In practice, SA assessment in air battle management can be usefully subdivided into the assessment of an individual air battle manager attempting to build his or her own tactical picture and the assessment of how well that picture is shared within a team of air battle managers.

Individual Air Battle Manager SA Assessment There is a wealth of tools for assessing either product or process of an individual's SA (see for examples, Endsley and Garland, 2000; Vidulich et al., 1994; Vidulich, 2003). Among the techniques available, procedures based on memory probe assessment can be considered prototypical (Endsley, 2000; Vidulich, 2003). These techniques, although very demanding to use, would appear to provide the best avenue for dealing with Endsley's caution that a gap in any individual's SA is also an indicator of a problem in the team SA. Executed in the traditional fashion with random freezes of the simulation, blanking of the participant's displays, and presentation of random questions from a large pool of potential questions, the memory probe technique has been demonstrated to be a sensitive measure (Endsley, 2000; Vidulich 2000). At the time at which the memory probe data are assessed, it provides a clear snapshot of the participant's SA at that moment. In other words, the typical memory probe procedure seems appropriate for assessing the momentary product of the participant's SA process, but not necessarily insightful on the nature of that participant's process for generating his or her awareness of the situation. Also, the issue of possible interruption effects of SAGAT remains controversial (e.g., McGowan and Banbury, Chapter 10, this volume).

A variant of the memory probe procedure that might provide insight is the situation-present query approach (Durso and Dattel, Chapter 8, this volume; Durso, Truitt, Hackworth, Crutchfield, Nikolic, Moertl, Ohrt, and Manning, 1995). In this technique, the freezing of the simulation associated with memory probe SA assessment does occur, but the situation information is not taken away from the participant. Rather than focusing on the accuracy of the participants' responses from memory, the situation-present procedure assesses and analyzes the reaction time required by participants to answer the experimenter's questions. Although this procedure has not been attempted in an air battle management environment, it might be an excellent method for assessing the air battle manager's abilities to efficiently 'drill-down' to the appropriate level of information. This could be interpreted as a test of the air battle manager's SA processes and how well they are supported in an air battle management simulation. In a data-rich air battle management environment, it is probably unreasonable to expect that any air battle manager will always be aware of all relevant information, but he or she must be able to access efficiently the relevant information needed to monitor mission progress and to alter plans when necessary.

Air Battle Manager Team SA Assessment It is improbable that any air battle in the foreseeable future will be managed by an individual air battle manager. Air battle management is a team activity with at least several and usually many air battle managers dividing up responsibilities and AORs. Further, while it is possible that the various air battle managers participating in an action might be co-located, for example on a single AWACS aircraft, it is far more likely that the team will be distributed across several ground-based and airborne locations. Conceptually, Endsley's suggestion of using memory probe measures to test the SA of all, or at least a representative sample, of the team members is an attractive one. In practice, however, simulations of adequate size and with acceptable fidelity to conduct evaluations that would be convincing to the organizations responsible for acquiring air battle management systems would be so expensive as to be impractical. Evaluations of selected subsets might be able to address some of the most crucial connections within planned air battle management systems, but they should be buttressed with other measurement approaches where possible. On the other hand, although getting a snapshot of the momentary SA product throughout a large distributed team is likely to be impractical, studying the processes by which SA is distributed among team members might be a reasonable and useful option. Probably the best avenue for studying the SA process in a team environment would be to investigate the pattern and content of communications between team members during mission performance. Several researchers have already demonstrated the potential for using communications analysis in SA research (Bowers, Braun, and Kline, 1994; Christ and Evans, 2002; Evans and Christ, 2003; Garbis and Artman, Chapter 15, this volume; Orasanu, 1995). Although the existing research has not addressed the area of air battle management, some of it has been conducted in a C^2 environment. Furthermore, current technological trends in air battle management might facilitate the collection and analysis of inter-team communications data.

Implicit in this discussion of an air battle management team's SA is the idea that the team is composed of one or more weapons components and a surveillance component operating in support of other air assets, such as fighters, bombers, and tankers. However, it may also be useful to consider the SA of the pilots of the aircraft being controlled as a function of the SA of the air battle management team, since a significant portion of a weapons director's job is to impart SA to the pilots.

SA Research Needs for Air Battle Management Teams

The discussion of the historical evolution of air battle management and the importance of SA for air battle managers, as well a review of the means of measuring this SA, does not immediately suggest a list of research questions demanding pursuit. However, careful consideration of the changing task domain and the potential influence of forthcoming technologies thereupon may intimate several classes of issues worth investigating.

First, it may be argued that the optimization of SA requires a comprehensive knowledge of the work domain. Specifically, if one does not understand the cognitive needs of the operator, one does not know how to meet these needs. While there have been investigations along these lines using cognitive systems engineering methodologies such as cognitive task analysis (e.g., Fahey, Rowe, Dunlap, and deBoom, 2001; Klinger, Andriole, Militello, Adelman, Klein, and Gomes, 1993), these have typically focused on AWACS weapons directors. To date, other AWACS roles, as well as those of air battle managers operating aboard other platforms, have been less frequently investigated. Similar analyses of other roles may be in order. Furthermore, techniques have been developed for conducting cognitive requirements analyses for systems that have not been completely designed (Naikar, Pearce, Drumm, and Sanderson, 2003). These might prove useful for developing interface concepts supporting SA for next-generation platforms like MC2A.

While additional research may be motivated by an understanding of the cognitive demands of the operator, it may also be inspired by developments in technology. This might manifest itself as a collection of studies investigating the effects on SA of novel operator-machine interface technologies, such as spatial intercoms, multi-layer displays, and multi-modal displays, the performance and workload effects of which have been studied by researchers in the context of air battle management in US Air Force and Navy laboratories (Bolia, 2003a, 2003b; Bolia, Nelson, Gardner, Vidulich, and McLaughlin, 2003; Guilliams, McLaughlin, Vidulich, Nelson, Bolia, and Donnelly, 2004; Nelson and Bolia, 2003; Nelson, Vidulich, Bolia, McLaughlin, Guilliams, and Donnelly, 2003; Osga, van Orden, Campbell, Kellmeyer, and Lulue, 2002). This is based on the assumption that improvements in SA demonstrated for individual operators would likely translate to enhanced team SA.

Furthermore, the fact that air battle managers operate as distributed teams in environments characterized by a high communications workload suggests that research on the effects of collaborative technologies on SA may be desirable. Along these lines, there are numerous commercially-available collaboration tools that may prove useful for enhancing team SA, information sharing, and overall ABM effectiveness. Collaborative communication tools include video and audio conferencing, chat and messaging tools, and automatic broadcast and alerts. The purported advantages of these technologies include face-to-face communications, real-time private and group conversations, and the capability to publish and receive critical information. Moreover, when combined with file sharing, these technologies enable users to collaboratively review and discuss text, images, and video. Additionally, asynchronous communication tools such as bulletin and message boards, and even email, may serve to further enhance team communication and information exchange.

Several collaboration technologies may also significantly enhance shared battlespace visualization. These include shared situation displays and customized dashboards, which may be augmented with virtual whiteboards and data capture and replay technologies. The latter may be particularly effective for mission rehearsal and debriefing, in addition to enriching the shared SA of the ABM team during operations. It should be noted that frequent and repetitive replay and rehearsal are critical to the development of expert decision making skills (Salas and Klein, 2001), which maybe be regarded as a spill-over benefit of this technology.

An additional category of collaborative technologies involves tools that include intelligent agents as collaborators. Specifically, decision aids and agents may be used for data mining and knowledge location, content and knowledge management, and automated workflow and scheduling. Given the time-critical and complex nature of network-centric ABM, the importance of effective dynamic replanning and rescheduling will continue to increase. To the extent that these technologies support the shared visualization and understanding of the dynamically-shifting spatial and temporal landscape of current and future operations, they will promote self-synchronization and result in more efficient prosecution of targets.

Despite the promise of these technologies, empirical research is needed to determine their most appropriate uses. Although researchers are beginning to postulate a relation between collaborative interface technologies and team SA (Bolstad and Endsley, 2003), few studies have addressed this issue explicitly. For example, it is conceivable that technologies such as video-teleconferencing may promote presence and face-to-face teamwork, while chat – already used extensively by the US Navy (Jara and Lisowski, 2003) – may reduce verbal communications and improve recall. However, the effectiveness of these technologies has not been quantified. Furthermore, the overall success of collaborative technology in the ABM domain will likely be a function of task appropriateness, technical maturity and usability, and organizational culture. The latter includes user acceptance and trust in the technology and an appreciation of its utility for net-centric operations. Along these lines, a recent survey conducted at the Air Force Research Laboratory (Nelson, Bolia, Vidulich, and Langhorne, 2004) asked trained US and Australian air battle managers to evaluate which collaborative technologies would be most useful to them in conducting current and future missions. These included, but were not limited to, the technologies described above. Surprisingly, all technologies in the survey were rated as at least potentially useful, but some (e.g., automated work flow and mission timelines, data capture and replay capabilities, file and application sharing) were clearly considered more promising than others (e.g., large-scale displays, automated decision support, video conferencing), suggesting directions for future work.

In addition to the integration of novel technologies on the interface side, and the introduction of collaborative technologies, proponents of NCW have insinuated that enhanced SA will be a by-product of sensor-netting and data fusion. Future research should explicitly address this hypothesis, across multiple scenarios, within the context of the NCW concept of operations. Research of this ilk has the potential to influence not only the realization of NCW, but also the development of tactics and doctrine for the prosecution of time-critical targets by future air battle management systems.

References

ABC News Primetime Live, (1995), *Avoidable Errors*, Broadcast 8 March 1995, Transcript #392.

Armistead, E.L. (2002), *AWACS and Hawkeyes: The Complete History of Airborne Early Warning Aircraft*, MBI Publishing Company, St. Paul, Minnesota.

Ashmore, E.B. (1929), *Air Defence*, Longmans, Green and Co., London.

Bolia, R.S. (2003a), 'Effects of Spatial Intercoms and Active Noise Reduction Headsets on Speech Intelligibility in an AWACS Environment', *Proceedings of the Human Factors and Ergonomics Society 47th Annual Meeting*, Human Factors and Ergonomics Society, Santa Monica, CA, pp. 100-103.

Bolia, R.S. (2003b), 'Spatial Intercoms for Air Battle Managers: Does Visually Cueing Talker Location Improve Speech Intelligibility?', *Proceedings of the 12th International Symposium on Aviation Psychology*, Wright State University, Dayton, Ohio, pp. 136-139.

Bolia, R.S., Nelson, W.T., Gardner, C.M., Vidulich, M.A. and McLaughlin, A.B. (2003), 'A Visual Depth Display for Air Battle Managers: Effects of Depth and Transparency on Performance and Workload,' *Setting the Standards: Proceedings of the Sixth International Australian Aviation Psychology Symposium.* Australian Aviation Psychology Association, Melbourne, Australia.

Bolia, R S., Vidulich, M.A., Nelson, W.T. and Cook, M.J. (in press), 'A History Lesson on the use of Technology to Support Military Decision-Making and Command and Control', in M.J. Cook (ed.), *Human Factors of Complex Decision Making*, Lawrence Erlbaum Associates, Mahwah, New Jersey.

Bolstad, C.A. and Endsley, M.R. (2003), 'Tools for Supporting Team Collaboration', *Proceedings of the Human Factors and Ergonomics Society 47th Annual Meeting*, Human Factors and Ergonomics Society, Santa Monica, California, pp. 374-378.

Bowers, C.A., Braun, C. and Kline, P.B. (1994), 'Communication and Team Situational Awareness', in R.D. Gilson, D.J. Garland, and J.M. Koonce (eds), *Situational Awareness in Complex Systems*, Embry-Riddle Aeronautical University Press, Daytona Beach, Florida, pp. 305-311.

Busch, D. and Grant, C.J. (2000), 'Changing the Face of War: The Cooperative Engagement Capability', *Sea Power*, Vol. 43(3), pp. 37-39.

Cebrowski, A.K. and Garstka, J.J. (1998), 'Network-Centric Warfare: Its Origin and Future', *US Naval Institute Proceedings*, Vol. 124(1), pp. 28-35.

Christ, R.E. and Evans, K.L. (2002), *Radio Communication and Situation Awareness of Infantry Squads during Urban Operations,* Technical Report 1131, United States Army Research Institute for the Behavioral and Social Sciences, Alexandria, Virgina.

Coakley, T.P. (1992), *Command and Control for War and Peace*, National Defense University Press, Washington.

Deighton, L. (1979), *Fighter: The True Story of the Battle of Britain,* Castle Books, Edison, New Jersey.

Dominguez, C. (1994), 'Can SA be Defined?', in M. Vidulich, C. Dominguez, E. Vogel, and G. McMillan (eds), *Situation Awareness: Papers and Annotated Bibliography*, Armstrong Laboratory Technical Report AL/CF-TR-1994-0085, Air Force Material Command, Wright-Patterson Air Force Base, Ohio.

Douhet, G. (1927), *The Command of the Air* (trans. D. Ferrari), in D. Jablonsky (ed.), *Roots of Strategy, Book 4*, Mechanicsburg, PA, Stackpole Books, 1999, pp. 265-407.

Durso, F.T., Truitt, T.R., Hackworth, C.A., Crutchfield, J.M., Nikolic, D., Moertl, P.M., Ohrt, D. and Manning, C.A. (1995), 'Expertise and Chess: A Pilot Study Comparing Situation Awareness Methodologies', in D.J. Garland and M.R. Endsley (eds), *Experimental Analysis and Measurement of Situation Awareness*, Embry-Riddle Aeronautical University Press, Dayton Beach, Florida, pp. 295-303.

Endsley, M.R. (1995), 'Toward a Theory of Situation Awareness in Dynamic Systems', *Human Factors*, Vol. 37(1), pp. 32-64.

Endsley, M.R. (2000), 'Direct Measurement of Situation Awareness: Validity and Use of SAGAT', in M.R. Endsley and D.J. Garland (eds), *Situation Awareness Analysis and Measurement*, Erlbaum, Mahwah, New Jersey, pp. 147-173.

Endsley, M.R. and Garland, D.J. (eds) (2000), *Situation Awareness Analysis and Measurement*, Erlbaum, Mahwah, New Jersey.

Evans, K.L. and Christ, R.E. (2003), *Development and Evaluation of Communication-based Measures of Situational Awareness*, Technical Report 1803, United States Army Research Institute for the Behavioral and Social Sciences, Alexandria, Virgina.

Fahey, R.P. Rowe, A.L., Dunlap, K.L. and deBoom, D.O. (2001), *Synthetic Task Design: Cognitive Task Analysis of AWACS Weapons Director Teams*, Air Force Research Laboratory Technical Report AFRL-HE-AZ-TR-2000-0159, Human Effectiveness Division, Mesa, Arizona.

Franks, N. (2003), *Dog-Fight: Aerial Tactics of the Aces of World War I*, Greenhill Books, London.

Fredette, R.H. (1976), *The Sky on Fire: The First Battle of Britain 1917-1918 and the Birth of the Royal Air Force*, Harcourt, New York.

Freeman, R.A. (1984), *The Mighty Eighth War Manual*, Cassell, London.

Fulghum, D.A. (2002), 'Key Decisions Remain for New Intel Program', *Aviation Week and Space Technology*, Vol. 157(4), pp. 178-179.

Futrell, R.F. (1989), *Volume I, Ideas, Concepts, Doctrine: Basic Thinking in the United States Air Force 1917-1960*, Air University Press, Maxwell Air Force Base, Alabama.

Garnett, G. (2001), 'The Canadian Forces and the Revolution in Military Affairs: A time for change', *Canadian Military Journal*, Vol. 2(1), pp. 5-10.

Guilliams, N.M., McLaughlin, A.B., Vidulich, M.A., Nelson, W.T., Bolia, R.S. and Donnelly, B.P. (2004), 'An Evaluation of Speech Recognition Technology in a Simulated Air Battle Management Task', *Proceedings of the Second Conference on Human Performance, Situation Awareness, and Automation*.

Hallion, R.P. (1992), *Storm Over Iraq: Air Power and the Gulf War*, Smithsonian, Washington, DC.

Hirst, M. (1983), *Airborne Early Warning: Design, Development and Operations*, Osprey, London.

Jara, T. and Lisowski, M. (2003), 'Don't Silence Navy Chat', *US Naval Institute Proceedings*, Vol. 129(9), pp. 52-55.

Kerno, R. (1999), 'CEC and the Interoperability Challenge', *Sea Power*, Vol. 42(3), pp. 45-47.

Klinger, D.W. Andriole, S.J., Militello, L.G., Adelman, L. Klein, G. and Gomes, M.E. (1993), *Designing for Performance: A Cognitive Systems Engineering Approach to Modifying an AWACS Human Computer Interface*, Armstrong Laboratory Technical Report AL/CF-TR-1993-0093, Air Force Material Command, Wright-Patterson Air Force Base, Ohio.

Kruzins, E. and Scholz, J. (2001), 'Australian Perspectives on Network Centric Warfare: Pragmatic Approaches with Limited Resources', *Australian Defence Force Journal*, No. 150, pp. 19-33.

Kuhl, G.C. (1993), *Wrong Place! Wrong Time! The 305th Bomb Group and the 2nd Schweinfurt Raid, October 14, 1943*, Schiffer, Atglen, Pennsylvania.

Michel, M.L. (1997), *Clashes: Air Combat over North Vietnam 1965-1972*, Naval Institute Press, Annapolis, Maryland.

Naikar, N., Pearce, B., Drumm, D. and Sanderson, P.M. (2003), 'Designing Teams for First-of-a-Kind, Complex Systems using the Initial Phases of Cognitive Work Analysis: Case Study', *Human Factors*, Vol. 45(2), pp. 202-217.

Nelson, W.T. and Bolia, R.S. (2003), 'Evaluating the Effectiveness of Spatial Audio Displays in a Simulated Airborne Command and Control Task', *Proceedings of the Human Factors and Ergonomics Society 47th Annual Meeting*, Human Factors and Ergonomics Society, Santa Monica, CA, pp. 202-206.

Nelson, W.T., Bolia, R.S. and Vidulich, M.A. and Langhorne, A.L (2004), 'User-Centered Evaluation of Multi-national Communications and Collaborative Technologies in a Network-Centric Air Battle Management Environment', *Paper submitted for presentation at the 48th Annual Meeting of the Human Factors and Ergonomics Society*.

Nelson, W.T., Vidulich, M.A., Bolia, R.S., McLaughlin, A.B., Guilliams, N.M. and Donnelly, B.P. (2003), 'Designing Speech Interfaces for Command and Control Applications', *Setting the Standards: Proceedings of the Sixth International Australian Aviation Psychology Symposium*, Australian Aviation Psychology Association, Melbourne, Australia.

Orasanu, J. (1995), 'Evaluating Team Situation Awareness through Communication', in M.R. Endsley and D.J. Garland (eds), *Situation Awareness Analysis and Measurement*, Erlbaum, Mahwah, New Jersey, pp. 283-288.

Osga, G., Van Orden, K., Campbell, N., Kellmeyer, D. and Lulue, D. (2002), *Design and Evaluation of Warfighter Task Support Methods in a Multi-Modal Watchstation*, SPAWAR Systems Center Technical Report 1874, SPAWAR Systems Center, San Diego, California.

Prange, G.W. (1981), *At Dawn We Slept: The Untold Story of Pearl Harbor*, McGraw-Hill, New York.

Salas, E. and Klein, G. (2001), *Linking Expertise and Naturalistic Decision Making*, Lawrence Erlbaum Associates, Mahwah, New Jersey.

Salas, E., Prince, C., Baker, D.P. and Shrestha, L. (1995), 'Situation Awareness in Team Performance: Implications for Measurement and Training', *Human Factors*, Vol. 37(1), pp. 137-148.

Scott, W.B. and Hughes, D. (2003), 'Nascent Net-Centric War Gains Pentagon Toehold', *Aviation Week and Space Technology*, Vol. 158(4), pp. 50-53.

Severs, H.G. (1997), The *Controversy Behind the Air Corps Tactical School's Strategic Bombardment Theory: An Analysis of the Bombardment versus Pursuit Aviation Data between 1930-1939*, Air University Technical Report AU/ACS/97-0126c/97-03, Maxwell Air Force Base, Alabama.

Snook, S.A. (2000), *Friendly Fire: The Accidental Shootdown of US Black Hawks over Northern Iraq*, Princeton University Press, Princeton, New Jersey.

Squire, P. (2003), 'Air Power into the 21st Century', *Air Power Review*, Vol. 6(1), pp. 1-9.

Stout, R.J., Endsley, M.R., Vidulich, M.A., Orasanu, J. and Flach, J.M. (1997), 'Team Situational Awareness: Is this Old Wine in New Bottles', in R.S. Jensen and L. Rakovan (eds), *Proceedings of the Ninth International Symposium on Aviation Psychology*, The Department of Aviation, The Ohio State University, Columbus, pp. 1460-1463.

Toomey, C.J. (2003), 'Army Digitization: Making it Ready for Prime Time', *Parameters*, Vol. 24(4), pp. 40-53.

Tyler, K. (1944), *Joint Committee Exhibit No. 146 – Navy Court of Inquiry*, pp. 446-460, downloaded 2 January 2004, from: http://www.ibiblio.org/pha/myths/radar/index.html.

United States Air Force (1997), *Air Force Basic Doctrine: Air Force Doctrine Document 1*, Headquarters Air Force Doctrine Center, Maxwell Air Force Base, Alabama.

van Creveld, M. (1985), *Command in War*, Harvard University Press, Cambridge, Massachusetts.

Vergun, D. (2001), 'On-Scene Report: Kernel Blitz (Experiment) 01, 'An Incredible Level of Situational Awareness'', *Sea Power*, Vol. 44(8), pp. 54-57.

Vidulich, M.A. (2000), 'Testing the Sensitivity of Situation Awareness Metrics in Interface Evaluations', in M.R. Endsley and D.J. Garland (eds), *Situation Awareness Analysis and Measurement*, Erlbaum, Mahwah, New Jersey, pp. 227-246.

Vidulich, M.A. (2003), 'Mental Workload and Situation Awareness: Essential Concepts for Aviation Psychology Practice', in P.S. Tsang and M.A. Vidulich (eds), *Principles and Practice of Aviation Psychology*, Erlbaum, Mahwah, New Jersey, pp. 115-146.

Vidulich, M., Dominguez, C., Vogel, E. and McMillan G. (1994), *Situation Awareness: Papers and Annotated Bibliography*, Armstrong Laboratory Technical Report AL/CF-TR-1994-0085, Air Force Material Command, Wright-Patterson Air Force Base, Ohio.

Wall, R. (2002), 'USAF Revamps 10 Top Programs', *Aviation Week and Space Technology*, Vol. 156(16), p. 54.

Woodward, S., with P. Robinson (1997), *One Hundred Days: The Memoirs of the Falklands Battle Group Commander*, Naval Institute Press, Annapolis, Maryland.

Zimmerman, D. (2001), *Britain's Shield: Radar and the Defeat of the Luftwaffe*, Sutton Publishing, Gloucestershire.

Chapter 14

Infantry Situation Awareness

Han Tin French, Michael D. Matthews and Elizabeth S. Redden

Introduction

Background

In combat a clear mental picture of the current situation and accurate projections of likely future conditions are necessary before effective decisions can be made. For infantry soldiers and their leaders, this means knowing the strength and combat power of one's own forces, and the location, strength, capabilities and intent of the enemy. It also involves accurate and timely communication – and comprehension – of orders and intelligence information. Historically, these needs were met with line-of-sight observation of the battle, the use of couriers to relay information, and the use of bugles, drums, and flags to signal the commander's intent. In the 20th century, more sophisticated command, control, and intelligence technologies, including the radio and radar, were introduced. Nevertheless, Command and Control (C^2) was still characterized by a sharply hierarchical and sometimes ponderous organizational structure. Decisions were often based on outdated information, and by the time orders were issued and communicated to subordinate units, conditions had often changed to the point that mission effectiveness was compromised.

In recent years, armies began introducing sophisticated and complex digital C^2 technologies into their forces. These technologies promise to alter the very nature of C^2, and change the way that battles and wars are fought. As General Edwin Burba, who observed armor units equipped with emerging digital technologies engage non-digitized units at the US Army's National Training Center, stated: '*Clearly, situation awareness has overriding combat aspects. It's decisive when used properly . . . it isn't a modest enhancement, it's a decisive enhancement!*' (Burba, 1999). More recently, the successes of US forces in defeating Iraqi units in the second Gulf War underscore the advantages of real-time C^2 capabilities provided by systems like the Forward Battle Command Brigade and Below (FBCB2) that provides up-to-date information on the location and combat power of component units. The following comments were provided by a battalion commander (name withheld to protect privacy):

> FBCB2 has revolutionized tactical battle command in many ways. I've already mentioned the digital maps and imagery as being a tremendous capability. I literally had

254

the entire country of Kuwait and Iraq at my fingertips. I could pan across the maps, zoom in, change to imagery (and zoom in on the imagery too), change scale, and even change the color of the grid lines on the map (actually a very handy feature). I didn't have to worry about changing map sheets- the screen updated as I moved. I didn't need a flashlight to read the maps and imagery since the screen had an adjustable backlight. The FBCB2 imagery wasn't quite as clear as a hard copy product but it was definitely suitable for every mission we executed. It enabled us to navigate through the narrow streets and alleys of Baghdad or determine if a canal road was suitable for tracked vehicle movement. I relied solely on FBCB2 imagery for all urban operations.

Infantry forces are also exploiting digital technologies to enhance C^2. The US Army is in the process of fielding its Land Warrior System, providing each soldier and leader with a wearable computer through which digital maps, messages, location data, and other information can be communicated. A wireless local area network radio communication system allows all soldiers to be in constant voice communication with each other and key leaders. Digital technologies are being infused into a great many aspects of infantry operations.

Situation Awareness

Human decision-making is a complex process and must depend on key perceptual and cognitive processes that precede the actual decision that is made. Situation Awareness (SA) is a construct developed to describe and account for the prerequisite processes that good decision-making is founded on. Within academic definitions of SA, it is generally held that SA involves basic information processing components including perception, attentional mechanisms, and both working memory and long-term memory functions. US Army doctrine defines SA as 'the ability to have accurate real-time information of friendly, enemy, neutral, and non-combatant locations; a common, relevant picture of the battlefield scaled to specific levels of interest and special needs' (TRADOC, 1994). Thus, effective decision-making depends on accurate and timely perceptions of the current situation, forming an accurate understanding of the current situation, and the ability to predict what is likely to occur in the near future (Endsley, 1995a).

The introduction of digital technologies are thought to improve SA by providing much more accurate and timely information to commanders and soldiers, and to allow near real-time communication of orders and vital information. However, to optimally leverage these technologies toward the desired end-state of vastly improved SA, decision-making, and mission effectiveness, they must be designed with both the constraints and skills that the human operators of these systems possess. In order for this design to proceed, a comprehensive and accurate understanding of SA is needed.

The purpose of this chapter is to review SA from the infantry perspective, recognizing that in most operations the infantry is part of a combined arms team. A discussion of the infantry operational environment is provided. This is followed by a review of infantry-centric SA models and infantry-specific SA metrics. Recent research on team SA is summarized. Finally, the role of SA in future infantry combat operations is discussed. A proper understanding of SA may be the cornerstone for combat success.

Infantry Operational Environments

The infantry profession has been in existence for three millennia. It is a physically, cognitively, and morally challenging profession. Soldiers are exposed to extremely dangerous situations, sometimes with little or no physical barrier between themselves, the enemy, and environment.

The armed forces are called upon to conduct operations in support of government objectives, ranging from warfighting to military operations other than conventional war. The latter include peacekeeping, peace enforcement, contribution to search and rescue operations, contribution to humanitarian and disaster relief operations, and providing assistance to the recovery and evacuation of people. To deal with the various tasks, the soldiers need to be 'tough, courageous and aggressive in combat, they can also show flexibility and initiative, and demonstrate subtlety and compassion when called upon to do so' (Australian Army, 2002, p.27).

Armed conflicts provide a challenging environment in which to operate. They are dynamic, unpredictable, difficult to control and therefore chaotic. The latter is caused by the complex interaction of friction, danger and uncertainty, which are enduring features of war (Australian Army, 2002). Friction results in difficulties in achieving the simplest of tasks due in part to the dangers posed by the adversaries. The 'fog-of-war' or uncertainty due to incomplete, inaccurate or even contradictory information, impedes a clear understanding of the situation.

The infantry operates in every conceivable terrain, including deserts, jungles, swamps, rural environment and cities. The urban environment presents one of the most challenging environments to operate within; characterized by the presence of streets, single and multi-storey buildings; infrastructure such as power and water supply, communication system; and combatants and non-combatants who may belong to a variety of groups, cultures and religions (Medby and Glenn, 2002). In urban areas, movement and fire is restricted; line-of-sight observation and communication is difficult. Conflicts may involve irregular forces that cannot be identified readily and for whom there are no rules and inhibitions. A US soldier's sentiment in the operation in Iraq is probably echoed by many of his counterparts. 'The hardest part ... is not knowing who it is or where they're at. Standing here right now you feel vulnerable. Somebody could shoot. You'd never see it coming' (Campbell, 2003).

Soldiers are exposed to psychological as well as physical stresses. Deaths of combatants and non-combatants, mass destruction of dwellings and infrastructure, dispossessed, distressed and angry crowds can cause varying degrees of horror and disgust.

Whilst lower level commanders are likely to be involved in close combat, the higher commanders are generally more remote from the battles. A higher commander, assisted by the headquarters staff, is responsible for larger areas of operation and for achieving a specific mission within it. The two primary tasks are to conduct C^2 functions of existing operations and planning for future operations. At the combat team or higher level, the commander has a variety of assets, which may include infantry, armor, artillery, engineer, air defense, logistics support, medical assets and other sub-units. The command post must ensure that these elements are coordinated to perform their respective tasks and orchestrated to achieve the overall effects. They have to monitor the evolving situations, keeping track of a range of matters including the subordinates' movements and activities, enemy disposition and movements, the activities of combat teams on adjoining areas, troops' conditions, equipment and supplies, and potential changes to the higher commanders' plan. Information received from the various elements in the battlespace has to be interpreted. Circumstances may change dramatically requiring adjustments to the original plan. Even though the situation may be unclear, the commander is often under time pressures to make decisions, for the consequences of not making any decision may be harmful.

The decision to commit a land force is not made lightly. Its deployment in a conflict is a demonstration of the determination to effect an outcome. Under these scenarios the infantry will continue to operate in dangerous, dynamic, unpredictable environments and be subjected to high levels of physical and psychological stresses. To be meaningful, research on infantry SA must take this operational setting into account.

Models of Infantry SA

Endsley, Holder, Leibrecht, Garland, Wampler and Matthews (2000) provide an infantry-specific model of SA based on her general SA model (Endsley, 1988, 1995a) that views SA as consisting of a core of basic cognitive states and processes. These include accurate perception of cues and events occurring within a given environment (level 1 SA), comprehending their meaning in terms of significance to the problem being faced (level 2 SA), and the ability to make accurate projections concerning the course of events in the near future (level 3 SA). These three levels of SA are cumulative in nature and represent increasingly sophisticated perceptual and cognitive appraisals of a situation. These three SA levels are viewed by Endsley as prerequisite for optimal decision-making and the selection of actions that are most appropriate to the situation at hand. Endsley et al., (2000) extend this model to the infantry domain by carefully analyzing the unique challenges of the infantry environment, task and organizational structures, and the team-based nature of infantry operations.

Because the Endsley model is widely known, and is described elsewhere (Rousseau, Tremblay and Breton, Chapter 1, this volume, for example) we describe instead a dynamic model of situated cognition developed by Shattuck and Miller (2004). Whereas Endsley et al.,'s (2000) model represents an information processing approach to SA, Shattuck and Miller's model blends the information processing approach with a cognitive engineering view of SA. The model includes Endsley's three levels of SA but also looks at the funneling of environmental data through digital data sensors and C^2 systems, prior to being viewed and acted upon by the leader. The model is particularly relevant to SA from the standpoint of designing sensor and digital C^2 systems that improve the leader's ability to make sense of potentially huge amounts of information bombarding the commander through increasingly pervasive and complicated digital information systems.

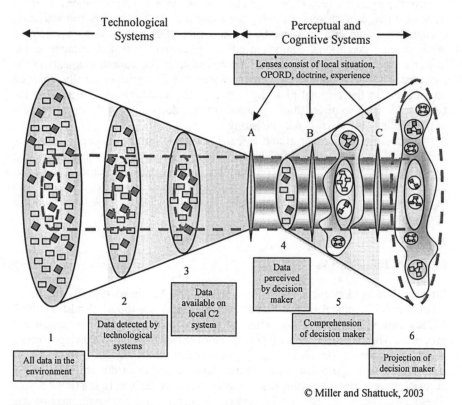

© Miller and Shattuck, 2003

Figure 14.1 Dynamic model of situated cognition

Shattuck and Miller's (2004) dynamic model of situated cognition is shown in Figure 14.1. On the left is depicted the technological systems cone of awareness. The diameter of the left-most portion of the cone – representing all the data in the environment – is quite large. This data, in an unfiltered format, would overwhelm the ability of a commander to make sense of it. The second part of this cone is smaller in diameter, and represents data collected by technological systems and sensors. Even much of these data are extraneous to the information requirements of the commander and his battle staff and must be filtered out. The remaining data, represented by the smallest diameter portion of the technological systems cone, is that which is presented to the commander on the local C^2 system. The importance of the left side of this model is that researchers and war fighters must decide what information a commander and his staff need for a particular mission, and provide just that information – and no more – on the digital C^2 system. The lenses (A, B, C) on the model underscore this notion, suggesting that systems must be designed to tailor information as a function of the local situation, the mission, doctrine, and the experience or preferences of the user.

The right side of the model, referred to as perceptual and cognitive systems cone of awareness, reflects the information processing side of SA. The technological systems cone focuses on engineered systems, and provides a conceptual model for filtering and organizing information. In contrast, the right side of the model focuses on intra-psychic factors, or mental processes of the commander and other users of the digital systems described above. This aspect of the model is heavily influenced by the Endsley's (1995a) information processing approach. The smallest diameter part of the perceptual and cognitive systems cone includes only the data perceived by the user. It should be noted that this would not necessarily include all of the data actually presented on the C^2 system. The second part of this cone, with a larger diameter, involves the user's ability to make sense of the information that is perceived. The highest level of SA is represented by the large diameter portion of the cone, located on the extreme right of Figure 15.1, and involves the ability of the user to make accurate projections of what is likely to occur in the near future.

The dynamic model of situated cognition suggests several approaches for improving data synthesis and presentation. These include tailoring displays in such a way as to cope with cognitive workload or overload. A related approach involves aggregating data rather than displaying all information from sensors. Miller and Shattuck (in press) reviews research that suggests that experienced battalion commanders do not view data equally across a battlefield. Rather, they focus on areas of high activity. As Miller and Shattuck (in press) observed 'in a sense, they tuned up the volume on the portion of the battlefield to which their attention was drawn and tuned down the volume on other portions of the battlefield.' Shattuck, Talcott, Matthews, Clark and Swiergosz (2002) also found that experienced commanders focused more on enemy activity, as opposed to inexperienced officers who focused on their own friendly forces. Shattuck and Miller's (2004) model thus provides a way of conceptualizing system design with implications toward enhanced SA and mission effectiveness.

In sum, an infantry-centric SA model is important because it may suggest and guide general approaches to SA development and enhancement for all infantry personnel. For example, Endsley et al.,'s (2000) information processing model suggests several avenues for SA training. One way would be through the development of mental models or scripts appropriate to a specific type of mission in infantry leaders, as traditionally provided by Army training programs. However these training procedures are often too slow or do not allow for sufficiently diverse experiences for effective scripts to be encoded. The use of an innovative immersive platoon/squad level infantry virtual combat simulator overcomes the problem (Pleban, Matthews, Salter and Eakin, 2002). In a few hours, a platoon leader could go through numerous missions, and receive feedback both digitally and from expert trainers. Theory guides research, the results of which in turn modify theory.

Situation Awareness Requirements

An initial effort to determine SA requirements for infantry operations ranging from those of individual combatants to brigade commanders and staff was undertaken in 1998 when the US Army Research Institute for the Behavioral and Social Sciences sponsored the Infantry Situation Awareness Workshop at Fort Benning, Georgia (Graham and Matthews, 1999). The Workshop brought together a unique blend of noted SA scholars, retired infantry general officers, and active duty and retired infantry subject matter experts. Fairly detailed SA requirements were reported for individual combatants and squads (Richardson, 1999), and for platoons, companies, and battalions (Holder, 1999). More general needs and issues facing brigades (Salter, 1999) and future combat teams (Gorman, 1999) were discussed. The theme that emerged was that SA information requirements vary as a function of echelon and mission, and a single generic list of requirements is of little use in determining needs for specific units operating in specific missions.

Thus, in order to develop psychometrically sound SA metrics, specific information requirements for a given mission or type of mission is needed. This requires a different approach. Matthews, Strater and Endsley (in press) report results of an infantry SA requirements analysis designed to determine the specific information requirements for infantry platoons operating in an urban environment. A goal-directed task analysis that involved interviews with six infantry subject matter experts was conducted. These interviews yielded seven primary mission goals and multiple sub-goals, which were then analyzed to determine specific information requirements needed to accomplish these goals. For example, one primary goal was to 'avoid casualties.' This consisted of five sub goals, including maintain troop readiness, defend against attack, avoid fratricide, establish and maintain security, and avoid detection. The sub goals suggested specific information requirements. For instance, in order to avoid fratricide, the platoon leader and soldiers must know the location of their own troops, and those of adjacent units. These SA requirements were tabulated and broken down by SA level – perception, comprehension, and projection. A similar approach to determining SA requirements at the brigade level was described by Bolstad, Riley, Jones and Endsley (2002).

Matthews, Eid, Johnsen, Meland and Talcott (2004) report results of a similar infantry SA requirements analysis. This was aimed at 'attack an objective' missions in forested terrain, as part of summer training exercises conducted at the Royal Norwegian Naval and Army Academies. Eight subject matter experts were interviewed in depth. The research focus was toward developing SA requirements that would be reliable indicators of a squad leader's SA in these types of missions. Eighteen such indicators were obtained, including factors such as communicating effectively with squad members and higher echelons, posting scouts to provide information while moving toward the objective, and the leader directly observing and assessing the objective prior to making key decisions. SA metrics based on these SA requirements were predictive of squad-leaders' performance and decision-making in the exercise.

Another empirical approach to determining SA requirements for infantry units was reported by Redden (2002). This experiment focused on SA requirements (referred to as critical information requirements, or CIRs) for infantry personnel up to platoon leaders for missions conducted in urban settings. Eight squad-sized elements of soldiers and their platoon leader participated in this study. Each element completed a series of missions in an immersive virtual combat simulator described in detail by Pleban et al., (2002). An initial and extensive list of candidate SA requirements was developed through interviews with a panel of infantry subject matter experts. Following each mission, participants rated these items on a seven-point Likert scale with respect to each item's importance to the mission. Items rated at five or above were considered necessary for mission performance. Major findings from this study showed that the information provided to squad members should only concern items that can be responded to or that affect their choice of a particular course of action. Squad members need less information than leaders at higher echelons. Moreover, the criticality of information about the opposing force beyond 50 meters increases with the leadership level. Squad members are interested in their immediate objective and are somewhat interested in the location of opposing force elements within 50 meters of the objective. In contrast, platoon leaders are interested in the location of the opposing force up to one kilometer away because this knowledge is important in their planning.

Mission-specific SA requirements of the sort reported in this section are critical because they provide the information needed to develop psychometrically sound SA metrics. However, it should be noted that SA requirements must be derived as a function of mission, echelon, and environment. That is, SA requirements key to a platoon level mission in an urban environment may be of less relevance to a company sized operation in a desert environment. The methodologies reported by Matthews and his associates and Redden may be employed to develop performance indicators for a variety of missions and echelons. Without such metrics, meaningful progress in infantry SA is not possible. Metrics based on these two analyses are described next, along with other approaches to measuring SA in infantry operations.

Measurement of Infantry SA

Background

The study and measurement of SA began using realistic simulators in the aviation field (Endsley, 1987, 1994; Pew, 1991). Endsley (1995b) suggested that her Situation Awareness Global Assessment Technique (SAGAT) can be used in any domain in which a reasonable simulation of task performance exists. However, the full range of the infantry domain is quite difficult to simulate considering the complex, interactive, and dynamic performance of the ground warrior in his environment. At present no simulators exist that allow the warrior to perform the full range of combat tasks, accurately replicate individual and team tasks, and are of sufficient granularity to query the warrior's cognitive processes. Advanced technology simulation systems, currently under development, can still only roughly approximate the situation in which infantry soldier operates. Consequently these should only be used for studies of infantry SA where the factors under consideration can be isolated from the complex multi-operational environment without significant impact on outcomes. The following paragraphs discuss how different SA measurement approaches have been applied in infantry field studies as well as in these advanced simulation systems.

Objective SA Measures and Environments

Objective measures of infantry SA strive to measure SA directly, based on specific SA requirements of a particular domain or scenario and at specific points in time during the problem as discussed in the previous section. Warriors are queried throughout the scenario so that accurate responses are not dependent upon memory, but instead, capture current awareness of the situation.

Objective measures of infantry SA differ mainly as a function of the complexity and richness of the enabling environment [free-play, Assessment Center (AC), virtual environment, gaming environment]. The challenge is to develop critical SA requirements within carefully scripted scenarios a priori. The next section describes objective measures of SA that have been developed and implemented in studies of infantry performance. It also describes various types of environments, developed for the objective assessment of infantry SA.

SAGAT SAGAT was originally developed for analysis of pilot SA, focusing on orientation and awareness of assets and targets. It is described in detail elsewhere (Endsley, 1995b). Typically, at a critical point in the scenario, the operator would be requested to describe his or her environmental features. In addition, in concurrence with her framework of SA, Endsley developed questions that probed not only perception of information (location, orientation, assets, targets) but also comprehension of information and projection. SAGAT does not necessarily result in a global SA score. For example, the per cent of aircraft reported correctly to individual items such as 'knowledge of aircraft location (by azimuth)' are used as the quantitative result (Endsley, 1987). The SAGAT approach can be used to generate a comprehensive array of SA probes. However, it is up to the researcher to ascertain the basis for an overall evaluation of operator SA, if one is needed.

Strater, Endsley, Pleban and Matthews (2001) developed an infantry performance version of the SAGAT protocol that was modified to reflect SA requirements for infantry platoon leaders in military operations in urban terrain (MOUT) missions. They used a list of 21 probe questions that were based upon an earlier SA requirements analysis (Matthews, Pleban, Endsley and Strater, 2000). Strater et al., (2001) found a relationship between the experience levels of the platoon leaders and the SA measure.

French and Hutchinson (2002) investigated the applicability of SAGAT for measuring SA in a simulated C^2 environment at the infantry brigade level. They reported that the method showed potential, but was disruptive. As the operational tempo was relatively low, they suggested that it might be possible to take the players out of the simulation to respond to SA probes without freezing the simulation. Placing probe questions on C^2 computer systems may reduce disruption and streamline the process.

Critical Information Knowledge Assessment (CIKA) Technique CIKA systematically scripts a story-line to generate a scenario that captures CIRs, affords operationally relevant and challenging mission events, and provides diagnostic, individual level of SA and overall SA assessment based on a weighted analysis of questionnaire-based item probes. CIKA stresses the need for front-end analysis of CIRs and development of an easily interpreted SA assessment tool that can be quickly used in the field. Therefore, the emphasis is on careful construction of questionnaire-based tools that will provide overall assessments of SA, in addition to a more diagnostic array of results. CIKA was developed and validated for the investigation and evaluation of infantry SA, which are discussed in the following section.

- *SA Free-play Environment* In 1998, the MOUT Advanced Concept Technology Demonstration (ACTD) commissioned the US Army Research Laboratory's (ARL) Human Research and Engineering Directorate (HRED) to develop a realistic method to assess infantry SA (Blackwell and Redden, 2000; Redden and Blackwell, 2000). Research determined that a free-play, force-on-force approach using freeze frames and assessment of knowledge questionnaires would be the most realistic way to assess infantry SA. Each set of SA queries (between ten and 12 questions) was tailored to the specific type of vignette that was used. Domain sampling was used to ensure the full spectrum of ground warrior activities and inclusion of each SA level. Several embedded events were included to elicit key situation assessment responses. Ground truth served as the basis of comparison for what the subject perceived the situation to be. In two joint exercises, Army and Marines Companies conducted day and night vignettes during baseline (using their current equipment) and technology conditions (using the MOUT ACTD technology). The same scenario (with different opposing force (OpFor) plans and obstacles) was then re-run. The percentage of correct questions for each freeze frame was computed for the two conditions. Successful discrimination between conditions was obtained. The SA measure exhibited parallel form test-retest reliability, content validity, and face validity.

- *SA Assessment Center (AC)* The success of the free-play methodology in the MOUT ACTD experiments led to the examination of methodologies that augmented the strengths (realism, reliability, and validity) and minimized the weaknesses (time required, uncontrolled variables) of free-play activities. The

AC approach to SA measurement offered a standardized set of situations; for example, a live MOUT scenario with scripted OpFor actions to which a person could respond and an SA score or scores derived (Redden and Blackwell, 2001).

As the context of the AC was based on a MOUT environment, a review of the Department of the Defense MOUT literature and a job analysis were performed and an initial task inventory developed. After tasks were selected for inclusion in the AC, an SME panel was convened to generate three scripted vignettes (two offensive and one defensive) that contained the highest priority tasks. These scripted vignettes defined 'ground truth' CIRs, specifications for the number of freeze frames and where to place them, and sets of SA queries were developed. These queries covered the three SA levels for each major element of infantry operations in a MOUT environment.

The use of the AC methodology rather than a free-play methodology resulted in fewer uncontrolled variables; furthermore the time to gather information was shorter. The tactics and reaction of the OpFor and the location of enemy contact were standardized by the use of scripted OpFor movement. The capabilities of the leadership at platoon and higher levels were held constant by using a scripted white cell (the group of individuals used to play higher headquarters in order to control the scenario).

- *Virtual Environment* Late in 2000, advancements in the capabilities of simulators led the ARL-HRED to plan and conduct a series of experiments to define requirements for infantry information systems in the Dismounted Battlespace Battle Laboratory's Squad Synthetic Environment (Redden, 2002). A validation study was run in the McKenna MOUT Site and in the simulator replicating the site, to ensure that results from the simulator would not differ from results in a live environment. The simulator was validated for cognitive tasks, through comparison of cognitive performance in both situations.

   The global SA of the infantrymen participating in the experiments was used as the measure of effectiveness to evaluate information system requirements such as display modality, the effect of sensor mix and density. While not as realistic and flexible as the free-play and AC methodology, this virtual environment methodology did allow a more controlled study of the effect of information input configurations on infantry SA.

- *Gaming Environment* The study of infantry SA has since expanded to consider SA in teams. Redden, Elliott, Turner and Blackwell (in press) are developing a CIKA measure for infantry collaborative SA (CSA). A scenario was created in a modified version of a networked gaming environment that emulates the McKenna MOUT Site. The CSA construct involves hierarchical team structures, where leaders must coordinate, decide, and perform quickly. The leader has the ability to plan, rehearse and disseminate battle plans in real time, as changes occur on the battlefield. The leader is the manager, coordinator, and executer of an evolving plan while the individual soldiers focus on execution of tasks and the gathering of data. The emphasis on the leader as the central component in CSA, led to development of a CSA measure that follows Schwartz's (1990) proposal that team SA is moderated by leaders in hierarchical teams. Individual SA is calculated in the measure to reflect the individual team member's SA. The effect of the individual SA and the collaboration between the team members is tracked and measured at the leader level by measuring the leader's comprehension of the situation and projection of a future course of action.

Location Information for Battlefield Awareness Measures Soldiers' spatial awareness, consisting of the awareness of enemy, friendly and their own locations, is critical to infantry performance. Location SA constructs emphasize aspects of spatial SA, with direct measures of the infantryman's spatial orientation. This is accomplished by probe questions regarding location. Recently Defence Research and Development Canada commissioned a study as part of their Soldier Information Requirements Technology Demonstration to investigate the effects of using augmented reality visual, 3D audio and 3D tactile display modalities for providing battlefield location information. The study evaluated the effectiveness of location information systems when both the wearer and the target were moving. It documented the differences in SA between location modalities by placing the infantryman in a live MOUT environment, changing the situation (placing snipers on the route) or changing the infantryman's orders. Objective measures of SA evaluated the effect of various devices on the soldier's spatial SA by assessing his ability to change routes and his knowledge of distance and azimuth to the waypoints and objectives.

Glumm, Branscome, Patton, Mullins and Burton (1999) assessed the SA of infantrymen for location information by administering probe questions via computer-generated audio during the conduct of a land navigation mission. These questions were used to assess the soldier's awareness of position with respect to waypoints, targets, and other units without allowing them to consult a map or display. Results indicated that the participants maintained greater SA when information was presented visually on a Head-Mounted Display than when the same information was presented through auditory messages.

Subjective SA Measures

Situation Awareness Behaviorally Anchored Rating Scale (SABARS) Strater et al. (2001) developed a subjective measure based upon an SA requirements analysis of infantry platoon leaders (Matthews et al., 2000) that used expert observers to rate the platoon leaders on behaviors linked to SA. The SABARS metric consisted of 27 behaviors and actions linked to SA in MOUT missions. In four missions conducted in a virtual MOUT environment, experienced and inexperienced platoon leaders interacted with three 'live' squad leaders and associated computer-generated forces. Performance was rated by Observer/Controllers (O/Cs) on a five-point scale. SABARS differentiated SA as a function of the platoon leaders' experience level.

Matthews and Beal (2002) subsequently tested SABARS during a field training exercise at the US Military Academy. In this study, SABARS did not differentiate SA between leaders and subordinates, perhaps because the cadets involved in the exercise were all relatively inexperienced at MOUT missions. The global SA item on the SABARS was, however, highly predictive of the leader's decision-making effectiveness, ability to communicate effectively with subordinates, and overall performance. Moreover, SABARS was assessed by the O/Cs using it as including items relevant to SA, being easy to use, providing useful feedback for after action reviews, and providing feedback on SA that is an important goal in improving training.

Matthews, Eid, Johnsen and Meland (2004) tested SABARS during field training exercises conducted by the Royal Norwegian Army and Naval Academies. A 19 item SABARS was developed specifically for the missions. O/Cs evaluated the performance of the squad leaders and completed SABARS ratings at the conclusion of each mission. Four SABARS subscales, developed by a factor analysis, were significant predictors of the squad leader's decision-making and communication effectiveness, as well as overall SA.

SABARS is relatively unobtrusive, the items describe concrete behaviors that are readily observable by the O/Cs rather than the subject's internal cognitive state, and thus, is relatively direct and objective. It is viewed by users as relevant and acceptable. The main drawback to using SABARS is that its items are mission specific, requiring an SA requirements analysis to generate items for each mission type that is being evaluated. Nevertheless, SABARS has great potential for assessing SA in field settings, and research exploring its psychometric properties continues.

Situation Awareness Rating Technique (SART) The SART is one of the best-known and thoroughly tested subjective measures of SA (Jones, 2000). SART assumes that operators use understanding of situations in making decisions, that this understanding is consciously available, and that it can be quantified and made unambiguous (Taylor, 1990). In 2003, the ARL-HRED Fort Benning Field Element administered this technique during a demonstration of an infantry information system developed under the Warrior's Edge program. The technique showed promise for the subjective measurement of infantry SA during situations that do not allow access to the soldiers during the scenario, or which entail multiple rehearsals of the same scenario.

Mission Awareness Rating Scale (MARS) MARS (Matthews, Beal and Pleban, 2002) is based on the Crew Awareness Rating Scale (CARS) described in depth by McGuinness and Foy (2000). The instrument consists of two subscales, one to assess SA content and another to assess SA workload, both on a four-point scale. The content subscale questions require the respondent to rate how well they can identify, comprehend, predict, and decide in the given mission. The workload subscale questions require the respondent to indicate how much mental effort is required to identify, comprehend, predict, and decide in the given mission.

MARS has been demonstrated to differentiate among four different methods for simulating night fighting in a virtual combat simulator (Matthews et al., 2002) and to assess SA among Norwegian Army and Navy cadets during summer field training exercises (e.g., Matthews and Eid, 2003). When used during field training exercises, it was found that leaders rated their SA as higher than subordinates on both content and workload (Matthews and Beal, 2002). MARS ratings are even predicted by a personality variable, optimism (Matthews, Eid, Johnsen and Meland, 2004). MARS is generic and does not have to be tailored to each specific mission or usage. It is easy for respondents to understand and use, and is acceptable to trainers due to its unobtrusiveness.

Summary

Objective techniques need significant efforts to develop and administer, requiring front-end considerations of CIRs and development of scenarios that provide operationally relevant and challenging experiences. However they provide a valuable measure when in-depth and diagnostic SA assessment is required. The techniques and scenarios provide rich experience and feedback to all participants, thus enhancing training and mission rehearsal. They also serve to facilitate development and evaluation of new soldier systems, using scenarios and instruments validated for the performance domain. Great progress has been made in establishing valid and diagnostic assessments of multi-operator SA in challenging and dynamic infantry scenarios. A drawback of objective techniques is that they can be somewhat disruptive.

While subjective SA measures have obvious limitations, there are instances when they may be the only type of data that can be obtained practically. In field training exercises, for example, trainers may be reluctant to allow obtrusive measures that require the stopping of action to allow probe questions to be administered. Although subjective measures have yet to show strong correlations with objective SA, they can be cost effective and practical. Their predictive ability of leader experience and performance is promising.

Team SA

It is important to consider team SA as the infantry works in a team environment. At the lowest hierarchical level the squad or section is regarded as the basic building blocks of an infantry unit. The squad is provided with its own mission, albeit normally functioning within a larger group, usually a platoon. At the higher echelons, the leaders are supported by increasingly larger headquarters teams in their C^2 function. Complex teaming arrangements occur not only within the immediate groups, but also with other groups on the horizontal level, as well as up and down the command chain. These may involve personnel from other corps in the combined arms team, such as artillery, engineering, medical, etc. Each member of infantry teams, irrespective of echelons, has specific tasks that contribute to the overall team goal. Well-developed individual SA, team SA and shared SA are needed to enable the team to achieve its mission.

In performing their tasks, members of infantry teams are often dispersed. At the lowest echelon level hand signals are still common as the means for communication. At the higher levels, radios and more sophisticated information technology support systems become more prevalent. Leaders rely in part on the reports received from their subordinates for SA. A highly skilled one will be able to develop SA, even though the team members are geographically dispersed and communication is constrained.

Discussions on team SA in other domains are provided by Vidulich, Bolia and Nelson, Chapter 13, and by Garbis and Artman, Chapter 15, of this volume. The most detailed study of infantry team SA is that by Endsley et al., (2000). Team SA is defined as 'the degree to which every team member possesses the SA required for his or her responsibilities' (Endsley, 1995b, p.39). According to this definition, team SA is the overall SA developed in the whole team to achieve its mission. Shared SA, which is the overlap between team members' SA, and is a subset of team SA, is defined as 'the degree to which team members possess the same SA on shared SA requirements' (Endsley and Jones, 1997, p.47). Four components underlie shared SA, namely shared SA requirements, shared SA sources, shared SA mechanisms and shared SA processes (Endsley et al., 2000). Shared SA requirements refer to the information, covering all three SA levels, that needs to be shared. Verbal and non-verbal communication, shared displays and shared environment are the sources for shared SA. Shared mental models are important mechanisms for developing shared SA. Shared SA processes are the many team processes that allow team members to gain shared SA.

Shared SA and shared mental models are part of cognitive competencies required for effective teamwork (Salas and Cannon-Bowers, 2000). Shared mental models are defined as 'knowledge structures held by members of a team that enable them to form accurate explanations and expectations for the task, and, in turn, to coordinate their actions and adapt their behavior to demands of the task and other team members' (Cannon-Bowers, Salas and Converse, 1993, p.228). Stout, Cannon-Bowers, and Salas (1996) contended that in effective teams, the members possess shared knowledge bases, in terms of the overall mission and the members' roles for achieving it, the required sequencing of activities, and the ability to take accurate actions that are expected by their team mates based on environmental cues. It was hypothesized that 'effective teams draw on shared knowledge bases to arrive at a common or team level of situational awareness among members' (p. 99). It appears that these knowledge bases allow infantry teams to develop team and shared SA and to operate effectively even under the most challenging conditions.

The infantry domain has not received much attention in team SA research. Shared SA requirements for army brigade officers were elicited by means of goal directed task analysis (Bolstad et al., 2000). Artman (2000) investigated the impact of information distribution on battalion staff's SA brought about by different technology architectures. A study on infantry team collaborative SA has been undertaken by Redden, Elliott, Turner and Blackwell (in press) and is described in the previous section.

With the introduction of advanced technology tools to the infantry, from the soldiers up to the highest echelon, research is needed to provide a good understanding of team SA, shared SA, their relationship to team performance and the factors that affect the development and maintenance of team SA and shared SA.

Infantry SA in Future Operations

In future wars it is envisaged that elements in the battlespace will be extensively networked, allowing the sharing of a large amount of information. The result of information sharing and collaboration is enhanced information quality and shared situation awareness. The latter enables self-synchronization, thereby dramatically increasing mission effectiveness (Network Centric Warfare Department of Defense Report to Congress July 2001 cited in Alberts, 2002). The vision for future warfare is shared by many western countries, although differences are expected in the extent of the networking.

The implementation of Network Centric Warfare (NCW) capability requires changes in the way the military conducts its business (Alberts, 2002). Personnel at all echelons will have access to a wide range of information, which commanders cannot control. This promotes shared SA that empowers those involved and enables distributed decision-making based on command intent. Decision-making is no longer the responsibility of a single commander. A new type of C^2 concept, one that is no longer strictly hierarchical, needs to be developed for a flattened organizational structure. To deal with the vast amount of information a variety of automation and decision aids are required, including those that fuse data from sensors, and the linking of sensors to shooters. Ultimately it is the ability of the elements in the battlespace to collaborate and self-synchronize that enables the efficient achievement of mission.

The ability to access a whole range of information will make a profound difference to infantry SA. Advanced sensor technology will be able to provide information on the position, movement and disposition of friendly, enemy and neutral entities in the battlespace. Whilst the 'fog-of-war' will not be eliminated, the available information will facilitate decision superiority against an adversary who does not possess advanced information technology tools.

There is a potential danger of information overload in NCW. Soldiers engaged in close combat and under time pressure need to be able to obtain information and gain situational understanding in the shortest possible time. Headquarters staff will have to make timely plans and decisions in order to step within the adversary's decision cycles. Information systems need to be designed carefully to ensure that data is fused into a comprehensible format and is presented in a manner that is consistent with the individual characteristics of the users, the type of data being presented, and the prevailing phase of the battle.

Data fusion capability, decision support systems and automation will be part of the future command posts to assist the operators in dealing with and making sense of the vast amount of information. The issue of 'out-of-the-loop' performance should not be overlooked (Endsley and Kiris, 1995). It is important for automatic systems to be designed carefully, to ensure that appropriate functions are allocated to the human and machine in order that each of their capabilities are utilized in the most efficient way. The reliance on information systems also creates vulnerability. The integrity of these systems must be guaranteed.

The mission command philosophy provides subordinate commanders with the autonomy to act independently to achieve command intent, within the stated constraints and available resources. This places much more responsibility on junior commanders, who must possess good global and local SA in order to make appropriate decisions. On the other hand, higher commanders can access detailed information such as they never could in the past. This may lead to 'big picture blindness' as a consequence of focusing on too low a level rather than the big picture. In addition 'micromanagement' by higher commanders may pose a serious problem.

The battlespace in the future will be more dispersed and more variable in density involving smaller and more adaptable forces. Operational tempo will increase and battles can continue without stopping because of advanced sensor technologies and devices that aid night vision. The challenge for commanders is to ensure the soldiers receive adequate rest. The lack of sleep and fatigue has adverse effects on cognitive performance including SA.

Adding to the stress experienced by soldiers and commanders is media pervasiveness. Combatants' actions will be under intense scrutiny, the outcome of which may work for or against the friendly forces in terms of public opinion. The battle to win the hearts and minds of communities where the operation takes place and the forces' countries of origin will be intense. Combatants will have access to information and news from within the battlespace, with positive or negative impact on morale.

In the future it is predicted that battles will be conducted in a multidimensional space, involving the air, land, sea, space, electromagnetic and information domain. The integration of the three services operating jointly with other nations will be the norm. The use of misinformation and deception to influence the adversaries' SA will be a weapon in future battles, as it has been in the past. Cyber wars will be conducted through blatant means, but potentially much more damaging on SA is the use of insidious, subtle methods that makes infiltration difficult to detect. Future battles will involve teams that are geographically dispersed but will have shared SA through collaboration and the sharing of information. As our understanding of distributed teams is limited, research in this area is required.

The capabilities of NCW can only be realized if potential problems are addressed through research and development of theories and application in a range of areas. In relation to infantry SA, the relevant areas include: design of information systems; interface design including battlespace information display; data fusion; automation and decision support systems; training; co-located and distributed teamwork, team performance, team SA, shared SA, shared mental models; collaboration within and between teams; collaborative tools; team structures; self-synchronization; command intent, sleep deprivation and fatigue.

References

Alberts, D.S. (2002), *Information Age Transformation: Getting To A 21st Century Military*, CCRP, Washington DC.

Artman, H. (2000), 'Team Situation Assessment and Information Distribution', *Ergonomics*, vol. 43, pp. 1111-1128.

Australian Army (2002), *Land Warfare Doctrine 1: The Fundamentals of Land Warfare (LWD1)*, Land Warfare and Development Centre, Puckapunyal, Victoria.

Blackwell, C.L. and Redden, E.S. (2000), 'Toward a Methodology for Evaluating the Impact of Situation Awareness on Unit Effectiveness of Dismounted Infantrymen', in *Proceedings of the Research and Technology Organization Human Factors in Medicine Panel Symposium*, Oslo, Norway, pp. 57.

Bolstad, C.A., Riley, J.M., Jones, D.G. and Endsley, M.R. (2002), 'Using Goal Directed Task Analysis With Army Brigade Officer Teams', in *Proceedings of the 46th Annual Meeting of the Human Factors and Ergonomics Society*, Human Factors and Ergonomics Society, Santa Monica, California, pp. 472-476.

Burba, E.H., Jr. (1999), 'Keynote Address: Army XXI Insights', in S.E. Graham and M.D. Matthews (eds), *Infantry Situation Awareness: Papers from the 1998 Infantry Situation Awareness Workshop*, US Army Research Institute for the Behavioral and Social Sciences, Alexandria, VA.

Campbell, M. (2003), 'Team Assassin's the Name but the Game Has Changed – Fear is the Daily Companion of the Young Americans Patrolling the Streets of Baghdad', *The Australian*, 4 August, p. 11.

Cannon-Bowers, J.A., Salas, E. and Converse, S. (1993), 'Shared Mental Models in Expert Team Decision Making', in N.J. Castellan (ed.), *Individual and Group Decision Making*, Erlbaum, Hillsdale, NJ, pp. 221-246.

Endsley, M.R. (1987), *SAGAT: A Methodology for the Measurement of Situation Awareness*, NOR DOC 87-83, Northrop Corporation, Hawthorne, CA.

Endsley, M.R. (1988), 'Design and Evaluation for Situation Awareness Enhancement', in *Proceedings of the Human Factors Society 32nd Annual Meeting*, Human Factors Society, Santa Monica, CA, pp. 97-101.

Endsley, M.R. (1994), 'Situation Awareness in Dynamic Human Decision Making: Measurement', in R. Gilson, D. Garland, and J. Koonce (eds), *Situational Awareness in Complex Systems*, Embry-Riddle Aeronautical University Press, Daytona Beach.

Endsley, M.R. (1995a), 'Toward a Theory of Situation Awareness in Dynamic Systems', *Human Factors*, vol. 37, pp. 32-64.

Endsley, M.R. (1995b), 'Measurement of Situation Awareness in Dynamic Systems', *Human Factors*, vol. 37, pp. 65-84.

Endsley, M.R., Holder, L.D., Leibrecht, B.C., Garland, D.J., Wampler. R.L. and Matthews, M.D. (2000), *Modeling and Measuring Situation Awareness in the Infantry Operational Environment*, Research Report 1753, US Army Research Institute for the Behavioral and Social Sciences, Alexandria, VA.

Endsley, M.R. and Jones, W.M. (1997), *Situation Awareness, Information Dominance and Information Warfare*, AL/CF-TR-1997-0156, United States Air Force Armstrong Laboratory, Wright-Patterson Air Force Base, OH.

Endsley, M.R. and Kiris, E.O. (1995), 'The Out-of-the-Loop Performance Problem and Level of Control in Automation', *Human Factors,* vol. 37, pp. 381-394.

Evans, K.L. and Christ, R.E. (2003), *Development and Validation of Communication-based Measures of Situation Awareness,* Research Report 1803, US Army Research Institute for the Behavioral and Social Sciences, Alexandria, VA.

French, H.T. and Hutchinson, A. (2002), 'Measurement of Situation Awareness in a C4ISR Experiment', in *Proceedings of the 7th International Command and Control Research and Technology Symposium.* CCRP, Washington DC.

Glumm, M.M., Branscome, T.A, Patton, D.J., Mullins, L.A. and Burton, P.A. (1999), *The Effects of an Auditory Versus a Visual Presentation of Information on Soldier Performance,* ARL-TR-1992, US Army Research Laboratory, Aberdeen Proving Ground, MD.

Gorman, P.F. (1999), 'Situation Awareness', in S.E. Graham and M.D. Matthews (eds), *Infantry Situation Awareness: Papers from the 1998 Infantry Situation Awareness Workshop,* US Army Research Institute for the Behavioral and Social Sciences, Alexandria, VA.

Graham, S.E. and Matthews, M.D. (1999, eds), *Infantry Situation Awareness: Papers from the 1998 Infantry Situation Awareness Workshop,* US Army Research Institute for the Behavioral and Social Sciences, Alexandria, VA.

Holder, L.D. (1999), 'Situation Awareness in Infantry Battalions', in S.E. Graham and M.D. Matthews (eds), *Infantry Situation Awareness: Papers from the 1998 Infantry Situation Awareness Workshop.* US Army Research Institute for the Behavioral and Social Sciences, Alexandria, VA.

Jones, D.G. (2000), 'Subjective Measures of Situation Awareness', in M.R. Endsley and D.J. Garland (eds), *Situation Awareness Analysis and Measurement,* Lawrence Erlbaum Associates, Mahwah, NJ.

Matthews, M.D. and Beal, S.A. (2002), *Assessing Situation Awareness in Field Training Exercises,* Research Report 1795, US Army Research Institute for the Behavioral and Social Sciences, Alexandria, VA.

Matthews, M.D., Beal, S.A. and Pleban, R.J. (2002), *Situation Awareness in a Virtual Environment: Description of a Subjective Assessment Scale,* Research Report 1786, US Army Research Institute for the Behavioral and Social Sciences, Alexandria, VA.

Matthews, M.D. and Eid, J. (2003), *Assessing Situation Awareness in a Norwegian Naval Training Exercise,* paper presented at the Annual Convention of the American Psychological Association, Toronto, Canada.

Matthews, M.D., Eid, J., Johnsen, B.J. and Meland, N.T. (2004), *Optimism Predicts Situation Awareness in a Military Training Exercise,* paper presented at the Annual Convention of the American Psychological Association, Honolulu, Hawaii.

Matthews, M.D., Eid, J., Johnsen, B.J., Meland, N.T. and Talcott, C. (2004), *Situation Awareness: Predicting Small Uni Leader Performance During a Combat Fatigue Course,* paper presented at the 7th Defense Analysis Seminar, Seoul, Korea.

Matthews, M.D., Pleban, R.J., Endsley, M.R. and Strater, L.D. (2000), 'Measures of Infantry Situation Awareness for a Virtual MOUT Environment', in *Proceedings of the Human Performance, Situation Awareness, and Automation Conference,* SA Technologies, Savannah, GA, pp. 262-267.

Matthews, M.D., Strater, L.D. and Endsley, M.R. (in press), 'Situation Awareness Requirements Analysis for Infantry Platoon Leaders', *Military Psychology.*

McGuinness, B. and Foy, J.L. (2000), 'A Subjective Measure of Situation Awareness: The Crew Awareness Rating Scale', in *Proceedings of the First Human Performance, Situation Awareness and Automation Conference,* SA Technologies, Atlanta, GA, pp. 286-291.

Medby, J.J. and Glenn, R.W. (2002), *Street Smart: Intelligence Preparation of the Battlefield for Urban Operations,* RAND, Santa Monica, CA.

Miller, N.L. and Shattuck, L.G. (in press), *Situation Awareness in the Future Force,* Naval Postgraduate School Technical Report, Naval Postgraduate School, Monterey, CA.

Pew, R.W. (1991), 'Defining and Measuring Situation Awareness in the Commercial Aircraft Cockpit', in *Proceedings of the Conference on Challenges in Aviation Human Factors,* American Institute of Aeronautics and Astronautics, Washington DC.

Pleban, R.J., Matthews, M.D., Salter, M.S. and Eakin, D.E. (2002), 'Training and Assessing Complex Decision-Making in a Virtual Environment', *Perceptual and Motor Skills,* vol. 94, pp. 871-882.

Redden, E.S. (2002), *Virtual Environment Study of Mission-based Critical Information Requirements,* Technical Report 2636, US Army Research Laboratory, Aberdeen Proving Ground, MD.

Redden, E.S. and Blackwell, C.L. (2000), 'Measurement of Situation Awareness in Free-play Exercises', in *Proceedings of the First Human Performance, Situation Awareness and Automation Conference,* SA Technologies, Atlanta, GA, pp. 131-136.

Redden, E.S. and Blackwell, C.L. (2001), *Situational Awareness and Communication Experiment for Military Operations in Urban Terrain: Experiment I,* Technical Report 2583, US Army Research Laboratory, Aberdeen Proving Ground, MD.

Redden, E.S., Elliott, L.R., Turner, D.D. and Blackwell, C.L. (in press), 'Development of a Metric for Collaborative Situation Awareness', in *Proceedings of Human Performance, Situation Awareness and Automation Technology Conference,* Daytona Beach, FL.

Richardson, W.R. (1999), 'Situation Awareness Requirements for Individual Combatants and Squads', in S.E. Graham and M.D. Matthews (eds), *Infantry Situation Awareness: Papers from the 1998 Infantry Situation Awareness Workshop.* US Army Research Institute for the Behavioral and Social Sciences, Alexandria, VA.

Salas, E. and Cannon-Bowers, J.A. (2000), 'The Anatomy of Team Training', in S. Tobias and J.D. Fletcher (eds), *Training and Retraining: A Handbook for Business, Industry, Government, and the Military,* Macmillan Reference, New York, pp. 312-335.

Salter, M.S. (1999), 'Situation Awareness Requirements for Infantry Brigades', in S.E. Graham and M.D. Matthews (eds), *Infantry Situation Awareness: Papers from the 1998 Infantry Situation Awareness Workshop,* US Army Research Institute for the Behavioral and Social Sciences, Alexandria, VA.

Schwartz, D. (1990), *Training for Situational Awareness,* Flight Safety International, Houston, TX.

Shattuck, L.G. and Miller, N.L. (2004), 'A Process Tracing Approach to the Investigation of Situation Awareness', in *Proceedings of the Human Factors and Ergonomics Society's 47th Annual Meeting,* Human Factors and Ergonomics Society, Santa Monica, CA.

Shattuck, L.G., Talcott, C., Matthews, M.D., Clark, J. and Swiergosz, M. (2002), 'Constructing Battlefield Understanding: A Comparison of Experienced and Novice Decision Makers in Different Contexts', in *Proceedings of the Human Factors and Ergonomics Society's 46th Annual Meeting,* Human Factors and Ergonomics Society, Santa Monica, CA, pp. 443-447.

Stout, R.J., Cannon-Bowers, J.A. and Salas, E. (1996), 'The Role of Shared Mental Models in Developing Team Situational Awareness: Implications for Training', *Training Research Journal,* vol. 2, pp. 85-116.

Strater, L.D., Endsley, M.R., Pleban, R.J. and Matthews, M.D. (2001), *Measures of Platoon Leader Situation Awareness in Virtual Decision Making Exercises,* Research Report 1770, US Army Research Institute for the Behavioral and Social Sciences, Alexandria, VA.

Taylor, R.M. (1990), 'Situational Awareness Rating Technique (SART): The Development of a Tool for Aircrew Systems Design', in *Situational Awareness in Aerospace Operations,* AGARD-CP-478, NATO-AGARD, Neuilly Sur Seine, France, pp. 3/1-3/17.

TRADOC (1994), *Force XXI Operations,* TRADOC PAM 525-5, United States Department of the Army, Washington DC.

Chapter 15

Team Situation Awareness as Communicative Practices

Christer Garbis and Henrik Artman

Introduction

Today an ever-increasing number of dynamic systems, such as nuclear power plants, air traffic control, industrial process plants etc. rely on the accurate performance of teams rather than on individuals. A dynamic system is here characterized by the fact that the state of a system changes both autonomously as well as a consequence of the decision-makers´ actions and that several interdependent decisions in real time are required if the system is to be controlled (Brehmer, 1992). A common feature which most dynamic systems share is that events happen fast, are often complex, consist of several components and require rapid analysis and decision making under severe time pressure (Orasanu and Connelly, 1993). It follows that the management of dynamic systems require considerable teamwork which often requires a substantial amount of communication. The fact that many decisions have to be made in parallel and actions have to be taken in real time requires that the operator teams need to maintain a rather accurate overall awareness of the process managed on a continuous basis. In addition, it is desirable that this continuous awareness is mutually shared among the team members.

Even though several studies have addressed the issue of team situation awareness (Swezey and Salas, 1992, Salas, Prince, Baker and Shrestha, 1995; Wellens, 1993; Artman, 2000; French, Matthews and Redden, Chapter 14, this volume) there is in general little knowledge about the local practices underlying the formation and maintenance of the overall situation awareness in dynamic systems (for exceptions see Heath and Luff, 1996; Artman and Waern, 1999; Sebok, 2000). In our empirical material derived from an underground line control room, we aim to understand team situation awareness in terms of the communicative and coordinative practices used within teams. We focus on the underlying mechanisms for the active construction of mutually shared situation awareness, its maintenance and even its momentary loss as a result of the communicative practice between team members.

'Having the Bubble' and Mutual Situation Awareness

'Having the bubble' is the expression used by those who man the combat operations centers in US Navy ships to indicate that they have managed to construct a cognitive understanding of the ship's overall situation and operational status in order to make the necessary decisions and take appropriate actions (Rochlin 1997).[4] To say that one has the bubble means that that person has successfully integrated the combat status, information from various sensors, the ships position and movement, and the status and performance of the weapon systems into a single overall 'picture' of the ship's situation and operational status. The expression is not merely a metaphor for a cognitive representation; rather it indicates that one is in control of a bubble and thereby in control of a delicate situation. To have the bubble is in other words equivalent to having situation awareness. Having the bubble is however a description which needs to be extended in several ways if we are to be able to understand team situation awareness in relation to the management of dynamic systems.

First, we need to go beyond the individual operators and include whole teams. A lot of the research in situation awareness has focused on the unaided individual operator and how he or she obtains the bubble (see for example Endsley 1995, Sarter and Woods 1995). This approach implies that situation awareness can be conceived of as a subjective phenomenon within an individual. However to understand team situation awareness we need to consider the concerted efforts of several team members. As a consequence of this we argue that we must expand the unit of analysis from individual task performers to encompass a whole operator team and their actions while it is engaged in what Waern (1998) calls cooperative process management.

Second, we need to take into account the fact that cooperative process management is based on the existence of a mutually shared goal between the team members. The management of dynamic systems is often achieved by a team where each individual has specific responsibility and roles which however are interdependent of each other (Heath and Luff, 1992; Hutchins 1995; Rasker, Post, Schraagen, 2000; Artman and Persson, 2000). The reason for this is that many incident-related processes are interwoven. Even though each member might have his own area of expertise and responsibility it is only through their mutual understanding that they can coordinate their resources and actions to accomplish the task. Thus team situation awareness requires the articulation of each individual's activity so that every team member can synchronize his/her actions with those of the others to reach a collectively shared goal. Understanding how the common goal is created and shared between team members is a necessary step in describing and understanding team situation awareness.

---

[4] According to Rochlin the term seems to derive from earlier times when the sighting of guns, and the movement of a ship were read from mechanical level-reading devices consisting of a bubble of air in a curved tube full of fluid, just like a carpenter's spirit level.

Third, team situation awareness relies on the extensive use of various artifacts. These artifacts, which represent information to the team, are often computer screens and various displays. The team members have often different information resources, which need to be combined and coordinated into a mutual understanding (Vidulich, Bolia, Nelson, Chapter 13, this volume). However the meaning of the information presented by these artifacts is not always clear and needs therefore to be interpreted and negotiated among the team members. Therefore team situation awareness calls for negotiation and communication between team members with and through these artifacts. By including the artifacts used and focusing on the interactional and negotiational practices as the primarily unit of analysis we can better understand what team situation awareness is and its role in the team (Rogalski and Samurçay, 1993; Sebok, 2000).

For the casual observer the amount of activity going on and information flowing around in a typical control room can be truly overwhelming. It is difficult to imagine that any operator can make an overall status assessment and piece together all those disparate bits of information into a large, coherent understanding. It therefore comes as no surprise that an individual operator alone cannot easily have the bubble, simply because there is just too much information that needs to be processed in a too limited time frame. In addition to this the situations dealt with are processes, which are likely to continuously change status, making it even more difficult to have the bubble. It would therefore seem as natural to address the issue of having the bubble during the management of dynamic systems as a collective phenomenon, which involves the interactions and communication between several team members, with the help of various technological artifacts.

The Process of Constructing, Maintaining, Losing and Reconstructing Team Situation Awareness

Team situation awareness has been defined by Wellens (1993) as the sharing of a common perspective between two or more individuals regarding current environmental events, their meaning and projected future. Salas, Prince, Baker, Shrestha (1995) defined team situation awareness as what is in part a shared understanding of a situation among team members a particular point in time. Taking our starting point in these definitions we would like to *extend the scope and further emphasize the interpretative and constructive nature* of team situation awareness to include the active construction of a situation understanding.

So far we have argued that team situation awareness in cooperative process management should be seen as a collective rather that an individual phenomenon, which rest on, a mutually shared goal and which is accomplished though the use of artifacts. To say that a team has reached common situation awareness can give the impression that we are dealing with a state, which is static and can easily be maintained. However, as we will try to show in this chapter, team situation awareness cannot easily be characterized by a static description. It is notable that in hindsight analysis, in which situation awareness has been regarded as a state and measured accordingly, the results tend to be interpreted in a binary sense, i.e., either the perception of elements in the environment is good or it is found to be poor (Flach, 1995; Woods, Johannesen, Cook, Sarter, 1994; Sarter and Woods, 1991). Intermediate positions have been notoriously hard to account for since this requires a considerably more elaborate conception of what it means to have team situation awareness of a complex process. To account for situation awareness as a state will not tell us anything about how the team formed, maintained or lost that awareness. This can only be done if we consider the awareness formation mechanisms as a dynamic process. We therefore need to account for the mechanisms through which the shared understanding is constructed, maintained, and sometimes even lost.

Once the common awareness is formed it is equally important for a team to maintain the overall understanding of the development of the situation as it unfolds. Maintaining the situation awareness during cooperative process management is often complicated by the fact that each situation is different from the previous one and that it unfolds in real time, giving the operator team little or no time at all to evaluate received information. Given the complexity of the process managed, the critical nature of the task at hand, the large amount of information which needs to be processed, and the time pressure, forming and maintaining the mutual situation awareness in cooperative process management constitutes an essential part of the work. Naturally, forming and maintaining this awareness in a control room poses a considerable strain on the people and the organization. Apart from requiring effort to construct and maintain the bubble, it is equally important to acknowledge that the bubble can be lost and reconstructed in the course of the work. Accounting for these mechanisms and transitions between the various bubble stages is an important part of understanding the role of the bubble. Therefore it is not surprising that many major accidents and catastrophes over the years have been the result of operators in coordination centers having lost the bubble because they could not comprehend a critical situation or even misunderstood it. In summary, we need to reconsider the unit of analysis and the very nature of the bubble formation and maintenance – that is we need to understand how teams create and maintain situation awareness as a distributed communicative phenomenon.

Data Collection and Setting

The setting for the study presented in this chapter is the control room of the Green underground line in Stockholm, Sweden. In the following we will briefly present the organization of the work as well as some of the most commonly used cognitive artifacts. We will also account for the methodology used for the data collection.

The operator team, who works in the control room of the Green line, and is responsible for the safe and timely conduct of underground traffic along the 48 stations of the line, consists of five operators. This comprises the Traffic Controller (TC) and the Shift Operator (SO), who are both responsible for controlling the trains, the Information Assistant (IA), who provides information to the passengers at the stations through the public address system, and two Signal System Operators (SSO) (Figure 15.1). Even though the title and formal task description of the operators vary, they have all gone through similar training. This means that they can all take over each other's tasks whenever this is needed. In addition to this the recruitment policy of the Stockholm underground is such that operator are recruited from within the organization, meaning that they have probably previously been working as a station manager, train driver, etc. The implication of this recruitment policy is that operators share a great deal of the history of the organization at the same time as they possess a detailed understanding of the day-to-day work which makes the underground system work.

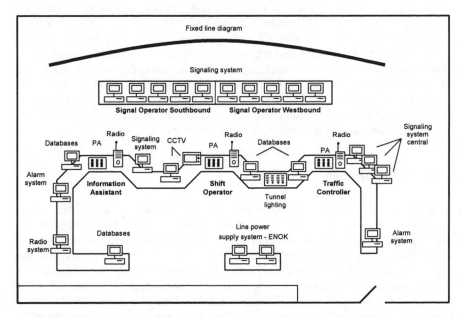

Figure 15.1 The layout of the control room with the positions of the operators and the informational artifacts available to them

The daily work of the operators is structured around a number of technological artifacts, which serve different purposes. The radio constitutes the main means of communication between the operators and the train drivers. Apart from the radio, the control room is equipped with numerous PCs which contain a variety of different sub control systems, such as an alarm system, various databases, a power line supply and control system, etc. The mimic panel, which is a large electronic board measuring 10m x 2m, displays each train as a sequence of lights moving on the line along with an identification number which indicates the destination of the train and its turn in the timetable. The mimic panel also displays all the signals and switches on the track. The mimic panel is, with its size, the dominant artifact in the room, and is placed in front of the operators, clearly visible to all of them. Two operators who, under normal operations during the day, handle the signals of the western and the eastern part of the track handle the signaling system. It should be noted that the signaling system was recently upgraded from an analogue to a fully digital one. Finally, the time table, which is often referred to, displays each train as a set of a numbers which denote variables, such as time of departure from the starting station, time of arrival at the final station, and when intermediate stations will be visited.

The analysis presented in this chapter is based on a field study conducted at the Green underground line control room in Stockholm, Sweden. The study took place during the spring of 2000. Data were collected and analyzed through the use of cognitive ethnography, which is a method that combines sociointeractional and cognitive aspects of work into one analysis. On the one hand cognitive ethnography is based on qualitative methods of sociology, which try to show how work is socially constituted and reconstituted, while on the other hand, it retains the analytical framework of cognitive science. In essence, the method implies that cognitive phenomena can be described and analyzed in qualitative terms. The gathered data include direct observations in the control room during operator shifts as well as video- and audio recordings. In addition, extensive field notes were collected based on informal interviews with operators.

Creating and Imposing the Bubble

The operators in the control room are supposed to have an adequate situation awareness, or as we prefer a consistent bubble, of the happenings on the underground line. Although how they create and maintain a bubble is dependent on both different technologies and the eyes and reports of the train drivers and other personnel in the field. We will here first look at a quite simple and common form of communication between a train driver and the operators at the control room. The excerpt will show how each of the two interlocutors who communicate tries to impose ones own understanding of the situation, or maybe to think that 'the other' have the same understanding as one self. We will also see how the operators in the control room together negotiate the possible meanings of the reported situation.

The situation is common – the driver wants to unlock the emergency brake. The emergency brake can be turned on by either a passenger or by the security system. The security system enforce the emergency brake if the train is accelerating to much, if there is an incongruence between the statuses between train and the security systems or if the friction between the wheels and the track is to low etc. In order to unlock the emergency brake the driver first has to call the control room and ask to permission to unlock it. Unlocking it means that the train can be driven in 15 km/h a certain stretch until the train is noticed by the security system again. Unlocking of the emergency brake is registered in the databases.

The excerpt starts with a rather indistinct call to the control room about a transport to Vällingby, a station (Table 15.1). The mimic panel displays '00000' between Vällingby and the wagon park. There is also another unidentified train but on the other end of the track. There have also been two announcements of transports from the wagon hall.

Table 15.1 A train driver makes an indistinct call to the control room

Time	Who to Whom	Transcript
12.37.17	Driver on radio.	Transport to Vällingby fro[..] ark, over.
12.37.24	TO to driver over radio	Transport to Vällingby
12.37.28	SO to TO	From!?

Transcription notations:

Shift Operator	SO
Traffic Operator	TO
Signal System Operator - Eastbound	SSO-East
Signal System Operator - Westbound	SSO-West
Non working visiting Shift Operator	NWSO

As mentioned the call in Table 15.1 is indistinct and the legible words are 'Transport' and 'Vällingby' [the destination station]. The driver does not identify his train but rather expects the operators at the control room to know which train he is calling from. The regulations say that you should identify your call by the train identification, but since the mimic panel was introduced praxis has been to omit this information as the control room operators often can interject this information from the mimic panel. Furthermore, as the transport has been announced it could well be anticipated that the operators would know this. Before answering the drivers call (time 12.37.24), the TO is scanning the mimic panel in order to identify which driver called. The destination is of course an important cue when scanning. He then answers the call by the information he has or can interject from the call and the panel. SO, who overheard the call, did not hear whom it came from and asks right out to the room while scanning the mimic panel. The driver quickly asks permission to unlock (see Table 15.2).

Table 15.2 Driver asks for permission to unlock the emergency brake. The control room operators collectively try to locate the train

Time	Who to Whom	Transcript
12.37.30	Driver on radio.	The train is put to emergency, I want to unlock.
12.37.34	TO to SO	Is it him on the approach there?
12.37.35	SO to TO	Yes, exactly
12.37.36	TO to driver over radio	Yes, you have permission to unlock, the approach to Vällingby, between the tracks, over.
12.37.44	Driver on radio	That is understood.

After the driver has asked for permission to unlock the emergency brake TO asks SO if it can be the train on the approach to Vällingby (Table 15.2, 12.37.34). SO confirms. Interestingly, it is now TO who asks SO even if SO first initiated the query. This is a common kind of articulating the information, in the process of analyzing the information at hand. This mundane form of communicating is a way of inviting others into ones cognitive processes and at the same time gives the other operators a chance to confirm or reject ones thoughts (Garbis, 2002; Artman and Waern, 1999).

TO then gives the driver permission to unlock the emergency brake, but in the same message is imposing his understanding of where the train is on the driver. By this he gives the driver a possibility to reject his understanding, or by just accepting the information confirming it. In this case the driver is accepting the information by telling that it is understood.

This case shows how the operators create an understanding of the situation, in this case a simple and common situation, by combing different forms of information e.g., the call, prior announcement, the information on the fixed line diagram. We can also see how the process is distributed over the different operators. The imposing of ones understanding (or when articulating ones questions) is a kind of practice that opens up the possibility to communicate ones understanding effectively, but at the same time give interlocutors the possibility to interpolate and correct ones understanding. The next case we will present is much more complex and will illuminate how the bubble is hard to create, and maintain when more information must be superimposed.

The Bubble is Punctured

The analysis presented below, describes how the operator team in the Green line control room, in Stockholm, Sweden dealt with an incident that occurred during an unusual type of engineering work. This work involved the repair and replacement of the westbound track over one of the major bridges connecting central Stockholm with the west areas of the city. The engineering work was scheduled to start at 19.00 hours on a Saturday when the traffic intensity is low. It was calculated that the replacement of the track section on the bridge would take approximately three hours. During these hours, both east- and westbound traffic would have to be led over the remaining eastbound track. This meant that both east- and westbound trains would have to be directed manually over the single remaining track on the bridge; this would have required that the switches and signals were controlled manually. Since one third of the Green line is located to the west of the bridge, any disruption of the traffic over the remaining eastbound track could, within a few minutes, turn the bridge into a troublesome bottle neck. Thus, over the next hours timely traffic was going to depend on the smooth flow of trains over the bridge.

Running underground line traffic counter-track is an operation that requires a significant amount of skill of the signaling system operators. It should be pointed out that no kind of written procedures exist for such operations. For this reason the management of the control room had decided to assign an extra signaling system operator for the particular evening whose only mission would be to manually manage the trains and the signaling system over the bridge where the engineering work was to be undertaken. The operator that would be responsible for the counter-track traffic took the position normally occupied by the signaling system operator west (c.f. Figure 15.1), while the control of the signals and switches on the rest of the track was divided between the signaling system operator east and the Traffic Controller.[5] The counter-track traffic maneuver had been carefully planned several days in advance including multiple briefings and discussions within the operator team. The presentation and analysis of the episode below starts a few minutes before counter-track traffic is scheduled to start. The emphasis is on how the bubble is lost and then constructed and maintained through the collective and distributed use of the informational artifacts available.

Prior to the replacement of the westbound track on the bridge the operators need to cut off the power supply to that particular section of the track. The operators at the control room are the only persons in the entire underground organization that have authorization to do this. In order to cut off the power, the operators have to call the control room of the electricity company delivering power to the underground line and demand to cut power at specified sections of the track. To their help the underground line operators have a line power supply system. This system displays the entire line in terms of the electrical feeding points of the track (Figure 15.2). The operators refer to the line power supply system as the ENOK system (in Swedish ElNätets Order och Kontrolsystem). At 19.15 the Traffic Operator calls the control room of the electricity company and requests that power supply is cut for the section over the bridge. The Traffic Operator communicates the relevant information by reading over the phone the numbers of the electrical feeding points of the relevant section of the line that he can see on the ENOK screen.

During the following couple of minutes, the Traffic Operator waits for the power on the track sections over the bridge to be cut. Even though it can represent the change in the status of the electrical feeding point, the ENOK system does not really mean anything for the operator, unless he is able to superimpose the information presented on it with the one displayed on the mimic panel. There exist two reasons for this. First, the operators use the ENOK power supply system very rarely. This means that it is unlikely that the operators at any time will remember the meaning of all functions on that system. Second, the ENOK system was originally designed for the electrical power supply organization rather than for the underground line. The system in the control room is just a duplicate of the system which the electricity supplier has in their control room. It was not originally designed to be operated by underground line control room operators. Therefore, the Shift Operator looks at the mimic panel to receive confirmation of the executed power cut. If everything is done correctly, the line section over the bridge will start to blink on the mimic panel; this means that it is powerless. In the meanwhile, the rest of the operator team continues its preparations for counter-track traffic

---

[5] As can be seen in Figure 15.1 the traffic controller has also access to the signaling system. If needed he/she can take over certain sections of the signaling system.

operations. Two minutes later the operator of the east signaling area notices on the mimic panel that the size of the track section, on both sides of the bridge, that has become powerless is larger than it should be. This, in its turn, makes it impossible for trains to approach the bridge and even less to cross it. The Signaling Operator first checks the screens of the signaling system in front of him and then looks at the mimic panel to confirm his observation. The powerless section is now blinking repeatedly with red lights on the mimic panel and thereby starts to draw all operators' attention to it (Table 15.3).

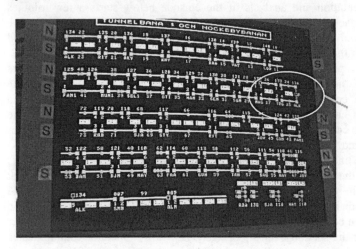

The bridge section as seen in the ENOK power line control system

Figure 15.2 The line power supply system (ENOK). Each electrical feeding point to the tracks is represented as a four digit number, for example 132-4

Table 15.3 The power is erroneously cut off at several sections of the track

Time	Who to Whom	Transcript
19.17.58	SSO-East to the SSO-West	there it goes [the power is cut off]
19.18.00	SSO-East to the other operators	oh, oh oh, no, no, no
19.18.00	The SSO-East and the SO simultaneously point to the part of the mimic panel where the power has been cut	
19.18.06	SO to her colleagues (while on the phone) pointing to the mimic panel	has something happened there?
19.18.10	TO (who is still on the phone with the electrical company) to the SO	we have lost power all the way to Kristineberg [name of station]

In the following, the operator of the east signaling area hits his palm loudly on the desk in an act of frustration. This operator has not only detected the particular situation but is also in a position to fully understand what it means. The reason is that he is the most senior in the room in terms of experience and age. As an operator with several decades of underground line control experience he can anticipate the problems that will follow when too many sections of the track are made powerless and traffic is disrupted. When interviewed afterwards he stated that in situations like these he can 'see' with his inner eye the kind of complications that will follow. At this stage it is interesting to note that not all operators have yet discovered, even less understood, what has happened. Even though the mimic panel is immediately accessible to the whole operator team, it is only the operator of the east signaling area who can first see and understand it.

At this stage the team is faced with two problems. The first and most urgent problem is to restore the power on all sections of the track that should not be powerless. This requires that the operator team understands what went wrong and how the problem can be fixed. As mentioned, at this stage not all team members have even noticed the problem. The second problem concerns the passenger trains that are approaching on each side of the bridge. Since there is no power on the tracks on several stations on each side of the bridge, the trains must be halted. The ultimate problem lies in the repercussions this stop might have on the total traffic situation. The Shift Operator normally knows that an incident like the current one can result in substantial traffic delays and most likely require considerable work from the team to restore the traffic once the power has been put back. However, at the moment she is engaged in a telephone call, only vaguely noticing that something seems to be wrong (Table 15.3, 19.18.06).

In the meanwhile, the Traffic Operator, who is still on the telephone with the control room of the electricity producer, attempts to solve the problem. To do this he stands in front of the ENOK system and tries to map the information displayed on it with the picture displayed on the mimic panel across the room. By trying to superimpose the information from these two informational artifacts, he hopes to be able to see what exactly has gone wrong. However, a considerable amount of interpretation is required to do this. The reason is that the representation of the division of the Green line in the ENOK system, does not correspond with the divisions of the track sections displayed on the signaling system, nor with the track and station sections displayed on the mimic panel. In other words, the power line supply system, the mimic panel, and the signaling system all provide the operators with different representations of the Green underground line. The above described incompatibility of the different representations of the Green line, in the various informational artifacts in the control room, has already resulted in that the Traffic Operator lost the bubble since he did not understand what went wrong. The lack of communication between the Traffic Operator and the rest of the team also results in the fact that no common understanding of the situation can be created yet.

As part of the preparation for the engineering work, all construction and maintenance trains have positioned themselves on a side-track at the station nearest to the bridge. These trains were positioned so that, when the engineering work on the bridge was about to begin, they should be able to move quickly into the working area. However, due to the erroneous cutting of the power supply, these trains can not enter the construction area.[6] At this stage the operators seem to almost have forgotten about the engineering work since they need to concentrate on restoring the power on the parts of the line where it was erroneously cut off. It is notable that the signaling operator of the west area, who has especially been brought in to manage the counter-track traffic, is alternating his gaze between the mimic panel and the signaling system in front of him. However, from where he is sitting he has no access to the information represented on the ENOK system nor has he been involved in any communication with the Traffic Operator or Shift Operator as to get an update on the situation (Table 15.4).

Table 15.4 The operator of the west signaling area realizes that construction and maintenance trains are also paralyzed

Time	Who to Whom	Transcript
19.19.32	The driver of one of the construction trains calls the control room	we are on track B in the Bromma depot / can we get out [on the main track] now?
19.19.39	SSO-West taps in to the communication. He then points to the blinking part of the mimic panel and talks to the room	but that is in the middle of the powerless part of the track
19.19.45	TO replies to the driver of the construction train after having heard the SSO-west	you will have to stay right where you are

Like in most dynamic real-time systems, once something goes wrong, problems start to accumulate. Under normal operations, when a train moves along the line, a combination of red digits and numbers is displayed in the mimic panel just above the set of lights indicating the actual train (Figure 15.3). This digit and number combination, which moves along with the train on the mimic panel, shows the destination of the train and its turn in the timetable. Under normal operations, this system for train identification is of great help for the operators since it allows them to, at a glance, identify each train on the mimic panel. However, construction and maintenance trains are not equipped with such electronic train identification systems. The train identification system, unable to read any data from the construction and maintenance trains, displays the trains as a set of six zeroes on the mimic panel. This means that the operators have to keep the identity of the train

---

[6] It should be pointed out that certain construction trains are diesel powered since many times they need to operate on occasions when the electrical power is cut off on the track. These trains usually run at night when most of the maintenance work takes place. However, not all trains involved in the replacement of the tracks on the bridge are diesel powered.

represented as six zeroes in their memory or write the identity down. In any case, this information is not publicly represented and available through the mimic panel. Things are further complicated by the fact that there are several trains parked one after the other at the same side track waiting to move on to the bridge in order to undertake the engineering work. In this particular case an operator who sees the six zeroes in the identification display on the mimic panel, just to the west of the bridge, should know that there are actually three engineering trains standing there. But the additional information needed to interpret the actual meaning of the six zeroes is not displayed anywhere on the mimic panel. Interestingly enough, no single team member has all this information. Ultimately, the knowledge of the position and status of the construction and maintenance trains, which are parked to the west of the bridge and which are being displayed as six zeroes on the mimic panel, is distributed between the team members and the mimic panel.

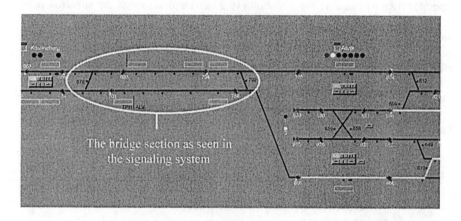

Figure 15.3 Screen shot from the signaling system of the area around the bridge. The field with six zeroes represents several construction and maintenance trains which are parked at the same section of the track

Up until this point the necessary information to understand the exact status of the power supply system and the traffic on the line is distributed between various informational artifacts. However, there is no single artifact in the control room which can display the consolidated status of the entire situation. Even worse is the fact that the operators seem to have lost their meta-knowledge. There are two significant aspects of the communication patterns between operators, which indicate this. First, operators do not seem to know which operator who has what information. Operators do not know which colleague knows what about the erroneous cutting of the power to the line. Neither do they know who knows the number, type, nor position of the construction and maintenance trains displayed as six zero's on the mimic panel. Second, it is clear that operators do not know whether the rest of the team is aware of what it is they are doing. According to

Rogers (1993) this kind of meta-level knowledge is an essential part of performing distributed and complex teamwork. To coordinate teamwork requires that a team member knows what another member knows, so that relevant information can be communicated. This type of communication and coordination problem has also been called the 'mutual knowledge' problem (Krauss and Fussell, 1990).

The Shift Operator now decides to call back to the electricity company that delivers power and ask that power feeding point no 132-4 to the track should be reconnected (Table 15.5). But this only solves part of the problem since the Traffic Operator notes that there are still sections of the track which are powerless (19.23.48). As a result, no engineering or passenger trains can pass through the station immediately to the west of the bridge. In the following minutes, we can see how the Signaling System Operator for the east part of the line who as mentioned earlier, is the most experienced one in the team, is becoming frustrated and declares that it is all going to hell (19.24.35). A few minutes later, the Shift Operator tries to evaluate the situation (19.27.26) and says that the situation does not look good at all. It is notable that up until now there has not really been any discussion about the cause of the erroneous cutting off of the power. Various members have their own understanding of the situation; based on which informational artifacts and representations they have access to, while little or no communication between team members has taken place. Ten minutes have now passed since power was erroneously cut off.

Table 15.5 Parts of the line supply are restored. However, parts of the line are still powerless

Time	Who to Whom	Transcript
19.23.35	SO (Part of the line where power was erroneously cut off is now restored)	now / we have got it [the power] back
19.23.48	TO to the SO	but there is still no power in the entire Alvik area [to the immediate west of the bridge]
19.24.35	SSO-East answers a telephone call	it is going straight to hell, what do you want?
19.25.30	SSO-East to the SO	which one [feeding point] did you reconnect?
19.25.31	SO	132-4
19.27.16	The situation is stabilized and a discussion starts in order to localize what went wrong. TO to the SO	which circuit was it that he reconnected?
19.27.26	SO to the room	132-4 / this is not good at all

In summary, the operator team is confronted with an unexpected situation which is rapidly unfolding and affecting the traffic flow as well as the maintenance work. At this stage each operator has little communication with the rest of the team and rather poor knowledge and awareness of exactly who knows what and who is currently engaged in what task. A significant part of the problem stems from the fact that some of the central informational artifacts involved in this situation provide the operators with different representations of the Green underground line. The difficulty to map the various representations of what is actually going on in the underground line, and the additional cognitive workload this results in for the operators, leaves little room for the formation of the bubble. The result is that the operators are rapidly losing the bubble without necessarily being aware of this fact at a team level. At the team level they do not seem to have a proper understanding of what went wrong, no estimation of how long the situation is going to last, and no prediction including possible solutions to the problems which are rapidly piling up.

Reconstructing the Bubble

Two more minutes of troubleshooting pass until the power is restored in the sections where it was erroneously cut off. In total, the incident took 12 minutes, a time span which might not strike the reader as especially long. However, the incident was long enough to significantly disrupt the traffic pattern according to the timetable. Even though the power is now restored, most team members still have a poor understanding of what exactly went wrong and how the problem was solved. The team has no time to consider these issues since two problems arose as a result from this incident and must be dealt with immediately. The first problem is how to move the construction trains onto the bridge so that they can start the engineering work. The second problem is to restore the passenger traffic on the line. In this section we will take a closer look at how the team members use the informational artifacts available to reconstruct the bubble with regard to the latter problem, i.e., restoring the passenger traffic.

The team needs to restore passenger traffic, which has come to a halt for close to a quarter of an hour. It is obvious that by now there exists a considerable discrepancy between the information in the timetable and the one on the mimic panel. Trains are simply not where they are supposed to be. The team needs to establish common ground with regard to the positions of the trains and then agree on which way is the best possible to run the traffic. The important thing for the team is to ensure that trains arrive at stations according to the timetable. A commonly used solution, practiced by operators in situations involving bigger delays in traffic, is to rearrange the identification numbers of the trains on the line. By assigning new identification numbers to the trains, operators can make the actual status of the underground traffic to match, as close as possible, the one stated in the timetable. In one sense we could say that operators modify the train positions by virtually assigning new identities to the trains. An example of how this is done can be found in the excerpt in Table 15.6 (19.30.17) where the Shift

Operator decides that the train that is indicated as 18-6 on the mimic panel, should switch its identification number with train number 19.

Table 15.6 The operators change the identity of the trains and assign them new ones so that the traffic status will resemble the one prescribed in the timetable

Time	Who to Whom	Transcript
19.30.17	SO to the room	where is 18-6 / is it standing on the middle track in Vällingby? It could switch numbers with 19
19.30.23	SSO-west	so old 18-6 is standing at the entrance to Vällingby / and the broken 70 stands on the middle track in Vällingby
19.30.40	SO	oh, is it [70] broken?
19.30.40	SSO-west	yeah
19.30.41	SO to SSO-west	ok I leave it [the task of switching the numbers] up to you then

The excerpt in Table 15.6 shows how the Shift Operator assigns the task of executing the identity switch to one of the signaling system operators. Changing the identification numbers of the trains is something, which can easily be done, in the new digital signaling system. Through a special command, a Signal System Operator can assign a new identification number to a particular train. The change will take effect immediately and become visible on the train driver's computer screen as well as on the mimic panel. Even though the signaling system is accessed by an individual operator through a 17 inch PC screen, it is worth noting that the changes becomes publicly available through the mimic panel which is clearly visible to everybody in the room (Figure 15.4). Here we have a situation where the combination of the mimic panel and the signaling system are integrated and used in such a way that they support the creation of a mutual awareness of the updated situation, and thereby directly contribute to the reconstruction of the bubble.

To understand better the importance of being able to make changes to the train identification numbers, in the mimic panel, we can briefly consider the situation up until three years ago when the signaling system was analogue and not connected to the mimic panel. In the analogue system the identification number of the trains was not displayed on the mimic panel since the system had not yet been implemented. When traffic disruptions occurred and the operators changed the identification numbers of the trains, these changes could not become immediately and publicly available. There was simply no single place in the control room were the operators could access the new status of the traffic on the line. Rather, each operator had to memorize which set of red lights on the mimic panel that had which identity. This task required considerable attention, which posed a considerable informational effort. To write down the relevant information on a piece of paper was hardly helpful since the lights that represented the trains on the mimic panel were constantly moving. In other words, after that an identification number changes, the operators had to closely follow the traffic, or they would risk losing track of the new identities of the trains. An interesting difference between the old and the new signaling system is that, in situations like the one described previously, the analogue system required considerable communication exchange between operators. The reason for this is that the knowledge about the most current traffic situation was distributed between them. In the new system, all the relevant information, concerning the updated identity of the trains, is visible is a rectangular display under each train on the mimic panel.

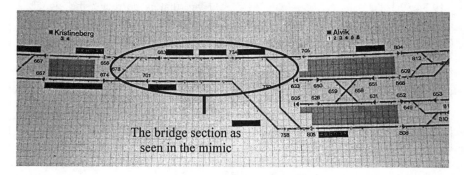

Figure 15.4 Picture form the mimic panel displaying the track sections over the bridge where the incident took place

As soon as the passenger trains are given permission to start to roll again, the driver of train 19-37 calls the control room on the radio and states that he is facing a signal indicating that he should go counter-trackwise over the bridge (Table 15.7, 19.34.44).[7] While the Traffic Operator grants the driver access to pass the signal and go counter-trackwise (Table 15.7, 19.34.50), the Shift Operator, who has overheard the exchange on the radio, intervenes and advises the driver to wait. The Shift Operator then addresses the Signaling System Operator, who is responsible for controlling the traffic over the bridge, and asks whether the signals around the area where the train is, are correctly set. In addition, the Shift Operator also asks the driver what color the signal in front of him is. At this point all information about the status of the signals and switches is publicly available on the mimic panel for all operators to read. But it is important for the team not to take this availability of information for granted assuming that other operators have understood it.

---

[7] Whenever an unusual thing happens, such as facing a signal that indicates that a train should go counter-trackwise, it is practice that the train driver contacts the control room to check that he or she has properly understood the situation and that no technical or human mistakes have occurred.

Table 15.7 The Shift Operator intervenes in the exchange between a train driver and the Traffic Operator in order to make absolutely sure that the signal, which the train is about to pass, is properly set. Since all involved parties have different representations of the particular signal, the Shift Operator ensures that they construct a shared understanding

Time	Who to Whom	Transcript
19.34.44	Train 19-37 on the radio	the signal says I should go counter-track
19.34.50	TO	yes that is correct / the signal is correct / you are welcome to enter counter-track southbound
19.35.07	SO on the radio	wait I need to talk to Peter [name of SSO-west] / you had blocked 720 right? switch 720
19.35.12	SSO-west	720 and 710 are blocked
19.35.19	SO on the radio	switch 720 and 710 are blocked / and you have white and red [signal] there? ok we will fix it

As mentioned earlier, the mutual knowledge problem states that it is difficult to know which piece of information has been observed and understood by whom. Given the fact that the team members are still busy in the aftermath of the power cut incident, it is likely to assume that their attention span is rather limited. Therefore, before letting a train go counter-trackwise, it is necessary for the Shift Operator to see to that the involved persons establish a mutually shared understanding of the information represented in the various parts of the underground line system. These parts are the actual signal on the tracks, the mimic panel, and the signaling system. Since the Traffic Operator, the Signaling System Operator, and the train drivers all have access to different and distributed representations, the only reasonable way to create a common understanding is through explicit verbal communication. By doing this, the Shift Operator draws the attention of all involved parties to the same problem verbally. The Shift Operator's verbal comment ensures that the proper and redundant awareness around the situation is negotiated and constructed and that the necessary common conceptual ground is created (Clark and Brennan, 1991). The actions of the Shift Operator thereby function to synthesize the different representations of the status of the signal into a mutually shared one. This is a fine example of how knowledge becomes socially distributed, and the bubble (situation awareness) is reconstructed.

Conclusions

The management of the Green underground line is a distributed cognitive process in at least two different ways. First, the control work is distributed between the operators of the team and second, it is distributed between the operators and the informational artifacts they use. Creating and maintaining the bubble of the status of the traffic as well as of the status of the control system in the underground line control room can be a significant challenge. In the incident described in this chapter the operators lost the bubble and had to reconstruct it. The previous sections have tried to describe the role of the informational artifacts which are involved during the loss as well as during the reconstruction of the bubble. The analysis of the communicative turns within the team reveals that the construction and loss of team situation awareness is a rather complex process. In particular there are three aspects, which are worth noticing.

First, the various artifacts have been designed and implemented over a long period of time which means that they tend to function as stand-alone artifacts rather than as integrated parts (see Vidulich, Bolia, Nelson, Chapter 13, this volume). For example, the electrical supply system (i.e., the ENOK system), the mimic panel, and the signaling system all provide rather different representations of the status of the line. The operators need different knowledge in order to interpret the meaning of each representation and their relation to other ones. During normal operations this does not pose a problem since the different systems are not normally used together all the time. Only when the power is erroneously cut in too big a section of the tracks and a breakdown occurs, does it become necessary to coordinate the information from the various informational artifacts into a single coherent understanding of the status of the line. But because of the informational incompatibility of the artifacts in the control room, the operators must create new representations which can help them create the bubble and take control of the situation. This is accomplished by superimposing the information displayed on the systems they have and thereby creating a new conceptual representation of the status. Superimposing information from various sources, in the absence of a shared record, turns out to be difficult and requires a substantial amount of communication within the team. The importance of having access to publicly shared information during collaborative problem solving has also been argued by Whittaker and Schwarz (1995), Whittaker, Geelhoed and Robinson (1993) and Sebok (2000). As Berndtsson and Normark (1999) have shown, the successful use of multiple computer systems in a cooperative process management is often depended on that these systems provide the operators with effortless visualization.

Rogers (1993) has shown that when breakdowns occur in workplaces, which are socially and technically distributed, the operators need to create a public record of the process they are in charge of. This is also the second observation in this study. In the case of the underground line, the operators could not access publicly shared information directly regarding which activities and tasks that had been completed and by whom. Neither could they access information about which trains were actually situated where. Since the power supply system, the mimic panel, and the signaling system cannot be integrated to create a permanent public record, the team had to engage in extensive communication to create a mutually shared understanding. The purpose of the extensive verbal communication was not only to update individual operators but, seen from the whole teams' perspective, to create a public record of the situation. The advantage of such socially distributed coordination is that the information is immediate. Verbal communication is probably the quickest means of communication for a collocated team, and it can provide a public mean of distributing information inadvertently throughout the team. As Rogers's notes the disadvantage is its transience (ephemerality), which makes it difficult for team members to go back to and check information. In contrast technologically mediated pathways provide permanent records and representations.

Analyzing the communicative turns during the incident, we can also clearly see a mismatch of expectations between the operators. According to Orasanu and Salas (1993), a mutually shared understanding of the situation at hand must include expectations and explanations as elements, which must be shared by all members within a team. In addition, Orasanu and Salas note that it is important that the shared understanding in the team provides the members with shared anticipations of the system. Without mutual expectations, a team will not be able to strategize on the future and decide what actions to take. To reach the state where a team has a mutual anticipation of the system, i.e., has managed to have a shared bubble; the different individual understandings of the team members have to converge enough so as to form a commonly shared understanding. It seems clear that even though a physical public record of the situation at hand might not have solved the whole problem, it could have helped the team to anchor each operator's expectations and understanding significantly. We have seen that when the socially distributed bubble construction mechanisms are not sufficiently supported by the publicly shared artifacts, the team had to engage in significant communicative and coordinative work to reach common ground. The communicative pathways include transformation of information between different modes; such as looking at the mimic panel and the signaling system, and comparing this information with the one on the power supply system. Synthesizing information in this way into a new understanding can delay the bubble reconstruction process and create further problems for the team.

Third, the available systems, which during normal operations help the team to construct and maintain the bubble, can take on a new and different meaning when the bubble is lost and needs to be reconstructed. As we saw, the interfaces and informational architecture of the various systems, which have been designed to support normal operations, could not help the team during this incident. Since the bubble is not a static condition but must, on a continuous level, be maintained and sometimes even reconstructed, informational artifacts for cooperative process management should be designed with this fact in mind. It is therefore important that future designs of informational tools for cooperative work take such unanticipated overheads into account (Bowers 1994). Control room work is normally a socially distributed process, which often functions without central coordination. During breakdowns and when the bubble is lost the team needs some sort of publicly available record of the situation and progress; preferably a physical one which they can refer to. However, introducing a computerized solution, which could be used by each operator, cannot solve all problems. Ultimately, computerizing the updating procedure could affect the way knowledge is communicated within the group. If such a computerized solution would have a shared record of the activities of each of the users and could aggregate information from the various other systems, the users would risk losing the meta-level knowledge of knowing that someone else knows what it is that they are doing.

Acknowledgements

We wish to thank Johan Eliasson and Olle Granat for collecting parts of the data material. We are also grateful to the underground personnel and management for letting us do the data collection.

References

Artman, H. (2000), 'Team Situation Assessment and Information Distribution', *Ergonomics*, vol. 43(8), pp. 1111-1128.

Artman, H. and Persson, M. (2000), 'Old Practices - New Technology: Observations of how Established Practices Meet New Technology', in R. Dieng, A. Gibson, L. Kersenty, G. De Michelis (eds), *Designing Cooperative Systems*, Ios Press Ohmsha., Amsterdam, pp. 35-49.

Artman, H. and Waern, Y. (1999), 'Distributed Cognition in an Emergency Co-ordination Center', *Cognition, Technology and Work*, vol. 1, pp. 237-246.

Berndtsson J. and Normark M. (1999), 'The Coordinative Functions of Flight Strips: Air Traffic Control Work Revisited', in *Proceedings of the Conference on Supporting Group Work - GROUP '99*, Phoenix, AR, USA, pp. 101-110.

Bowers J. (1994), 'The Work to Make a Network Work: Studying CSCW in Action', in *Proceedings of the Conference on Computer Supported Cooperative Work - CSCW '94*, Chapel Hill, NC, USA, ACM Press, pp. 287-297.

Brehmer, B. (1992), 'Dynamic Decision Making: Human Control of Complex Systems', *Acta Psychologica*, vol. 81, pp. 211-241.

Clark, H.H. and Brennan, S.E. (1991), 'Grounding in Communication', in L.B. Resnick, J.M. Levine and S.D. Teasley (eds), *Perspectives on Socially Shared Cognition*, American Psychological Association Press, pp. 127-149.

Endsley, M. (1995), 'Toward a Theory of Situation Awareness in Dynamic Systems', *Human Factors*, vol. 37(1), pp. 32-64.

Flach, J.M. (1995), 'Situation Awareness: Proceed with Caution. *Human Factors*', vol. 37, pp. 149-157.

Garbis, C. (2002), 'Exploring the Openness of Cognitive Artifacts in Cooperative Process Management', *Cognition, Technology and Work*, vol. 4, pp. 9-21.

Heath, C. and Luff, P. (1992), 'Collaboration and Control - Crisis Management and Multimedia Technology in London Underground Line Control Rooms', *Computer Supported Co-operative Work (CSCW)*, vol.1, pp. 69-94.

Heath, C. and Luff, P. (1996), 'Convergent Activities: Line Control and Passenger Information on the London Underground', in Y. Engeström and D. Middleton (eds), *Cognition and Communication at Work*, Cambridge University Press, pp. 96-129.

Hutchins, E. (1995), *Cognition in the Wild*, MIT Press, MA.

Krauss, R.M. and Fussell, S.R. (1990), 'Mutual Knowledge and Communicative Effectiveness' in J. Galegher, R.E. Kraut, C. Egido (eds), *Intellectual Teamwork*. Lawrence Erlbaum, pp. 111-145.

Orasanu, J. and Connolly, T. (1993), 'The Reinvention of Decision Making', in G. A. Klein, J. Orasanu, R. Calderwood and C. E. Zsambok (eds), *Decision Making in Action*, Ablex Publishing Company, pp. 3-20.

Orasanu J. and Salas E. (1993), 'Team Decision Making in Complex Environments', in G. A. Klein, J. Orasanu, R. Calderwood and C. E. Zsambok (eds), *Decision Making in Action*, Ablex Publishing Company, pp. 327-345.

Rasker, P.C., Post, W.M. and Schraagen, M.C. (2000), 'Effects of Two Types of Intra-Team Feedback on Developing a Shared Mental Model in Command and Control Teams', *Ergonomics*, vol. 43(8), pp. 1167-1189.

Rochlin, G.I. (1997), *Trapped in the Net - The Unanticipated Consequences of Computerization*, Princeton University Press, Princeton, New Jersey.

Rogalski, J. and Samurçay, R. (1993), 'Analysing Communication in Complex Distributed Decision Making', *Ergonomics*, vol. 36(11), pp. 1329-1343.

Rogers Y. (1993), 'Coordinating Computer-Mediated Work', *Computer Supported Cooperative Work (CSCW)*, vol. 1, pp. 295-315.

Salas, E., Prince, C., Baker, D.P. and Shrestha, L. (1995), 'Situation Awareness in Team Performance ', *Human Factors*, vol. 37(1), pp. 123-136.

Sarter, N.B. and Woods, D.D. (1991), 'Situation Awareness: A Critical but Ill-defined Phenomenon', *International Journal of Aviation Psychology*, vol. 1, pp. 45-57.

Sarter, N.B. and Woods, D.D. (1995), 'How in the World did We Ever Get Into That Mode? Mode Error and Awareness in Supervisory Control', *Human Factors*, vol. 37(1), pp. 5-19.

Sebok, A. (2000), 'Team Performance in Process Control: Influence of Interface Design and Staffing Levels', *Ergonomics*, vol. 43(8), pp. 1210-1236.

Swezey, R.W. and Salas, E. (1992), *Teams: Their Training and Performance*, Ablex Publishing Corp, Norwood, New Jersey.

Wærn, Y. (1998), *Co-operative Process Management – Cognition and Information Technology*, Taylor and Francis, London.

Wellens, A.R. (1993), 'Group Situation Awareness and Distributed Decision Making: From Military to Civilian Applications'. in N.J. Castellan (ed.), *Individual and Group Decision Making: Current Issues*, Erlbaum, pp. 267-287.

Whittaker S. and Schwarz H. (1995), 'Back to the Future: Pen and Paper Technology Supports Complex Group Coordination', in *Proceedings of the Conference on Human Factors in Computing Systems CHI '95*, ACM Press, pp. 495-502.

Whittaker S., Geelhoed E. and Robinson E. (1993), 'Shared Workspaces: How do They Work and When are They Useful?', *International Journal of Man Machine Studies*, vol. 39, pp. 813-842.

Woods, D.D., Johannesen, L.J., Cook, R.I. and Sarter, N.B. (1994), *Behind Human Error: Cognitive Systems, Computers, and Hindsight*, CSERIAC-report.

Chapter 16

The Role of Situation Awareness in Sport

Nic James and John Patrick

Introduction

The term Situation Awareness (SA) has received scant explicit recognition within the Sports Psychology literature, which is surprising given the task requirements of many sports. The 'awareness' component of sports performance can easily be understood through the commonly used exemplar of SA i.e., the fighter pilot (e.g., Endsley, 1993), even a major difference is that the pilot indirectly perceives many variables through instrumentation whereas the sports player relies on direct perception of the environment. We know that the fighter pilot is required to have considerable spatial knowledge (awareness) of the dynamic, externally-paced, three dimensional environment. This is precisely the type of environment that faces players of invasion games (e.g., soccer, basketball or American football) and racket sports. The fighter pilot has to have spent many hours practicing manipulating the controls of the aeroplane to allow fast and partially implicit control such that the aeroplane and its weapons systems can be engaged with extreme precision and speed. This is also the nature of expertise in the aforementioned sports. The expert soccer player can control and pass the football whilst the squash player can hit the ball with the racket with similar levels of precision and speed as would be expected from an expert performer of any domain where a large number of hours of deliberate, purposeful practice have been undertaken (Ericsson, Krampe and Tesch-Römer, 1993; Ericsson, 1996). Of course higher order cognitive functions are also required of the fighter pilot to enable a temporal mapping of the controlled elements i.e., the plane and its weapons systems, with the external features beyond control (the enemy aircraft and the terrain in which the dogfight takes place). These attentional demands as well as the ability to shift focus as required, the ability to recognize pertinent information from the visual display to allow anticipatory behavior, and rapid decision-making to elicit the best course of action describe the tasks necessary for successful operation of a fighter plane. Once again these requirements directly relate to the tasks undertaken in invasion and racket sports. For example, the soccer player must be able to attend to both the opponent trying to take the ball away and be aware of the team-mate making a run into space so that the ball can be passed at the appropriate time. A racket sports player must monitor the opponent's play to the extent that very small changes in the opponent's racket and arm preparation can be observed, enabling an anticipatory movement toward the intended shot direction and consequently a more accurate return shot

(Abernethy and Russell, 1984, 1987). Thus the expert performer, within many sports, has been defined by the ability to be aware of certain aspects of play and make more appropriate decisions when faced with a number of options usually under severe time constraints (Ward and Williams, 2003). These requirements have been well researched in sports psychology although little reference has been made to SA. This chapter will therefore review the appropriate sports psychology literature to make explicit the link to SA.

Chapter Overview

Given the paucity of research that investigates explicitly the role of SA in sport, this chapter will concentrate on the various paradigms that have been used to study, primary perceptual processes and anticipation, all of which are in scope to SA. These include the use of various occlusion techniques that attempt to identify what cues are significant and are used by expert players, eye registration techniques and verbal reports. The varying SA requirements and accompanying SA processes of various sports situations are described, including individual and team, racket and invasion sports. An important distinction is drawn between the findings from laboratory studies and real game situations. Some different approaches are discussed for training important perceptual and anticipation skills associated with high levels of skill. Finally some new methods are discussed that may facilitate the investigation of SA in sports contexts.

Sports Situations and SA

This chapter adopts the task-oriented perspective concerning the achievement of SA, as elaborated by Patrick and James (Chapter 4, this volume). Consequently the achievement of SA comprises three sub-tasks, corresponding to Endsley's (1995) three hierarchical phases. Consider the situation where a squash player is waiting to return the opponent's forthcoming shot. In terms of achieving SA the player needs to perceive the opponent's movements (toward the ball and stroke mechanics) in conjunction with the flight of the ball whilst simultaneously monitoring his/her own position on the court. This corresponds to the performance of task 1.1.1 in Patrick and James, Chapter 4, this volume, Figure 4.1. Success in this task would mean making sense of this information such that the opponent's movements would be co-ordinated with the ball trajectory to allow some mapping of this visual information with a knowledge base of general information related to typical behaviors in similar situations as well as more precise information regarding the opponent's previous actions in similar situations (task 1.1.2 in Patrick and James, Chapter 4, this volume, Figure 4.1). Successful accomplishment of these tasks will then support some form of decision making to anticipate the likely outcome of the opponent's stroke (task 1.1.3 in Patrick and James, Chapter 4, this volume, Figure 4.1). The extent to which this is possible seems to increase fairly linearly with time up until the point when a decision has to be made

(Howarth, Walsh and Abernethy, 1984; Abernethy, Gill, Parks and Packer, 2001; James and Bradley, in press). It has been suggested that pattern matching together with some probability assessment enables such anticipatory decisions to be made followed by decision making concerning what consequent behavior should be selected in order to anticipate the opponent's next shot (task 1.2, Patrick and James, this volume, Figure 4.1). How these tasks are undertaken is highly sport and situation-specific and rapidly evolves during any one dynamic sport situation. Given the extent to which information changes over a small space of time, it has been hypothesized that processes occur in a parallel rather than in a serial manner (Williams, Davids and Williams, 1999).

The information source available to the squash player is largely visual-spatial but is critically determined by temporal cues. For example, an opponent will have to boast (play the ball onto the side wall so that it travels to the opposite side and usually to the front of the court) when the ball is located behind the back foot at the point of contact. Any small deviation from this (i.e., the ball is located to the side or in front of the back foot at point of contact) allows any number of shots to be played and hence renders anticipation improbable. Thus the critical task in terms of SA is predicting the point of contact, in relation to the opponent and the court, as early as possible as well as determining whether the stroke mechanics and situational probabilities enable the determination of where the ball will be hit. The importance of the opponent's playing standard should not be overlooked as expert players will be better than lesser players at producing a greater variety of shot and minimizing anticipation by utilizing very similar stroke mechanics (James and Bradley, in press).

Different psychological processes are required when the squash player is about to hit the ball as opposed to when he or she is waiting to receive it. In this situation the task to perceive elements of the current situation involves primarily monitoring the flight of the ball along with his/her own movements to enable the forthcoming shot to be played. To a lesser extent, and probably only at more advanced levels of play, some perception of the opponent's movement is necessary because of tactical considerations concerning where to hit the ball. Monitoring this information enables the recognition of the impeding shot's difficulty (determined by the ball location at the point of contact and the evolving spatial relationship between the player and ball). A decision has to be made at some point as to what shot is to be played and frequently players select a familiar shot on the basis of patterns stored in long-term memory (Hughes and Robertson, 1998).

The two examples cited above indicate how Endsley's (1995) three hierarchical phases of SA can be conceptualized as three sub-tasks of the task of 'achieving and maintaining SA' (see Patrick and James, Chapter 4, this volume). Each sub-task can involve the full range of cognitive processes even though the SA labels themselves can be confused with the information processing stages in cognitive models. Thus there may be a need for some decision making, for example, in the selection of what information sources provide useful cues to support anticipation (Abernethy and Russell, 1987).

SA Requirements of Different Sports

Improving sporting performance depends upon identification of the subtle and changing awareness required, often through investigation of expert performance. In this Section, the nature of these SA requirements will be explored from a review of various empirical studies. However the diversity of sporting situations (invasion, net/wall/racket, fielding/striking, target and combat) makes generalizations about SA requirements impossible. Various methodologies have been employed including use of de Groot's (1946/1978) chess memory paradigm. Others involve limiting the information available to the sportsperson in order to determine its effect on performance (temporal and spatial occlusion; liquid occlusion spectacles), assessing eye movements, and collecting verbal reports (concurrent and/or retrospective). These studies have usually taken place in laboratory settings although some studies have used real game situations.

A total of fourteen studies are summarized in Table 16.1 together with some important SA requirements that have emerged. Five of these studies concern soccer, three relate to squash, and the remaining ones cover badminton, tennis, ice hockey, cricket, volleyball and basketball. The various methods used by these studies are also summarized. Some of these studies are discussed in detail below, including both individual and team sports, illustrating their varying SA requirements and accompanying SA processes.

Memory of Sporting Situations

Historically, a great deal of the research in sports psychology that concerns perception can be traced back to the pioneering work of de Groot, (1946/1978). His research methodology, which was later refined by Chase and Simon (1973), assessed chess expertise by requiring players of different standards to reproduce from memory the chess pieces of a typical mid-game scenario viewed for a few seconds. Sports researchers have utilized this methodology using static slides and film clips of various sports situations and have found that, as with the chess experiments, experts have superior recall and recognition of sport-specific patterns of play (e.g., Allard, Graham and Paarsalu, 1980; Starkes, 1987; Williams, Davids, Burwitz and Williams, 1993). Typically experts' advantage over novices has been restricted to structured representations of their sport (e.g., offensive patterns of play ending in a shot at goal) depicted via video clip (Williams et al., 1993). Unstructured representations (e.g., players walking off the pitch) have not discriminated differences between experts and novices (for a review of these studies see Starkes and Allard, 1991).

These researchers have thus come to the same conclusions as Chase and Simon (1973), namely that experts have more accomplished knowledge resources, stored as complex patterns (chunks), accumulated through many years of experience within the domain from which they are able to pattern match. This observation is well established in the sports domain although the pattern recognition model clearly does not comprehensively explain expert performance. Indeed Ericsson (2003), a leading researcher into the nature of expertise, suggests that these

Table 16.1 A selection of sports studies identifying some SA requirements

Authors	Sport	Method	SA requirements
1. Invasion games			
Helsen and Pauwels (1993)	Soccer	Eye tracking for attacking scenarios in a dynamic film	• Novices focus on attackers, the goal and the ball • Experts additionally focus on the sweeper and areas of free space
Tyldesley, Bootsma and Bomhoff (1982)	Soccer	Eye tracking of penalty kick on static slides	• Experienced goalkeepers' scan behavior initially directed to hips and kicking leg (thought to be useful for prediction of ball direction) followed by upper body orientation
Ward and Williams (2003)	Soccer	Highlight key players from film stopped 120 ms before player in possession passes the ball	• Elite players used each key opposition player's level of threat, assessed by expert coaches, as a relative index of attention allocation
Williams and Davids (1998)	Soccer	Eye tracking of film-based simulations of 11 v 11; 3 v 3 and 1 v 1 player scenarios	• Experienced players had more fixations of shorter duration in the 11 v 11 situation compared to the inexperienced • No difference in eye fixations between experienced and inexperienced players for 3 v 3 situations • Experienced players fixated on the hip region more in the 1 v 1 situation
Williams, Davids, Burwitz and Williams (1994)	Soccer	Eye tracking of film based simulations of 11 v 11 players	• Experienced players fixated more on movements and positions of players not in control of the ball whereas inexperienced players fixated on the ball and player passing the ball
Bard and Fleury (1981)	Ice hockey	Eye tracking of live model performing slap shot or sweep shot	• Proportional fixations on the puck or stick were Sweep shots 35per cent :65per cent Slap shots 35per cent :65per cent - experts; 70per cent :30per cent - novices

Table 16.1 (continued)

Authors	Sport	Method	SA requirements
2. Net/wall/racket sports			
Abernethy and Russell (1987)	Badminton	Film of rally and final shot played is spatially occluded	• Experts can use more proximal visual cues i.e., the arm holding the racket whereas novices rely on the racket
Abernethy et al., (2001)	Squash	Live on court wearing liquid occlusion spectacles	• Expert players were able to determine the ball's trajectory prior to the opposing player commencing his movement into position
Crognier, Veret, and Féry, 2003)	Tennis	Live on court anticipation task wearing liquid occlusion spectacles	• Shot prediction was significantly better in realistic situations than unrealistic ones with only visual information up to the end of the backswing given
Howarth et al., (1984)	Squash	High speed film analysis of real matches	• Experts made earlier anticipatory movements than novices
James and Bradley (in press)	Squash	High speed film analysis of real matches	• Visual cues not apparent until 70 ms before expert player hits the ball and in some situations visual information up to ball contact not sufficient to allow anticipation
3. Fielding/striking sports			
Renshaw and Fairweather (2000)	Cricket	Film of bowler temporally occluded at fixed times	• Expert batters had greater perceptual discrimination of bowl type, related to prior experience of bowl type • Additional ball flight information not useful
4. Target sports			
Vickers and Adolphe (1997)	Volleyball	Eye tracking of service	• Experts track the ball by fixating just in front of the ball but not on point of contact with hands
Vickers (1996a, b)	Basketball	Eye tracking of free throw	• Experts fixated on the hoop longer ('quiet eye' period between first fixation on target to first movement of hands)

laboratory tasks fail to capture the experts' superior performance and its mediating mechanisms because of their artificiality. He also points out that even the most fundamental conclusions should be treated with caution, as recent studies have shown that after only fifty hours of practice novices can match the recall performance of chess masters with thousands of hours of chess-playing experience (Ericsson and Harris, 1990). Also with a limited amount of practice, chess experts could display consistently superior performance on 'random' chess configurations (Ericsson, Patel and Kintsch, 2000). Awareness, through recall of prior sporting events is, however, undoubtedly useful for determining the appropriate response. For example a defender may recall previous encounters with an attacker who favors taking on an opponent down the right side of the body and thus can select the optimal manner for defense. However the recall/recognition paradigm does not shed light on the nature of the psychological processes involved. Other limitations of this methodology include the relatively arbitrary way in which a snapshot is taken of what is a fast dynamic sport and the fact that the response required from participants fails to accommodate the crucial information related to what has happened, is happening and will happen. Furthermore no information is sought regarding what parts of the visual display are useful. Therefore this type of study is limited in how much light it can shed on the SA requirements of different sports situations.

Perception and Anticipation in Sports Situations

Researchers have been interested in perceptual awareness associated with sports expertise, particularly in relation to the ability to anticipate an opponent's next move. In many sports each player is required to be aware of the surrounding, quickly evolving, situation and make an assessment of it to determine the next course of action. The visual display will typically contain information in the form of players' movements (possibly one's own team as well as the opposition), ball location and trajectory, as well as other features of the terrain which may be important. Perception and understanding of these visual cues are critical for anticipation and future action.

Sports studies that have considered the visual information available to players have found that experts can detect objects e.g., the ball within the visual field faster (e.g., Allard and Starkes, 1980). Also, they can anticipate better than novices, opponents' intentions based on partial information, produced by a spatial occlusion technique that removes part of the visual display to determine it's utility, (Abernethy and Russell, 1987) or limited information , where a temporal occlusion technique stops the unfolding action at set times (e.g., Jones and Miles, 1978; Abernethy, 1990). These findings have been replicated many times typically in film and slide studies where the naturally evolving time-line has been curtailed. However such conclusions are, and should be treated cautiously because of the selectivity and artificiality of the methodology. On the other hand, these studies have great potential for elucidating SA requirements and associated information with the prediction of future events (task 1.1.3 in Patrick and James, Chapter 4, this volume, Figure 4.1). Whilst many of these studies retain the dynamic nature of the sports involved, the artificiality of removing much of the background knowledge that players would normally have regarding opponents, team-mates, environment etc., is likely to disrupt the natural cognitive processes involved (Williams, Davids and Williams, 1999).

Some efforts have been made to replicate these studies in more realistic settings. For example, Paull and Glencross (1997) compared expert (batting average of 0.3 or better) and novice (played B grade) baseball batters' ability to anticipate pitching direction. They found that experts made quicker and more accurate predictions about the pitch. However, in an attempt to include the information available in real games, strategic information was included concerning number of balls, strikes and batters out. It was thought that this information would enable the use of probabilistic information, regarding likely pitch outcome that would be available during real games. Both experts and novices improved their performance to the same extent. This somewhat unexpected finding was thought to be due to the fact that this information is fundamental to baseball and consequently a ceiling effect occurred. The authors also tested for expert-novice differences by temporally occluding the pitches at times relative to the ball release by the pitcher (– 80 ms, + 80 ms, + 160 ms and + 240 ms). Overall no expert-novice difference was found although further analysis revealed that different pitch types (curve ball, fast ball and breaking ball) required differing amounts of information and therefore firm conclusions were difficult to make. The authors concluded that, for a fast sport such as baseball, the experts had developed a superior knowledge base which enabled them to (a) access knowledge for anticipation quicker, (b) identify better the useful cues within the visual display and (c) allow the player to assign probabilities regarding the forthcoming action.

These findings are typical of the sports psychology literature and identify not only that experts have better SA but also begin to suggest the nature of the SA requirements that are important for different sports situations. However it is unclear from these studies precisely what information is critical and how this is processed? How do experts make judgments regarding future events? One popular theoretical explanation in the sports domain is the idea that different knowledge structures are used dependent upon the skill level of the performer. Anderson's ACT model (e.g., 1990) describes the transition between using declarative knowledge (factual information) by the novice to procedural knowledge (suggested as 'chunked' in a string to enable quick production of coordinated movement) used by the expert. Thus it is suggested, in cricket for example, that any particular ball delivery would access in an expert cricketer, a relevant knowledge structure that produces a condition-action response based on the ball trajectory (if – then rule). This would occur without conscious thought and therefore would be inaccessible for verbal report by the performer. Another theory that has much support is Ericsson and Kintsch's (1995) theory that experts circumnavigate the limits of short-term memory (Simon and Chase, 1973) by acquiring skills that allow a prediction of future long-term memory retrieval by utilizing flexible representations that can rapidly adapt to situational demands. In a similar vein it has been suggested that expert players may assign probabilities to forthcoming actions that would effectively prime the knowledge structures to enable quicker responses (Alain and Sarrazin, 1990). Thus the setting of probabilities could act to direct attention to the parts of the display in which cues are expected to appear (Paull and Glencross, 1997) as well as prime the knowledge held in long-term memory for retrieval (Anderson, 1990; Ericsson and Kintsch, 1995).

These theoretical notions have merit but as Ericsson (2003) points out the nature of expertise in sports is so complex, having evolved over many years of practice, that insights may only be possible by examining not only the phenomena in their natural settings but also the performance of experts. It is certainly important that the nature of SA in sports situations is investigated by ecologically valid approaches.

Eye Movements

In order to assess which visual cues are informative for an anticipatory response and to determine what parts of a visual display are perceived and attended to, some researchers have used eye movement registration methodologies. Some of these involve a head mounted camera system that enables an accurate assessment of eye line of gaze (via displacement between pupil and corneal reflection, position of eye in head, and position and orientation of head in space). Measures taken typically involve assessment of fixation duration with respect to different areas of the display and the search pattern undertaken. It is generally assumed that the most informative aspects of the display will be gazed at the longest although looking and perceiving are not necessarily related. Williams, Ward, Knowles and Smeeton (2002) found no significant differences in fixation locations, durations or frequencies between skilled (club players) and less skilled (recreational) tennis players. They did, however, find that the skilled players tended to use more successive fixations within and between the head-shoulder and trunk-hip regions than the less skilled players who tended to alternate their gaze between the racket and ball areas. This supports the earlier work in badminton by Abernethy and Russell (1987) who suggested that better players tend to gain more awareness from more proximal information sources (the arm in this instance) compared to more distal sources (the racket) for the less skilled. Similarly Helsen and Pauwels (1993) found that expert soccer players fixated on the position of the sweeper, and potential areas of 'free space' whereas novices concentrated on less sophisticated sources such as other attackers, the goal and the ball. The general consensus of opinion from this type of study is that experts tend to have search strategies that are relevant to the task i.e., fixate on the hypothesized informative areas and employ fewer fixations of longer duration (Helsen and Pauwels, 1993; Williams and Davids, 1998).

Eye movement studies have been informative in determining the nature of the SA requirements with respect to perceiving important elements in various sports situations (i.e., performing task 1.1.1 in Patrick and James, Chapter 4, this volume, Figure 4.1). We know, for example, that contrary to popular belief, baseball batters do not watch the ball hit the bat (Hubbard and Seng, 1954), volleyball players track the ball by fixating just ahead of the ball (Adolphe, Vickers and Laplante, 1997), and expert basketball players fixate on the basket earlier during the free throw than novices (Vickers, 1996a, 1996b). We also have knowledge, although not unequivocal, that experts look at different things with different search patterns than novices (e.g., Williams and Davids, 1998). However it is difficult to conclude that because a football player is fixating on the hip region of an opponent that this is an informative visual cue. The whole of the visual field at any one time should be considered as a potential source of information as one cannot rule out the possibility that information in the periphery is not informative. More research is needed to identify what it is within the visual field that is informative, particularly for experts, defined as world class and not just semi-professional players and the like, and furthermore how much information is used at any one time. Also, given the dynamic nature of many sports, it is unlikely that studies relating only to visual search will fully capture SA requirements and processes. Rather a detailed examination is needed of the shifting focus of attention coupled to the evolving game situation.

Combined Assessments

Some researchers have proposed that individual measures of performance cannot capture the nature of expertise since expertise in any sport requires a number of outstanding attributes such as the cognitive and motor skills required for soccer. Consequently, Helsen and Starkes (1999) used a multidimensional approach to try to understand the nature of expertise in soccer players. A range of perceptual, anticipation and motor tasks were assigned to expert players (semi-professional) and intermediate players (undergraduates with soccer skills but no competitive experience). Non-specific (to soccer) perceptual measures did not tend to discriminate the two groups as predicted (Allard, Graham and Paarsalu, 1980; Starkes, 1987; Allard and Starkes, 1980; Helsen and Pauwels, 1993). Soccer specific measures (response accuracy and number of eye fixations to solve tactical game problems represented as multi-choice film scenarios) did discriminate between the two groups. Of particular interest was the finding that each of the different game situations (the film was stopped as the player with the ball was about to pass, shoot or dribble) seemed to require different approaches with respect to anticipation. It was suggested that different offensive plays result in differential cue availability e.g., the eye fixation durations were significantly shorter for passing situations than shooting or dribbling situations. Also, on trials where the correct anticipation was not elicited, participants tended to fixate on the player with the ball longer than during correct trials. These findings suggest that, in a fast dynamic team sport such as soccer, the ability to select the critical information sources from the visual array is essential and furthermore if attention is not allocated appropriately then future anticipation is severely affected. Clearly this demonstrates the variability even within offensive plays in soccer and gives credence to the view that SA should be studied in situation specific ways as the varying task demands will require different cognitive strategies.

In a similar study, Ward and Williams (2003) tested the perceptual and cognitive skill development of expert (English Premier League Academies) and sub-elite (schools) soccer players via film-based simulations. The temporal occlusion approach assessed participants' ability to anticipate the direction of a dribble or pass. The recall paradigm assessed encoding and retrieval ability for typical patterns of structured and unstructured play (Williams et al., 1993). Finally, using a novel technique, participants were asked to highlight key players in a good position to receive the ball after the film had been stopped 120 ms before the player in possession passed the ball. Expert coaches rated the players so that key and non-key players could be identified. The results suggested that these measures could accurately predict elite status in approximately 80 per cent of cases, from as early as age nine. In terms of situation awareness, the novel assessment technique was suggested to have shown that participants were able to assign an appropriate probability hierarchy to the most important players and use each key player's level of threat as a relative index of attention allocation. This also proved to be the most discriminating factor of skill level and for the elite participants this index improved between nine and fifteen years of age.

These studies have yielded more specific information concerning the nature of SA requirements. The different eye fixations required to solve different tactical game problems (Helsen and Starkes, 1999) offers some insight into the complexity of the processes required to achieve SA. However the fixed choice paradigm that concerns predicting direction is limited in its usefulness as the important mechanisms responsible for successful achievement are not explored. The two papers discussed above (Helsen and Starkes, 1999; Ward and Williams, 2003) do consider the multidimensional nature of expertise although the rationale for the selection of game scenarios is critical and deserves further consideration.

The studies discussed so far have taken place within controlled laboratory conditions, which as Ericsson (2003) has suggested cannot elucidate expert performance because the complex and tightly integrated mechanisms that mediate expert performance, gradually acquired over many years of preparation and training, only surface when performing under the relevant conditions. He points out that whilst chess performance can withstand the laboratory setting, the same cannot be said for soccer or squash as real-time constraints and perceptual requirements for reproducing precise motor actions exist.

Real Game Situations

Ericsson (2003) has argued that laboratory studies with fixed tasks may constrain the expert performer. As evidence of this, Mcleod (1987) has shown that expert cricketers can adapt to varying situations, in this case reducing the unpredictability of a bouncing cricket ball by approaching it, something that would not be possible in the laboratory setting! Thus it would seem that the adage from the SA literature that 'the situation and the awareness are inseparable' has common ground with leading researchers in the sports domain. However, the biggest hurdle to overcome for assessing perceptual skill in realistic sports settings is the obvious problem of stopping or disrupting the event. Fortunately technology and ingenuity have allowed some insights into real-world performance.

Abernethy et al. (2001) had expert (at least highest level of district) and less skilled (lowest league) squash players play matches against the same opponent who was of an intermediate standard. The participants wore PLATO liquid-crystal occlusion spectacles (Milgram, 1987) and were required to attempt to return the shot of their opponent after the spectacles had been remotely altered from transparent to opaque. Since the experimental procedure required the experimenter to judge when to switch the spectacles to opaque, it was impossible to standardize this timing, in terms of time prior to the ball being struck, between the two standards of player. Post-event it was possible to relatively accurately determine (within 20 ms error) when the switching took place in relation to the ball contact by the use of one camera (50 Hz) fixated on an LED activated by the switch synchronized with another camera (50 Hz) fixated on the participant. The findings suggested that expert players were able to determine the ball's trajectory prior to the opposing player commencing his movement into position. In this study, the fact that experts were playing opponents weaker than themselves, whilst novices played opponents who were better, makes evaluation of the expert-novice difference problematic. However it may be concluded that the experts were able to use advance cues to enable anticipation although the source of this information in terms of visual cues and/or subjective event probabilities is unclear.

James and Bradley (in press) assessed anticipatory behavior in elite squash players (at least top 80 in the world), filmed during matches with a high speed camera operating at 250 frames per second. By controlling for shot difficulty (only easy shots were sampled), they showed that even elite players, when playing opponents of a similar standard, cannot always anticipate shot direction without some ball trajectory information. The conclusion drawn from this study was that expert squash players can disguise their intention by using a similar stance and swing, thus making accurate prediction very difficult. Also, when a person is presented with an easy shot, it is more difficult for the opponent to predict the location of the return because of the wide range of shots that are potentially in scope and the lack of different visual cues between them. Thus visual cues are not always sufficient at elite level to support anticipation. Previous studies (Howarth et al., 1984) have consistently shown that experts could anticipate ball trajectories but did not consider shot difficulty or adequately account for opponent's standard of play. Thus previous conclusions that visual information was sufficient to enable anticipatory behavior were considered too simplistic. Rather James and Bradley maintained that much of the anticipation seen in previous studies was a result of participants' assessments of situational probabilities based on previous knowledge of likely shot selection given the situation, rather than visual cues derived from body and racket orientation. It would seem that these two sources of information differ in their utility depending on the situation and the standard of the player. Further research is needed to assess their relative importance.

Féry and Crognier (2001) addressed some of the methodological problems previously identified by having expert (at least ten years intensive experience) tennis players engage in rallies, some of which were high fidelity with respect to real tennis rallies and other that were more artificial. The reason for including realistic rallies was that, during these, the player could better accumulate probabilistic information concerning his opponent's shot selection. One player wearing liquid occlusion spectacles hit an approach shot and, in the more realistic rallies, assumed a position at the net. When the opponent returned a passing shot the glasses were automatically turned opaque 100 ms after ball contact. In order to maximize ecological validity, the player then had to mimic playing the volley and simultaneously indicate, via a hand held selection device, where he thought the ball would have landed. The results showed that these players were able to determine where the ball would have landed through observation of their opponent's stroke movements and the ball trajectory combined with situation specific probability assessments. Féry and Crognier's initial hypothesis that the more realistic the game situation the better the prediction was not supported. One interpretation for this finding is that the available ball trajectory information was sufficient to enable a better than chance prediction of shot outcome irrespective of the realism of the rally. In a follow up study, Crognier, Veret, and Féry, (2003) used a protective blanket that was raised immediately following the passing shot made by the opponent so that the ball was prevented from traveling over the net. On this occasion the spectacles were turned opaque when the opponent had withdrawn the racket to the top of the backswing so that the hitting action and ball trajectory could not be seen. Using this methodology the more realistic situations were anticipated significantly better than those with lower realism. In this experiment, no ball trajectory information was available and so participants had to rely on the opponent's stroke movements and situation specific probability assessments. It could thus be argued that the highly realistic rallies increased the ecological validity and consequently enabled a more accurate probability weighting for the upcoming shot. This suggests that anticipation with respect to scenarios in fast ball sports may depend on the sports person developing a comprehensive set of heuristics.

The use of real game situations clearly advances the possibility of understanding how experts demonstrate their superior skills. However the complexity of the sporting situation makes general statements difficult to make. For example, James and Bradley (in press) have shown that it is too simplistic to suggest that experts can always make sense of the situation with enough understanding to allow a prediction of future events and hence have good SA. Whilst it is obvious that in some situations this is the case, from a coaching perspective, it is equally important to identify a lack of SA as it is to specify the strategies necessary to achieve SA. The real game studies reviewed have addressed the fundamental problems associated with laboratory studies, but without further attempts to understand the mechanisms involved in achieving SA, no advances will be made on how SA is acquired.

A final methodology that can be used in real game situations is the collection of verbal reports together with actions sometimes referred to as process tracing (for a review see Patrick and James, in press). Much debate has been forthcoming over the validity and reliability of this process (e.g., Ericsson and Simon, 1993; Nisbett and Wilson, 1977) although a consensus opinion suggests that concurrent and retrospective verbal reports of thinking aloud during and immediately following performance may offer some useful insights. McPherson and Thomas (1989) collected verbal reports between points during tennis competitions. They simply asked players what they had been thinking about during the previous point and what they were currently thinking about. McPherson (1999, 2000) extended this research and consequently found that adult experts' problem representations were found to be more tactical in terms of action plans and current event profiles than representations of youth experts or novices of any age. It was suggested that both action plans (e.g., serve to the forehand) and current event profiles (e.g., success rate of backhand drives) influenced the nature of information attended to. The use of verbal reports would seem to provide another possible technique for shedding light on SA requirements and accompanying SA processes despite the limitation that some of these may be implicit and not available for verbal scrutiny.

Training for Awareness

There are two approaches to training awareness. Awareness can be developed through either general practice or specific perceptual training procedures. With respect to the former approach, Ericsson and colleagues (e.g., Ericsson and Charness, 1994; Ericsson et al., 1993) suggest that ten years of *deliberate practice* is necessary to attain expertise. Another suggestion is that expertise in sport develops from engagement in more than one activity, which is contrary to the suggestion in music (Ericsson et al., 1993). Coté, Baker and Abernethy (2003) tested this theory by sampling 28 elite athletes (National teams) from a range of sports selected by the coaches as being superior in their capability to 'read the game' as opposed to being more athletic or skilful. A sample of 13 non-expert decision-makers, taken from the same teams, hence matched for experience, provided control data. Structured interviews were used to assess athlete's involvement in sports and other activities. Experts were found to have experienced similar hours of sport-specific training to non-experts until approximately 11 years of involvement. At this point the experts dramatically increased their involvement such that, after 15 years involvement, experts had accumulated nearly double the number of hour's practice of the non-experts. It was also evident that some athletes had engaged in activities other than their main sport and it was suggested that participation in these may have circumvented, or partially substituted for, some of the many hours of sport-specific practice. Hence it was suggested that dynamic anticipation and decision-making during play in confined spaces e.g., when playing basketball, developed well-defined pattern recognition and spatial awareness that transferred well to the athlete's chosen sport.

The second training approach is directed specifically at improving perceptual skills (for a review see Williams and Grant, 1999). They suggested that studies aimed at improving the visual 'hardware' of sports participants were generally difficult to endorse since there was no convincing evidence that highly skilled athletes have superior visual abilities than less skilled athletes, maybe due to a 'ceiling effect'. Sport-specific perceptual training programs have generally had more success although these have typically used video-based simulation, footage shot from the player's perspective and selectively edited to provide differing amounts of pre-contact cues and ball flight information, but these programs have not considered whether findings transfer to the real task (e.g., Farrow et al., 1998). Williams, Ward and Chapman (2003) attempted to address the problems associated with laboratory-based training by assessing how well experienced outfield hockey players, with little or no goalkeeping experience, were able to save penalty flicks presented live and as film clips (from four seconds before ball contact to the point when the ball crossed the line). The live test involved transporting a real hockey goal into the laboratory so that accurate filming of responses could take place. Training involved viewing a film, similar to the test situation, where tuition was given regarding the important cues. A control group received no instruction and a placebo group watched an instructional video on goalkeeping skills. Results showed that only the training group improved their anticipation time pre- to post-test. This improvement was significant on both the laboratory and live tasks, suggesting that the perceptual improvements due to film based training do transfer to the real task.

Recently sports scientists have assessed the most appropriate method for training sports performers in visual cue usage. The question has been posed as to whether participants of training studies need to be explicitly told what to look at within a display or whether they could learn the meaning of the cues equally well, or better, without formal instructions i.e., implicitly. There is some debate in the literature regarding the mechanisms involved in the skill learning process between the two learning approaches. Where specific instructions (explicit learning) are given it is hypothesized that a large verbalizable knowledge base would be concurrently generated whereas this would be relatively absent in the implicit learning situation (Maxwell, Masters and Eves, 2000). Debate exists about the impact of explicit rule formation during motor learning with Masters (2000) advocating a minimization of this process through implicit learning strategies whereas Beek (2000) argues that verbalizable knowledge is not necessarily damaging to motor performance. Liao and Masters (2001) suggested the concept of analogy learning whereby an analogy or metaphor is used to explain the task demands, hence reducing the need for explicit verbal information. Whilst implicit learning seems to have support in sports science, the difficulty of creating an implicit learning situation should not be underestimated (Maxwell et al., 2000). Furthermore methodological problems arise regarding participants' natural learning approach (Bennett, 2000).

Farrow and Abernethy (2002) assessed implicit and explicit learning strategies whereby 32 schoolboy tennis players (intermediate level) learnt to return the tennis serve over four weeks. Ability to predict the direction of the tennis serve was tested in a realistic setting, wearing liquid crystal spectacles, utilizing a progressive temporal occlusion approach. The number of explicit rules possessed by participants was tested pre- and post-training using a verbal protocol procedure developed by Masters (1992). Participants in the explicit group were told about the relationship between location of ball toss, racket head angle and other features related to the tennis serve. The implicit group was asked to guess the speed of the serve as this was thought to encourage the monitoring of the service action without consciously processing the anticipatory information. A control group and a placebo group were also used, the latter watching competitive matches. Verbal protocols suggested that explicit learning resulted in more explicit rule formation compared to the other three groups. The assessment of anticipatory behavior between the four groups revealed some significant differences although the conclusions made have been questioned (Jackson, 2003).

In a similar study, Williams et al., (2002) assessed thirty two recreational tennis players who either received explicit training on advance cues associated with a tennis serve or were given information concerning where to look but no formal rules regarding relationships between cues and outcomes. As in the previous study, a placebo and control group were used. Both training groups subsequently improved their anticipations and decision times, unlike the placebo and control groups, as assessed by both laboratory and field tests. These more robust findings suggest film-based training is useful for learning the utility of visual cues although more research is needed into the effectiveness of explicit and implicit training methods.

Future Research in SA for Sporting Situations

The difficulties associated with assessing SA in sport are primarily concerned with deriving measures that retain ecological validity as well as capturing the diversity of the sporting situations. James, Patrick and colleagues have been working towards this goal by developing two methodologies. One approach involves the use of video recordings of matches being viewed by expert coaches who rate the extent that SA is not achieved. Where inter-rater agreement is satisfactory, scenarios can be grouped together according to common reasons for lack of SA. This information can then be used in a second experimental approach that involves players wearing liquid occlusion spectacles (Milgram, 1987) whilst playing small-sided games. These scenarios can be carefully devised so as to retain the same rules, playing conditions and patterns of play associated with the full-sided version of the games. Both these approaches provide new methods for the investigation of awareness in sports situations.

References

Abernethy, B. (1990), 'Expertise, Visual Search and Information Pick-Up in Squash', *Perception*, vol. 19, pp. 63-77.

Abernethy, B. and Russell, D.G. (1984), 'Advance Cue Utilisation by Skilled Cricket Batsmen', *Australian Journal of Science and Medicine in Sport*, vol. 16(2), pp. 2-10.

Abernethy, B. and Russell, D.G. (1987), 'Expert-Novice Differences in an Applied Selective Attention Task', *Journal of Sport Psychology*, vol. 9, pp. 326-345.

Abernethy, B., Gill, D.P., Parks, S.L. and Packer, S.T. (2001), 'Expertise and the Perception of Kinematic and Situational Probability Information', *Perception*, vol. 30, pp. 233-252.

Adolphe, R.M., Vickers, J.N. and Laplante, G. (1997), 'The Effects of Training Visual Attention on Gaze Behaviour and Accuracy: A Pilot Study', *International Journal of Sports Vision*, vol. 4(1), pp. 28-33.

Alain, C. and Sarrazin, C. (1990), 'Study of Decision-Making in Squash Competition: A Computer Simulation Approach', *Canadian Journal of Sport Science*, vol. 15(3), pp. 193-200.

Allard, F., Graham, S. and Paarsalu, M.L. (1980), 'Perception in Sport: Basketball', *Journal of Sport Psychology*, vol. 2, pp. 14-21.

Allard, F. and Starkes, J.L. (1980), 'Perception in Sport: Volleyball', *Journal of Sport Psychology*, vol. 2, pp. 22-33.

Anderson, J.R. (1990), *Cognitive Psychology and its Implications* (3rd ed.), W.H. Freeman, New York.

Bard, C. and Fleury, M. (1981), 'Considering Eye Movement as a Predictor of Attainment', In I.M. Cockerill and W.W. MacGillvary (eds), *Vision and Sport,* Stanley Thornes, Cheltenham.

Beek, P.J. (2000), 'Toward a Theory of Implicit Learning in the Perceptual-Motor Domain', *International Journal of Sport Psychology*, vol. 31, pp. 547-554.

Bennett, S.J. (2000), 'Implicit Learning: Should it be used in Practice?' *International Journal of Sport Psychology*, vol. 31, pp. 542-546.

Chase, W.G. and Simon, H.A. (1973), 'The Mind's Eye in Chess', In W.G. Chase (ed.), *Visual Information Processing*, Academic Press, New York, pp. 215-281.

Coté, J., Baker, J. and Abernethy, B. (2003), 'From Play to Practice: A Developmental Framework for the Acquisition of Expertise in Team Sports', In J.L. Starkes and K.A. Ericsson (eds), *Expert Performance in Sports: Advances in Research on Sport Expertise*, Human Kinetics, Champaign: Illinois, pp. 89-113.

Crognier, L., Veret, N. and Féry, Y.A. (2003), 'Is Anticipation in Tennis Related to Specific Knowledge', In Proceedings of the 8th International Table Tennis Federation Sports Science Congress and the 3rd World Congress of Science and Racket Sports, pp. 16.

de Groot, A. (1978), *Thought and Choice in Chess*, The Hague, Mouton. (Original work published 1946).

Endsley, M.R. (1993), 'A Survey of Situation Awareness Requirements in Air-to-Air Combat Fighters', *International Journal of Aviation Psychology*, vol. 3, pp. 157-168.

Endsley, M.R. (1995), 'Toward a Theory of Situation Awareness in Dynamic Systems', *Human Factors*, vol. 37(1), pp. 32-64.

Ericsson, K.A. (ed.) (1996), *'The Road to Excellence'*, Lawrence Erlbaum Associates, New Jersey.

Ericsson, K.A. (2003), 'How the Expert Performance Approach Differs from Traditional Approaches to Expertise in Sport: In Search of a Shared Theoretical Framework for Studying Expert Performance', In J.L. Starkes and K.A. Ericsson (eds), *Expert Performance in Sports: Advances in Research on Sport Expertise*, Human Kinetics, Champaign: Illinois, pp. 371-402.

Ericsson, K.A. and Harris, M.S. (1990), *Expert Chess Knowledge without Chess Knowledge: A Training Study.* Poster presented at the 31st Annual Meeting of the Psychonomic Society, New Orleans, Louisiana.

Ericsson, K.A., Krampe, R.T. and Tesch-Römer, C. (1993), 'The Role of Deliberate Practice in the Acquisition of Expert Performance', *Psychological Review*, vol. 100, pp. 363-406.

Ericsson, K.A. and Simon, H.A. (1993), *Protocol Analysis: Verbal Reports as Data*, (Rev. ed.), MIT press, Cambridge, MA.

Ericsson, K.A. and Charness, N. (1994), 'Expert Performance: Its Structure and Acquisition', *American Psychologist*, vol. 49, pp. 725-747.

Ericsson, K.A. and Kintsch, W. (1995), 'Long-Term Working Memory', *Psychological Review*, vol. 102, pp. 211-245.

Ericsson, K.A., Patel, V.L. and Kintsch, W. (2000), 'How Experts' Adaptations to Representative Task Demands Account for the Expertise Effect in Memory Recall: Comment on Vicente and Wang (1998)', *Psychological Review*, vol. 107, pp. 578-592.

Farrow, D., Chivers, P., Hardingham, C. and Sachse, S. (1998), 'The Effect of Video-based Perceptual Training on the Tennis Return of Serve', *International Journal of Sport Psychology*, vol. 29, pp. 231-242.

Farrow, D. and Abernethy, B. (2002), 'Can Anticipatory Skills be Learned through Implicit Video-based Perceptual Training?' *Journal of Sports Sciences*, vol. 20, pp. 471-485.

Féry, Y.-A. and Crognier, L. (2001), 'On the Tactical Significance of Game Situations in Anticipating Ball Trajectories in Tennis', *Research Quarterly for Exercise and Sport*, vol. 72(2), pp. 143-149.

Helsen, W.F. and Pauwels, J.M. (1993), 'The Relationship between Expertise and Visual Information Processing in Sport', In J.L. Starkes and F. Allard (eds), *Cognitive Issues in Motor Expertise*, Elsevier, Amsterdam, pp. 109-134.

Helsen, W.F. and Starkes, J.L. (1999), 'A Multidimensional Approach to Skilled Perception and Performance in Sport', *Applied Cognitive Psychology*, vol. 13, pp. 1-27.

Howarth, C., Walsh, W.D. and Abernethy, B. (1984), 'A Field Examination of Anticipation in Squash: some Preliminary Data', *The Australian Journal of Science and Medicine in Sport*, vol. 16(3), pp. 7-11.

Hubbard, A.W. and Seng, C.N. (1954), 'Visual Movements of Batters', *Research Quarterly*, vol. 25, pp. 42-57.

Hughes M.D. and Robertson, C. (1998), 'Using Computerised Notational Analysis to Create a Template for Elite Squash and its Subsequent use in Designing Hand Notation Systems for Player Development', In A. Lees, I. Maynard, M. Hughes and T. Reilly (eds), *Science and Racket Sports II*, E and FN Spon, London, pp. 227-234.

Jackson, R.C. (2003), 'Evaluating the Evidence for Implicit Perceptual Learning: A Re-analysis of Farrow and Abernethy (2002)', *Journal of Sports Sciences*, vol. 21(6), pp. 503-509.

James, N. and Bradley, C. (in press), 'Disguising Ones Intentions: The Availability of Visual Cues and Situational Probabilities when Playing against an International Level Squash Player', In A. Lees, J-F. Kahn, and I. Maynard (eds), *Science and Racket Sports III*, Routledge, Taylor and Francis Books, London.

Jones, C.M. and Miles, T.R. (1978), 'Use of Advance Cues in Predicting the Flight of a Lawn Tennis Ball', *Journal of Human Movement Studies*, vol. 4, pp. 231-235.

Liao, C.-M. and Masters, R.S.W. (2001), 'Analogy Learning: A Means to Implicit Motor Learning', *Journal of Sports Sciences*, vol. 19, pp. 307-319.

Masters, R.S.W. (1992), 'Knowledge, Knerves and Know-How: The Role of Explicit versus Implicit Knowledge in the Breakdown of a Complex Motor Skill under Pressure', *British Journal of Psychology*, vol. 83, pp. 343-358.

Masters, R.S.W. (2000), 'Theoretical Aspects of Implicit Learning in Sport', *International Journal of Sport Psychology*, vol. 31, pp. 530-541.

Maxwell, J.P., Masters, R.S.W. and Eves, F.F. (2000), 'From Novice to no Know-How: A Longitudinal Study of Implicit Motor Learning', *Journal of Sports Sciences*, vol. 18, pp. 111-120.

Mcleod, P.N. (1987), 'Visual Reaction Time and High-Speed Ball Games', *Perception*, vol. 16, pp. 49-59.

McPherson, S.L. (1999), 'Expert-Novice Differences in Performance Skills and Problem Representation of Youths and Adults During Tennis Competition', *Research Quarterly for Exercise and Sport*, vol. 70, pp. 233-251.

McPherson, S.L. (2000), 'Expert-Novice Differences in Planning Strategies during Collegiate Singles Tennis Competition', *Journal of Sport and Exercise Psychology*, vol. 22, pp. 39-62.

McPherson, S.L. and Thomas, J.R. (1989), 'Relation of Knowledge and Performance in Boys' Tennis: Age and Expertise', *Journal of Experimental Child Psychology*, vol. 48, pp. 190-211.

Milgram, P. (1987), 'A Spectacle-Mounted Liquid Crystal Tachistoscope', *Behaviour Research Methods, Instrumentation and Computers*, vol. 19, pp. 449-456.

Nisbett, R.E. and Wilson, T.D. (1977), 'Telling More than we can Know: Verbal Reports on Mental Processes', *Psychological Review*, vol. 84, pp. 231-259.

Patrick, J. and James, N. (in press), 'Process Tracing of Complex Cognitive Work Tasks', *Journal of Occupational and Organizational Psychology*.

Paull, G. and Glencross, D. (1997), 'Expert Perception and Decision Making in Baseball', *International Journal of Sport Psychology*, vol. 28, pp. 35-56.

Renshaw, I. and Fairweather, M.M. (2000). 'Cricket Bowling Deliveries and the Discrimination Ability of Professional and Amateur Batters', *Journal of Sports Sciences*, vol. 18, pp. 951-957.

Simon, H.A. and Chase, W.G. (1973), 'Skill in Chess', *American Scientist*, vol. 61, pp. 394-403.

Starkes, J.L. (1987), 'Skill in Field Hockey: The Nature of the Cognitive Advantage', *Journal of Sport Psychology*, vol. 9, pp. 146-160.

Starkes, J.L and Allard, F. (1991), 'Motor-Skill Experts in Sports, Dance and other Domains', In K.A. Ericsson and J. Smith (eds), *Toward a General Theory of Expertise: Prospects and Limits*, Cambridge University Press, Cambridge, pp. 126-152.

Tyldesley, D.A., Bootsma, R.J. and Bomhoff, G.T. (1982), 'Skill Level and Eye Movement Patterns in a Sport Orientated Reaction Time Test', In H. Reider, H. Mechling and K. Reischle (eds) *Proceeding of an International Symposium on Motor Behaviour: Contribution to Learning in Sport*. Cologne: Hofmann.

Vickers, J.N. (1996a), 'Visual Control while Aiming at a Far Target', *Journal of Experimental Psychology: Human Perception and Performance*, vol. 22, pp. 342-354.

Vickers, J.N. (1996b), 'Control of Visual Attention during the Basketball Free Throw', *American Journal of Sports Medicine*, vol. 24, pp. S93-S97.

Vickers, J.N. and Adolphe, R.M. (1997), 'Gaze Behaviour during a Ball Tracking and Aiming Skill', *International Journal of Sports Vision*, vol. 4(1), pp. 18-27.

Ward, P. and Williams, A.M. (2003), 'Perceptual and Cognitive Skill Development in Soccer: The Multidimensional Nature of Expert Performance', *Journal of Sport and Exercise Psychology*, vol. 25, pp. 93-111.

Williams, A.M., Davids, K., Burwitz, L. and Williams, J.G. (1993), 'Cognitive Knowledge and Soccer Performance', *Perceptual and Motor Skills*, vol. 76, pp. 579-593.

Williams, A.M., Davids, K., Burwitz, L. and Williams, J.G. (1994), 'Visual Search Strategies in Experienced and Inexperienced Soccer Players', *Research Quarterly for Exercise and Sport*, vol. 65(2), pp. 127-135.

Williams, A.M., Davids, K. (1998), 'Visual Search Strategy, Selective Attention and Expertise in Soccer', *Research Quarterly for Exercise and Sport*, vol. 69, pp. 111-128.

Williams, A.M., Davids, K. and Williams, J.G. (1999), *Visual Perception and Action in Sport*. Spon Press, London.

Williams A.M. and Grant, A. (1999), 'Training Perceptual Skill in Sport', *International Journal of Sport Psychology*, vol. 30, pp. 194-220.

Williams, A.M., Ward, P., Knowles, J.M. and Smeeton, N.J. (2002), 'Anticipation Skill in a Real-World Task: Measurement, Training and Transfer in Tennis', *Journal of Experimental Psychology: Applied*, vol. 8(4), pp. 259-270.

Williams, A.M., Ward, P. and Chapman, C. (2003), 'Training Perceptual Skill in Field Hockey: Is there Transfer from the Laboratory to the Field?' *Research Quarterly for Exercise and Sport*, vol. 74, pp. 98-103.

Chapter 17

Situation Awareness: Progress and Directions

Mica R. Endsley

Introduction

Research on Situation Awareness (SA) continues to flourish in a wide variety of fields from driving to military command and control demonstrating its wide applicability outside of its original aviation origins. Indeed, we have found analogous language that has naturally arisen in other domains, such as 'the picture' in air traffic control (Endsley and Smolensky, 1998) or 'the bubble' in control rooms (Garbis and Artman, Chapter 15, this volume). Treatises on SA can be found in materials for mountaineering, educators and the martial arts. The ubiquitous nature of this work speaks primarily to the ubiquitous nature of SA – it underlies much of human performance in both man-made work operations, such as aircraft piloting, and non-engineered but challenging situations, such as warfighting. In this light, I would like to talk about where we are in terms of research on SA – the progress that has, or has not, been made and the research that is still needed to provide useful inputs to the job of training, or designing systems, that will foster SA in a difficult and challenging world.

Theory

I have reviewed and compared models of SA elsewhere (Endsley, 2000b), including their many commonalities, and will not repeat that assessment here. I will, however, first address several problems I have observed related to a misinterpretation of my 1995 model (Endsley, 1995c) and discuss interesting progress on SA within the context of this model.

Endsley's Model of SA

The 1995 model (Endsley, 1995c) of SA (Figure 17.1) has been sometimes praised and sometimes maligned, but most frequently cited as forming a foundation for discussion on SA, the cognitive processes underlying its formation, and the factors affecting it. In this regard it forms a useful starting point for many research objectives. Yet, I have noted of late certain misperceptions about the model (perhaps I have not conveyed things clearly enough), that instead hamper research progress. I will first discuss some of these misperceptions and correct the record.

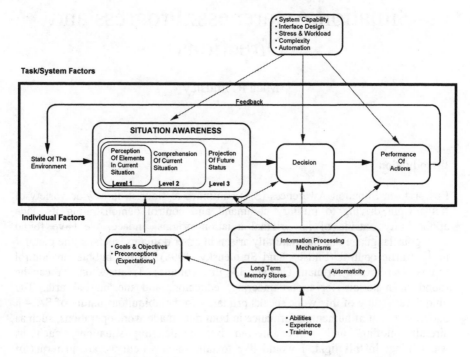

Figure 17.1 Model of Situation Awareness in dynamic decision making (Endsley, 1995c)

In summary, the model consists of several key factors:

- perception, comprehension and projection as three levels of SA;
- the role of goals and goal-directed processing in directing attention and interpreting the significance of perceived information;
- the role of information salience in 'grabbing' attention in a data-driven fashion, and the importance of alternating goal-driven and data-driven processing;
- the role of expectations (fed by the current model of the situation and by long-term memory stores) in directing attention and interpreting information;
- the heavy demands on limited working memory restricting SA for novices and for those in novel situations, but the tremendous advantages of mental models and pattern matching to prototypical schema that largely circumvent these limits;

- the use of mental models for providing a means for integrating different bits of information and comprehending their meaning (relevant to goals) and for allowing people to make useful projections of likely future events and states;
- pattern matching to schema (i.e., prototypical states of the mental model) that provides rapid retrieval of comprehension and projection relevant to the recognized situation and in many cases single-step retrieval of appropriate actions for the situation.

Levels of SA The three levels of SA, perception (level 1), comprehension (level 2) and projection (level 3), represent ascending degrees of SA. A person who understands or comprehends the significance of information has a higher level of SA than one who only perceives the basic data, and the person who is able to project what will happen in the situation has an even higher level of SA. Their SA can be said to be of a higher quality. So the person who understands that at an altitude of 10,000 feet a collision with terrain is imminent has better SA than one who only knows the aircraft is at 10,000 feet.

This does not mean that perception, comprehension and projection necessarily occur in linear discrete stages. In fact, the model clearly states that this is not necessarily the case. In general it is easy to see that level 2 builds on level 1 and level 3 builds on level 2. That is, a person needs to see or hear a signal (level 1), interpret what it means (level 2) and then project what will happen next (level 3). This is from a data-driven perspective. The reality, however, is that a simple 1-2-3 progression (i.e., data-driven) is not an efficient processing mechanism in a complex and dynamic system, which is where expertise and goal driven processing come into play.

The model also represents that many times people are goal-driven. So based on their goals or their current understanding or projections (level 2 and 3) the individual will go looking for data to either confirm or deny this assessment or to fill in questions (look for level 1 data). This is an iterative process, with understanding driving the search for new data and new data coming together to feed understanding, as represented by the feedback arrow in the model in Figure 17.1. These processes are considerably different than the depiction of linear stages presented by Dekker and Lützhöft (Chapter 2, this volume) or by Patrick and James (Chapter 4, this volume), for example.

In addition, the model specifies the use of 'defaults' in mental models that have a significant role. SA is composed of many different situation elements in most domains and people never really have complete SA across many of those level 1 elements. They must constantly try to update their SA to the degree that they can from available data (employing scan patterns or data-search behaviors), and often 'fill in' where they do not have available data through defaults in the mental model. That is they use their level 2/3 SA to generate assumptions regarding level 1 representations (either rightly or wrongly).

... default values for certain features of a system can be used if exact current values are not known. Fighter pilots, for example, usually get only limited information about other aircraft. They therefore must operate on default information (e.g., it is probably a MIG-

29 and therefore likely traveling at certain approximate speed). When more details become available, their SA becomes more accurate (e.g., knowledge of the exact airspeed), possibly leading to better decisions, but they are still able to make reasonable decisions without perfect information. (Endsley, 1995c, p. 45)

In this way people can have level 2 and 3 SA, even when they do not have complete or accurate level 1 SA, and can use the higher levels of SA to drive the search for and acquisition of level 1 SA. There exists the potential for error in this process – people may erroneously attempt to fit data into a pre-existing representation of the situation, misinterpreting the true significance of that data (Carmino, Idee, Larchier Boulanger, and Morlat, 1988; Jones and Endsley, 2000). The problems of anchoring and confirmation bias have been well discussed. None-the-less, this provides much efficiency in processing in a complex world with missing information, and appears to be a very robust part of cognition.

Elements of SA A second area of confusion seems to lie in what are meant by the 'elements' in the definition of SA 'the perception of the elements in the environment within a volume of space and time, the comprehension of their meaning and the projection of their status in the near future' (Endsley, 1988). These elements are of course very domain specific. Examples for air traffic control are shown in Table 17.1. N ote that these elements are all clearly observable, meaningful pieces of information for an air traffic controller. Thin gs such as aircraft type, altitude, heading and flight plan; restrictions in effect at an airport or conformance to a clearance are all fairly concrete and meaningful attributes of the situation to the air traffic controller.

This is in direct opposition to a false portrayal of SA elements as mere stimuli. 'Information processing theories begin with the primitive, meaningless nature of stimuli in the world (they are 'elements' in the words of one SA theory)' (Dekker and Lützhöft, Chapter 2, this volume, pp. 25-26). There is nothing primitive or meaningless about even level 1 SA, much less the higher levels. There is much to be done to move science forward in the area of SA research. It is not well served by such misrepresentations which only add confusion in the name of pushing a philosophy, rather than adding light by truly exploring meaningful similarities and differences in competing theories.

Product vs. Process A final area of confusion seems to center around the distinction between SA as a product and the processes involved in achieving SA.

> Whilst we agree that situation awareness involves knowledge that is task-relevant, attempting to separate processes from products in a rigorous manner is not feasible even with experimental and psychophysiological techniques. We therefore conclude that any useful understanding of SA has to embrace not only a person's knowledge of a situation but also the processes responsible for producing such knowledge, which will depend on the situation and its context. (Patrick and James, Chapter 4, this volume, p. 63)

Table 17.1 Elements of SA in Air Traffic Control (Endsley and Rodgers, 1994)

LEVEL 1

Aircraft
aircraft ID, CID, beacon code
current route (position, heading, aircraft turn rate,
 altitude, climb/descent rate, groundspeed)
current flight plan (destination, filed plan)
aircraft capabilities (turn rate, climb/descent
 rate, cruising speed, max/min speed)
equipment on board
aircraft type
fuel/loading
aircraft status
 activity (enroute, arriving, departing, handed-
 off, pointed-out)
 level of control (IFR, VFR, flight
 following, VFR-on top, uncontrolled
 object)
 aircraft contact established
 aircraft descent established
 communications (present/ frequency)
 responsible controller
 aircraft priority
 special conditions
 equipment malfunctions
 emergencies
 pilot capability/state/ intentions
 altimeter setting

Emergencies
type of emergency
time on fuel remaining
souls on board

Requests
pilot/ controller requests
reason for request

Clearances
assignment given
received by correct aircraft
readback correct/complete
pilot acceptance of clearance
flight progress strip current

Sector
special airspace status
equipment functioning
restrictions in effect
changes to standard procedures

Special Operations
type of special operation
time begin/ terminate operations
projected duration
area and altitude effected

ATC Equipment Malfunctions
equipment affected
alternate equipment available
equipment position/ range
aircraft in outage area

Airports
operational status
restrictions in effect
direction of departures
current aircraft arrival rate
arrival requirements
active runways/approach
sector saturation
aircraft in holding (time, number, direction,
 leg length)

Weather
area affected
altitudes affected
conditions (snow, icing, fog, hail, rain,
 turbulence, overhangs)
temperatures
intensity
visibility
turbulence
winds
IFR/VFR conditions
Airport conditions

LEVEL 2

Conformance
amount of deviation (altitude, airspeed, route)
time until aircraft reaches assigned altitude,
 speed, route/heading

Current Separation
amount of separation between
 aircraft/objects/airspace/
 ground along route
deviation between separation and prescribed
 limits
number/timing aircraft on routes
altitudes available

Timing
projected time in airspace
projected time till clear of airspace
time until aircraft landing expected
time/distance aircraft to airport
time/distance till visual contact
order/sequencing of aircraft

Deviations
deviation aircraft/ landing req.
deviation aircraft /flight plan
deviation aircraft/pilot requests

Other Sector/ Airspace
radio frequency
aircraft duration/reason for use

Significance
impact of requests/clearances on:
 aircraft separation/safety

own/ other sector workload
impact of weather on:
 aircraft safety/ flight comfort
 own/ other sector workload
 aircraft flow/routing (airport arrival r
 flow rates, holding requirements
 aircraft routes, separation
 procedures)
 altitudes available
 traffic advisories
impact of special operations on sector
 operations/procedures
location of nearest capable airport for aircr
 type/emergency
impact of malfunction on: routing,
 communications, flow control,
 aircraft, coordination procedures,
 other sectors, own workload
impact no. of aircraft on workload
sector demand vs own capabilities

Confidence Level/ Accuracy of Info
aircraft ID, position, altitude, airspeed,
 heading
weather
altimeter setting

LEVEL 3

Projected Aircraft Route (Current)
position, flight plan, destination, heading,
 route, altitude, climb/ descent rate,
 airspeed, winds, groundspeed,
 intentions, assignments

Projected Aircraft Route (Potential)
projected position x at time t
potential assignments

Projected Separation
amount of separation along route
 (aircraft/ objects/ airspace/ground)
deviation between separation and prescril
 limits
relative projected aircraft routes
relative timing along route

Predicted Changes in Weather
direction/speed of movement
increasing/decreasing in intensity

Impact of Potential Route Changes
type of change required
time and distance till turn aircraft
amount of turn /new heading, altitude,
 route change required
aircraft ability to make change
projected no. of changes necessary
increase/decrease length of route
cost/benefit of new clearance
impact of proposed change on:
 aircraft separation

It apparently bears repeating that the distinctions drawn between process and product have to do with clarifying our language and terminology when discussing SA.

As a matter of consistent terminology, it is first necessary to distinguish the term 'situation awareness' as a state of knowledge, from the processes used to achieve that state. (Endsley, 1995c, p. 36)

> We wish to distinguish the process of achieving situation awareness, which is sometimes called situation assessment, from its product or consequences. The state of awareness with respect to information and knowledge is the product. (Tenney, Adams, Pew, Huggins and Rogers, 1992, p. 2)

It does not mean that somehow an artificial line has been drawn stating that only one is important or that they do not intricately affect each other.

> I am full in agreement with Adams, Tenney and Pew (this issue) that there is great benefit from examining the interdependence of the processes and the resultant state of knowledge, however, in order to clarify discourse on SA, it is important to keep the terminology straight. (Endsley, 1995c)

In fact, both of these models (Endsley, 1988, 1995c; Tenney et al., 1992) discuss the processes involved in achieving and maintaining SA as a state of knowledge (as a product of those processes), and the ways in which the current product affects those processes in turn.

The reasons for clarifying the language and terminology have more to do with historical problems in miscommunication among different researchers and with different approaches for measuring SA. Some measures such as eye movement recordings or communications tracing clearly seek to understand the processes that people use to achieve SA, but tell us little about the product or the level of SA they achieve through those processes. Other measures, such as the Situation Awareness Global Assessment Technique (SAGAT) or testable response measures seek to measure or quantify the level of SA a person possesses, but do not tell us anything about the processes that were used. Depending on the goals of the researcher, exploration of cognitive processes or design of systems, a different set of measures is more appropriate. In some cases, a combination may be needed to really get at a full understanding. For instance, process-oriented measures may be useful for understanding the types of information seeking behaviors that different groups of people use. When coupled with SAGAT, we would also have a diagnostic measure of how successful these processes were in deriving different elements of SA.

Projection

Some of the more interesting progress of late increasing our understanding of SA pertains to the third level of SA – projection. In and of itself, projection is an interesting aspect of SA, but has been a somewhat murky one. Projection can be seen to be very useful, allowing for proactive decision making rather than mere reactive existence. Evidence suggests that those who have high levels of SA engage in an active process of projection and contingency planning that allows their performance, even under emergency or rare event conditions, to appear effortless. Yet, how far one needs to be able to project has never been clear. And the types of processes used to achieve projection could certainly benefit from more research.

Horswill and McKenna (Chapter 9, this volume) present a detailed analysis of anticipation of hazards in driving. 'Hazard perception can be viewed as drivers' situation awareness for potentially dangerous incidents in the traffic environment' (Horswill and McKenna, Chapter 9, this volume). It is one element of projection in driving that they have clearly demonstrated is highly relevant to performance in term of accident avoidance. It is worth pointing out that anticipating hazards is not all that matters in driving. Other factors relate to the vehicle (speed, fuel, etc.), to navigation (location of self and objective), and to maneuvering in traffic (distance from other vehicles) (Bolstad, 2001). None-the-less, in terms of the likelihood of being involved in an accident, this aspect of SA appears to be highly significant in driving.

Of particular interest, they investigated the degree to which hazard anticipation was effected by concurrent tasks. While experienced drivers are better at anticipating hazards than less experienced drivers, they were even more negatively affected by dual tasks that tapped into the central executive. This implies that:

> ... good hazard perception is better conceived as an effortful, proactive process. Those drivers who are best at hazard perception actively search for hazards using a dynamic mental model of the traffic environment. Using the working memory framework, evidence suggests that hazard perception, as performed by expert and experienced drivers, is a central executive task. When experienced drivers no longer apply these central resources, their hazard perception ability appears to be reduced to the level of novices ... effective hazard perception is cognitively demanding and does not possess the requisite properties of an automatic task. (Horswill and McKenna, Chapter 9, this volume, pp. 166-167)

This finding fits well with recent research on projection by Jones and colleagues (Jones, Quoetone, Ferree, Magsig and Bunting, 2003) involving weather forecasters. They compared two hypotheses regarding the processes used for projection: (i) using mental models to run a mental simulation of what might happen with the system over time, and (ii) pattern matching between features of the situation and schema of known similar situations in order to base projections on the outcomes of these situations.

The first case represents an active process requiring central executive processes. The later is more characteristic of an automatic process. They found evidence for both processes in their study: '... they adjusted their strategy as needed to provide the best assessment of the environment' (Jones et al., 2003). In this study it appeared that pattern-matching to similar situations could yield acceptable results in some cases if the right cues were focused on for the pattern match, yet the successful forecasters also needed to shift to more active mental simulations when the needed cues were not particularly salient in the situation (needed to be inferred from other cues) or when the situations required mental simulation to fully understand the implications.

Those whose forecasts were incorrect often tended to focus on different cues in the situation. It is not known whether they lacked sufficient resources for mental simulation, prematurely latched on to a pattern based on insufficient assessment of its fit, lacked sensitivity to relevant features, or merely lacked sufficient patterns in memory to match correctly. In the hazard anticipation studies, evidence suggests that novices did not direct their attention to as wide a range of information in the environment, potentially due to a more impoverished mental model directing that search (Underwood, Chapman, Bowden, and Crundall, 2002).

When put together with the review of driving hazard anticipation by Horswill and McKenna (Chapter 9, this volume), it would appear that while experience can breed the development of a mental library of prototypical situations that allows very rapid situation recognition and decision making, it is insufficient to provide robust mental projections. Mental simulations that produce likely projections of events appear to be required in at least some cases, and an active effort at considering potential future situations is a skill that must be actively engaged in. These assessments require further research and validation.

Alternately, Banbury, Croft, Macken and Jones (Chapter 7, this volume) propose a model of cognitive streaming to explain projection. As both cognitive streaming and theories based on mental models provide for the use of relational probabilities between elements to generate projections of likely events (e.g., see development of Bayesian networks of SA by Zacharias, Miao, Illgen, Yara, and Siouris (1996) it is unclear what the implications of cognitive streaming's depiction of memory as a process rather than a store provide to explaining this aspect of SA.

On Sense Making and Situation Awareness

Recently there has been interest in the concept of sense making (Weick, 1995; Weick, Sutcliffe, and Obstfeld, 1999) and how it relates to SA. While some portray this as a different and alternative view of cognition (Dekker and Lützhöft, Chapter 2, this volume), in fact sense making more closely refers to a subset of the processes involved in SA. Focused on processes at the organizational level, Weick and his colleagues have focused on how people work to make sense of the information and systems they find themselves in. In this aspect it is the process of forming level 2 SA from level 1 data through effortful processes of gathering and synthesizing information, using story building and mental models to find some formulation, some representation that accounts for and explains the disparate data.

Sense making undoubtedly represents an activity engaged in to formulate level 2 SA in some cases, however, it needs to be pointed out that in many cases such effortful, highly intentional deliberation and assessment does not appear to be carried out. Kaempf, Klein, Thordsen and Wolf (1996), for example found in a study of tactical commanders, 95 per cent used a recognition decision strategy. This involved either feature matching to situation prototypes (87 per cent) or story building (13 per cent). In the vast majority of cases the situation recognition was instantaneous and reflexive. The speed of operations in activities such as sports, driving, flying and air traffic control practically prohibits such conscious deliberation in the majority of cases, but rather reserves it for the exceptions. It is quite possible that the ability to determine when such deliberative processes are needed may be a key indicator of skill and expertise in many environments.

It should also be pointed out that sense making is necessarily backward looking, forming reasons for past events and diagnosing the causative factors of observed faults. These are certainly needed processes, particularly in the usual events and high consequence systems under Weick's focus. Yet SA, as an active ongoing model of the situation that is in place during routine as well as novel situations, is also focused on the future. Maintaining SA involves constantly updating what is known about the present and projecting what is likely to happen in order to inform effective decision processes. Active sense making is engaged in when needed, but represents only a portion of the picture.

Finally, it should be noted that sense making has largely been discussed at the organizational level. Its description and focus have looked to the organizational barriers and successful factors associated with organizations that are successful, including issues such as an organizational culture of mindfulness, focus on the potential for failures and commitment to organizational resilience (e.g., error trapping and recovery). These are indeed interesting concepts and likely to represent some of the task and organizational factors that can impact on SA (in individuals and in teams), none-the-less, the level of analysis is quite different than that at which most SA research has been conducted. The sense making research discusses processes at an organizational level, but not at a cognitive level, as that was not its intent. It has instead, looked to models of SA to provide more detail at the cognitive level (Kaempf et al., 1996). Therefore, I would put forth that this parallel body of work is complimentary to SA research, but not directly at odds with it, nor possessing an alternate view at the cognitive level.

Ecological Theories and Situation Awareness

A theory of human performance that is very different than the model of SA is the ecological psychology approach (Flach, 1990; Vicente and Rasmussen, 1992) based largely on the work of Gibson (1979). Ecological psychology rejects the view of turning data into information in the head of the observer or operator and instead views aspects of the world as being seen directly in terms of their affordances to the operator. 'Ecological approaches tend to focus on meaning in terms of functional significance' (Flach and Hancock, 1992, p. 1057). It has evolved as a rebellion from the practice of experimental psychology which for many years had divorced the study of cognitive functions from the environment and the complex tasks in which they normally occur (Flach 1990). In doing so, it explicitly avoids discussion of cognitive constructs (such as attention or memory) and instead focuses on the attributes of the work domain (its structure and constraints) and the affordances that domain offers based on operator goals.

At a surface level it is difficult to reconcile these two very different theoretical approaches: Ecological psychology which explicitly rejects cognitivist considerations, and SA which is essentially a cognitive construct. For this reason, it is easy to see why it is that while these two bodies of research have evolved during essentially the same time frame (the late 1980s though the present day), they have provided very little transfer of information back and forth.

In actuality though, despite their very different formulations, I think there are some significant similarities between these areas of research. Hancock and Diaz (2002) have recently stepped forth to fill this void, going back to Gibson's work on field of safe travel (FST). They state:

> ... both SA and FST are identified with perceptions and interpretations from those perceptions ... The first is that ambient environments provide distinct characteristics which stand out from the rest of the surround to motivate response and generate intent: this is denoted as 'objects or features' in FST and as 'elements' in SA. Secondly, it provides a more general level of information about the actor's surroundings in terms of space and time, which is characterized in FST as 'an indefinitely bounded fielded... at any given moment' and as 'a volume of time and space' in the definition of SA ... The two definitions are also consistent in their idea that an actor responds to the environment based upon the consequences that are expected to follow. This notion is manifest in FST as a 'negative valence' and as 'comprehension of [the] meaning [of environmental elements]' in SA ... Lastly, both definitions described anticipative reasoning or strategizing; this is indicated by the idea in FST of use of the term 'protruding forward' and by Endsley's notion of SA as applicable to the near future'. (Hancock and Diaz, 2002, p. 120)

Thus, they demonstrate commonality, at least with Gibson's original work in motion perception, at a fairly basic level of the elements or features of the environment, the development of meaning or affordances, and of some projection of future status.

These two bodies of work also have considerable similarity on their focus on operator goals and meaning. In the language of ecological psychology, this is in terms of the affordances. In SA, the comprehension of the elements is all about meaning which derives from operator goals.

> Level 2 SA goes beyond simply being aware of the elements which are present, to include an understanding of the significance of those elements in light of pertinent operator goals. Based upon knowledge of Level 1 elements, particularly when put together to form patterns with the other elements (gestalt), the decision maker forms a holistic picture of the environment, comprehending the significance of objects and events. (Endsley, 1995c, p. 37)

Aside from these significant similarities, other differences also exist:

- SA theories place more emphasis on the dynamic, changing goals of the operator – drawing on the interplay between data-driven and goal-driven processing to explain changes in operator attention and information priorities over time. Lacking cognitive constructs to work with, ecological frameworks remain largely silent on this issue;
- SA theories also place more emphasis on future projections – looking not only at how well elements of the environment are meeting my current goals, but

also on projections of how those will change in future, a constant issues for operators of dynamic systems. While this is not necessarily excluded in an ecological framework (as demonstrated by FST), it has not received as much direct consideration in the literature or in its design applications. While ecological theory would seem to encompass the projection of an observed element into time, it does not appear to directly consider the mechanisms whereby observations of changes in two parameters would lead to projections of changes in a third. This cannot be immediately explained by a flow field or similar construct;

- Ecological frameworks do appear to allow for the presence of mental models (although how that squares with a rejection of cognitive constructs is not clear). Ecological interface design (EID), for example, focuses on delineating a system model (its functional purpose, abstract function, generalized function, physical function and physical form) and then using this description to design interfaces that will lead to veridical operator mental models of that system, with system states mapped to that model in a way that hopefully makes the affordances perceptually salient (Lee, Kinghorn and Sanquist, 1995; Vicente, 1999). SA-oriented design similarly puts emphasis on designing to directly portray level 2 and 3 SA, but also on the use of the goal structure to group and aggregate information in meaningful ways on displays and on the use of information salience to trigger critical cues relevant to key system states.

I do not believe these two parallel bodies of work are antithetical, rather I view them as coming to many of the same conclusions from very different routes. Whereas the current ecological faction has largely arisen from the world of power plant operators, SA research was born from the world of the aircraft pilot. Hence ecological design focuses on defining the underlying system structure (perfectly logical in an engineered system such as a power plant which is driven by underlying laws of physics) to determine an interface. In the work of aviation, military operations and driving, however, despite the presence of some mechanical and systems aspects, a wide range of human, cultural and organization factors are also highly relevant to the problem domain. There is no clear consistent model that can be independently and objectively determined. The best representations available may be those of the operator – the best experts available. Thus the problem of system design must consider not only creating effective information integrations for particular subsets of data in an effort to map to operator goals and level 2 and 3 SA requirements, but also the interplay of various goals and subgoals, and the display features needed to support those changing prioritizations.

Whereas, EID has been based on the ecological perception work of Gibson (1979), SA theory has formed in light of the studies of real world decision making (Dreyfus, 1981). Both are well in line in terms of their emphasis on human cognition and behavior in real world settings rather than in artificial laboratory tasks. Although the ecologists have felt the need to cast off cognitive constructs in order to get out of the laboratory and to shift focus to the environment instead, SA theory has instead broadened cognitive theories, modifying them to fit the realities of real world settings. While ecological theories arise from the field of psychology

– moving out of the laboratory and its artificialities; SA theory comes primarily from the world of engineering – designing systems that will better provide operators with this commodity that they crave. It does not suffer from the need to reject laboratory artificialities because it was never there to start with.

Many individual displays arrived at in the name of SA-Oriented Design (SAOD) look very similar to those arrived at through methods called ecological. While EID has been mostly applied to specific subsystem displays (Lee et al., 1995), SAOD places more consideration on the whole system, and the designs needed to keep operator awareness and understanding high across sub-systems. That is not to say that such differences are intractable or even necessarily a function of their underlying theoretical approaches, but perhaps are as much a function of history and the different paths taken to arrive at this point. Overall, I think there are far more similarities than differences in these models and recommend in favor of actions such as that of Hancock and Diaz (2002) to find unification or to determine where real factual differences actually lie.

From Descriptive Models to Prescriptive Models of SA

Moray (2004) has issued a stirring call for the need for predictive models of SA, echoed here by Rousseau, Tremblay and Breton (Chapter 1, this volume) and Bryant, Lichacz, Hollands and Baranski (Chapter 6, this volume). Existing theories of SA are largely descriptive rather than prescriptive. That is while we think we have some notion of the mechanisms at play in building and maintaining SA, we have very little ability to determine a priori what level of SA an operator will achieve with a given system design, or to predict the ways in which one system design will affect SA as compared to another.

Workload models have enjoyed some success in the design world, largely due to their promise to allow designers and managers to predict in advance the effect of some design concept on human workload and thus performance. The ability to predict performance effects through a model (rather than requiring detailed design prototyping and user testing) is a Shangri-la in the design community; a capability that would put human factors largely on the same playing field as the other engineering disciplines which value predictive analytic tools and eschew empiricism.

SAE (1997) calls for the following attributes of an SA model: acceptable to users; accurate; detailed to include internal and external states of the system, the environment and the relationship between the system and its environment, and the three levels of SA; diagnosticity; flexibility; inexpensive; objective; providing qualitative output; reliable; sensitive; simple and valid. In addition, it should account for several characteristics of humans that effect SA, including: attention, perception, memory, automaticity, goal driven and data driven processing, individual differences, system characteristics, system design, stress and workload, complexity and automation. The characteristics of models being developed in order to test psychological theories provide design recommendations or to provide intelligent aids to augment human performance may also vary considerably.

While a worthwhile goal, this desired Nirvana has been hard to achieve in the human factors discipline, for both models of human performance and workload. It is certainly a tall order for SA. None-the-less many notable modeling efforts can be pointed out, including MIDAS, IMPRINT, SOAR, ACT-R and Belief Nets, which have fearlessly begun to carve up bits of the wilderness:

- Shively, Brickner and Silbiger (1997) expanded on the MIDAS model, considering perceived SA as a function of relevant situational elements available, an SA manager regulating search behaviors, and an SA error component. Their calculation is a ratio of operator's relevant knowledge to the information needed for the mission. Burdick and Shively (2000) tested this measure in an aircraft simulation at three task difficulty conditions and found a high degree of correspondence between the model's predictions and SAGAT data on various factors such as ownship heading, bearing to an accident site, and altitude;

- Walters and Yow (2000) used measures of SACRI based on SAGAT from a power plant study at the Halden Man-Machine Laboratory to include SA measures in a MicroSaint™ task network model. Their model captured the monitoring and memorizing of system values by operators over time, and calculates and future trend based on historical data. They found no statistical difference between the A' (sensitivity calculated from signal detection theory) of five crews and the model;

- Archer, Warwick and Oster (2000) developed a representation of SA in a MicroSaint™ task network model based on an 'information driven decision making' architecture that reflected SA based on what elements of information the operator has been presented with and 'how fresh' that information may be to the operator. They represented changes in information quality based on initial quality and the volatility of the information over time to create decay functions for the parameters;

- more recently, Juarez and Gonzalez (2003; 2004) have worked to extend the ACT-R model to deal more explicitly with the cognitive factors affecting SA;

- Zacharias and colleagues (Zacharias et al., 1996) have also created a number of computer models using Bayesian belief nets. These programs use inputs on system state to create classifications of the situation that map to level 2 and 3 SA. Their intent has not been to predict human SA, but to create intelligent aids for augmenting human SA in complex systems;

- Moray (2004) proposes that we have many of the requisite capabilities needed to create prescriptive SA models, including models of strategic modeling and methods of knowledge representation, and building on classical control theory.

While I am not sure that any of these approaches, by themselves, are capable of completely modeling the complex cognitive processes that underlie SA, it appears that each may be able capture parts of it and as such move us closer to our goal. Most certainly if we are ever able to have useful human performance models for predicting the joint human/system performance associated with complex systems and challenging environments, then they certainly will need to take into consideration the SA needed to perform as well as the allowable workload levels. The movement of the field towards predictive models will, I believe, characterize much of the next decade.

Training to Improve SA

Considerable progress has been made in the area of developing methods for training SA. Robinson (2000) developed a two-day program for training SA at British Airways. This program combined training on the three levels of SA in an inspired combination with error management research (in terms of avoidance, trapping and mitigation) from the work of Helmreich, Merritt and Sherman (1996) and Reason (1997). The program involved classroom training focused on practical strategies followed by a simulator training scenario.

> High Crew SA does not necessarily lead to high performance, especially if the decision making process is flawed, however, as Endsley's taxonomy illustrated, there would appear to be a correlation between high SA and the avoidance of incidents. The developmental points are that Crews should try to achieve the highest possible SA, to allow for the best chance of avoiding threats/errors at an early stage. The best time to share projection level information would appear to be at times of low workload, when there is the time and capacity to process the information (e.g., at the briefing stage). By having high Crew SA and avoiding the majority of known threats, the Crews then have more spare capacity to trap and mitigate errors and threats as they develop, thus avoiding the potential onset of overload. (Robinson, 2000)

In addition to very positive subjective feedback on the training (78 per cent strongly agreed the program had practical value), pilots who received the training were rated as having significantly better team skills and showed a significant increase in operating at level 3 SA (as compared to level 1 or 2 SA). British Airways subsequently implemented the program across its fleet.

Building on Robinson's work, the European Commission funded the Enhanced Safety through Situation Awareness Integration (ESSAI) program for improving SA and threat management in airline pilots. The program includes a high quality multi-media DVD of the training material (in several languages), followed by a low-tech exercise and two simulator-based exercises. As reported here by Hörmann, Banbury, Dudfield, Soll and Lodge (Chapter 12, this volume), using a system of performance markers to rate SA, pilots who received the training had significantly higher SA as compared to a control group in a simulator test scenario. They also found that trained pilots were operating more at level 3 SA and demonstrated superior threat management performance in comparison to the control group.

Following on this development and validation effort, two major European airlines, Alitalia and Aero Lloyd, have implemented the ESSAI training program. Hörmann, Blokzijl, and Polo (2004) found that 99 per cent of the pilots report the training was very useful and the majority of pilots responding three months following training reported they were actively using the training in their daily operations.

Aero Lloyd stated that the ESSAI training did show measurable effects on flight safety within the company. At the same time it was confirmed by almost all pilots that ESSAI was 'something really different and useful compared to the normal training'... [at Alitalia] 96 per cent requested more of this kind of training. (Hörmann, Blokzijl and Polo, 2004)

These results indicate a very positive move forward in commercial aviation training that provides knowledge and skills on SA which has been found to be a leading factor in flight performance. While collecting uncontroversial data in field settings is always difficult, it will be very informative to follow-up on this training to see if differences in flight safety measures are observed in future operations.

The work of McKenna and his colleagues on training hazard awareness in drivers is also very encouraging, McKenna and Crick (1991; 1994) found that hazard awareness could improve through a training course.

Training involved participants watching video-based scenes of traffic situations and being encouraged to look further ahead down the road. At various points, the video was paused and drivers were asked to generate possibilities for what might happen next. McKenna and Crick (1994) compared training schedules with and without this prediction task and found significant improvements only when the prediction task was included. (Horswill and McKenna, Chapter 9, this volume)

Verbal commentary, including emphasis on looking ahead, critical hazard areas and anticipating hazards, accompanying the driving scenes was also reported to be valuable in their review which included at least ten different studies showing improvements in hazard projection with training. Given the strong body of research showing a relationship between hazard anticipation and accident rates, this work probably has the most data showing that SA can be trained and that such training can improve operator performance. In this light, driving tests in the United Kingdom and Australia now include hazard anticipation assessments.

In a different approach, we developed a set of computer-based training modules designed to build some basic skills underlying SA for new general aviation pilots (Bolstad, Endsley, Howell, and Costello, 2002). Unlike commercial pilots, general aviation pilots have received far less training and attention and typically have far less experience. These modules include training in time-sharing or distributed attention, checklist completion, ATC communications, intensive preflight planning and contingency planning, and SA feedback training which were all found to be problems in new pilots. In tests with low-time general aviation pilots it was found that the training modules were generally successful in imparting the desired skills. Some improvements in SA were found in follow-on simulated flight trials, but the simulator was insensitive to detect flight performance differences. More research is warranted to track whether this type of skills training can improve SA in the flight environment.

In a different domain, Strater, Jones and Endsley (2004) developed a computer based training program for improving SA in new army platoon leaders. This program sought to help build-up the mental models and schema that are needed for pattern recognition to produce situation understanding and projection. In addition it taught skills related to building SA through team communications and contingency planning. In initial testing with cadets performing exercises at the Royal Norwegian Naval Academy, we found that trained cadets were more likely to correctly refuse to attack a refugee camp than untrained cadets, indicating better SA. In addition, trained cadets indicated that they spent more mental effort developing Level 3 SA and determining how to best meet their goals.

Patrick and James (Chapter 4, this volume) report that they improved diagnosis of multiple faults (level 2 SA) through a training program that encouraged operators to explore multiple fault explanations for observed symptoms.

Overall, it would appear that significant progress is being made in developing programs that enhance skills related to SA. Developed in different domains, and for different classes of operators (novices to highly skilled), these programs show much promise for improving SA through training. Given the complexity of factors underlying SA and the differences in factors affecting SA in different domains, it is unlikely that a one-size-fits-all approach to SA training will be appropriate. It may be possible to learn things from these various approaches, however, that can be used to develop stronger SA training programs for populations who need it.

Measurement of SA

The proliferation of SA measures appears to be continuing unabated. French, Matthews and Redden (Chapter 14, this volume) for example, discuss ten different approaches to assessing SA in an army setting. Some of these have been around for some time (e.g., SART, SAGAT), and others appear to be customized versions of either probes set into scenarios, performance measures, or subjective rating scales (either by self assessment or outside observer). As such they fall into the categories of measures previously explored (Endsley and Garland, 2000), but customized for the conditions of the domain and the test environments.

One relatively unique measure is discussed in the literature on hazard anticipation (see review by Horswill and McKenna, Chapter 9, this volume). While having observers press a button when they think there is a potential hazard can be thought of as an extraneous task, it is none-the-less a clear objective measure. Although it only measures one aspect of SA in this domain (awareness of hazards), they demonstrated high predictive validity and considerable work provides a convincing story for its psychometric properties. A similar approach may be interesting to investigate in different domains.

James and Patrick (Chapter 16, this volume) present some interesting challenges in trying to measure SA in the fast moving setting of sports. While it can be argued that driving and flying also involve activities with rapid dynamic motion and psycho-motor actions, these settings are mediated by an engineered world (the dashboard or cockpit) that lends itself well to simulators and thus far more experimenter control. The real time action of sports, however, relying heavily on cues in the body movements and expressions of other players and motion vectors of the ball, is more difficult to simulate realistically. They review a number of different studies that use some techniques familiar to SA research such as eye tracking to determine key cues focused on and probes (e.g., indicate the key players) in stop action on video tapes. In addition, they review some unique approaches, such as visual occlusion of certain information, to determine how those cues affect performance. This interesting body of literature (mostly conducted to study expertise in sports rather than SA per se) demonstrates unique approaches to examining SA in this challenging domain.

Most of these techniques are better suited to examining level 1 SA, however, the stop action probes used with video can get at higher level SA assessments. Given the significant role of highly automatized motor movements in sports activities, many aspects of the game may be not available to conscious awareness (thus techniques such as those above are needed to extract out relevant factors). Yet, anecdotal information from expert players (e.g., sports interviews with professional athletes) also demonstrates a high level of cognitive awareness of certain strategic aspects of the game that also bear examination. It would be interesting to see if the higher levels of SA can also be tapped into in sports studies.

I am less impressed with a reliance on strictly observational or 'ethnographic' assessments of SA (or other cognitive behaviors for that matter). While observations of relevant work environments and human behaviors in these environments is a very important first step in coming to understand any new domain, this activity in and of its self is not sufficient to constitute scientific research. It is fraught with problems of subjective bias in the observer. We (like the experts we study) often see what we expect to see, we interpret the world through our own personal lens. Thus we are extraordinarily open to the trap of apophenia.

Observations and interviewing the operators in a domain is a long standing tradition (e.g., see work of Gilbreth in industrial engineering and the Tavistock studies in Europe), not something particularly new. When going beyond observations of physical movements or social interactions (as demonstrated by verbal and non-verbal communications), however, to discussions of cognitive processes or states, these techniques have their limits. Observations in the work domain should be used to gain an initial understanding of the environment and the strategies and processes operators may be using, allowing researchers to develop good hypotheses. These hypotheses still need to be tested and validated, however, to determine their veracity. Thus they really should be followed up with more scientific testing and measurement, else we build castles out of sand.

There has been some progress on research related to two measures: SAGAT and real-time probe measures.

Situation Awareness Global Assessment Technique (SAGAT)

In general, SAGAT has been successfully used to measure SA in a wide variety of domains, including piloting, air traffic control, driving, power plant operations and military command and control. Vidulich's (2000) meta-analysis of SA measurement techniques found high sensitivity of probe type techniques, as long as they covered a wide variety of questions. Our testing of the measure has shown content validity (basing results on detailed cognitive task analyses in the domain) and predictive validity (Endsley, 1990). In addition, we have conducted numerous tests and found no evidence of the freezes to collect SAGAT data affecting later performance in the testing trial (1995a; 2000a; Endsley and Bolstad, 1993).

Despite this, one often repeated concern is that the measure is 'intrusive' (Sarter and Woods, 1991), although neither they nor anyone else has demonstrated this to be the case. McGowan and Banbury (Chapter 10, this volume), to their credit, have conducted a detailed and careful experiment to attempt to get to the bottom of this. They question 'how situation awareness – a phenomenon akin to consciousness that may involve a sophisticated mix of central executive and automatic processes – can be resistant to the effects of interruption'. To test this, they conducted a study in which SAGAT data was collected and compared to the hazard perception test (recording how quickly participants responded to a potential hazard, indicating the location with a mouse) in a recorded video tape of a driving scenario. They compared trials in which freezes were used to collect SAGAT data against those in which they were not (the hazard perception RT was collected in all trials). Of concern was whether (i) the interruptions would disrupt ongoing task performance and (ii) whether the questions would unduly orient participants to certain information thus improving ongoing task performance.

They found a slight (but significant) decrease in amount of anticipation to the hazard, on the order of about 1/2 second, in trials that included an interruption as compared to those that did not for subject groups receiving either SA probes, orienting questions (pointing out information of relevance) or irrelevant probes. Several possibilities must be considered for this finding. It is likely that the 1/2 second interference affect was associated with psychomotor response time due to the interruption. In a speeded reaction time test like the hazard anticipation measure, this would not be unexpected. Although the hazard anticipation RT is not in and of itself a realistic part of performance in a real driving situation, one could easily argue that this effect would also be found in other psychomotor concurrent measures, such as braking response time or RMS error in track control for a second or so around the interruption as subjects regain control of the vehicle (if in a simulation rather than a video). While it would be easy to quibble with this finding, due to the conditions of the test, in fact I would not be surprised to see something similar if an actual simulator with human-in the-loop participation was used rather than the passive monitoring situation in their study.

I do question its relevance to whether SAGAT affects performance in the way we have generally applied it however. In these studies we generally allow the subject a short period to 'reorient' to the situation following the freeze before starting up again. The types of concurrent performance measures collected do not involve fine RMS error or RT. They usually have more to do with concrete mission related performance (e.g., ATC aircraft separation errors). If a study truly used RT to measure task performance (such as in the sports studies), then I certainly agree that an interruption would affect that type of measure based simply on interference in the psychomotor aspects of the task. I would not recommend combining SAGAT with other types of measures of this kind (e.g., testable response measures or RT to real time probes) in the same time intervals for this reason – the measures interfere with each other. This does not mean, however, that the SAGAT queries create a problem for normal performance of the types of tasks where it is usually employed and the performance measures relate more to cognitive task performance.

Of even more interest is the slightly greater anticipation times (approximately two seconds) exhibited by those participants who received the SA queries and the orienting queries, both in the interrupted events where the probes occurred and also on other events which did not include a probe. This indicates a higher sense of awareness in these conditions overall (which did not occur in the condition when irrelevant information was the subject of the probe). The probes themselves were effective in directing the participants' attention to relevant information.

Of relevance to this observation is the finding by Vidulich (2000) that probes with a narrow range were less successful than those with a broad range of questions such as SAGAT. That is, when the probes direct participants' attention to a subset of information in the environment, it is likely that the measures will primarily pick up on this redirection of attention, rather than SA overall. This same lesson is of some importance here. The anticipation measure is relevant to a subset of SA in the driving task. Similarly, the probes were directed at this same information subset. An appropriate follow-on study should examine the effect of a broad range of probes (i.e., those that covered material relevant to many aspects of SA in driving).

A related question has to do with whether the probes are able to tap into the full range of SA, or are limited from getting at 'implicit knowledge'. The majority of the implicit memory data is derived from very artificial and simplistic tasks (e.g., sentence completion being affected by previously exposed words), however, and many question whether such differences are real or an artifact of the testing conditions and measures used (see Gugerty, 1997). Its relevance for SA, within dynamic and complex operations of systems also remains unclear. Gugerty (1997) for example found a high degree of correlation between implicit measures of SA and an explicit measure in a driving task.

I continue to find that SAGAT is designed to get at as much of information in memory as possible (either implicit or explicit), due to its use of recognition and not just free recall in the probe response measures. It is impossible to say if it gets at all knowledge, however, without another measure to compare it to. As yet, more sensitive and detailed objective measures of SA have not been derived for comparison. Croft, Banbury, Butler and Berry (Chapter 5, this volume) propose some possible implicit measures. It will be interesting to see if these are indeed plausible or able to get at a more robust assessment of SA that would be useful. The practical use of such measures would also need to be demonstrated.

Real-time SA Probes

As an alternate approach to freezing the simulation, probes questioning the participant on his or her SA could be provided in real-time during the trial at the same time that they are carrying out their other tasks. I have in the past been concerned that this approach would be overly intrusive – taking away attention from ongoing tasks and therefore affecting SA (Endsley, 1996). Durso and Dattel (Chapter 8, this volume) report here on the research they have conducted using this methodology which they call the Situation Present Assessment Method (SPAM).

We have also conducted several studies to examine the validity of this technique for measuring SA (Jones and Endsley, in press). We compared SA as measured by real-time probes to SA as measured by SAGAT in several studies. In a direct comparison of SA on match queries or probes, we found a weak but significant correlation between the two measures. The sensitivity and validity of the real-time probe measures is highly affected by the number of repeated measures of the same probe or question during the trial. Because SAGAT can provide multiple queries during a freeze (typically 10-15), it can collect more repeated measures across a wider variety of SA elements during a session. With real-time probes, only one question at a time can be provided and the number of times it is reasonable to interrupt with probes is limited. Therefore, in order to collect information across the same range of situation elements during a trial of the same length, very few repeats of a particular probe can be provided. This severely limits the robustness of the measure provided of the participant's SA on various elements of the situation. It is difficult to tell if low SA on a particular probe is an indicant of a real problem with the system design, or if it is merely the effect of a momentary redirection of attention away from that element. Repeated measures on each individual query or probe are needed to insure that a reliable assessment of SA is obtained. When a sufficient number of repeats of a given probe are provided in a session, then the correlation with SAGAT seems to improve. It is of import to note that our study participants did not find the probes to be overly intrusive into their normal tasks.

In our studies we also found a weak correlation between the real-time probes and workload measures. However, Durso and Dattel (Chapter 8, this volume) also recommend providing an initial warning queue, dissociating the response time to the probe content from the time taken to address the probe as an interruption to other ongoing work. This technique may help improve the validity of real-time probe measures, by making it less a secondary workload measure and more associated with SA knowledge.

In situations where it is not feasible to interrupt a simulation, for instance if SA data is needed in real-world situations, real-time probes may be feasible as long as care is taken to collect enough data to provide a robust measure on each probe, but not to use such a limited range of probes as to skew participants' attention to certain aspects of the situation. In those situations where freezes are possible, SAGAT still seems to provide a more robust and validated approach to SA measurement.

Systems Design

Of most confusion is the assertion that SA does not contribute to an understanding of human performance or human error. Dek ker and Lützhöft (Chapter 2, this volume) misrepresent studies of SA as being about casting blame for error – a concern about end product alone. Flach (1995, p. 150) states 'How does one know that SA was lost? Because the human responded inappropriately? Why did the human respond inappropriately? Because SA was lost'.

If the only measure of SA is performance, then quite frankly I too find the construct circular and of little utility. For this reason, I have always used SAGAT as a direct measure of SA in my research and design studies. SA is useful precisely because it tells us much more about the effect of system designs than does just performance alone. This type of direct measure differentiates the cause of performance error due to SA from those due to poor strategies or decision making or poor task execution. Breaking apart these factors can be very relevant in tests of new technologies.

More importantly what both of these arguments ignore is that SA was not developed as a construct for the interest of psychologists. Rather it came from the operational domain of the pilot – they are deeply concerned about losing SA because if they do, they know they stand a significantly greater chance of making a critical error. Studies of SA error have not sought to cast blame on operators, or even to end the analysis there, but rather have looked at the underlying factors behind the SA error in order to identify the environmental, organizational or task factors that lead to these losses of SA (Endsley, 1995b; Jones and Endsley, 1996). The clear focus of most SA research has been quite practical in nature – developing system designs and training solutions that help operators attain the highest levels of SA possible.

Figure 17.2 **SA-Oriented Design Process (from Endsley, Bolte and Jones, 2003)**

The most interesting frontier for SA remains in the design arena. New technologies and displays of many kinds continue to be investigated as means of improving SA. More recently, we have significantly expanded the concept of SAOD, Figure 17.2, to provide not only a structured process for designing to improve SA, but also 50 design principles (Endsley, Bolte and Jones, 2003). Most human factors design guidelines are directed at the component level – text height, contrast ratios, gauge design. SA-Oriented Design principles, based on SA theory and research to date on SA, focus more on to creating an overall integrated system that supports SA. It addresses not just the perceptual and physical characteristics of systems, but on the content they need to have and the way in which that information needs to accessed and presented to support the cognitive processes of their users.

Summary

In conclusion, the field of study regarding SA continues to grow. Not only in terms of the domains to which it has been applied, but in terms of the theoretical and practical problems that surround it. New research has pushed the boundaries from individual SA toward team or shared SA (see McNeese, Salas and Endsley, 2001), training SA and furthering our knowledge on designing systems that support SA. Volumes such as the present can contribute significantly to those goals by furthering our understanding of how human cognition works to achieve and maintain SA (or fails to do so in some cases) and by strengthening the underlying methodological research base. I continue to encourage such efforts to move beyond speculation and further the solid scientific research that must be conducted to address the real issues that will sufficiently further our knowledge of this and other cognitive behaviors.

References

Archer, S., Warwick, W. and Oster, A. (2000), 'Current Efforts to Model Human Decision Making in a Military Environment', in *Proceedings of the Advanced Studies Simulation Technologies Conference*, Washington, DC.

Bolstad, C.A. (2001), 'Situation Awareness: Does it Change with Age?', in *Proceedings of the Human Factors and Ergonomics Society*, Santa Monica, CA.

Bolstad, C.A., Endsley, M.R., Howell, C. and Costello, A. (2002), 'General Aviation Pilot Training for Situation Awareness: An Evaluation', in *Proceedings of the Human Factors and Ergonomics Society*, Santa Monica, CA.

Burdick, M.D. and Shively, R.J. (2000), 'Evaluation of a Computation Model of Situational Awareness', in *Proceedings of the IEA 2000/HFES 2000 Congress*, Santa Monica, CA.

Carmino, A., Idee, E., Larchier Boulanger, J. and Morlat, G. (1988), 'Representational Errors: Why Some May Be Termed Diabolical', in L.P. Goodstein, H.B. Anderson and S.E. Olsen (eds), *Tasks, Errors and Mental Models*, Taylor and Francis, London, pp. 240-250.

Dreyfus, S.E. (1981), *Formal Models versus Human Situational Understanding: Inherent Limitations on the Modeling of Business Expertise*, Technical Report No. ORC 81-3, Operations Research Center, University of California, Berkley.

Endsley, M.R. (1988), 'Design and Evaluation for Situation Awareness Enhancement', in *Proceedings of the Human Factors Society*, Santa Monica, CA.

Endsley, M.R. (1990), 'Predictive Utility of an Objective Measure of Situation Awareness', in *Proceedings of the Human Factors Society*, Santa Monica, CA.

Endsley, M.R. (1995a), 'Measurement of Situation Awareness in Dynamic Systems', *Human Factors*, vol. 37(1), pp. 65-84.

Endsley, M.R. (1995b), 'A Taxonomy of Situation Awareness Errors', in R. Fuller, N. Johnston and N. McDonald (eds), *Human Factors in Aviation Operations*, Ashgate, Aldershot, pp. 287-292.

Endsley, M.R. (1995c), 'Toward a Theory of Situation Awareness in Dynamic Systems', *Human Factors*, vol. 37(1), pp. 32-64.

Endsley, M.R. (1996), 'Situation Awareness Measurement in Test and Evaluation', in T.G. O'Brien and S.G. Charlton (eds), *Handbook of Human Factors Testing and Evaluation*, Lawrence Erlbaum, Mahwah, NJ, pp. 159-180.

Endsley, M.R. (2000a), 'Direct Measurement of Situation Awareness: Validity and Use of SAGAT', in M.R. Endsley and D.J. Garland (eds), *Situation Awareness Analysis and Measurement*, Lawrence Erlbaum, Mahwah, NJ, pp. 147-174.

Endsley, M.R. (2000b), ' Theoretical Underpinnings of Situation Awareness: A Critical Review', in M.R. Endsley and D.J. Garland (eds), *Situation Awareness Analysis and Measurement*, Lawrence Erlbaum, Mahwah, NJ, pp. 3-32.

Endsley, M.R. and Bolstad, C.A. (1993), 'Human Capabilities and Limitations in Situation Awareness', in *Combat Automation for Airborne Weapon Systems: Man/Machine Interface Trends and Technologies* (AGARD-CP-520), NATO – AGARD, Neuilly Sur Seine, France, pp. 19/11-19/10.

Endsley, M.R., Bolte, B. and Jones, D.G. (2003), *Designing for Situation Awareness: An Approach to Human-Centered Design*, Taylor and Francis, London.

Endsley, M.R. and Garland, D.J. (eds), (2000), *Situation Awareness Analysis and Measurement*, Lawrence Erlbaum, Mahwah, NJ.

Endsley, M.R. and Rodgers, M.D. (1994), 'Situation Awareness Information Requirements for En Route Air Traffic Control', in *Proceedings of the Human Factors and Ergonomics Society*, Santa Monica, CA.

Endsley, M.R. and Smolensky, M. (1998), 'Situation Awareness in Air Traffic Control: The Picture', in M. Smolensky and E. Stein (eds), *Human Factors in Air Traffic Control*, Academic Press, New York, pp. 115-154.

Flach, J.M. (1990), 'The Ecology of Human-Machine Systems I: Introduction', *Ecological Psychology*, vol. 2(3), pp. 191-205.

Flach, J.M. (1995), 'Situation Awareness: Proceed with Caution', *Human Factors*, vol. 37(1), pp. 149-157.

Flach, J.M. and Hancock, P.A. (1992), 'An Ecological Approach to Human-Machine Systems', in *Proceedings of the Human Factors Society*, Santa Monica, CA.

Gibson, J.J. (1979), *The Ecological Approach to Visual Perception*, Houghton-Mifflin, Boston.

Gugerty, L.J. (1997), 'Situation Awareness during Driving: Explicit and Implicit Knowledge in Dynamic Spatial Memory', *Journal of Experimental Psychology: Applied*, vol. 3, pp. 42-66.

Hancock, P.A. and Diaz, D.D. (2002), ' Ergonomics as a Foundation for a Science of Purpose', *Theoretical Issues in Ergonomics Science*, vol. 3(2), pp. 115-123.

Helmreich, R.L., Merritt, A.C. and Sherman, P.J. (1996), 'Human Factors and National Culture', *ICAO Journal*, vol. 51(8), pp. 14-16.

Hörmann, H.J., Blokzijl, C. and Polo, L. (2004), 'ESSAI – A European Training Solution for Enhancing Situation Awareness and Threat Management on Modern Aircraft Flight Decks', *Proceedings of the 16th Annual European Aviation Safety Seminar of the Flight Safety Foundation and European Regions Airline Association*, Barcelona, Spain.

Jones, D.G. and Endsley, M.R. (1996), 'Sources of Situation Awareness Errors in Aviation', *Aviation, Space and Environmental Medicine*, vol. 67(6), pp. 507-512.

Jones, D.G. and Endsley, M.R. (2000), 'Overcoming Representational Errors in Complex Environments', *Human Factors*, vol. 42(3), pp. 367-378.

Jones, D.G. and Endsley, M.R. (in press), 'Using Real Time Probes for Measuring Situation Awareness', *International Journal of Aviation Psychology*.

Jones, D.G., Quoetone, E.M., Ferree, J.T., Magsig, M.A. and Bunting, W.F. (2003), 'An Initial Investigation into the Cognitive Processes Underlying Mental Projection, in *Proceedings of the Human Factors and Ergonomics Society*, Santa Monica, CA.

Juarez, O. and Gonzalez, C. (2003), 'MASA: Meta-Architecture for Situation Awareness', in *Proceedings of the 2003 Conference on Behavior Representation in Modeling and Simulation (BRIMS)*, Scottsdale, AZ.

Juarez, O. and Gonzalez, C. (2004), 'Situation Awareness of Commanders: A Cognitive Model, in *Proceedings of the 2004 Conference on Behavior Representation in Modeling and Simulation (BRIMS)*, Arlington, VA.

Kaempf, G.L., Klein, G.A., Thordsen, M.L. and Wolf, S. (1996), 'Decision Making in Complex Naval Command and Control Environments', *Human Factors*, vol. 38(2), pp. 220-231.

Lee, J.D., Kinghorn, R.A. and Sanquist, T.F. (1995), *Review of Ecological Interface Design Research: Applications of the Design Philosophy and Results of Empirical Evaluations*, Battelle Research Center.

McKenna, F. and Crick, J.L. (1991), *Hazard Perception in Drivers: A Methodology for Testing and Training*, Technical Report for the Transport and Road Research Laboratory, University of Reading, Reading.

McKenna, F.P., and Crick, J.L. (1994), *Developments in Hazard Perception*, Department of Transport, London.

McNeese, M., Salas, E. and Endsley, M. (2001), *New Trends in Cooperative Activities: Understanding System Dynamics in Complex Environments*, Human Factors and Ergonomics Society, Santa Monica, CA.

Moray, N. (2004), 'Ou sont les neiges d'antan?' in *Proceedings of the Human Performance, Situation Awareness and Automation*, Daytona Beach, FL.

Reason, J. (1997), *Managing the Risks of Organizational Accidents*, Ashgate Press, London.

Robinson, D. (2000), 'The Development of Flight Crew Situation Awareness in Commercial Transport Aircraft', in *Proceedings of the Human Performance, Situation Awareness and Automation: User-Centered Design for a New Millennium Conference*, Marietta, GA.

SAE (1997), *Requirements for Models of Situation Awareness*, Technical Report No. ARD50050, SAE International, Warrendale, PA.

Sarter, N.B. and Woods, D.D. (1991), 'Situation Awareness: A Critical But Ill-Defined Phenomenon', *International Journal of Aviation Psychology*, vol. 1(1), pp. 45-57.

Shively, R.J., Brickner, M. and Silbiger, J. (1997), 'A Computational Model of Situational Awareness Instantiated in MIDAS', in *Proceedings of the Ninth International Symposium on Aviation Psychology*, Columbus, OH.

Strater, L.G., Reynolds, J.P., Faulkner, L.A., Birch, K., Hyatt, J., Swetnam, S., et al. (2004), 'PC-Based Tools to Improve Infantry Situation Awareness', in *Proceedings of the Human Factors and Ergonomics Society*, Santa Monica, CA.

Tenney, Y.T., Adams, M.J., Pew, R.W., Huggins, A.W.F. and Rogers, W.H. (1992), *A Principled Approach to the Measurement of Situation Awareness in Commercial Aviation*, Technical Report No. NASA Contractor Report 4451, NASA Langely Research Center, Langely, VA.

Underwood, G., Chapman, P., Bowden, K. and Crundall, D. (2002), 'Visual Search While Driving: Skill and Awareness During Inspection of the Scene', *Transportation Research*, Part F(5), pp. 87-97.

Vicente, K. (1999), ' Cognitive Work Analysis: Towards Safe, Productive and Healthy Computer-Based Work', Lawrence Erlbaum, Mahwah, NJ.

Vicente, K.J. and Rasmussen, J. (1992), 'Ecological Interface Design: Theoretical Foundations', *IEEE Transactions on Systems, Man and Cybernetics*, vol. 22(4), pp. 589-606.

Vidulich, M. (2000), 'Testing the Sensitivity of Situation Awareness Metrics in Interface Evaluations', in M.R. Endsley and D.J. Garland (eds), *Situation Awareness Analysis and Measurement*, Lawrence Erlbaum, Mahwah, NJ, pp. 227-248.

Walters, B. and Yow, A. (2000), 'An Evaluation of Task Network Modeling for Use in Simulating Situation Awareness', in *Proceedings of the IEA 2000/HFES 2000 Congress*, Santa Monica, CA.

Weick, K.E. (1995), *Sensemaking in Organizations*, Sage Publications, Thousand Oaks, CA.

Weick, K.E., Sutcliffe, K.M. and Obstfeld, D. (1999), 'Organizing for High Reliability: Processes of Collective Mindfulness', *Research in Organizational Behavior*, vol. 21, pp. 81-123.

Zacharias, G., Miao, A., Illgen, C., Yara, J. and Siouris, G. (1996), 'SAMPLE: Situation Awareness Model for Pilot-in-the-Loop Evaluation', in *Proceeding of the First Annual Conference on Situation Awareness in the Tactical Air Environment*, Patuxent River.

Author Index

Subject Index